Praise for

THE COMMANDERS

"Engaging . . . Military history buffs and those wanting to learn about leadership and management styles from three important men of the 20th century will likely eagerly consume this tremendous work."
—*Library Journal* (**starred review**)

"A veteran military historian delves into the leadership qualities of three iconic World War II commanders . . . Astute and entertaining."
—*Kirkus Reviews*

"Utterly fascinating. Lloyd Clark demonstrates his deep and wide-ranging knowledge in this compelling new look at three of the most iconic commanders of World War II. With genuinely fresh insights, immense wisdom and thought-provoking analysis, this is a superb account of these three men, divided by different nationalities but with uncanny similarities in ambition, character and motivation."
—**James Holland, author of *Normandy '44* and *Brothers in Arms***

"Lloyd Clark continues his run of first-class military history with this insightful investigation of the best three generals from each of the major armies on the Western Front in the Second World War. This treble-biography highlights both the interaction of these commanders with each other, and where they stood in the constantly shifting command structure of their own sides. It's intensely readable, well-researched and stuffed full of leadership lessons for the modern day, plus the intense rivalry of Monty and Patton is one of the great stories of the war, and has never been told better."
—**Andrew Roberts, author of *Churchill: Walking with Destiny***

"Lloyd Clark is a skillful raconteur weaving together the military biographies of three of WWII's crucial commanders. Through new scholarship and expert analysis, Clark provides a fresh look at these men and their leadership that changed history. Fast-paced, vivid, and compelling, the book belongs in the hands of anyone interested in the importance of leadership in the midst of conflict."
—**Patrick K. O'Donnell, bestselling author of**
Dog Company* and *The Indispensables

THE
COMMANDERS

Also by Lloyd Clark

Blitzkrieg:
Myth, Reality and Hitler's Lightning War – France, 1940

The Battle of the Tanks:
Kursk, 1943

Crossing the Rhine:
Breaking into Nazi Germany 1944 and 1945 –
The Greatest Airborne Battles in History

Anzio:
Italy and the Battle for Rome – 1944

THE COMMANDERS
LLOYD CLARK

THE LEADERSHIP JOURNEYS
OF GEORGE PATTON,
BERNARD MONTGOMERY
AND ERWIN ROMMEL

Grove Press
New York

The author would like to thank Haus Publishing for permission to quote from Ralf Georg Reuth's *Rommel: The End of a Legend* and Pen & Sword for the quotes from Bernard Montgomery's *The Memoirs of Montgomery of Alamein*; material quoted from *Patton* by Carlo D'Este, copyright © 1995 by Carlo D'Este, is used by permission of HarperCollins Publishers. While every effort has been made to contact copyright holders of material reproduced in this book, the author would be pleased to rectify any omissions in subsequent editions should they be drawn to his attention.

First published in hardback in Great Britain in 2022 by Atlantic Books, an imprint of Atlantic Books Ltd.

Published simultaneously in Canada
Printed in the United States of America

First Grove Atlantic hardcover edition: November 2022
First Grove Atlantic paperback edition: October 2023

Layout and typesetting benstudios.co.uk
Map artwork by Keith Chaffer

Library of Congress Cataloging-in-Publication data is available for this title.

ISBN 978-0-8021-6123-9
eISBN 978-0-8021-6023-2

Grove Press
an imprint of Grove Atlantic
154 West 14th Street
New York, NY 10011

Distributed by Publishers Group West

groveatlantic.com

23 24 25 26 27   10 9 8 7 6 5 4 3 2 1

For Catriona, with much love.
Now and forever.

Contents

Maps

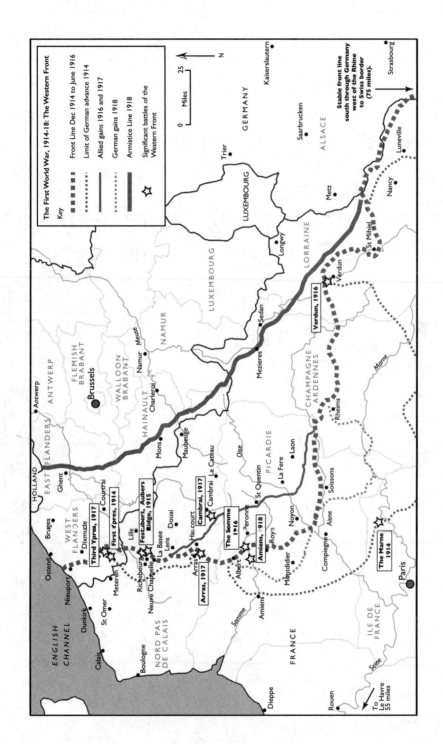

The First World War, 1914-18: The Western Front

Key

- Front Line Dec 1914 to June 1916
- Limit of German advance 1914
- Allied gains 1916 and 1917
- German gains 1918
- Armistice Line 1918
- ☆ Significant battles of the Western Front

N

0 ————— 25
Miles

Stable front line south through Germany west of the Rhine to Swiss border (75 miles).

ENGLISH CHANNEL

HOLLAND

Antwerp

EAST FLANDERS
FLEMISH FLANDERS
Bruges
Ostend
Nieuport
Dixmude
Courtrai
WEST FLANDERS
St Omer
Meteren
Dunkirk
Calais
Boulogne
NORD PAS DE CALAIS
Dieppe
Rouen

FLEMISH BRABANT
WALLOON BRABANT
Brussels
HAINAULT
Ghent
Charleroi
Mons
Maubeuge
Lille
La Basée
Lens
Douai
Arras
Albert
Amiens
Somme
Montdidier
Roye
Noyon
Compiègne

NAMUR
Namur
Meuse
Charleroi
Le Cateau
Cambrai
St Quentin
Oise
La Fère
Laon
Soissons
Aisne
PICARDIE

LUXEMBOURG
Sedan
Mezieres
CHAMPAGNE ARDENNES
Rheims
Marne

GERMANY
Trier
Luxembourg
Longwy
St Mihiel
Verdun
LORRAINE
Metz
Nancy
Luneville
Saarbrucken
Kaiserslautern
ALSACE
Strasbourg

Third Ypres, 1917
First Ypres, 1914
Festubert, Aubers Ridge, 1915
Richebourg
Neuve Chapelle
Arras, 1917
Hazebrouck
Cambrai, 1917
The Somme 1916
Amiens, 1918
Péronne
Verdun, 1916
The Marne 1914

Paris
ILE DE FRANCE
FRANCE
Seine
To Havre Le Havre 55 miles

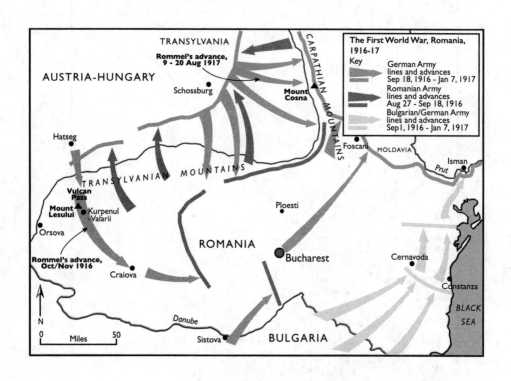

The First World War, Romania, 1916-17

Key

German Army lines and advances Sep 18, 1916 - Jan 7, 1917

Romanian Army lines and advances Aug 27 - Sep 18, 1916

Bulgarian/German Army lines and advances Sep1, 1916 - Jan 7, 1917

TRANSYLVANIA

AUSTRIA-HUNGARY

Rommel's advance, 9 - 20 Aug 1917

Schossburg

CARPATHIAN MOUNTAINS

Mount Cosna

Hatseg

TRANSYLVANIAN MOUNTAINS

Foscani

MOLDAVIA

Isman

Prut

Vulcan Pass

Mount Lesului

Kurpenul -Valarii

Ploesti

Orsova

Rommel's advance, Oct/Nov 1916

ROMANIA

Craiova

Bucharest

Cernavoda

Constanza

BLACK SEA

N

0   Miles   50

Danube

Sistova

BULGARIA

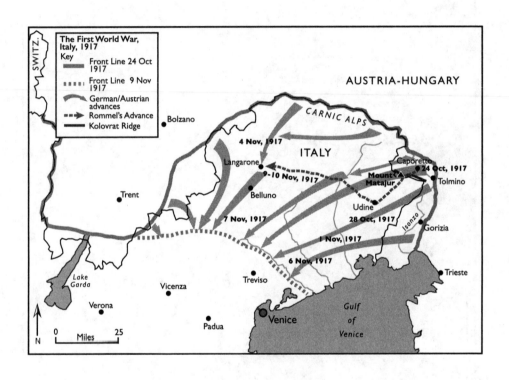

The First World War,
Italy, 1917
Key
━━━ Front Line 24 Oct
1917
▪▪▪▪ Front Line 9 Nov
1917
⟩⟩⟩ German/Austrian
advances
▪▪▶ Rommel's Advance
━━━ Kolovrat Ridge

SWITZ.

AUSTRIA-HUNGARY

CARNIC ALPS

ITALY

Bolzano

4 Nov, 1917

Langarone

9-10 Nov, 1917

Caporetto

24 Oct, 1917

Mount
Matajur

Tolmino

Trent

Belluno

7 Nov, 1917

Udine

28 Oct, 1917

Gorizia

Isonzo

1 Nov, 1917

6 Nov, 1917

Treviso

Trieste

Lake
Garda

Vicenza

Verona

Gulf
of
Venice

N

0   Miles   25

Padua

Venice

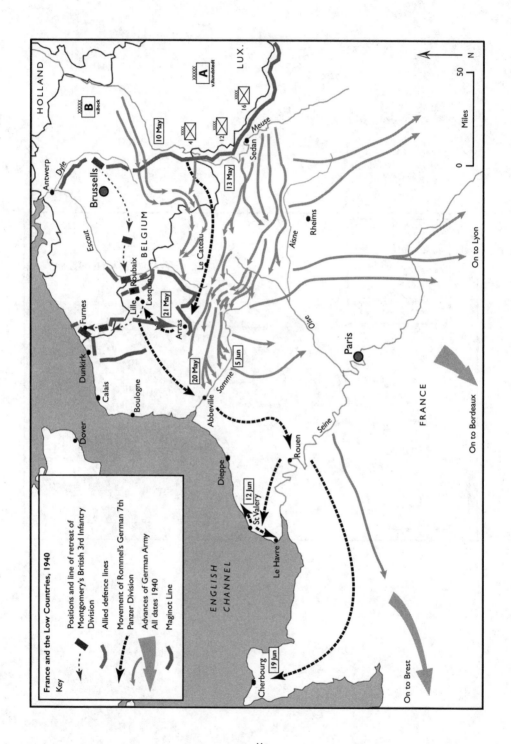

France and the Low Countries, 1940

Key

- - - Positions and line of retreat of Montgomery's British 3rd Infantry Division

▬ ▬ Allied defence lines

- - - Movement of Rommel's German 7th Panzer Division

➤ Advances of German Army All dates 1940

◗ Maginot Line

HOLLAND

LUX.

BELGIUM

FRANCE

ENGLISH CHANNEL

N

0   50

Miles

Antwerp

Dyle

Brussells

Escaut

Dunkirk

Calais

Boulogne

Dover

Furnes

Lille

Roubaix

Lesquin

Arras

Le Cateau

Abbeville

Somme

Dieppe

St Valery

Le Havre

Rouen

Seine

Cherbourg

Oise

Aisne

Rheims

Sedan

Meuse

Paris

On to Lyon

On to Bordeaux

On to Brest

A v.Rundstedt

B v.Bock

16

12

4

10 May

13 May

21 May

20 May

5 Jun

12 Jun

19 Jun

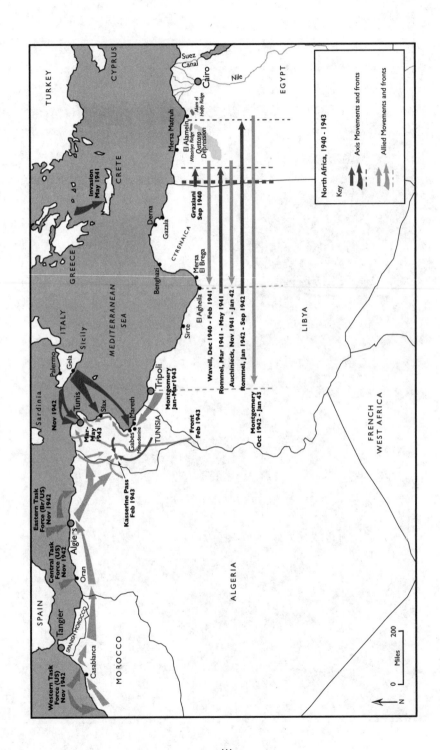

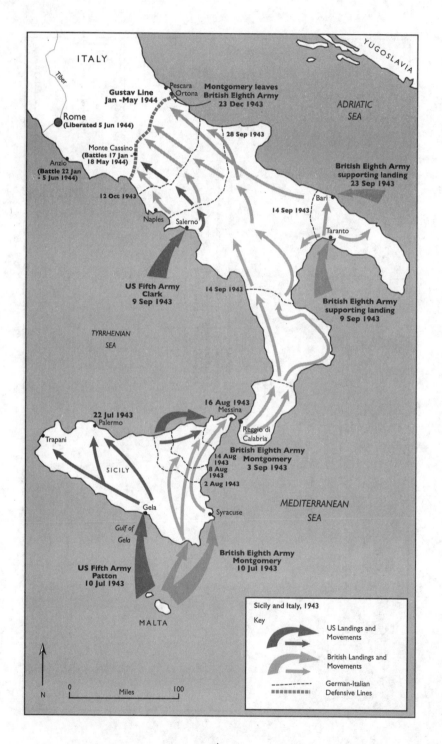

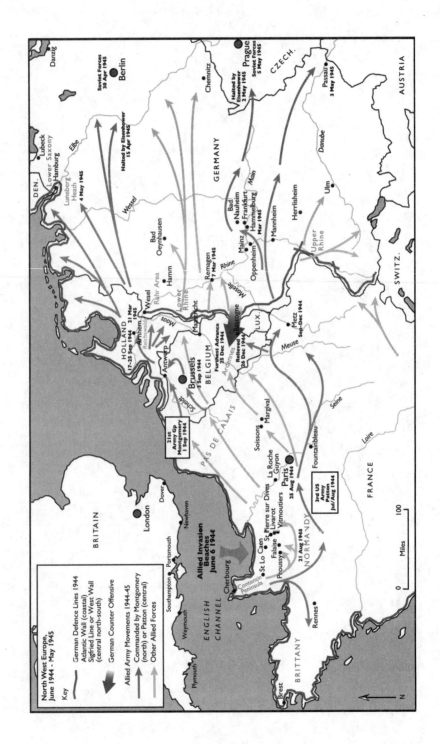

Key

North West Europe, June 1944 - May 1945

German Defence Lines 1944
— Atlantic Wall (coastal)
— Sigfried Line or West Wall (central north-south)
→ German Counter Offensive

Allied Army Movements 1944-45
— Commanded by Montgomery (north) or Patton (central)
→ Other Allied Forces

Danzig

DEN.

Lübeck

Lower Saxony Hamburg

Elbe

Berlin

Soviet Forces 30 Apr 1945

Chemnitz

Prague

Soviet Forces 5 May 1945

CZECH.

Halted by Eisenhower 2 May 1945

Halted by Eisenhower 15 Apr 1945

Luneberg Heath 4 May 1945

Wesel

Passau 3 May 1945

AUSTRIA

GERMANY

Danube

Bad Oeynhausen

Ruhr Area

Hamm

Remagen 7 Mar 1945

Rhine

Lower Rhine

Bad Nauheim

Frankfurt

Hammelburg Mar 1945

Mainz

Oppenheim

Mannheim

Herrlisheim

Ulm

Upper Rhine

SWITZ.

Main

Moselle

Wesel 21 Mar 1945

Arnhem 17-25 Sep 1944

Reichswald

Maas

Maastricht

HOLLAND

Antwerp

Brussels 1 Sep 1944

BELGIUM

Scheldt

Bastogne

Relieved 26 Dec 1944

Furthest Advance 25 Dec 1944

Ardennes

LUX.

Metz Sep-Dec 1944

Meuse

21st Army Gp Montgomery 1 Sep 1944

PAS DE CALAIS

Soissons

Margival

Seine

Loire

FRANCE

Fountainbleau

3rd US Army Patton Jul/Aug 1944

Dover

Newhaven

BRITAIN

London

Portsmouth

Southampton

Weymouth

Plymouth

ENGLISH CHANNEL

Cherbourg

Contentin Peninsula

St Lo Caen

St Pierre sur Dives

La Roche Guyon

Livarot Vimoutiers

Falaise

Proussy

21 Aug 1944

NORMANDY

Paris 25 Aug 1944

Rennes

BRITTANY

Brest

Allied Invasion Beaches June 6 1944

0   Miles   100

N

Introduction

TOWARDS THE END of his long and distinguished life I visited Field Marshal The Lord Bramall at his home in Hampshire. Although he was over ninety years of age, I found that Dwin, as he insisted I call him, had lost none of his passion for discussing military affairs and, in particular, leadership. His precise and persuasive arguments that morning about what he felt made an effective leader drew heavily from a career that began leading a 35-man platoon in Normandy on 8 June 1944 and ended forty years later as Chief of the Defence Staff, the professional head of the British Armed Forces. As the field marshal plunged deep into history to illustrate the importance of apt leadership styles and why it is vital to win trust, I began to understand more why he was one of the most accomplished military leaders Britain has ever produced.

Dwin deployed an argument as deftly as a general might manoeuvre his principal fighting division, as he expounded on the enduring nature of leadership across the millennia, referencing Bernard Montgomery heavily during our conversation. 'Monty could be an exceptional leader,' he explained, 'with a great talent for putting his message across and getting things done how he wanted – but could also be *extremely* difficult.'[1]

There was no doubt that Dwin admired much about Montgomery. The field marshal presented a young Lieutenant

Bramall with the ribbon for a Military Cross awarded for his leadership in October 1944, when he cleared a German post with grenades and his Sten gun. Before Bramall met the great man at the presentation, one of Montgomery's aides had given him some advice: 'The Field Marshal will ask you whether you and he have ever met before. He will not mind if you say "Yes" or "No", but he *will* mind if you say you can't remember.'[2] Dwin chuckled at the memory, shaking his head.

As our discussion progressed, Dwin became keen to discuss what he termed 'the privilege of responsibility'. Whether leading a small team in combat to seize tactically important ground, or clashing with Whitehall mandarins over the implications of budget cuts, 'the personal sense of responsibility,' Dwin expounded, 'does not *feel* different and nor does the sense that one is extremely fortunate to be faced with such challenges and looked to by others for a way forward.'

Taking a pause to gather his thoughts but looking me straight in the eye, he continued: 'It does not matter what one's appointment is or the tests that one faces, leadership is essential. Leadership underpins everything the Army does and involves everybody. Success is always founded on good leadership while with failure the opposite is very often true. It is vital, *absolutely vital*, to find a way to inspire men to do the mundane as well as the extraordinary. Yes, *inspire* is the correct word – inspire and motivate.' The field marshal then explained how he, and those who inspired him, encouraged men to follow. He emphasized his belief that the methods and style adopted by an individual leader have to take account of many variables if they are to be successful.

Academics David Day and John Antonakis concur, having written that leadership is shaped by 'the leader's dispositional characteristics and behaviours, follower perceptions and attributions of the leader, and the context in which the influencing process occurs'.[3] Yet while obvious attributes such as moral courage, decisiveness and calmness under pressure are essential for leader effectiveness, it is leader*ship* skills – such as the ability to communicate, empathize and create an *esprit de corps* – which will make a leader potent.[4] Successful military leaders therefore need to possess both *intra-* and *inter*-personal skills if their leadership is to work, and this requires constant attention to the art of leading and constant attention to how they might improve their abilities. As Harry S. Laver and Jeffrey J. Matthews note in *The Art of Command*, a study of nine commanders from George Washington to Colin Powell: 'Their careers demonstrate that the quality of one's leadership ability develops over years, even decades. None of them began their careers in the military as exceptional leaders. They did, however, have the good fortune to serve under effective mentors, and, more significantly, each had the good sense to learn from the examples set by these role models.'[5]

With each new role, every advance in rank and each new context, it is particularly important that officers and soldiers think again about their leadership and what is demanded of them. While an army will do what it can to prepare individuals for the next stage in their career (for traditionally armies *grow* their own leaders), self-development remains indispensable because there is always a need to translate organizational training and education into something that reflects the leader as an individual. Even if enlisted soldiers make up by far the greater proportion of an army, finding time to improve one's leadership is particularly important to officers because they dominate command appointments in which they have legal responsibility for the 'direction, coordination and control of military forces'.[6] Leadership is an indispensable constituent of command – which makes its own heavy demands on an individual's professional and personal competencies – but no matter what role or context an officer happens to be working in, proficient leadership drives military effectiveness, for as the ancient Greek writer Herodotus wrote nearly two and a half thousand years ago, 'Circumstances rule men; men do not rule circumstances.'[7] In being recognized as the personification of an army's values, standards and leadership philosophy, a leader not only creates a positive local climate but helps to reinforce the healthy organizational culture upon which the army's fighting power depends.[8] It is a poorly advised army, therefore, that does not take heed of Jörg Muth's assertion in his book *Command Culture* that 'troops fight the way they are led'[9] and, ultimately, fighting is what an army exists to do.

During our discussion about military culture, Dwin Bramall began to speak with great knowledge about the impact of three particular leaders: George Patton, Bernard Montgomery and Erwin Rommel. Born between 1885 and 1891, they came into the world at the height of an industrial revolution which powered the Age of Empire in Europe and the Gilded Age in the United States, and fuelled the First World War. All three officers participated in the 1914–18 cataclysm, and like millions of others, the field marshal emphasized, were so affected by their wartime experiences that it became a fundamental influence on their lives. Yet neither Patton, Montgomery nor Rommel were dissuaded by the carnage from seeking military careers when the guns finally fell silent, and in time the army became their great passion. Each became wholly dedicated to the profession of arms and, being exceptional officers and leaders, they prospered. Yet despite the broad similarities between the three men, there were marked differences in their approaches to leadership due to the individuality bestowed on them by their genes, upbringing, life experience and relationships. Together, these stimuli created three unique personalities – which, in turn, determined each man's leadership style.[10]

During our discussion about the complex and nuanced web of what makes one man willingly follow another, the field marshal suggested that I use the lives of Patton, Montgomery and Rommel to reveal 'the short steps on the long journey of leadership'.[11] The result is this book, which seeks, through the eyes of a military historian, to explore the many and various influences that shaped Patton, Montgomery and Rommel as men, as soldiers and, principally, as leaders. It will chart their leadership development through war and peace and through good times and bad. It is a military biography of three officers, viewed through the prism of leadership, as they became among the most prominent officers in their armies and, eventually, in early 1943, all fought in Tunisia. North Africa, however, did not mark the end of the leadership odyssey for Patton, Montgomery or Rommel; it instead acted as a waypoint on the route to a final confrontation in northern Europe, at the end of which, two of these remarkable men would be dead.

CHAPTER ONE

Early Years and Junior Leaders, 1880s–1914

I N LATE SPRING 1905, the body of shoemaker Hiram Cronk was displayed in the main lobby of New York City Hall. Cronk was given this honour not because he had been 105 years of age at the time of his passing, but because he had been the last surviving veteran of the War of 1812. When his body was finally removed from view (after some 925,000 people visited to pay their respects), Cronk was transported through New York streets lined with thousands of onlookers, in a hearse drawn by four gleaming black horses and escorted by men who had fought in the Civil War. Remarking on a scene that he felt marked the end of a more noble era, the correspondent of West Virginia's *Bluefield Daily Telegraph* recorded that the old soldier was 'the last link connecting the simplicity of Jefferson's day with the strenuous complexity of the present'.[1]

The Second Industrial Revolution and the rapid economic growth that accompanied it had ushered in a new age. Advances in manufacturing technology were supported by a rapidly developing railway network that linked modern cities and had, along with the telegraph and telephones, transformed the nation by the dawn of the twentieth century.[2] An aspirational society agitated for government-led reform, while men of influence called for the United States to exert itself more forcefully in the international arena. A stronger, more confident nation with a clear identity had emerged, and it rippled with ambition. By 1905 the balance of the world's power was shifting, and in this dangerous but opportunity-laden arena George S. Patton, Bernard Montgomery and Erwin Rommel sought to make their mark.

The nineteenth century was filled with dominant figures – colossi that strode the world stage and, whether politicians or generals, artists or businessmen, explorers or sportsmen, kept increasingly literate populations absorbed by their achievements – and in that patriarchal society, exceptionally successful specimens of the male sex were used by their respective nations as inspirational figures in a competitive era. Indeed, in 1841 the philosopher Thomas Carlyle published *On Heroes, Hero-Worship, and the Heroic in History* in which he argued that 'Great Men should rule and that other men should revere them'.[3] Yet while Carlyle believed that 'the great' should be role models for the young, he also theorized that their successful emulation was limited to those blessed with inherently 'heroic' dispositional traits at birth. A generation later, however, the notion that an individual's ability to achieve the remarkable was determined solely by what we now know as genetics was challenged by those who postulated that the creation of leaders also depended on the environment into which they were born. In 1873, for example, Herbert Spencer opined in *The Study of Sociology* that early social conditioning moulded personalities, outlook and approach, and that 'before [a Great Man] can remake his society, his society must make him'.[4]

Patton, Montgomery and Rommel were, therefore, born to an era in which the dominant belief was that privileged upper-middle-class professional and aristocratic families alone formed the 'leadership class' – for it was thought offspring not only inherited the most favourable genes for the task, but were also exposed to the positive societal influences that were required to develop the necessary traits.

— ◻ —

George S. Patton Jr was born to a wealthy family of high-achievers. In the century before his birth, his ancestors included Brigadier General Hugh Mercer, Democrat congressman John Mercer Patton, and the latter's son, George Smith Patton – who, with seven of his brothers, fought under the Confederate flag during the Civil War. An accomplished leader who displayed great personal courage, coolness and decisiveness, George Smith Patton was mortally wounded aged thirty-one while commanding a brigade in the Third Battle of Winchester in September 1864. He was laid to rest next to his brother, Waller Tazewell Patton, who himself had died of wounds during Pickett's Charge at Gettysburg in July the previous year, while commanding the 7th Virginia Infantry Regiment.

The stories of their heroism and sacrifice were well known to George Smith Patton's four children – including George S. Patton, whose impoverished mother, Susan, instilled in him a set of strong values during his upbringing in California. Based on loyalty, hard work and discipline, Mrs Patton's principles were to stand her son in good stead for his time at the Virginia Military Institute (VMI) during the mid-1870s. There George became the first-ranking officer cadet in his class, before returning to California to study law where, in 1884, he passed the California bar examination and married Ruth Wilson. Ruth was the daughter of the late Benjamin Wilson, one of California's founding fathers, the first elected mayor of Los Angeles, a great landowner and a successful businessman. Together, George and Ruth raised two children on Benjamin's glorious Lake Vineyard estate. The first, born on 11 November 1885, was given the Patton family's traditional name for a first son: George.

'Georgie', as George Junior became known, enjoyed an idyllic childhood with his sister Anne (known as 'Nita'). The pair revelled in the freedom they had to explore the countryside, ride and do whatever else they could find to entertain and exhaust themselves. They were blissfully unaware that their father had sacrificed his burgeoning legal career to run the by-then-ailing Wilson empire and that he constantly struggled to maintain his family's lifestyle, which included the frequent and lavish entertainment of guests in their large home boasting both servants and stables.

One house guest became a permanent fixture, and worked assiduously to dominate the household. Annie, or 'Nannie' as she was known to the family, was Ruth's tyrannical spinster sister. She quickly established herself as a primary influence on young Georgie, whom she mollycoddled as if he were her own. His parents tolerated this, not least because Nannie was a great stimulant to Georgie's imagination by encouraging his role-playing of the fictional characters she read about to him from Homer, Scott, Kipling and Shakespeare, as well as historical figures including Alexander the Great, Napoleon Bonaparte, Robert E. Lee and Stonewall Jackson.[5] His was an informal education until entering school at the age of eleven, where some previously identified difficulties with reading, writing and spelling were confirmed.

Biographers disagree over the cause of these learning difficulties, some arguing that they were the result of dyslexia while others merely the result of his late entry into school.[6] Whatever the cause, the situation demanded that George find ways to overcome the challenges his learning difficulties produced, and he largely succeeded. Although his spelling remained poor for the rest of his life, George S. Patton Jr became a fluent writer and a voracious reader. Nevertheless, his lack of educational 'normality', and lack of early socialization with other boys in the formal, structured setting of an educational establishment, did see George marked out as 'different' during his early years at school, and therefore vulnerable to peers who pounced unsympathetically on anybody unlike themselves. Consequentially he felt slow, stupid and something of an outsider while at school, and this, in turn, created within him a need for approval, reassurance and acknowledgement.[7] These were also circumstances that fuelled George's fiery desire to succeed and – of great importance to him – not disgrace his family name. An intelligent boy who recognized the value of hard work, in time he was able to successfully manage his complicated relationship with words. Indeed, by the age of sixteen he began the work required to win a coveted place at the United States Military Academy West Point.

Although West Point then trained a minority of US Army officers, a disproportionate number of its graduates achieved the most senior ranks.[8] Patton prepared for the gruelling entrance examination while at VMI, and his father set about mobilizing his agents of influence to win for his son the single West Point nomination that his senator, Thomas R. Bard, could make each year. Application to the task and not inconsiderable sacrifice on the part of both Georges led to success: Patton passed the entrance examination in March 1904 and Bard awarded the eighteen-year-old his nomination soon after. This success reinforced in George that, with discipline, industry and the right connections, he could achieve anything he wanted. To that end, George wrote to his father that summer determined that he would become a general, stating, 'I will do my best to attain what I consider – wrongly perhaps – my destiny.'[9]

Whatever his destiny, George knew that the four-year West Point course would be a severe test of his body and mind as well as a formative experience. The syllabus was heavily academic with an emphasis on mathematics, the sciences and engineering (to Patton's chagrin, no specific military history course was offered and nothing on infantry tactics), all delivered in a dry style by passionless military staff who lacked expertise in what they were teaching.[10] The academy was less a haven of critical thinking and more a crammer-cum-finishing-school which exalted discipline and drill. George had no difficulty with 'bull and starch', but he found the absorbing of vast quantities of knowledge to pass the examinations particularly challenging. Moreover, although he desperately wanted to become a leader, Patton found that West Point offered little developmental opportunity because its officer cadets were admitted on the assumption that they already possessed the necessary traits to be effective leaders. The first ('plebe') year was notorious for its 'hazing' – bullying by senior cadets – which was designed to break some cadets and help staff identify those who failed to show the required stoicism. The West Point experience, therefore, produced resilient, courageous, disciplined officers with strong academic credentials, but who knew precious little about soldiering, officership or leadership. Indeed, George C. Marshall, the future Chief of Staff of the US Army, later identified the academy as having a negative influence on the Army because it taught 'how to give commands and to look firm and inexorable' and, what is more, the cadets 'largely had to find [their] knowledge of leadership and command from… the disciplining of "plebes".'[11]

West Point was very different from the comfortable world Patton had previously inhabited, where his foibles were accepted, his demands acceded to and his intolerances went unchallenged. The narrow-minded and soft young George, therefore, failed to endear himself to his fellow cadets, whom he derided as of 'lesser character' and 'not quite gentlemen', and he was severely bullied in return.[12] Thus, he remained an outsider, devoid of both the close friendships that West Point promoted and the appreciation of his talents that he had come to rely on as a child. Surrounded by capable, bright, fit peers who enjoyed each other's company, Patton wrote frequent self-pitying letters to his father, including one at the end of 1904 which stated, 'I am a characterless, lazy, stupid, yet ambitious dreamer; who will degenerate into a third rate second lieutenant and never command anything more than a platoon.'[13] Such missives were most frequently written at times of stress or failure, which meant, therefore, that a flurry of letters arrived in California at the end of his first year when, having failed his mathematics examination, he was required to retake the entire year.

Already tenacious and convinced that failing to graduate from West Point was unconscionable, the increasingly obstinate young man redoubled his efforts. In the small black notebook that he took to carrying during his time as an officer cadet in order to record his thoughts, his first entry read simply: 'Do your damdest [sic] always.'[14] Over the next four years, whenever his academic grades dipped – which they frequently did – he managed to raise them just before his examinations. However, he consistently failed to create any warmth between himself and his fellow officer cadets. When promoted to second corporal in the spring of 1906, for example, Patton's overzealousness and ability to irritate soon saw him demoted to sixth corporal. It was a chastening experience but he gradually recovered the ranks – the West Point staff showing they valued his military demeanour – to become sergeant major in his third (classman) year, and was then promoted into the role he coveted most: regimental adjutant. He was effective in each of these appointments, but never popular because he delighted in punishing the minor infractions of his fellows while boasting that he would be a general by the age of thirty. In the back of a library textbook in April 1909 he wrote an unfinished list titled 'Qualities Of A Great General':

1. Tactically aggressive (loves a fight)
2. Strength of character
3. Steadiness of purpose
4. Acceptance of responsibility
5. Energy
6. Good health and strength
7. ____[15]

By the time he had written these words, Patton had already decided that, like the great generals of history, he would wear a mask of command. This mask, he believed, conveyed an authority that he might otherwise lack, and imbued him with a gravitas and an aura that made his leadership compelling. In George's case, however, the mask was less a means of changing persona and more a means of making up for his leadership deficiencies – most notably his poor ability to win the respect of his subordinates. However, in adopting what biographer Carlo D'Este has called 'his authoritarian, macho, warrior personality',[16] Patton remained out of step with other officer cadets, even though he believed they were out of step with him.

Patton graduated 46th in a class of 103 in June 1909, revealing a solid but unspectacular performance at the Academy despite his grand ambitions. He joined the cavalry, a traditional and glamorous organization well suited to an accomplished rider who had admired the dashing boldness of soldiers on horseback since childhood. The greatest immediate challenge facing Patton on commissioning was how to do what West Point had signally failed to prepare him to do: lead soldiers in the field army. During his five years at the Academy he had only very occasionally set eyes on an enlisted man, and had not received training in even the most rudimentary military skills, including shooting.[17] As a consequence, when Patton arrived at Fort Sheridan, Illinois, in September 1909 to begin his first tour of duty as a second lieutenant in the 15th Cavalry Regiment, there was some resentment among the men of his platoon that he had the authority and a sense of entitlement but was useless to them. It was essential, therefore, that Patton absorb as much professional knowledge as he could, as quickly as possible, and develop a strong relationship with his non-commissioned officers (NCOs) in the process.

The issue of poorly prepared junior officers was, however, just one of many that beset a US Army whose significant capability deficiencies had been exposed by the Spanish-American War (1898) and the Filipino-American War (1899–1902). The modernization programme that followed was well intentioned, but with a small budget. With its 85,000 officers and men scattered over a panoply of small, rundown garrisons, the US Army remained a demoralized and fragmented force when Patton joined.[18] Nevertheless, reform had begun before Patton joined the Army, with the ambition of developing it from an old-fashioned frontier police force into something fit for an innovative nation with growing power and expectations. The structural changes that followed, for example, saw the establishment of divisional formations that made the Army capable of undertaking swift expansion should the need arise. Progress was also made in 1903 with the creation of a General Staff to plan, investigate and coordinate military activity under the auspices of a Chief of Staff of the US Army, the professional head of the service. It was an initiative that gave the Army the cerebral and organizational firepower it had been lacking for so long, and produced a new emphasis on officer development that was designed to better prepare its people for specific career stages. The enterprise included cohered courses which ran in garrison and branch schools, the staff college at Fort Leavenworth, Kansas, and at the recently created US Army War College in Washington.[19] The turn of the century also saw a modern officer career-management introduced with responsibility for promotions, assignments and tours, and rotation between staff and command assignments punctuated by periodic professional training. In sum, the changes were a significant advance in the professionalization of the US Army and, ultimately, were of great advantage to ambitious, energetic and talented officers like George Patton.

Despite the change gripping the Army at the end of the first decade of the twentieth century, there was little to show for it at Fort Sheridan, which remained a small and dilapidated cavalry outpost thirty miles north of Chicago, home to Troop K of the 15th Cavalry Regiment. Patton found a lethargy in the Troop's attitude to soldiering which, under the mentorship of Captain Francis Marshall – the patient, professional and diligent commander of the unit – he sought to rectify. Second Lieutenant Patton inevitably made some elementary mistakes in the early days of his command, mostly the result of the young officer's desire to show the qualities of a strong leader rather than ensuring that his leadership was appropriate. Overplaying his rank, being exceedingly officious and losing his temper (particularly during his first introduction to leading soldiers) were all behaviours that had dogged his time at West Point, and now they haunted his platoon until a combination of NCOs and Marshall taught him the error of his ways. The lessons were hard, but Patton absorbed them. On one occasion, having humiliated an enlisted man in front of his colleagues for failing to properly tether a horse, when his rage subsided Patton returned and apologized personally to the man in question and then to all those who had witnessed the unsavoury scene. It was the first of many occasions during his long career in which Patton found it necessary to ask for the forgiveness of subordinates, colleagues or superiors. Marshall pointed out the need for leaders to be aware of their attitudes, behaviours and actions on others rather than merely expecting a positive reaction to an officer with authority. The wise troop leader also recommended that Patton should seek to have greater empathy with his subordinates – not just to be seen as an officer who took an interest, but to be better placed to energize, motivate and inspire them day to day.

Fort Sheridan was a learning ground for Patton in many ways, be it in the art of leadership, the skills that he expected his men to have, or how to use his spare time for self-improvement. To his credit, while other junior officers frittered away long hours loafing in the mess, Patton read deeply, reflected on the profession of arms and engaged in a vigorous theoretical correspondence with friends and colleagues. In so doing he was acting on his own advice, having written in his little black notebook while at West Point: 'I believe that in order for a man to become a great soldier… it is necessary for him to be so thoroughly conversant with all sorts of military possibilities that when ever an occasion arises he has at hand with out effort on his part a parallel.'[20] His assiduous attention to the profession of arms was to become an important part of Patton's life.

The young officer also found ample time to participate in a range of sports, particularly those involving horses but also fencing and pistol shooting, as well as enjoying a full social life in camp and in nearby Chicago. During his frequent trips to the city he became reacquainted with Beatrice Ayer, the beautiful and talented daughter of an eighty-year-old Boston multimillionaire and a distant relative who had visited Lake Vineyard several years earlier. A romance developed, and in May 1910, after a short courtship, the couple were married at Avalon, the Ayer family mansion in Prides Crossing, Massachusetts. Yet while for the young officer the match required relatively minor changes to his lifestyle, for Beatrice, taking a lowly paid junior Army officer as her husband and swapping comforts and glamorous society for cramped accommodation in the austere Fort Sheridan married quarters, it demanded considerable sacrifice. Beatrice had not only married George S. Patton, she had also married the US Army and she did not find the transition at all easy.

The arrival of the couple's first child, Beatrice (known as 'Bee'), in March 1911 did little to improve Mrs Patton's feeling of dislocation, for although the baby could have strengthened the union with her husband, it instead sent George into a jealous malaise, caused by Bee's monopolization of her mother, which lasted several months. By the autumn, George had come to recognize that Beatrice was not going to undermine the needs of her child to pamper a selfish husband and he transformed into the doting father that he was to remain, but the episode did reveal Patton's deep desire to be the centre of attention and his proclivity for bouts of poor mental health.

Although what precisely caused George's sudden acceptance of his daughter's needs is unknown, being given temporary command of Troop K in Marshall's absence may well have shaken him out of his misery. It was followed soon after by more good news – he had been posted to Fort Myer in Arlington, Virginia, just three miles from the White House. His new job with Troop A at the headquarters of the 15th Cavalry Regiment would put Patton within easy reach of the powerful men in the capital city, the society that his wife craved and an opportunity to combine both. Indeed, Fort Myer was the official residence of the Chief of Staff of the US Army and an array of other senior officers, and as soon as Patton arrived in December 1911 he wasted no time in ensuring that their paths crossed. It was a watershed event in Patton's career and 'his life and military development entered a wholly new phase, the real beginning of his rise to fame'.[21] With their larger and more comfortable quarters, the Pattons hired a full-time maid and a chauffeur to drive the family car, and Patton purchased a thoroughbred horse to add to his own burgeoning stable. He rode each morning for exercise and to make new and prestigious acquaintances. On one such ride Patton met Secretary of War Henry L. Stimson, with whom, despite their eighteen-year age difference, he began a friendship that was to last until the end of Patton's life.

Captain Julian R. Lindsey, the commander of Patton's troop, must have watched his new subordinate's approach to life at Fort Myer with some curiosity, because it was flamboyant even for the cavalry.

Yet Patton must have revealed more than just an ability to attract attention, for by the spring of 1912 he had been appointed squadron quartermaster, a much sought-after position, and his annual report rated him 'excellent' in his attention to duty, professional zeal, general bearing and military appearance, and 'very good' for intelligence, judgement, instructing, drilling and handling enlisted men.[22] Attentive to his duties but always keen to fill his time constructively, Patton began to write military articles and pamphlets to help develop himself, but also to get noticed. Although his first pieces (such as *Principles of Scouting*, published in February 1912[23]) were focused on the cavalry and well received, his aspiration was to examine issues of broader interest to the US Army.

Patton's ambition to be a man of influence was furthered by his selection to represent the United States in the new modern pentathlon event at the 1912 Summer Olympics in Stockholm. As the sport saw all competitors drawn from their nations' respective armies, the 26-year-old Patton was a natural choice for US selectors looking for an individual adept at swimming, pistol shooting, running, fencing and riding. Although finishing fifth was a frustration for the young officer, the US press gave Patton such significant coverage that by the time he returned he had become something of a celebrity, and he was the toast of prestigious dinner parties at which, as one fellow guest wrote, 'the young man needed little encouragement to tell his tales of his triumphs'.[24] The name 'Patton' rippled through Washington society and was known by the Chief of Staff of the US Army, Major General Leonard Wood, who by the autumn of 1912 was a regular on the rides that Patton and Stimson took together. It was company that gave George confidence as well as connections that he might mobilize in the future, but he remained a junior officer with a little local fame that he recognized was based on a limited achievement.

To make a real impact, Patton knew that he had to offer something that others found valuable, and this was also important to his leadership of his platoon at Fort Myer. There, however, he was often left exasperated by his subordinates' failure to show any improvement in their military skills despite his best efforts to train them. After one particularly unsuccessful day on the ranges, he wrote to Beatrice: 'Our great trouble is that men do not do what they are told. They think too much! This talk about the independence of the American soldier will cost a lot of lives, if we would teach them to obay [sic] we would do much better than teaching them to shoot.'[25] It was a challenge that reinforced his long-held belief that discipline was the cornerstone of military competency, and this had to be laid securely by leaders before a soldier could be commanded, far less led.

Patton was addressing such matters at the end of 1912 by asserting his will directly on those he commanded when, unexpectedly, he was plucked from regimental duties and dropped into a very different context, as a temporary assistant in the Chief of Staff's office, and became advisor to the Ordnance Department. On his way back from Stockholm, Patton had taken a sojourn at the French Cavalry School in Saumur to learn from the best fencing instructor in the French Army, and now, while waiting for his article 'The Form and Use of the Saber' to be published, he assisted in the development of what became known on its issue as the 'Patton Saber'.[26]

George Patton's stock was on the rise, and in the spring of 1913, when his short appointment came to an end, he had every right to feel that, at last, he was making a difference to the US Army as a specialist. His growing knowledge and skill as a swordsman continued with another course at Saumur that summer, following which he attended the Mounted Service School at Fort Riley, Kansas, not only as a student on a career course but also as 'Master of the Sword', an instructor to more senior officers on advanced programmes. Learning to use a sword had started with play when Patton was a child but had become a passion, and he had become a stylishly effective swordsman in his twenties. During the first class he delivered at Fort Riley, Patton was keenly aware that he was junior to those he needed to influence and so said, 'I realize how hard it must be to take instruction from a man you must regard as still a little damp behind the ears. But gentlemen, I am about to demonstrate to you that I have been an expert with the sword, if nothing else, for at least fifteen years, and in that respect I am your senior.'[27] He then waved in the air the two wooden swords that he and his sister used to play with as children at Lake Vineyard, to peals of laughter from the watching officers. Patton went on to demonstrate his skill and deep knowledge of swordsmanship, and held his audience in the palm of his expensively gloved hand.

Such were his abilities, moreover, that upon graduation from the course in May 1914, Patton was awarded one of just ten highly coveted places on the school's Troop Commander's course. There was no question of him refusing such an invitation even if it did mean more time away from his family and being remote from world events. Thus, as Europe descended into war, and second lieutenants from the belligerent armies took their chances, George Patton looked on enviously from a distant US Army camp in the middle of Kansas.

— ◻ —

Bernard Montgomery was from a solidly middle-class family that unwittingly shaped him into something of a rebel. Born in London on 17 November 1887 to Reverend Henry and Maud Montgomery, the fourth of their nine children, Bernard was expected by his family to contribute to a British Empire that was a source of gloating satisfaction among the privileged classes and of growing envy to international competitors. The Montgomerys could trace their roots back 900 years (although a little tenuously) to the Norman warrior Roger de Montgomeri, a trusted soldier and confidant of William the Conqueror who became one of the most influential men in England in the years after the 1066 invasion. More recently, Samuel Montgomery, Bernard's great-grandfather, had been a successful Irish merchant who by 1750 had acquired enough wealth to build New Park House on sixty acres at Moville in the northern Irish county of Donegal. Just weeks after Bernard's birth, the heavily mortgaged New Park was inherited by Reverend Henry after the death of his father, Sir Robert Montgomery, a former Lieutenant Governor of the Punjab. It was a huge financial burden for a junior clergyman, then vicar of St Mark's in Kennington in south London, who also had responsibility for a growing family. Henry did what he could to safeguard the family seat, but his endeavours demanded significant sacrifices by his children, who grew up in a family for which thrift was a virtue born of necessity. Maud consequently ran the family's finances while her husband conducted his ministry, allocating him a tiny weekly allowance and asserting a ruthless discipline on all – which was to affect Bernard for the rest of his life.

Maud Montgomery was the daughter of Frederic Farrar, a noted figure in Victorian society, a prolific author, a former head of Marlborough School and an esteemed clergyman who was destined to end his days as canon of Westminster Abbey. Maud met her future husband when she was just a girl and Henry worked under her father as a curate while Frederic was rector of St Margaret's, Westminster (Parliament's church). They married in 1881 and were soon producing a family, on which Maud sought to impose strict order and Christian values in what conservatives perceived as a 'rapidly changing and immoral world'.[28] She dominated the Montgomery household while Henry concentrated on his professional duties, which, due to his immense hard work and considerable talents, saw him promoted to Bishop of Tasmania in 1889. It was a great honour but demanded yet more sacrifice from his family, which was summarily uprooted from the urban sprawl when Bernard was two and transplanted to the tiny leafy city of Hobart on the other side of the world.

Here the Montgomery children were home-tutored and left free to explore the local countryside, glorying in their independence. They were always aware, however, that independence was allowed only within the confines of their affectionless mother's strict rules, which, if broken, would most likely end with a physical punishment. Of all the Montgomery household, Bernard was the most likely to stand up to his mother, which inevitably led to a confrontation between two immensely stubborn individuals and saw him later write, 'My early life was a series of fierce battles.'[29]

On returning to London in 1902 when his father took up a new appointment, Bernard and his older brother Donald were enrolled as day boys at St Paul's, a high-achieving and traditional English public school in London. On his arrival Bernard was not deemed as academically able as the majority of his contemporaries and was placed in what was commonly referred to as the 'Army Class' (for, as Montgomery later admitted, 'In those days the Army did not attract the best brains in the country'[30]). Bernard worked diligently at his studies, but although he remained a mediocre student in the classroom, he quickly gained a reputation for being a rule breaker who excelled on the games field. Slight, wiry and agile, the young Montgomery had the speed of thought and limb that made him an outstanding rugby and cricket player, while also being one of the school's top swimmers.

The sporting accolades that came his way over his years at St Paul's more than compensated for his lack of academic acumen in the eyes of other boys. Nevertheless, Bernard's extracurricular accomplishments did little to allay the concerns of his parents, who towards the end of his time at the school received a report which stated that their son was 'rather backward for his age'.[31] Young Montgomery, it seemed, was best suited to life as an army officer, and so in the autumn of 1906 he sat the entrance examinations for the Royal Military College Sandhurst (RMC). The fact that Montgomery passed a decent 72nd out of the 177 who sat the examination was all that Henry and Maud needed to confirm that a respectable career awaited their son, and they spared no effort in encouraging him to take up the Army's offer of a place on its commissioning course.[32]

The British Army in the first decade of the twentieth century was smarting after the unsettling experience of the 1899–1902 Anglo-Boer War. Although ending in victory against the two Boer republics that were demonstrating their anger at the British Empire's influence in southern Africa and despite a numerical superiority of nearly six to one, the British had struggled to impose their will in the face of the Boers' guerrilla warfare. The long and expensive war instigated several official enquiries, the recommendations of which prompted reforms which sought to make the Army more professional and broadly improve its fighting capabilities.[33]

Considering the increasing threat to Britain offered by Germany's military build-up and foreign policy ambitions, many influential commentators regarded such developments as not coming a moment too soon. With leadership having been identified as critical in the required transformation, measures focused on improving officer training were among the first to be initiated. Criticisms of the RMC had been made by a government committee which reported in 1902 that the college was more like a public school than an institution designed to turn out military professionals, and led to an immediate overhaul of its syllabus, teaching and assessments.[34] The aim, the committee explained, was to ensure that an RMC student was no longer instilled with a dislike of military study 'which too often remains with him throughout his career'.[35] Field Marshal Lord Kitchener, Commander-in-Chief of the British Army in India and founder of the Indian Staff College at Quetta, believed in the objective, as he regretted that there was 'too often a want of serious study of their profession by officers who are, I think, rather inclined to deal too lightly with military questions of moment'.[36]

As a consequence, when Bernard Montgomery arrived at the RMC on 30 January 1907 for his twelve-month course, he was entering an institution in the middle of a slew of important changes in how it produced young men fit for the challenge of leading in a twentieth-century army. Montgomery thoroughly enjoyed his early weeks at Sandhurst, was soon promoted to lance corporal, and by the summer was rated 'excellent' by the commandant.[37] He continued to excel at team sports, performed well in the practical exercises, and enjoyed a syllabus which now included tactics, military history and geography.[38] While there was no specific leader and leadership training or education, the entire course was driven by the need to develop an officer cadet's character and provide him with the basic military skills required in his first appointment. Specifically selected military instructors immediately made improvements to the course, and Montgomery was among the first to attend a new summer camp created to test leadership and practical military skills in the field. Encouraged to excel by the competition engendered by this new breed of instructor, Officer Cadet Montgomery nonetheless very nearly failed to commission.

In December 1907, just before their final examinations, a small group of officer cadets held down a colleague in his room while Montgomery set fire to his shirt tails. The injuries that the young man sustained required his hospitalization, and Montgomery's castigation was severe. He escaped expulsion from the RMC only after a personal plea by his mother, but was censured, demoted and 'back-termed' to repeat the final three months of the course. It was an embarrassing brush with disaster. Checking his behaviour and applying himself to his work, Montgomery eventually passed his examinations to graduate from Sandhurst a creditable 35th out of 150 in the spring of 1908.[39] His reward was a commission into the Royal Warwickshire Regiment, a traditional and inexpensive county regiment with a fine heritage in which talent would shine brightly. 'Monty', as he was known to friends and colleagues, left Sandhurst and moved away from his family without hesitation, determined to embrace fresh opportunities and a new life.

Second Lieutenant Montgomery's first posting was to the 1st Battalion Royal Warwickshire Regiment in the ancient city of Peshawar, then in India and located close to the strategically sensitive North-West Frontier of the British Empire. Threatened by Russia and Afghanistan and frequent raids by Pashtun tribes, the officers and men of the 1st Royal Warwicks had to be on their mettle. As a platoon commander responsible for fifty men, Montgomery soon learned that the culture in the battalion was not sympathetic to idleness.[40] It was an excellent environment for his development as a leader, and he set about discovering his troops' fighting capability and what, as he later wrote, 'made them tick'.[41] He also attended as many courses to improve his own skills and knowledge as time would allow, including musketry, machine gunnery and signals, while also taking lessons in Urdu and the local Pashtu dialect. In every spare moment, rather than relaxing in the mess with his peers, Monty read a wide range of books, articles and Army publications that would provide him with a better understanding of his profession. This distinguished him from most other officers in the battalion, but as he later wrote, 'Looking back, I would put this period as the time when it was becoming apparent to me that to succeed one must master one's profession.'[42]

As a junior leader, Montgomery was particularly keen to understand his soldiers and how to interact with them, paying particularly careful attention to his communication skills and what worked best to get a certain effect.[43] Many of his fellow officers treated the enlisted men with undisguised scorn and then complained that they were disobedient, whereas Montgomery endeavoured to be respectful and to show that he valued the efforts of his platoon. 'The men were splendid', he later wrote, 'they were natural soldiers and as good material as anyone could want. The British officers were not all so good.'[44]

His general disapproval of his fellow officers was based on the lack of professionalism that he judged to pervade the battalion, for although everybody seemed busy, he saw plenty of socializing and administration but precious little dynamism. Montgomery did not drink, nor did he enjoy the gossip or childish games that were endemic in an officers' mess that proscribed talking 'shop' and junior officers speaking their minds. To his peers, Montgomery was seen as a bit of a bore, too intense and too obviously energetic. Clement Tomes, a fellow subaltern, later recalled 'it is [Bernard's] keenness that seems to stand out most in my memory', while others felt he got too close to his men and derided his decision to ape his men by tattooing his forearms.[45] But Montgomery did not particularly care to be like other officers unless he could see a purpose in it, and far from being concerned about his colleagues' sneering remarks about his behaviour, he luxuriated in the knowledge that his platoon was developing into the best in the company and one of the most capable in the battalion.

From the outset of his career, Bernard Montgomery did not court popularity but rather respect, for he sought not to be measured by some mistaken belief in the need to conform but purely on his results. Had his sporting prowess not been quite so compelling, Montgomery may well have found himself exiled by his brother officers – a situation that was to be avoided at all costs in the complex world of the regimental family – but instead he was perceived as a distinctly odd young man, although with an attention to detail, self-discipline and sporting talent that demanded he be tolerated.

One of the traits Montgomery displayed while still in his first appointment that was sure to have raised an eyebrow among his fellow officers was his blatant ambition. Although promoted to full lieutenant in April 1910, he remained frustrated that, like in most other armies, promotion in the British Army was not predicated on talent but on time served (seniority) when a vacancy was open.[46] Montgomery reacted in the only way he could, to patiently make the most of the opportunities that came his way and to prepare assiduously for the day when his responsibilities would broaden. He therefore revelled in the battalion's move south to Bombay in October 1910 for its final two years of overseas duty. 'Bombay!' wrote a fellow officer at this time. 'It is the one station in the whole British empire about which nothing good has ever been heard.'[47] But Montgomery expected only useful challenges.[48]

The port city was a cauldron of humanity. Populous, vibrant and offering many temptations to the troops, it was also home to notoriously poor military facilities and sliding standards. Soon Montgomery was spending considerable time on disciplinary issues and had to finally accept that his moral standards were not shared by his men. Nevertheless, he seems to have been content to accept the behaviours that he found distasteful (including drinking, fighting and using prostitutes) if they did not undermine military performance.

This was a practical compromise that Montgomery was to make time and again through his career, because he saw no advantage coming from 'fighting a tide of well-set attitudes without good cause'.[49]

This, it seems, was appreciated by his platoon, who worked hard for their officer in what he called a 'quid pro quo sort of arrangement'.[50] Montgomery was particularly keen to ensure healthy competition among his men, and established prizes for the best platoon shot and the 200-yard dash. Thus, when appointed the battalion's sports officer and the German battleship *Gneisenau* arrived in port with the Crown Prince abroad, Montgomery immediately challenged its crew to a football match. Ignoring advice from headquarters to field a weakened side, Lieutenant Montgomery oversaw a 40-0 drubbing of the opposition, and justified his ruthlessness to a fellow officer by saying, 'Oh! I was taking no risks with those bastards.'[51]

By the time the 1st Royal Warwicks finally left Indian shores for England in November 1912, nobody was more relieved than Montgomery. Although his time overseas had been an excellent place to develop his leadership, he had become ever more irritated by being in what he perceived as a military backwater at a time when Europe was edging towards war.[52] Montgomery's next posting was to the battalion depot at Shorncliffe on the south coast of England, from where he could see the French coastline on a clear day. As assistant adjutant he did not get integrally involved in the training that took place at the camp, but it was a position that gave him his first taste of staff duties, a strong understanding of the workings and relationships within headquarters, and it put him in close proximity to the commanding officer. Recognizing that he would likely revert to platoon command should war break out, however, Montgomery pushed hard to be sent to an infantry officers' course at the School of Musketry (where he received a distinction) and then to a machine gunnery course to further develop his technical skills.

This was a dedication to his profession which was noticed by Captain B. P. Lefroy, who had just returned to regimental duties having attended the Camberley Staff College and soon found himself informally mentoring the enthusiastic Montgomery. So valuable was the relationship that Montgomery wrote, decades later, 'All this goes to show how important it is for a young officer to come into contact with the best type of officer and the right influences early in his military career.'[53] Lefroy seems to have fuelled the young officer's ambition, reinforcing that hard work would pay dividends, and left him keen for greater responsibility. As Monty's biographer, Nigel Hamilton, has said: '[Montgomery's] genius lay not so much in his natural gift for leadership – a quality not lacking in English history – as in his deliberate, almost insane pursuit of his goal: a goal he would achieve by unending pursuit of clarity and ruthless self-discipline.'[54]

— ◻ —

Erwin Rommel was born on 15 November 1891 in Heidenheim an der Brenz, an attractive provincial town in the state of Württemberg, in the south-western German region of Swabia. Renowned across the nation for being inhabited by unemotional, shrewd and hard-working people, Swabia enjoyed a distinct culture and had a suspicion of all things Prussian. The Rommels were a middle-class family broadly illustrative of these regional characteristics. Erwin's father – also named Erwin – was a mathematics teacher (as was his father) who rose to become headmaster of the secondary school in nearby Aalen. Erwin's mother, Helene, the daughter of an ennobled civic dignitary, was a housewife who bore five children. Erwin was particularly attached to his mother and she encouraged her small, pale, weak-looking son to explore the outdoors. 'As far as I can recall', Erwin wrote in his late teens, 'my early years passed very pleasantly as I was able to romp around our yard and big garden all day long.'[55] A natural athlete whose strength and stamina belied his puny appearance, he came to enjoy a range of sports, including rock climbing, hiking, running, skiing, cycling and swimming. Erwin's strength and endurance were a source of wonder to those who expected less from a boy of such a diminutive stature, but exposure to his fiercely competitive character soon made them aware that he was a fighter who never gave up and most definitely did not like to come second.

Erwin's love of the outdoors and his fighting spirit made the Army an obvious career choice for him in an age when the institution was so highly regarded in Germany, but he was not immediately drawn to it. His supportive parents were not wealthy, nor did they expect more of their son than the sort of success that was respectable for his class. Erwin was an average student – poor at those subjects in which he had little interest, but good at those that captured his imagination. With his strong grades in maths and science, Erwin was initially drawn to a career in engineering, and at age fourteen he constructed a full-sized glider with a friend which they managed to coax into flying a short distance. Ultimately, however, young Rommel joined the German Army, hoping that he might be able to combine his practical mind with a life in the open that could satisfy his growing desire for excitement.[56] It was also a solidly middle-class profession of which his parents approved, because a generation earlier the Army had provided the basis for a renewed national identity and unbridled ambition.

Indeed, young Erwin grew up in a nation with a booming economy and an intention to create a great overseas empire, which together were bound to antagonize the status quo. The establishment of a powerful army was, therefore, a considered investment in the future, and even the dour Swabians recognized the opportunities that the organization offered. Rommel's father did not hesitate in writing him a letter of recommendation to the artillery unit with which he himself had served during his compulsory military service. The Army vacillated before accepting Rommel, for no matter what his accomplishments, the selection of a Swabian teacher's son was not particularly attractive for an organization that was dominated by elitist Prussian standards, as that state was its largest and most instrumental contributor. Rommel was eventually offered a place to train as an officer, but not in one of the more fashionable arms or regiments, nor even in a technical arm such as the artillery, but instead in the line infantry where demand was highest and social standing mattered least. Having accepted an invitation to become an officer cadet in the 124th Württemberg Infantry Regiment, he was told to report to its base in the attractive medieval garrison town of Weingarten – and there, on 10 July 1910, Erwin Rommel began his Army career.

At 622,483 officers and men, the German Army that Rommel joined was developing to meet Germany's foreign policy ambitions.[57] This expansion was overseen by the Chief of the General Staff, Helmuth von Moltke (the Younger), who sought to ensure that when fully mobilized the Army could expand rapidly to 4 million.[58] In peace, the armies of four kingdoms of the united Germany (Prussia, Bavaria, Saxony and Württemberg) kept their own identities, but in time of war they would come together as a single entity commanded by the Kaiser. Prussia contributed 75 per cent of the German Army's manpower, but its broader influence stemmed from its long military tradition and recent military successes. Reforms enacted by the likes of August Neidhardt von Gneisenau, Gerhard von Scharnhorst and Carl von Clausewitz in the wake of Prussia's defeat by France in 1806 had been introduced by Moltke (the Elder), and were the platform on which victories against the Austrians in 1866 and the French four years later were constructed. By 1871, Germany was unified, and the Prussian Army had become a model of modern military professionalism.

Pulling on his officer cadet uniform for the first time, therefore, Rommel was joining a valued Prussian institution. His first six months were spent serving as a soldier – holding ranks from private to sergeant – to give him a grounding in army life and an insight into the Württemberg Regiment's values and standards. Ever since the 1820s training had sought to foster a 'mutual confidence between officers and men' designed to ensure that all could relate to serving as an enlisted man and so develop trust that would see the men 'respond with willing discipline'.[59] The 1908 field manual of the Prussian Army reflected this, and stressed that constant attention to the 'welfare of his men is the good and rewarding privilege of the officer' and, moreover, 'it is not enough that one orders, nor that one has right in mind; much more influential on subordinates is the way in which one orders'.[60] Both were to become hallmarks of Rommel's leadership style in the years to come, because he recognized that the rank and file of the Army were better-educated and drawn from a more demanding society than their predecessors, and so less likely to obey orders blindly. Thus Rommel made it his business to ensure his will was done by gaining the trust and respect of those he led, not only as an officer but as a soldier and as a man. His passing of a peer assessment at the end of his first phase of training was evidence that he was successful in this endeavour, and it was an experience that put him in a strong position to continue his leadership development.

Rommel's final eight months of officer training were conducted at the Königliche Kriegsschule (military school) located in the coastal town of Danzig in Prussia. Arriving in March 1911, the circumspect Swabian was immediately immersed in Prussian Army culture and was left in no doubt about the high standards expected of every officer. He thrived while other candidates were sent home. The course was primarily focused on the development and assessment of each cadet's 'character', which can broadly be seen as the ability to display key leader and leadership attributes (such as willpower, courage, integrity, professional knowledge, empathy and communication skills) in a manner appropriate to the context. Each attribute was exhaustively tested, with willpower, for example, needing to be revealed in the individual's desire to become a model officer, his determination to succeed at any task, the resolve to take a decision, the willingness to speak his mind and the mental strength to remain steady under pressure.[61]

Yet even if an officer cadet revealed a scintillating set of attributes in a broad range of circumstances, it would be for nothing if he failed to show a well-developed sense of responsibility towards his men and set an example at all times. At the Kriegsschule, therefore, Rommel was not only schooled in the requirements of Prussian military leadership, he was also educated in the practical application of leadership and assessed continually on his ability to deliver it effectively, in his own style, no matter where or when. Ultimately, the conduct of every officer cadet was examined at every turn for clues about his strengths and weaknesses, and how he behaved, how he responded to pressure and how he communicated his ideas were all noted. Everything an officer cadet did, both on and off duty, was viewed through the prism of leadership and informed his instructors about his development as a leader. The Königliche Kriegsschule was very clear about what it wanted to produce and why, but it was not in the business of supplying the Army with homogenized officers. In recognizing that each officer cadet was an individual as opposed to an automaton who merely needed to be programmed, the school could be justly proud of its tradition of delivering to the Army a spectrum of leaders who not only met common standards but, due to the harnessing of their own personalities and talents, could excel in a range of exacting environments.

Rommel passed out of the Kriegsschule in January 1912 with a report from the commandant that rated him 'good' at leadership and noted that he was 'Firm in character, with immense willpower and a keen enthusiasm… Orderly, punctual, conscientious and comradely. Mentally well endowed, [and with] a strict sense of duty'.[62] His instructors also found him to be a rather intense and, at times, overly serious young man who was inclined to be reclusive and bordered on the anti-social. This was a perceptive overview of Rommel considering the leader he was to become, but included no indication of the personal weaknesses that were soon to cause such pain.

Just eighteen months after his commission, and having taken up his first appointment with the Württemberg regiment in Weingarten as a trainer of new soldiers and returning reserve officers, he was in considerable turmoil. While in Danzig, the Protestant Rommel had fallen for a pretty Catholic woman named Lucia Mollin (known as 'Lucie' or 'Lu') and had proposed to her. She had accepted, but remained in Danzig while Rommel began his tour of duty over 600 miles away. In Weingarten during the spring of 1913, the betrothed Rommel fell into a relationship with a fruit seller named Walburga

Stemmer, who bore him a daughter, Gertrud, in December. Having announced to his parents that he intended to marry Stemmer, Rommel's mother intervened. Seeking to avoid the scandal that such a union would provoke – and the consequent negative implications for her son's career – Helene Rommel convinced her son to end the relationship. He would marry Lucie a few years later having told her about his child, but Gertrud's birth nearly ended Rommel's career just as it was starting.[63]

His work does not seem to have suffered, despite the strain in his personal life, and he threw himself into his duties with renewed vigour in 1913, in doing so winning the praise of his superiors and those he led. Rommel had a particular talent for teaching – the family business – and a gift for communicating complex ideas simply and in a way that stimulated those in his classes and created productive discussion. He showed the same dynamism when temporarily seconded to the 49th Field Artillery Regiment in Ulm as a battery platoon commander in the spring of 1914. If war was to come, Rommel knew how valuable it would be for an infantry leader to be able to co-operate effectively with the gunners. It was not a wasted effort, for by August he was in action for the first time and at the beginning of a remarkable series of leadership experiences.

CHAPTER TWO

First Combat, 1914–16

WHEN WAR BROKE OUT in Europe during August 1914, Second Lieutenant George S. Patton was more than 4,500 miles away attending the advanced programme of his Troop Commander's course at Fort Riley in Kansas. Despite its importance for an ambitious cavalryman, he was so keen to experience combat that he even explored the possibility of joining the army of a combatant nation. Having written to General Leonard Wood about taking a year of leave to fight in Europe, however, he received a disappointing but encouraging reply: 'We don't want to waste youngsters of your sort in the service of foreign nations.'[1] Yet, reading reports of the great early battles taking place at Mons, the Marne and Ypres, Patton looked with envious eyes across the Atlantic at those engaged in the developing carnage on the Western Front and dared to think of himself leading men to glory.[2]

He remained frustrated by his time at Fort Riley, which he found 'tedious', made worse by the fact that, having said he would be a general by the age of thirty, he was a 29-year-old second lieutenant. But Patton would have to remain patient, even if that virtue was not an attribute most readily associated with the man who set such unrealistic career milestones, and he immersed himself in work. In particular, he devoured military history, sometimes spending an unbroken twelve hours with his books, and he wrote to Beatrice in March 1915: 'The more I read, the more I see the necessity for reading. War now will not be gained by a highly educated "bottom" but by a well developed "top".'[3] He found even more time to devote to study while recuperating from a riding injury during the spring of 1915. Having been accident-prone since he was a child, Patton narrowly avoided death on several occasions as an adult – not all of them on the field of battle – including this incident at Fort Riley when he fell off his horse, which then rolled on him before kicking him in the head. His thinning crown was stitched with no obvious longer-term medical implications, but he was lucky not to have been killed, convincing Patton that he had been spared by God because he was destined for 'greater things'.[4]

In June 1915, the month after the sinking of the *Lusitania* had failed to convince President Woodrow Wilson that the United States should join the European war (a decision that Patton derided), Patton graduated successfully from his course at Fort Riley – and promptly had another accident. Returning from a polo match while on leave in Massachusetts, his car overturned and, in a remarkable coincidence (which he declared again was divine intervention), was saved from choking in a pool of oily gravel not by a stranger, but by Beatrice's brother. Another period of protracted convalescence – including the birth of another daughter when he had hoped for a son – did little to improve his mood, and he immediately objected to the news that his next posting would be with the 15th Cavalry Regiment in the Philippines. Fearing that he was being consigned to obscurity while there was fighting to be done, Patton lobbied the War Department hard to be transferred to the 8th Cavalry Regiment at Fort Bliss in Texas, where he would be grappling with Mexican bandits. His success in obtaining a transfer was, no doubt, at least in part due to Patton's latest report, which rated him generally as 'excellent' and 'a most promising young officer of high ideals, devotion to duty, and marked industry' even if the opinionated officer 'should be encouraged to practice self-restraint' in his dealing with superiors.[5] Thus, leaving his family in Massachusetts, a wide-eyed Patton arrived in Texas during

September 1915 looking for any opportunity to test his courage and make his name in action.

Located just outside El Paso, Fort Bliss had been monitoring events in Mexico since the outbreak of revolution in 1910, which had led to civil war four years later. By 1915, the United States supported the coalition headed by the ruthless Venustiano Carranza, but the country remained in turmoil; and in the north, Francisco 'Pancho' Villa sought to depose Carranza. Patton stepped into this fraught situation when he was assigned to his new regiment, which was tasked with securing the border with Mexico as part of John J. Pershing's 8th Brigade. Pershing, whose wife and three daughters had recently perished in a fire at his family home in San Francisco, was still grieving when Patton was given responsibility for the 8th Cavalry Regiment's Troop D, but the strait-laced general was soon to have a major impact on Patton and become one of the most significant mentors of his career. In the meantime, Troop D was sent into the Sierra Blanca Mountains on border patrol, where Patton's responsibility for manning outposts and protecting railway lines did not require inspirational speeches before glorious cavalry charges, instead demanding the tiresome management of mundane duties. He learned not to show his own boredom to his subordinates, and so adopted a demeanour that belied the fact that there was little prospect of any engagement with the bandits, so as 'to keep the men keen'.[6]

An uneventful winter followed, but in March 1916 the US Army involvement in Mexican affairs took a decisive turn after Villa's men attacked the 13th Cavalry Regiment barracks in Columbus, New Mexico, killing seventeen soldiers and civilians. President Woodrow Wilson finally authorized Pershing to capture Villa and an expedition party was formed, but Patton was hugely disappointed when he learned that his own 8th Cavalry Regiment was not to be involved. Yet while similarly thwarted peers lamented their bad luck, Patton wrote directly to Pershing offering his services in whatever capacity he thought fit. It was a calculated but bold move which caught the general's eye (Pershing had done something similar during the

Spanish-American War in 1898), and he replied to Patton asking him why he deserved to be chosen over so many others. Patton replied simply: 'Because I want to go more than anyone else.'[7] By return he received an invitation to join the party as Pershing's aide. In a job that entailed organizing the general's diary, accompanying him on visits, taking notes at meetings and drafting letters, Patton would gain valuable early insights into the world of a senior leader, while enjoying an unrivalled opportunity to learn from one of the US Army's rising stars.

Pershing's 6,600-man expeditionary force left camp in mid-March with the single aim of capturing Villa. The partially motorized force consisted of infantry, cavalry, horsed artillery, supporting troops and a squadron of aircraft, and it plunged into Mexico with all the agility and stealth that one might expect of a large and hastily assembled force lacking adequate intelligence. In the heat and demanding terrain, the task of seeking out a highly mobile enemy soon became a chastening experience for the US troops.

Pershing regularly sallied out from his forward headquarters seventy-five miles south of the border to lend his personal leadership to the venture, and could often be found far in advance of the main body of his troops reconnoitring the ground in an open-topped Dodge touring car that he used as a mobile command post. Patton travelled at the general's side, watching his every move, absorbing his style, and was impressed with what he saw. As he later wrote: '[Pershing's] commanding presence... and his utter disregard of danger overawed the Mexicans.'[8]

He began to copy some of Pershing's behaviours. The general was an officer who not only demonstrated personal courage but was also charismatic, decisive and always set an example. Patton was particularly impressed that, while Pershing could easily have chosen safety and comfort, he instead felt it essential to share the risks his men took and endure their discomforts even if it meant sleeping on the ground without a tent. The general showed a humility that Patton himself could only aspire to, and Pershing taught the young officer the value of finding the time to talk to people (no matter what their rank or role), show an interest in what they were doing and thank them. Patton also learned that Pershing's effectiveness did not come without great self-discipline. 'By constant study, [he] knew to the most minute detail each of the subjects in which he demanded practice', Patton later wrote, 'and by his physical presence and personal example and explanation, insured himself that they were correctly carried out.'[9]

The trust and understanding that Patton established in his relationship with Pershing had, by May 1916, encouraged the general to give his testy aide an opportunity to hunt down Julio Cárdenas, Villa's trusted lieutenant, and so the young officer created a raiding party. The first foray to Cárdenas's villa was frustrated when his quarry managed to escape, but when Patton and his team returned on 14 May they had more success. Having sent his men to their designated positions around the property, Patton himself began an approach towards the front of the building, determined to flush Cárdenas out and towards the waiting guns. He walked slowly, listening, watching, his hands clasping a rifle while two Colt .45 revolvers rested in their holsters on a cartridge belt slung low around his hips.

The silence was broken suddenly. Three Mexicans on horseback bolted out from the rear of the villa firing their weapons wildly. As the bandits thundered towards him, Patton discarded his rifle, drew his revolvers and returned fire. In the ensuing gun battle, Patton hit one of the riders in the arm, and as the man's horse was shot from under him, the wounded bandit was dispatched in a hail of fire. The remaining two Mexicans panicked, but as they sought to break through the lightly held American perimeter, one was killed and the second was wounded. The stricken man fell from his horse and attempted to hobble back towards the villa. Patton shot him with his rifle; Julio Cárdenas was dead before he hit the ground.[10]

In common with most of his brother officers, Patton had no principled objection to gunning down men he viewed with contempt, and a letter he wrote to Beatrice at this time made it clear that he viewed his Mexican adversaries as racially inferior to himself: '[They] are much lower than the Indians…They have absolutely no morals and there have been no marriages here for five years.'[11] He thus had no qualms about theatrically strapping the dead bodies of Cárdenas and his two men to the bonnets of his cars after his successful hunting party at the rebel's villa – the first US Army tactical action using automobiles. Pershing's reaction to the stunt is not known, but the event was described in a laudatory article in *The New York Times*, and a Boston daily featured a photograph of Patton taken outside his tent, pipe in mouth (*à la* Pershing), under a headline which led to a new moniker for the junior officer: the 'Bandit-killer'.[12] Patton was thrilled, and wrote to his wife that Pershing had told 'some of the officers that I did more in half a day than the whole 13th Cavalry did in a week'.[13]

With the excitement of the spring over, by July 1916 Patton was, once again, bored by the routine of his duties. 'We are all rapidly going crazy from lack of occupation and there is no help in sight',[14] George wrote to his father just as details about the great Somme offensive in France were reaching the expeditionary force, and he took up his studies once more. He viewed his peers who were less attentive to their self-development with an open derision that angered many, and this soon came to Pershing's attention. Writing to Patton in October while his clumsy subordinate was recuperating in hospital having set his tent and himself on fire when he over-pressurized a lamp, the general advised: 'Do not be too insistent upon your own personal views. We are at liberty to express our personal views only when called upon to do so or else confidentially to our friends, but always confidentially and with the complete understanding that they are in no sense to govern our actions.'[15]

Patton may have altered his behaviour around his colleagues, but there is little evidence that he felt it necessary to suppress his opinions in his published articles – two of which appeared in Army journals in late 1916 – that sought to make a contribution to the improvement of the US Army. The first concerned cavalry tactics and expressed his growing advocacy of mobility, boldness and aggression in military operations, while the second argued that leaders should initiate a rigorous training programme for their troops as an effective means of enhancing their fighting effectiveness.[16] George Patton, it seemed to his chain of command, was a man full of ideas, and he possessed a spirit which, although sometimes misplaced, marked him out. Such men were beginning to be identified for service overseas as the US inched towards involvement in the First World War.

— ¤ —

When Britain declared war on the German Empire on 4 August 1914, 26-year-old Lieutenant Bernard Montgomery was adjutant of the 1st Battalion Royal Warwickshire Regiment. Commanded by Lieutenant Colonel John Ford Elkington and stationed near Folkestone on the south coast of England, the regiment had been mobilized with the rest of the British Army during the previous week as it began its detailed preparations for a move to France. Montgomery was relieved that decisions were finally being made after months of tension. 'I can't help thinking that [war] will be a good thing', he wrote to his mother, '& much better to have it now & get done with it. A modern war would not last very long, & would be such an awful affair that there would be no more war for 50 years.'[17] His rather relaxed tone about the impending conflict was suggestive of a mood that was widespread at the time, for with Germany having to fight on two fronts the British and French in the west and Russia in the east – it was widely thought that her rapid defeat was inevitable. Montgomery was keen to be involved in a combat leadership role when the fighting began, and having made that clear to his commanding officer, his wish was granted with a reappointment to platoon commander.

As part of 4th Division's 10th Brigade, Elkington's battalion would be one of the first deployed to the continent with the British Expeditionary Force (BEF), where it would be expected to meet the huge German invasion and play its role in halting the enemy's advance. Knowing this, Montgomery wasted no time during the three weeks before the battalion departed for France in asserting himself over the sixty-seven men in his platoon. He started by establishing a strong bond with his subordinates – the basis of the deep trust that he knew would be essential when the fighting began. He was convinced that by showing concern for the welfare and safety of his platoon, he would gain its respect, improve its morale and so help create a fighting spirit. In a practical sense, he did his utmost to minimize the time that his young men spent on nugatory activities. By scheduling shooting practice, runs and tactical training, he ensured that the platoon was 'match fit'; and by creating a competition between his sections, he kept them engaged. 'Every morning we go for a long route march to get their feet hard', he wrote in mid-August, 'and finish up with manoeuvres of some sort. Then every evening we inspect the men's feet to see that they haven't got blisters etc… If your men can't march they are no use.'[18] Montgomery's methods were not designed to win the affection of his men but rather their respect. The young officer was gradually seen as a hard but fair officer and a thorough professional who could be relied on. His decisiveness and willingness to get his men what they needed (such as the time when a farmer denied them access to water to refill their canteens while on a march and, as he later recalled, 'I brought in my men and took it'[19]) was appreciated by the platoon, who repaid his care with hard work and loyalty.

On 22 August 1914, the day the vanguard of the 100,000-man-strong BEF reached the Belgian town of Mons, the 1st Battalion Royal Warwickshire Regiment left Southampton docks aboard SS *Caledonia*.[20] It docked at Boulogne the following morning and Montgomery learned that, outnumbered four to one, British, French and Belgian forces were withdrawing before the German onslaught. 'It is not a case of *if* but *when* the dam will collapse,' wrote Julien Beaumont, a translator working at the BEF's General Headquarters. 'We thought the war would be a short one, but one that would see Germany vanquished. How misguided we were!'[21]

Having arrived at the town of Le Cateau near the Belgian border on the morning of 24 August, the Warwicks joined the rest of the brigade and thus became part of the organized chaos that accompanied the BEF's retreat. While carrying out the withdrawal routine, at 04.30 on 26 August the Warwicks came under German artillery fire while bivouacking in a damp field in the village of Haucourt, some fifteen miles north-west of Cambrai. Their orders surprisingly did not involve another battalion withdrawal but, instead, a hasty attack to retake a ridge recently captured by the enemy. 'We advanced through a hail of bullets from rifles & machine-guns & through a perfect storm of shrapnel fire,' Montgomery later wrote of how he led his platoon as it advanced towards the enemy.[22] He shouted encouragement to his frightened men and waved his sword in the air (which even to Montgomery at the time seemed like a redundant gesture from a bygone era in the face of modern firepower) only then to trip over his scabbard. Scrambling to his feet, he found that most of his men were already dead or seriously wounded, but Montgomery pushed on again and in a blur of activity found himself isolated with the remaining eighty men of the company pinned down and with no means of communication to the rear.

They remained *in situ* all day, with Montgomery, the only officer, desperate for information and unaware that the small group had already been abandoned in a brigade withdrawal. Sensing something had gone awry and aware that the enemy would soon advance, he took the decision to use the cover of darkness to disengage and make haste towards friendly lines – wherever that might be. Over the next two days, Montgomery's party linked up with some 600 men from a variety of other units on the same quest, led by a Major Poole, and tried to evade capture by the pursuing Germans. They were finally reunited with the BEF on 28 August, and in doing so re-joined a strategic withdrawal without any sense of where and when it would end.

Montgomery's first taste of action in France had not been glorious, but it was distinguished in its own way and provided a robust introduction to the friction of war and leadership in combat.

His efforts were certainly appreciated by his surviving men and the wider regiment, which, having suffered such terrible losses, made Montgomery a temporary captain in command of a company. His elevation coincided with the Germans being checked to the east of Paris, where Allied counter-attacks forced them to make tactical withdrawals to more favourable ground. By mid-September the Germans had reached the north bank of the Aisne river in the BEF sector, and both sides began to dig in. Within weeks, intricate trench systems were being created, with the Warwicks playing a full part in 4th Division's defensive preparations, and new routines ensured that battalions were rotated in and out of the front line.

Always seeking to be a role model, and keen to see his company retain an aggressive edge, Montgomery wrote that autumn: 'I can see the Germans in their trenches & occasionally we exchange shots; I bagged one man this morning, and one horse.'[23] He never asked one of his men to do what he himself would not, but in return Montgomery expected his men to be on their mettle. Constantly touring his company's sector, Montgomery chatted with his officers and men, and so gained a good sense of his subordinates' mindset. There were dangers inherent in such an approach – on two occasions, men who had been standing next to Montgomery were shot dead – but he was convinced that being visible to the troops was the essence of junior leadership and he demanded that his platoon commanders do similar. His style was instinctively paternalistic, an approach that placed him firmly at the centre of everything. 'It is no small responsibility being in command of 250 men on active service & within 600 yards of the German Army', he wrote to his mother, 'it's really a major's command and I am lucky to have it. I have two officers under me, but the responsibility rests on me, & I am glad it does.'[24]

Stalemate developed along the line during the last months of 1914, but not before both sides had attempted to outflank each other to the north in what became known as the 'Race to the Sea'. At the end of this phase in mid-October, the Warwickshire battalion was relocated from the Aisne to a position thirty miles south of

Dunkirk, just inside the French border. Here, having been replaced as company commander by a more senior colleague fresh from England, Montgomery reverted to the command of his former platoon. In this role, on 13 October he participated in an attack on the village of Méteren, which was the Warwicks' objective in the first formal BEF attack of the war, involving some 50,000 troops. With no support from field artillery, Montgomery led his men over open ground on a damp, misty morning towards the German line just outside the village.[25] As soon as the battalion launched itself towards the first buildings, it fell prey to German field-gun shelling and small arms fire, but the men did not falter. Focused on his objective, Montgomery led his platoon from the front once more, but this time with a revolver instead of a sword, yelling encouragement at the top of his voice in the hope that he would be heard over the din of combat. His men followed, drawn forward by their officer's presence, and fell quickly on the Germans. Montgomery kicked a German rifleman hard in the stomach and won his first prisoner in the process, and after several minutes of close-quarter fighting the position was under control.

As the platoon was reorganizing it became clear that there had been success along the line. Keen to maintain pressure on the Germans, headquarters issued new orders for the battalion to play its part in a brigade attack to complete the taking of Méteren that evening. In preparation, Montgomery went forward on a lone reconnaissance. Running at the crouch, revolver in hand, he had covered twenty yards when his men heard a rifle crack and saw their officer slump to the ground. A round had passed through his right lung, and left him bleeding profusely and in a swirl of pain. One of his men ran forward to administer first aid but was shot through the head as he reached Montgomery and fell across his officer's body. Summoning up all his energy, Montgomery shouted that no more men should break cover and he remained in the middle of the battlefield throughout the resultant attempt to dislodge the enemy from the village. Unable to move, he was shot again, this time through the left knee, with other rounds being absorbed by the corpse of the man who even in death offered protection to his platoon commander. Not until after dark did Méteren fall and Montgomery could finally receive the medical attention he required. He was not expected to live.

Montgomery's survival astounded those who were responsible for his care. He lay for five days drifting in and out of consciousness, but once stabilized he was evacuated back to England for specialist treatment at the Royal Herbert Hospital in Woolwich, south London, close to his childhood home. His health slowly improved and he insisted on a return to France just as soon as the Army could arrange it. He dismissed the idea of being disabled out of the Army as 'ridiculous' and the possibility of an untaxing desk job in England as 'unconscionable', and so, promoted to the temporary rank of captain and having been awarded the Distinguished Service Order (DSO) for his 'conspicuous gallant leading',[26] he sought new challenges in uniform. The fact that medics correctly predicted that his shortness of breath would be chronic prompted a decision that he should not return to general duties but to a staff position.

Although a blow to his command aspirations, Montgomery recognized his physical limitations and was posted as brigade major (chief of staff) to the 91st Infantry Brigade (consisting of volunteers), which was then forming in Manchester. He returned to service in February 1915 as one of the 'red tabs', staff officers identified by their red collar patches who were commonly reviled by fighting units for their supposed physical and emotional detachment from the front. Having been a front-line soldier decorated for his gallantry gave Montgomery an advantage in the respectability stakes, but headquarters staff work in an operational context was a completely new challenge for him. His boss, Brigadier General G. M. Mackenzie, was described by Montgomery as 'a very nice person but quite useless' and the young officer was convinced that, despite his lack of appropriate training and experience, he would be better in the role himself.[27] The young major's professionalism and capacity for work were exceptional, but he did not hide his low opinion of others from colleagues, which led to criticisms of arrogance from within the staff team. For his part, Montgomery was not particularly concerned by the chorus of disapproval, for he knew that his work was respected by the general and his only concern was with improving the fighting effectiveness of 91st Brigade before it reached the front.

Montgomery started by setting new standards for training – some of which he organized in the rugged terrain of North Wales – and supervising all aspects of its application. Such was his success that before the brigade could be sent as a single entity to France, its four battalions were used to reinforce other formations, thus requiring that Mackenzie and his staff start building again with new troops. Heading the re-designated 104th Infantry Brigade, part of Major General Reginald Pinney's 35th 'Bantam' Division, Montgomery again set to work turning disconcerted civilians into capable soldiers. By August 1915 he had succeeded once more, with his leadership during a field exercise that month impressing Mackenzie, who complimented him on his 'fine work'. Although the general may not have been the most dynamic commander in the BEF, nor particularly bright, in a letter to Montgomery's father Mackenzie revealed that he could recognize talent and knew how to use it:

> I have the very highest opinion of [Montgomery]. He is equally good at Administration as at Training of Troops. He ought to have a brilliant future in the Army, and rise to high rank… He has taken a great deal of routine work and drudgery off my hands, doing the work in a quiet unobtrusive way… [I]t is not every Staff Officer that I have met, nor many, who have been so thorough and helpful in the work. General Pinney too knows his work and worth, and I am sure will look after his future interests.[28]

The brigade headquarters left Southampton for Le Havre on 29 January 1916, its four battalions following to attend the BEF's 'finishing school' at Saint-Omer and then moving into the line. The Western Front that Monty, as he was now commonly called, re-entered was different from the one that he had left on a stretcher fifteen months before, as the trench system had been solidified and established from the Belgian coast in the north to the Swiss border in the south, creating a deadlock which had reduced Allied strategy to an attritional slogfest based on great set-piece battles that were soon seared into Montgomery's consciousness. By 1916, the task of the increasingly civilian BEF was to learn fast, absorb losses and show tenacity in the face of huge carnage. Men like Montgomery had responsibility for the nation's precious young men, and it was their duty to use their leadership to prepare these men as well as they could for the trials – and, when required, be ready to lead them to their deaths. If anything, that responsibility increased Montgomery's efforts on behalf of those at the sharp end of combat.

On 7 March, having marched through the devastated rear area behind the BEF lines, 104th Brigade snaked its way through the communication trenches to take its position in rotation at Richebourg, near Neuve-Chapelle – three weeks in the line followed by a week in reserve to rest, train, and provide men for the war's insatiable need for working parties. It was a schedule that Montgomery had to manage carefully. 'After each phase it was important that the battalions had improved', he later wrote to David Drake, a staff captain back in England, 'and that they were better equipped to deal with whatever was thrown at them next time.'[29]

Acting as Mackenzie's eyes and ears on the ground, Monty's daily routine was shaped around his belief that it was essential to have daily contact with the brigade. Rising at 05.00, he first attended to administrative duties in his dugout in the trenches occupied by brigade headquarters, then left to visit the battalions (either in the trenches or in the rear area) from mid-morning to late afternoon. He felt conspicuousness was crucial to headquarters' efforts to win the trust of the fighting troops, and he listened to officers and soldiers alike as he assessed activities and morale. 'My war experience led me to believe', Montgomery later wrote, 'that the staff must be the servants of the troops, and that a good staff officer must serve his commander and the troops but himself be anonymous.'[30] He returned to his desk at headquarters at around 17.00 to write up and distribute his findings, before grappling with the issues of the day that required his attention, taking a brief dinner with his colleagues and then retiring to bed at around midnight. It was a gruelling seven-days-a-week regimen.

The arrival of the talented 42-year-old James Sandilands as a replacement for Mackenzie in the early summer of 1916 was doubtless the fillip that Montgomery and the brigade needed before it engaged in one of the wars' most demanding battles. A Staff College graduate who had commanded a battalion in combat and been mentioned in dispatches for his gallantry, Sandilands was just the sort of energetic officer that Montgomery respected, and he would come to regard him as 'the best general I ever served under'.[31] He was impressed with how Sandilands conducted himself, and particularly the extent to which he made time for visits, often on his own, partly to get first-hand knowledge of his troops but also to take some pressure off his tired brigade major. Both men knew that the brigade was soon to be severely tested at the Somme, where it was inserted in late July 1916. Having failed to break the German front earlier in the month, the casualty-heavy offensive continued with attempts to take vital ground that, it was hoped, would unhinge the enemy's defences. 104th Brigade entered this complex military situation at Guillemont, where it was to provide the reserve for an attack on Maltz Horn Farm on 20 July.[32]

Having engaged in a week of brutal fighting, the brigade suffered nearly 1,000 casualties for very limited territorial gains. Monty witnessed the mauling first hand during his daily rounds – during which he was knocked off his feet on more than one occasion by enemy shellfire – and Sandilands found his reports indispensable. On 10 August, when both Montgomery and Sandilands were at the front, they came under such regular bombardment that, dusting himself down after the latest shelling, the major turned to the general and said, 'I'm beginning to take all this enemy attention personally, sir. If we are both blown to pieces now, the Germans would have removed the best brigade major in the British Army, and a good brigadier general!'[33] On another visit, and to the very great admiration of those who watched him, Monty was told that a battalion withdraw had stalled due to officer casualties, so he instinctively jumped out of the trench and sprinted across No Man's Land to take control. Artillery shells exploded all around, small arms fire threw up soil at his feet and buzzed past his head, but his presence proved decisive in helping to extricate the unit. Stories about 'Mad Montgomery' soon became the talk of the brigade.

The close working relationship that Montgomery struck up with Sandilands was a model of its type, as they focused on training, promotions and their lesson-learning process to ensure that skilled leaders were in positions where they could exert their influence to best effect. This was particularly important with the need to integrate so many inexperienced replacements into the fighting battalions, and also when higher headquarters poached good staff officers from the brigade. Sandilands let some men go but he always fought hard to keep his brigade major, which meant that eventually Montgomery was the only remaining member of the original staff team.

The benefit of maintaining a capable and stable staff organization was an important lesson that Montgomery took from his time with 104th Brigade on the Somme. Another was the need for generals, no matter what their seniority, to be engaged with the front, their troops and the realities of war. 'There was little contact between the generals and the troops,' Montgomery later wrote. 'I never once saw the British Commander-in-Chief, neither French nor Haig, and only twice did I see an Army Commander.'[34] Only by actively participating in the war did Montgomery come to judge that the British Army had approached the conflict as if it were nothing more than a predictable table-top exercise rather than a complicated and unpredictable series of events concerning real people. As the Battle of the Somme came to an end in the mud of a Picardy November, he concluded that the root of the Western Front problem was the want of effective leadership.

— □ —

When the German Army mobilized for war on 1 August 1914, Erwin Rommel immediately left the artillery regiment to which he was attached and returned to Weingarten, where the 124th Württemberg Infantry Regiment was being put onto a war footing. Its commander, Colonel Otto Haas, immediately appointed Rommel a platoon commander in 2nd Battalion's 7th Company, responsible for eighty men he knew well. As part of 27th Division in Crown Prince Wilhelm's Fifth Army, the regiment was at the hub of the Schlieffen Plan's great wheeling movement that sought to sweep through Belgium and France to wrap around Paris.

The regiment's advance into the densely forested Ardennes region of south-east Belgium began after dark on 21 August, with many initially experiencing a surge of nervous excitement that was to leave them struggling to keep their focus by the following dawn. Rommel's First World War memoir, *Infantry Attacks*, was to bring his name to popular attention when it was published in 1937, and the book reveals the anticipation that he felt in the pit of his stomach as his platoon led the battalion at the start of a long journey into the unknown.[35] After several hours' marching, the company commander, Major Theo Bader, ordered Rommel and four fellow platoon members to reconnoitre forward while the column took a rest. With adrenaline coursing through his body on what was his first combat assignment, Rommel moved off into the blackness. His account of that night explains his nervousness: 'Much more cautious than in peace time exercises – as one is aware of the responsibility for the lives of one's men.'[36] The task was completed without incident, and Rommel spent the rest of the night running messages between various headquarters.

On the following day, 22 August, Rommel experienced his first much-anticipated combat, which provided an insight into the leader that he had become. In a two-battalion attack, his objective was a cluster of buildings in the village of Bleid, which was known to be occupied by French troops. Peering hard through the morning mist as he led the platoon to the enemy, Rommel heard a speculative shot scud over their heads from an unseen sentry, but his men pressed on to find cover a short distance behind a hedge. The platoon concealed itself while its commander led a small reconnaissance party towards a nearby farm. Peering around the corner of the first building, Rommel saw enemy soldiers emerge phantom-like from the mist – some twenty in all. The four men selected a target and, following their officer's order, opened fire. Rommel felled his man by the entrance to a house at a range of twenty yards. 'My shot cracked', he recalled in his memoir, 'the enemy's head slams heavily forward onto the step.'[37] Several Frenchmen sank to the ground, the remainder scattering towards safety while the reconnaissance party moved forward on Rommel's orders to exploit the psychological advantage that their surprise arrival had created, but they were soon forced to fall back with the main body of the platoon, which then mounted a hasty attack.

The subsequent fighting was typical of that conducted in a complex built-up area: intense, energy-sapping and difficult to control. Rommel directed his platoon to clear one building at a time using burning straw to smoke the defenders out, either taking them prisoner when they emerged or, if they remained combative, fighting them in the street. It was a slow process, but with other units breaking into the village, Bleid was soon secured.[38] Rommel's boldness had spearheaded a significant tactical victory for the regiment, but on receiving information that the enemy had been seen withdrawing, Rommel sought to chase them down. He once again led a reconnaissance party forward, and when the equivalent of a French company had been located, a fierce firefight ensued. Scores of enemy casualties littered the ground as Rommel's audaciousness was again vindicated and a disorientated enemy was forced to withdraw in considerable disorder. At this point, Rommel collapsed, falling unconscious, his body's reaction to his exertions over the previous twenty-four hours and to his having paid scant attention to his own basic needs. It was another valuable lesson learned, for after a short period of rest, a drink and some food, Rommel was back on his feet and leading his platoon once more.

The events at Bleid had given Rommel's men an early taste of what every combat leader requires to establish credibility with his subordinates: success. Not all leaders (no matter how good they may appear in barracks) excel in battle. Having gained a small victory with extremely low casualties, Rommel's men willingly followed him. He was briefly detailed from his platoon to serve as battalion adjutant, but by the autumn of 1914 he was back fighting, now with a different platoon in the densely wooded Argonne region of northeastern France. Because the group did not know him, he once again determined to set a standard and lead from the front. When his men were pinned down by an enemy machine gun during an attack across barren terrain and went to ground, he sensed that he needed to make the first move. Scrambling to his feet, he ran forward into the killing zone and shot two of the enemy dead with his rifle as his men roused themselves to follow. Having neutralized a machine gun, Rommel became a casualty himself. 'As I rushed forward, the enemy opened fire. I was hit and sent rolling over just a few feet from the enemy,' he later recalled. 'My left thigh had been torn apart by a rifle round and blood spurted from a fist-sized wound.'[39] He was extremely fortunate to have survived, but his gallantry that day was recognized with the award of the Iron Cross, Second Class – and a platoon that knew the young officer's selflessness had saved their lives.

On his return to active duty in January 1915, Rommel was given temporary command of a company manning the trenches in the Argonne. Fighting in the sector had been intense during the previous three months, and the company he acquired was dispirited after significant losses followed by unknown green replacements. Once again, his attention was on ensuring that the needs of the men were catered for as they rotated through the trenches and rear area – good food, rest and entertainment, as well as equipment, training and tactics – and that he got to know his soldiers personally. He needed to rebuild the unit's confidence, for once a leader had established confidence, he argued, his men would 'follow him through thick and thin'.[40] Gradually, the company regained its self-assurance with Rommel leading it in some small but morale-boosting tactical successes.

On one raiding party, however, Rommel faced a significant problem. Lying on the frozen ground of No Man's Land one bitterly cold winter's day, he scanned the enemy's dense protective wire for the single break in the obstacle, which had previously been identified as a place through which the company could pass before it fell on the enemy's position. He was the first through the gap, crawling on all fours as enemy small arms fire began to slam into the ground around him. 'I had previously ordered the company to follow me', he wrote in *Infantry Attacks*, 'but the leading platoon commander lost his courage and the entire company came to a halt in front of the obstacle.'[41] A furious Rommel, fearing the loss of valuable momentum and knowing that his men were vulnerable where they lay, returned to the offending officer to say that 'he would be shot if he didn't immediately obey my orders'.[42] The platoon commander began to move forward and the rest of the men did the same. Although the raid was not destined to be a great success, the new company commander had made a strong point: he would not tolerate disobedience. It was a relatively minor incident but it also revealed how Rommel's leadership was forged on the battlefield. He made no apologies for being a tough and uncompromising officer because he was being true to himself, had the best interests of his men at heart and got results. If leading meant that on occasion he had to issue threats to get the outcome he desired, then so be it.

The impact that Rommel had on his new command was significant. Awarded the Iron Cross, First Class for his leadership during the raid through the barbed wire (the first of his rank in the regiment to be awarded the honour), by the end of the winter he led a company with a powerful fighting spirit. While the other companies were identified by their number, his became known as 'Rommel Company', a singular honour which gave its members an identity that was indivisible from its commander. The loyalty of the men to their young officer was something that he cherished. Despite his hard edge, Rommel was known as a compassionate man, a leader who never became immune to casualties among his men and who always took time to reassure the wounded and bring comfort to the dying. He was a courageous, caring and charismatic officer with an uncanny military instinct and an outstanding fighting record. Lieutenant Theodor Werner, who served with Rommel during this time, later wrote approvingly:

> Anybody who once came under his spell of personality turned into a real soldier. However tough the strain he seemed inexhaustible. He seemed to know just what the enemy were like and how they would probably react. His plans were often startling, instinctive, spontaneous and not infrequently obscure. He had an exceptional imagination, and it enabled him to hit on the most unexpected solutions to tough situations. When there was danger, he was always out in front calling on us to follow. He seemed to know no fear whatever. His men idolized him and had boundless faith in him.[43]

Such was the bond that Rommel built with his men that when, as anticipated, he was supplanted as commander of the company that bore his name by an officer with greater seniority (albeit with no combat experience), Rommel accepted being his second in command. Although one can only surmise how difficult it was for the incoming officer to take over from Rommel while the man himself remained part of the team, the episode must have been hugely frustrating for the displaced Erwin, whose duty it was to help the new man make the company his own. Although patience is not a quality most readily associated with Rommel, during the summer of 1915 he nevertheless learned of its benefits and waited for his opportunity.

Venerated by his men and his superiors for his leadership effectiveness, and twice officially recognized for his gallantry, by the end of 1915 First Lieutenant Erwin Rommel's fortitude was repaid with an invitation to apply his skills in more open warfare, as a company commander in the elite Royal Württemberg Mountain Battalion. Consisting of men looking for a new challenge (with 10 per cent having been awarded bravery decorations), this new 2,000-man unit was forming in Münsingen, a small town thirty miles south-east of Stuttgart, and was tailor-made for a man of Rommel's abilities. His battalion commander was 45-year-old Major Theodor Sprösser, a talented and driven officer known for his own compelling leadership built on demanding standards and strict discipline. Sprösser had commanded a battalion of the Württemberg Regiment since the outbreak of war on both the Western and Eastern Fronts, where he had made his enviable reputation as a courageous and skilled commander. Now he led a Mountain Battalion that consisted of six rifle companies, each with an attached machine gun platoon and a higher quality of soldier than Rommel had previously experienced. It was being developed into a high-performing outfit by Sprösser in anticipation of a most demanding role in one of Europe's most hostile environments. Its initial training completed, the battalion was sent to the Vosges (the highest ground on the Western Front, just twenty-five miles from the Swiss border), where from early January 1916 through to the autumn it was shaped into a fighting organization with no rivals. Rommel thrived in the competitive culture that Sprösser created to get the best out of his subordinates, and by the end of the year those officers and their men were fighting in the Romanian mountains. It was a test like nothing Rommel had previously experienced.

Romania had entered the war at the end of August 1916 on the Allied side and, supported by the Russians, its forces fought to gain control of the mountain passes leading to the Transylvania region of eastern Austria–Hungary. They made good progress, forcing the Austro-Hungarian defenders back, but the latter's ally Germany sent reinforcements and together they counter-attacked.

The German Alpine Corps, of which the Württemberg Mountain Battalion was a part, was in the thick of the fighting. Despite its training, the unit found the conditions in which it had to live and operate extremely demanding: chilling weather, difficult resupply, minimal medical support, mountains to climb in full equipment and an enemy waiting to fight at the summit. Thomas Artmann, an Alpine Corps officer, began to keep a journal about his experiences, and on 1 November wrote: 'The increasing cold and damp gets into the bones. It takes hours to revive and fingers remain numb. Some men complain of painful feet for socks and boots are permanently wet. We often endure days on rations that do little for the morale or the physical well-being of chilled troops and we have many casualties.'

On the following day, he noted: 'There was no food last night or this morning. Exhaustion. I go to see the men. They smile but I know they are feeling low. The wind never stops. It screams. This is a terrible, terrible place.'[44]

Although living in the Western Front's trenches had perilous health implications for the troops, if anything they were exceeded by the danger that each man faced in the Transylvanian mountains. Although Rommel did what he could, morale plummeted during periods of prolonged sleeting rain when clothing froze to their bodies, and particularly when they had nothing to eat but emergency rations. In such circumstances it was as well that the enemy they initially engaged proved no match for the Swabian mountain battalion, but as autumn progressed and the German and Austro-Hungarian troops pressed into Romania, that changed and they became 'wild and dangerous opponents'.[45] Peak after peak had to be climbed, fought over, seized and consolidated. The assault on Mount Lesului on 11 November 1916 as part of the attempt to force the Vulcan Pass was typical of operations that the Mountain Battalion undertook. 'On our way to the line of departure', Rommel wrote, 'we ran into Rumanian sentries and had a short firefight'; it was his company's subsequent bold flanking movement that unhinged the position and created the conditions for success.[46] Despite the trying conditions, Rommel used the fact that there were no rigid defensive lines to his advantage – a broader canvas for his tactical creativity – and success was as good a motivator of men as anything else in the Romanian mountains.

Sprösser was impressed with Rommel's impact, knowing that he had been critical to the battalion's accomplishments, which had contributed to the German advance into northern and western Romania. For the Württembergers, the offensive continued on 13 November when the battalion made one of its periodic returns into the valley to clear the village of Kurpenul-Valarii, which lay on their axis of advance. Rommel personally led a reconnaissance party into the collection of sturdy farm buildings to ascertain the positions of the enemy, while the remainder of his men followed at a safe distance along with the supporting machine-gun platoon. When numerically superior enemy opened fire on Rommel's small party, he was concerned that they could be surrounded before the main body of his company arrived and so braved a hail of enemy fire and zigzagged back to inform his leading platoon about the situation he had just left. He ordered it and the machine guns to suppress the enemy so that the reconnaissance party could fall back, which it did at great speed, before forming his men into an all-round defensive position. It was quite clear to Rommel that the company had walked into a trap, and for the rest of the day the encircling Romanians tried to destroy the exposed Germans.

Hour after hour Rommel moved about his platoons to ensure that there was no weak link in the chain of positions, making adjustments where necessary, offering advice and encouragement where he could, and never being concerned for his own safety despite the incoming fire that his movement attracted. The fact that the company ultimately survived was due to Mountain Battalion reinforcements, but during that long day Rommel's leadership kept his men alive. What is more, the company's stand ensured that a vital entry-point into Kurpenul-Valarii remained open, and this was the route through which the majority of the Württembergers advanced in subsequent village-clearance operations. By evening Rommel counted the cost: twenty of his company had become casualties, but on the Romanian side, 'hundreds of dead covered the battlefield, with a division commander among them'.[47]

Sprösser was once again thoroughly impressed with his company commander, and with grateful thanks and best wishes he sent the 25-year-old Erwin Rommel back to Germany for some leave, during which time he could marry his great love, Lucie Mollin.

CHAPTER THREE

Hard-Won Experience, 1917–18

B Y THE TIME JOHN PERSHING'S expeditionary force began to pull out of Mexico in February 1917, George Patton had long since become bored by his routine and the lack of personal challenge. With no immediate prospect of capturing Pancho Villa, he was delighted to be quitting the country and wrote to Beatrice: 'This is the last letter I shall write you from Mexico. I have learned a lot about my profession and a lot about how much I love you. The first was necessary the second was not.'[1]

In April, while George was commanding a troop of the 7th Cavalry at Fort Bliss, the United States declared war on the Central Powers (Germany, Austria–Hungary, the Ottoman Empire and Bulgaria) and he turned his attention to how he might get to Europe and fight Germans. In this quest he was fortunate to know 'Jack' Pershing, recently promoted to major general and appointed as commander of the American Expeditionary Forces (AEF), and he extracted letters of recommendation from anybody of influence willing to write to the War Department that Patton should serve in the new organization.[2] As it turned out, Pershing had preselected his former aide to become part of his team as commander of the 'Headquarters Troops', consisting of some sixty-five enlisted orderlies, chauffeurs, engineers, medical personnel and signallers. It was not a glamorous role, but it got Patton on the ship to France, and he could not have been more delighted that he was, at least, to work in a theatre of war.

Just before he sailed from New York, the senior Patton family held a dinner in honour of Pershing in Washington, and a newspaper confirmed the public rumour that Pershing and Nita Patton were to be married, having met at a Fort Bliss social function the previous year. Although the engagement was soon broken when Pershing's attention became focused on the war (and other women), George Patton left the United States with a general who looked set to become his brother-in-law – a situation that gave the ambitious junior officer a sense of well-being as he steamed across the Atlantic. He also knew that if he was to attain the combat command after which he hankered, it would have to be earned.

Having arrived in England on 8 June, Patton was soon pulled into the uniformed whirlpool that was London in the fourth year of what had been dubbed 'the Great War'. Here he acted as Pershing's aide once more, accompanying him to a variety of high-profile events, including one with King George V and another with Prime Minister David Lloyd George, but he was also part of the advance party tasked with establishing an AEF headquarters in Paris. In the French capital, not for the first time in his career, Patton soon found his daily routine dreary and so endeavoured to enliven his experience by spending money that his wife had brought to their marriage. First, he took a grand apartment off the Champs-Élysées, and then, despite his short walk to work, purchased a pretentious 12-cylinder Packard automobile. To most, these affectations were grotesque indulgences in the middle of a war and signs of an ostentation that were insensitive to the circumstances. Yet as long as they could not influence his career prospects, Patton dismissed critics as 'jealous SOBs', 'mean and stupid men' and 'officers born in the gutter and likely to stay there'.[3] His supreme self-confidence in his own abilities and opinions was only enhanced by his proximity to war-fighting.

By late August the weight of the US effort had moved away from Paris as training establishments sprang up in the Lorraine sector, towards the southern end of the front, and AEF headquarters moved to Chaumont on the Marne river. Here Patton continued to lead his mixed team of soldiers, but he was also required to be at Pershing's side when the general visited the troops and attended meetings with subordinates and allies. Patton's respect for his boss only intensified during this period as he witnessed how Pershing took calm control of events and people, no matter where or when he encountered them. He was impressed by the way the general handled colleagues from other armies – always friendly towards them but never anything less than frank about his resolution to look after the interests of his own troops. Patton enjoyed being given a privileged place at such conferences but would have much preferred the opportunity to lead men in the battles the generals spent hours discussing. 'This war would be a lot more interesting if we could have some fighting,' he wrote home in September, lamenting America's lack of combat.[4]

Patton's desire for action was interrupted by a bout of jaundice which left him hospitalized and concerned that his circumstances might reduce his visibility to senior officers at a crucial time. He need not have worried, however, for during his recovery Lieutenant Colonel LeRoy Eltinge, Patton's former Fort Myer troop commander, visited him bearing a proposal from AEF headquarters. 'Patton, we want to start a Tank School,' Eltinge told him, 'but to get anything out of tanks one must be reckless and take risks. I think you are the sort of darned fool who will do it.'[5] Patton was so intrigued that when his visitor had left he picked up his pen and wrote to Pershing, pressing his case to become involved with the project: 'I believe I have quick judgement and that I am willing to take chances. Also I have always believed in getting close to the enemy and have taught this for two years at the Mounted Service School where I had success in arousing the aggressive spirit in the students.' He ended his letter by reminding the general about his success at the Julio Cárdenas villa: 'I believe that I am the only American who has ever made an attack in a motor vehicle.'[6]

The potential of tanks had been discussed since well before their introduction onto the Somme battlefield by the British in September 1916, but their patchy performance then and afterwards continued to raise questions about their utility. As a cavalryman, Patton was particularly seduced by the mobility provided by the faster, lighter French tanks that the US Army also preferred. For the remainder of his time in a hospital bed, Patton read all he could about tank design, tactics and the lessons drawn from their previous employment. Thus, a well-informed Captain George Patton became the first officer of the new US Tank Corps on 10 November 1917, the day before he turned thirty-two. His headquarters was at Langres, twenty miles south of Chaumont where, assisted by First Lieutenant Elgin Braine, he was tasked with establishing the AEF's Light Tank School in a few ramshackle farm buildings and with a handful of staff. There would be no tanks or students until the system could produce them, and Patton's first priority was to create an infrastructure that could support training when it began.

Leaving colleagues to deal with the day-to-day administration, Patton continued his efforts to become an expert in all things tank, visiting a French training centre where he took instruction in driving a two-man Renault FT light tank, using its gun and servicing its engine. He also travelled to the British sector to meet with Brigadier General Hugh Elles, commander of the Tank Corps, and his chief of staff (and military maverick) Lieutenant Colonel J. F. C. Fuller, to discuss the November 1917 Battle of Cambrai in which 476 heavy tanks were used en masse with mixed results – their initial surprise created tactical success, but it could not be developed into operational advantage.

From a standing start, Patton thus collated a fund of knowledge from which he could create a viable tank school and become a credible tank leader. 'Every thing must be created and there is nothing to start with, nothing but me that is,' he wrote home. 'Some times I wonder if I can do all there is to do but I suppose I can.'⁷ During this period Beatrice and his father received several letters from Langres laced with

Patton's concerns about his abilities, but both had long since come to recognize that such behaviour was merely a preamble to success.

Patton's work in establishing the tank school was well regarded at AEF headquarters and a 58-page report titled *Light Tanks*, delivered to his superiors in December 1917, provided a clear vision for the organization, structure, composition and tactics of the US light tank force.[8] Patton's work soon became the blueprint in creating the US Tank Corps, but before then he used the early winter to prepare the Light Tank School's training manuals, lessons and supporting materials, so that when the first eighteen officer instructors arrived in mid-January 1918 they could be issued with the full course content and supporting materials. Those failing to meet his expectations were sent back to their units. Some he liked personally but, he wrote, 'War is not run on sentiment', and he maintained a pool of replacements to ensure that there were no weak instructors.[9]

Of all his requirements for his instructors, discipline loomed large, because he believed that it was the foundation of all military activity. Discipline, he later argued, removed resistance to obeying commands and created a habit of 'instant, cheerful, unhesitating obedience'.[10] It was no surprise to the directing staff, therefore, that Tank School Memo No. 1, dated 27 January 1918, emphasized the importance of 'soldierly appearance and deportment', which he expected all to exhibit.[11] Most found his obsessive demands around neatness and what he called 'looking the part' exasperating – and, indeed, Patton wrote to his wife, 'I am getting a hell of a reputation for a skunk... I expect some of them would like to poison me.'[12] Yet despite his chronic micromanagement and sometimes overbearing demands, Patton's staff were loyal to him because he gave as much as he took. His subordinates were well cared for, and he bound them to the school (and therefore to him) in identity-building activities. Thus, when the Light Tank School arrived on a muddy field somewhere in northern France to play competitive sport against another school – such as the cross-country running event held in April at the officer candidate school in La Valbonne (near Lyon) – it was always a highly motivated team, its members well turned out in spotless uniforms or crisp playing kit proudly emblazoned with a blue, red and yellow triangular 'tank shoulder patch' of their commander's design.[13]

By the time the first two companies of troops arrived at the Light Tank School in February to be trained, the major part of Patton's operation had moved to Bourg, a village five miles south of Langres. Promoted to lieutenant colonel in March 1918, Patton played a significant role in delivering the six-week-long course, and split his time between teaching and the ongoing responsibilities at his headquarters. Before long, Patton's aphorism 'With DISCIPLINE you are IRRESISTIBLE' became the mantra at his school, and such was the impression the course made on its trainees that few ever forgot it.[14] One trainee, Lieutenant Julian Morrison, later wrote:

> Every day, some Sundays excepted, a fixed schedule was carried out from daylight to dark and then for the officers school at night. [I] always got a great deal of encouragement from these lectures, usually given by Colonel Patton. [I] was made to understand by the Colonel that a tank officer was meant to die. His favorite message to his officer was 'Go forward, go forward. If your tank breaks down go forward with the Infantry. There will be no excuse for your failure in this, and if I find any tank officer behind the Infantry I will ------.'[15]

The AEF Tank Corps' new commander, Colonel Samuel D. Rockenbach, was impressed with what his subordinate had created so quickly, although he was quietly disdainful of Patton's pomposity. Patton picked up on this, writing to Beatrice, 'I guess he does not care a whole lot for me.'[16] Yet Rockenbach had supported his promotion and protected him from higher headquarters meddling. He also kept pressure on AEF headquarters to get the Light Tank School the tanks it had been promised months before. The first ten French Renaults were delivered in the spring of 1918, but training still had to be conducted, and as they were of little defensive value they remained unused when a major new German offensive on the Western Front began in late March and continued deep into summer. Although the series of attacks initially caused great Allied alarm, the inability of the German Army to turn operational success into strategic victory blighted its last opportunity to strike a decisive blow, and it eventually petered out in mid-July. The offensive's impact was the opposite to that which the German high command had intended, as it exacerbated their field army's exhaustion and provided the ideal conditions for the Allies to strike back.

Anticipating the potential for some sort of counter-attack throughout the spring and summer, Patton redoubled efforts at the Light Tank School to ensure that light armour would play its part in whatever was planned. Consequently, he developed a conceptual basis on which the tanks could be employed – his *Brief Notes on the Tactical Employment of Tanks* was written in preparation for the school's first field exercises. Indeed, so committed was Patton to the employment of his tanks that, although he spent most of the summer attending the Army General Staff College at Langres, he returned to work at Bourg each evening to maintain progress.

In the staff college classroom, meanwhile, he learned from a series of experts about the structure, organization and workings of the Army, and was tutored in the variety of skills a staff officer required. Never one to miss an occasion to influence people, and with the cream of the US Army on the Light Tank School's doorstep, it was a relatively simple business for Patton to put on a tank show for the officers at Langres. Thus, at the end of the course in mid-August, the commandant, directing staff and students of the Army General Staff College were treated to a striking and highly successful light tank demonstration. It was a piece of theatre, 'the first tank Maneuver ever held in the US Army', and included an attack in which the machines buzzed around the field like angry wasps – their speed, agility and ability to unhinge defences amply supported by dramatic gestures from commanders.[17] Few who left Bourg that day were left in any doubt about what light tanks could achieve, and knew that in Patton they had a very capable commander. The question remained, however, whether the war would last long enough for the tanks to be deployed in combat.

By the end of August, with his staff course passed, Patton received a strong report from the now Brigadier General Rockenbach: 'The splendid results obtained by this officer in the Tank school show him to be zealous and of good judgement and intelligence. His command is well disciplined and very soldiery in appearance.'[18] As the outstanding candidate to lead the light tanks in battle, Patton was subsequently appointed commander of the 1st Brigade Tank Corps. The man who had arrived in France twelve months earlier leading a handful of enlisted men undertaking routine headquarters duties was now responsible for a cutting-edge formation consisting of two light tank battalions and nearly 1,000 officers and men.

Patton ached for his brigade to be tested, and made a nuisance of himself in his quest to find out more about developing operations and to convince senior officers of the advantages that his tanks could bring to the battlefield. Finally, he was told that an attack was being prepared to eliminate the German salient at Saint-Mihiel and the 1st Brigade Tank Corps, consisting of 144 tanks, would fight in support of the infantry as part of the US First Army commanded personally by Pershing. On the evening of 11 September, just hours before the attack was to be launched, Patton had headquarters issue his 'special instructions' to his troops:

> No tank is to be surrendered or abandoned to the enemy. If you are left alone in the midst of the enemy keep shooting. If your gun is disabled use your pistols and squash the enemy with your tracks... remember that you are the first American tanks. You must establish the fact that AMERICAN TANKS DO NOT SURRENDER... This is our BIG CHANCE; WHAT WE HAVE WORKED FOR... MAKE IT WORTHWHILE.[19]

Knowing his subordinate was keen to be personally involved in battle, Rockenbach's orders to Patton were that he was to remain in his command post and exert his influence remotely by radio. 'There is no question of personal courage in this war', he wrote to Patton, 'it is a business proposition where every man must be in his place and performing his part. Keep control of your reserve and supply, you have no business in a Tank, and I give you the order not to go into fight in a tank.'[20] Thus, when the last rounds of the four-hour-long preliminary bombardment had been sent hurtling towards the enemy, Patton was peering through his binoculars at the rain-soaked, smoke-filled battlefield for any sign of movement.

On the left he could just make out his 344th Tank Battalion supporting 1st Division, making good progress (indeed, a couple of hours later, its objective, the village of Nonsard, was taken). However, on the right, the 345th Tank Battalion and 42nd Division were struggling against the main German trench system, and at around 07.00 the brigade headquarters lost contact with the unit altogether. It was just the excuse that Patton needed to leave his post to find out what was happening for himself. With a pipe clenched firmly between his teeth, he set out, accompanied by an aide and four runners, enemy shells bursting all around. The party finally found the tanks held up behind infantrymen sheltering in shell holes and folds in the ground before their objective, the village of Pannes. Furious the attack had stalled, Patton found the senior infantry officer present – one Brigadier Douglas MacArthur – and the two men agreed to stimulate movement. While MacArthur exhorted groups of cowering infantry to follow him, Patton jumped onto one of his tanks and, perched precariously behind its turret, ordered it to advance. Slowly but surely, the attack resumed with Patton using a stick to direct man and machine, and his voice to shout commands and encouragement. The combined effort was so successful in reinvigorating the attack that Pannes fell two hours later. It was a victory for the sort of personal leadership that Patton had always advocated.

Patton was delighted at the outcome of the 1st Tank Brigade's initial action, for it had made a valuable contribution to operations in the Saint-Mihiel salient, which had been cleared by the evening of the second day of the US attack, and at the cost of just two tanks destroyed, five men killed and nineteen wounded. Rockenbach, however, was furious by what he perceived to be Patton's flagrant insubordination at having left his command post – a situation made worse when Patton tried to defend his actions and which culminated in the general threatening to remove his colonel from command. 'Gen. R gave me hell for going up but it had to be done,' Patton wrote to Beatrice. 'At least I will not sit in a dug out and have my men out in the fighting.'[21]

The actions at Pannes on 12 September 1918 revealed a chronic flaw in Patton's leadership: although he expected the utmost loyalty from his subordinates, he offered the same to his superiors only on his terms. As such, his chain of command increasingly realized that, although Patton was a fine leader, unless he was kept on a tight leash his impetuousness made him prone to wandering from the prescribed course and he could become a liability.

Patton was to have one last attempt at making his mark before the armistice curtailed his adventures. On 26 September 1918, the largest offensive undertaken by the AEF in the war began in co-operation with French forces in the Meuse-Argonne sector. It nearly cost Patton his life. Fighting once again as part of the First Army, but this time in support of 35th Division, the 1st Tank Brigade's role was for 344th Battalion to follow the spearhead infantry with 345th Battalion following a mile behind. Patton was again ordered to stay at his command post by Rockenbach, but he had no intention of doing so if circumstances dictated that he needed to be elsewhere.

Thus, an hour after the attack began, Patton found an excuse to leave his station and cross the battlefield through the fog and smoke to inspire his tanks forward. Finding himself in the village of Cheppy just as the attack was faltering before a determined enemy, Patton once again urged the frightened troops to advance. Reflecting on such situations later, he wrote: 'I have never seen a brave man. All men are frightened. The more intelligent they are, the more they are frightened. The courageous man is the man who forces himself, in spite of his fear, to carry on. Discipline, pride, self-respect, self-confidence, and the love of glory are attributes which will make a man courageous even when he is afraid.'[22]

Patton did 'carry on' at Cheppy, and crisscrossed the battlefield ordering the infantry to follow him using all sorts of threats, expletives and questioning of their manhood. At first, one or two men got to their feet, then a dozen more, and within minutes he attracted scores of men who found his leadership reassuring in the chaos. Patton led them towards the enemy until their fire became so intense that they were forced to shelter behind a small slope. Taking stock of the situation, the officer's eye fell on five of his tanks gathered nearby, and he set out to give them orders to support his attack. Approaching the machines, however, he realized that they were bogged in mud, and so Patton organized an extraction party to dig them out. He helped, enemy rounds ricocheting off the tank armour, and when it was suggested that he should take cover, he said, 'To Hell with them – they can't hit me,' but then went to find more men to help speed up the work.[23]

Encountering some infantry hiding in a ditch, he ordered them out, but one man would not move and so, as he later wrote, 'I hit him over the head with a shovel. It was exciting for they shot at us all the time but I got mad and walked on the parapet.'[24] All five tanks were eventually released; and then, gathering 150 infantrymen around him, Patton led them once more towards the German lines, shouting, swearing and waving his stick as though it were a sword and he were a child again at Lake Vineyard. Men fell all around him, forcing the diminished group to ground once more. Patton knew that they would be killed if they remained in that position. Suddenly overcome with a sense of calm, he said out loud, 'It is time for another Patton to die,' and having called for volunteers to accompany him, stood up.[25] Joe Angelo, his orderly, tried to stop his officer – 'I thought the Colonel had gone mad,' he later testified – but then followed him anyway, along with half a dozen others.[26] All became casualties except for Angelo, with Patton taking a bullet in his upper left thigh which exited through his backside, leaving 'a hole about the size of a dollar'.[27] Angelo dragged him into a small shell-hole which was then raked by fire as he administered the first aid that almost certainly saved Patton's life. The two men lay there for the next two hours with one of the tanks for protection, Patton giving Angelo orders to take to his battalions until, at last, Cheppy fell.

While the battle to clear the Argonne Forest continued, a febrile Patton lay in a base hospital in Dijon for three weeks before his wound was cleared of infection, and then needed another month to heal. Justifying his selflessness on the fateful day, he wrote to Beatrice: 'I had to go in when I did or the whole line might have broken. Perhaps I was mistaken but anyway I believe I have been sited [sic] for a decoration either the Medal of Honor or the military [Distinguished Service] cross. I hope I get one of them.'[28]

No disciplinary action was taken against Patton, either for the striking of a soldier on the battlefield or for once again disobeying Rockenbach's orders. His serious wound provided some protection from admonishment, and the end of the war effectively cloaked his misdemeanours. Patton returned to service at Bourg just in time for his thirty-third birthday, 11 November 1918, the same day the Armistice was signed. He celebrated both events, but in the days that followed he was struck by the feeling that he still had unfinished business with war and was determined to 'start getting ready for the next'.[29]

— ▫ —

When Captain Alan Maciver joined the 20th Battalion Lancashire Fusiliers as a company commander during the autumn of 1916, his new charges were still reeling from their recent participation in the Battle of the Somme, and he recognized the importance of raising their morale before they participated in any future offensive. It was his first time back in the front line in two years, after a German rifle round shattered his spectacles and seriously damaged his left eye when he was a platoon commander. Returning to service and still in considerable pain, Maciver had to re-acclimatize to combat quickly and lead four broken and dangerously undermanned platoons at Arras. With the enemy a mere twenty yards away, frequent reconnaissance of No Man's Land was vital to ensure that their defensive obstacles remained unbroken, but even such a routine activity had the potential to undermine his attempts to instil in his charges a renewed fighting spirit. Indeed, one such foray led to the death of one of Maciver's platoon commanders, who was shot and fell 'spread eagled over the barbed wire' where he soon began to bloat and was gnawed on by rats.[30]

As the officer responsible for every life under his command, Maciver keenly felt the loss of a colleague whom he knew well, and whose blackening face as he hung suspended on the barrier was like a silent, grisly reproach. The stress of this and other incidents mounted on Maciver as the weeks passed, and eventually, with his injuries continuing to hamper his effectiveness, he was transferred to a staff appointment in his parent 104th Brigade. His job was as assistant to the brigade major, Captain Bernard Montgomery, a man he had previously encountered during the officer's visits to the front line. Maciver soon learned that his boss's apparent bonhomie was in fact a studied behaviour that he largely saved for his interactions with the troops, and that at most other times he was a rather aloof individual who worked extremely hard, demanded a great deal of those around him and had a keen eye for detail. Few in the headquarters were drawn to Montgomery the man, but all recognized his talents and the positive impact he made on the brigade every day. As Maciver pointedly recalled decades later when asked about serving under Monty: 'His successor was a grand chap.'[31]

By January 1917, Bernard Montgomery had left 104th Brigade and was settling into a staff role as part of the 33rd Infantry Division headquarters in the Somme sector, transitioning successfully from decorated combat leader to a highly effective staff officer. The fighting on the Western Front itself had changed from its early mobility into an unedifying deadlock, but recent attritional slogs had significantly weakened the German Army, resulting in its withdrawal in February 1917 to the recently built defensive position known as the 'Hindenburg Line'. This immensely strong position posed a new test for military planners, and they were naturally curious as to whether developing British fighting methods – tactical innovations supporting sustainable all-arms operations, inspired by lessons learned from the Battle of the Somme – could provide an effective solution for future breakthrough attempts. The General Staff, however, remained what one commentator has called 'an inflexible, hierarchical structure [that] impaired the flow of information, hindered learning and stymied initiative'.[32] Recognizing this, the British Army made an attempt to improve the situation in early 1917 through a staff officer programme of attachments to a variety of headquarters, as well as wartime staff training schools, staff-focused lectures and a raft of manuals and aide memoirs.

Montgomery's own experience on joining 33rd Division was like that of many staff officers who had been appointed without any formal staff training (which was traditionally provided by the two-year-long Camberley Staff College course) as positions needed to be filled quickly. He was thus known as a 'staff learner', expected to pick up the critical skills while in a role, including those required for leading at headquarters. This demanded a different approach from that taken by those in fighting units – due to the need, for example, to work with a larger number of senior officers, collaborate with a variety of subject-matter experts, and provide leadership remotely and often from behind a desk.

Montgomery was among the first to benefit from the new training regime, and was selected as one of the first twenty students to attend a six-week staff course at one of the wartime schools. The establishment was commanded by Lieutenant Colonel Charles Bonham-Carter, who Montgomery felt was 'a very studious hard-working young man devoted to his profession and modest'.[33] Accommodated in the house of a prosperous doctor in the town of Hesdin near the Channel coast, Montgomery attended lectures and seminars designed to provide a grounding in theory, while exercises mirrored real scenarios. 'There was no exam at the end of the course nor at any time during the course,' Montgomery later wrote of his experience. 'We just went there to learn and we all helped each other and acquired knowledge from each other.'[34] It was a stimulating time, during which he found 'the strenuous brain work' taxing but hugely beneficial. He was returned to 33rd Division just in time to deploy his refined capabilities during the preparation for the formation's participation in the next great British offensive, to take place against the Hindenburg Line at Arras in the spring of 1917.

Montgomery's areas of responsibility as General Staff Officer Grade 2 (GSO2) were operations, training and associated activities, which necessitated frequent visits to the troops in the front line. He described the job in a letter to his father as 'very interesting', but demanding because he had to be 'an expert on every subject'.[35] The division was commanded by Major General Reginald Pinney, an experienced officer who emphasized the need for self-discipline and being teetotal, and who angered his troops by replacing their regular rum issue with tea. One NCO described him as a 'bun-pinching crank, more suited to command of a Church Mission hut than troops'.[36] Siegfried Sassoon's famous poem 'The General' was based on Pinney, describing how his cheery face was appreciated by two soldiers, Harry and Jack, before 'he did for them both by his plan of attack'.[37] Pinney was no buffoon, but when he committed his division into battle at Arras during the second week in April, the initial momentum of the offensive had been exhausted and the formation took barely a single mile of ground for the cost of nearly 3,000 men.[38] It was slaughter on a scale that appalled Montgomery, and scarred him so deeply that he bore the marks for the rest of his life. He was not alone, for Pinney exhorted headquarters to prepare for the next battle 'with care, learning from our experiences and giving the leadership the men expect and deserve'.[39]

Encouraged by the general's willingness to discuss issues of importance personally with his staff officers, Montgomery trusted that 33rd Division's next attack would not be so costly. It came on 20 May and was a success, but in a salutary lesson to Montgomery and everybody else who had worked hard to support the formation, the attack after that led to heavy casualties and the failure to achieve its objectives. Such was the challenge and unpredictability of fighting on the Western Front, and such was the lot of a staff officer: unappreciated and even scorned by those at the front, yet working under huge pressure and with enormous responsibilities. Montgomery added to his understanding that, without a strong and capable staff, a formation's effectiveness was fundamentally weakened – and even with one, the vicissitudes of war dictated that no outcome was guaranteed.

While to higher headquarters 33rd Division was an asset that had to be put to work, to Montgomery it was a living, breathing body of men who deserved the best support the British Army could provide. That perspective Captain Montgomery took with him to IX Corps in July; his experience had made him the ideal candidate for the role of senior GSO2 in its headquarters, with primary responsibility for training – a role in which he was becoming something of an expert, and which he enjoyed. 'I like my new job very much. I am very lucky to get it,' he explained in a letter to his father. 'There are three GSO 2s in a Corps and when the senior appointment fell vacant it would have been only natural if one of the other two had moved up. But it was given to me, although both the others are senior in rank to me, being Majors.'[40]

The corps was commanded by Lieutenant General Sir Alexander Hamilton-Gordon and was part of General Sir Herbert Plumer's Second Army. Plumer was at the forefront of the British Army's attempts to encourage closer co-operation between different arms – artillery, infantry, engineers, tanks and combat support – and an advocate of offensives with more limited objectives than had been the norm until then. Montgomery therefore found himself at the centre of the BEF's ongoing attempts to transform itself into a more effective force capable of breaking the deadlock. It was his responsibility to make certain that each of IX Corps' divisions not only understood their role in the approach, but could carry out that role efficiently, effectively, and with an emphasis on mutual co-operation. Gone were the days when troops were regarded as unthinking automatons incapable of sophisticated techniques; by mid-1917 decentralized decision-making was encouraged and combat leaders were given far greater freedom of action. This change was a victory not only for trust but for common sense, and came about when senior commanders harnessed the deep thinking that staff officers like Montgomery were engaged in, about how greater tactical flexibility and teamwork might be utilized to overcome the enemy's sophisticated defences.

The Second Army's success in the Battle of Messines the month before Montgomery arrived at IX Corps had vindicated the British Army's new approach, and he distilled its lessons. Montgomery's contribution to the influential *Instructions for the Training of Divisions for Offensive Action* was published that summer, and provided a practical guide to Plumer's fighting methods for immediate use by combat formations. The booklet's directives were closely followed by each of the corps' divisions as they prepared for the launch of the infamous Third Battle of Ypres, which began on 31 July 1917, and they subsequently played an important part in the successes achieved at Menin Road Ridge, Polygon Wood and Broodseinde, during which the infantry took an objective and consolidated their gains while supporting units then surged forward to take the next objective. This 'leap frog' method was woven into a plan that saw improved all-arms co-operation across the corps, with the infantry co-operating closely with the artillery and the Royal Flying Corps, which not only sought to defend the airspace over the battlefield but also to attack the enemy on the ground. Indeed, Montgomery wrote as much to his father on 9 October, saying that the battles were 'masterpieces and could not have been better'.[41] Just one month later, however, the battle had descended into the mud and slaughter before the village of Passchendaele, which at a stroke had the impact of wiping out the earlier successes and thereafter made the Third

Battle of Ypres a by-word for failure. The carnage that Montgomery witnessed that autumn reinforced what he had come to regard as a fundamental truth in the application of military force – a belief that he summarized in a letter to his mother on 8 November, when he explained that 'the whole art of war is to gain your objective with as little loss as possible'.[42]

The transfer of Plumer to a new command in Italy fuelled Montgomery's determination to do justice to the general's legacy. He wrote a series of IX Corps publications, one of the most important of which was titled *Instructions on the Defence*.[43] This booklet anticipated a major offensive by Germany in the West if the Russians dropped out of the war, and its contents were fully tested in the wake of the German peace treaty with Russia.

Launched on 21 March 1918, General Erich Ludendorff's 'Spring Offensive' forced British withdrawals first in Picardy and then in Flanders. By 11 April, with the French rushing to the aid of the BEF, the force's commander, Field Marshal Sir Douglas Haig, issued his famous special order of the day: 'Every position must be held to the last man: there must be no retirement. With our backs to the wall and believing in the justice of our cause each one of us must fight on to the end.'[44] Montgomery was intimately involved in attempts to hold the line in the Ypres sector when IX Corps successfully defended the Kemmel Ridge in mid-April at the cost of 27,000 casualties, and every staff officer was required to play a role in a priority effort no matter what their job title.[45] The formation was again in action at the end of May when the Germans attacked towards the Aisne river, where IX Corps had just taken over the dangerous Chemin des Dames sector.[46] Ultimately the attack was unsuccessful, and by mid-July the whole German offensive had failed despite its massive expenditure in men, materiel and morale. It was the strategic turning point for which the Allies had been waiting.

Although not an outright victory, the repelling of the protracted enemy onslaught in the first half of 1918 created the conditions for decisive Allied action. Despite the continued vigour of the 'lions led by donkeys' myth, the reality was that the challenges of industrialized warfare encountered by the British Army on the Western Front were something for which it was not prepared but ultimately saw through to victory.[47] Senior leaders inevitably made mistakes in the most demanding of circumstances, but gradually learned from them while taking responsibility for the development of a largely citizen army while it was in contact with the enemy. There were no simple answers to the deadlock, but the strategy of attrition, as unpalatable as it was, did create a disparity in men, materiel and morale at the front, and that change was exploited by effective new fighting methods – such as those adopted for the Battle of Messines in June 1917, or at Cambrai in November the same year, in which aircraft, artillery, tanks and infantry combined in narrow-fronted attacks only to a depth that could be quickly consolidated – which the severely weakened Germans could no longer resist by the summer of 1918.

It was a triumph of Allied leadership, willpower and organization from which Montgomery would draw strength in the years to come. In 1918, however, his personal reward for the part he played in the British Army's ability to withstand the German onslaught was initially promotion to brevet major and the commendation of his general, but soon after he was selected for the important job of chief of staff of the 47th (London) Division as a temporary lieutenant colonel. An experienced formation currently serving with the Fourth Army as part of III Corps, it was commanded by Major General Sir George Gorringe, who was widely acknowledged as a rude and unpleasant bully. As Gorringe's right-hand man – acting as an advisor, putting the commander's decisions into action and heading the division's staff – Montgomery was in a powerful position. He had been given the job because he was a strong character who had developed an ability to offer a well-reasoned challenge to senior officers ('uninformed criticism is valueless', he argued[48]) and the relationship worked well. Indeed, Gorringe quickly recognized Montgomery's talents and gave him the freedom to run the division day-to-day while he set the formation's course within the corps organization.

The Gorringe-Montgomery partnership soon became an excellent illustration of how a team could become far more potent than the sum of its parts, with the general's robust ideas filleted by his chief of staff to ensure they were practical and effective. Far from mellowing his general, Montgomery reinforced the man's intimidating demeanour and even adopted it himself as a means of getting what he wanted out of those he led. '[The division staff] all work very well together', he bragged in a letter home, 'and they do what I tell them like lambs.'[49] Gorringe and Montgomery made a tyrannical double act.

The strength of the relationship between the commander of 47th Division and his chief of staff was deepened by participation in the great Allied offensive that began on 8 August 1918 and was destined to end the war. Although the division was tasked with holding a flank during the initial phase of the attack launched from Amiens, Montgomery was integrally involved in the planning and preparation of all phases of the battle. It was his job to understand Gorringe's intent and concept of operations before then translating them into an operational plan. Applying Plumer's integrated fighting methods, the Battle of Amiens saw even greater emphasis placed on the role of airpower and armour, and Montgomery ensured that the Australian and the Canadian Corps' main effort was effectively co-ordinated with his division's supporting role.[50] His *Instructions for the Offensive* issued on 18 August emphasized collaborative teamwork through combined arms, and provided the framework for 47th Division's own attack four days later; and, with amendments, the document remained a central pillar of the division's approach to combat for the remaining three months of the war. The ever-changing circumstances required constant adaptation, and therefore Montgomery penned a pamphlet titled *Lessons Learnt in Operations undertaken in August and September 1918*, covering all aspects of the division's arms, which was used as the basis for training that Montgomery personally facilitated. 'These are stirring times and everyone is being pushed to the limit of their endurance,' he wrote to his mother as the fighting on the Western Front changed its character one final time. 'One is gaining wonderful experience in this advance.'[51]

The 47th (London) Division had enjoyed some considerable success in its contribution to pushing the Germans back over the Canal du Nord in early September, and by the time it returned to the front line again in early October, it did so with added confidence based on Montgomery's work in identifying areas for improvement and then developmental training. Although its burgeoning abilities were not fully tested as autumn set in and the division became part of the Fifth Army's offensive in Artois, its liberation of Lille was a major achievement, and one used deftly by Montgomery to raise the division's profile.[52] Thus, on 28 October 1918, a proud formation marched through the city of Lille in a parade organized by its wily chief of staff. The streets, packed with cheering locals, were festooned with bunting and plastered with posters proclaiming 'Honour and Glory for 47th Division our Deliverers'.[53] Gorringe and Montgomery, having led the division to the Grand Place, then joined civic dignitaries, senior officers and the Minister of Munitions, Winston Churchill, to watch the march pass.

Two weeks after the triumphant Lille display, the war was over. When the Armistice took effect on 11 November, Montgomery was at La Tombe, near Tournai, where he marked the event with a brief entry in the division war diary. Shortly after, he made an important resolution which he later wrote about in his memoirs: 'I decided to dedicate myself to my profession, to master its details, and to put all else aside.'[54]

— ◻ —

Having married Lucie in December 1916, Erwin Rommel returned to his company of Württemberg Mountain troops in Romania shortly after, and within days the young officer felt as though he had never been away. In the front line for several months without a rest, the increasingly weary battalion was showing signs of mental and physical tiredness, as the Alpine Corps advance continued in appalling weather. With its fighting efficiency diminishing as morale dipped, Major Sprösser finally informed Rommel that his company was being taken out of the line for a period of rest, organization and training, well away from the front. By the time the refreshed and reinvigorated company re-joined the Württemberg Mountain Battalion in Romania (via a short stint at the front in the Vosges sector to regain the 'fighting edge'), the winter had passed and, Rommel observed, 'the troops were probably then at the very peak of their performance'.[55]

By May 1917, German and Austro-Hungarian formations had overrun large parts of Romania, including the capital, Bucharest, and a summer offensive was being planned to complete its subjugation by wheeling north into Moldavia. In preparation, the invaders spent weeks improving their lines of communication, husbanding their stores and, at the front, seizing advantageous tactical positions. During this period, Rommel's responsibilities increased to embrace a three-company-strong force around which the rest of the battalion was organized. The 'Rommel Detachment' was to lead the Württembergers' contribution to the Bavarian Infantry Brigade's attack on Mount Cosna, a peak in the Carpathian range and a lynchpin in the Romanian defences. It began on 9 August 1917, and Rommel was a visible presence in the vanguard of his 500-man force. Using a trusted team of NCOs and runners to bring him information from across the unit and to communicate his orders, Rommel was adamant that the detachment retain its shape and sustain forward momentum. Having ascended the mountain using infiltration tactics and rebuffed several counter-attacks, the push for the summit took place the following day.

While directing his troops into position for the final phase, Rommel was struck in his left forearm by an enemy round. The bullet missed both bones but bled heavily, causing him to feel light-headed, yet even while he was being attended to by a medic and in severe pain, Rommel continued to give orders. Then enemy artillery rounds began to explode across the detachment's positions, the blasts generating a deadly debris of rock and steel which travelled at high velocity in all directions.

One German sergeant, Leo Krämer, who lived through innumerable similar bombardments, described it as 'a hellish experience as they produced a curtain of death'. There was no option but for those in the open to find whatever cover was available – a boulder or rocky outcrop – and take shelter. 'I was hit hard just above the right eye', Krämer recalled, 'and my comrades saw the blood and thought I was dead. I was unconscious for a while, lying in the open, but when I came to somebody ran out and dragged me behind a rock wall and bandaged my head. My platoon lost 10 men dead that day largely because being on a mountain is about as isolated a battlefield as can be found.'[56]

In such circumstances, all Rommel's men could do was take shelter, withstand the pummelling of the enemy's artillery and wait until the onslaught ended. 'I was exhausted from the loss of blood', Rommel later wrote of his predicament, 'and, hindered by my wound and an overcoat that hung loosely from my shoulders, I considered giving up command. After careful consideration of the detachment's difficult situation, however, I decided to remain at my post.'[57]

With the Romanians reinforcing under the cover of artillery support, and well-sited machine guns suppressing any attempt by the Germans to launch their final assault, not until after dark could Rommel receive situation reports from his companies, rework his plan and give new orders. One company created a noisy diversion, while a second swung around the enemy's flank and fell on their defences with deadly surprise. While the methods may have been traditional, the fact that a wounded Rommel had remained in command long enough to organize and execute a successful plan was impressive and won the plaudits of Sprösser, who brought the remainder of the battalion forward to consolidate the accomplishment.

In the week of fighting that followed, the Württembergers fought off repeated Romanian attempts to remove them from the mountaintop, with the wounded Rommel taking charge of the defensive efforts. He moved constantly around his exposed units to keep their spirits up and assess their situation, but the officer's pale, pained face told its own story. Even so, Lieutenant Theodor Werner later wrote admiringly of his boss: 'Although a leader without comparison, he was still one of us.'[58] Only after the enemy began withdrawing on 20 August did Rommel (who later admitted that by this point he was beginning to 'babble the silliest nonsense'[59]) hand over command to a subordinate and walk back down the mountain to medical care.

Rommel's performance on Mount Cosna did not reveal, as one biographer has argued, 'something disturbing about his unwillingness – or inability – to recognize that he was not indispensable',[60] but instead a self-awareness that his presence was a motivating factor in a fragile tactical situation, and as such far outweighed any risk of him remaining in command. The price of the battalion's contribution to the undermining of Romanian defences had been heavy, however, as the Württembergers lost 88 dead, 299 wounded and 6 missing.[61]

Having spent several weeks with Lucie in Danzig, regaining his health, Rommel returned to active service in mid-October, by which time the Alpine Corps was fighting in the Italian campaign, its third front of the war, along the mountainous border with Austria–Hungary.[62] Eleven battles of the Isonzo river had achieved little in over two years, other than nearly a million casualties, but as 1917 drew to a close and with Italian morale in steep decline, seven German divisions reinforced the Austro-Hungarians for a huge offensive. Fighting as part of the Fourteenth Army, the Alpine Corps was to spearhead the attack commencing on 24 October. Known as the 'Twelfth Isonzo', or more commonly the Battle of Caporetto, its goal was to make a breach in the Italian front line by neutralizing a series of enemy strongpoints and batteries along adjoining ridges, including the dominating Mount Matajur (5,400 feet), before sweeping down onto the broad Veneto plain towards Venice.

Designated the lead battalion once again, Sprösser's companies advanced behind a wall of gas and mortar bombs after a heavy artillery bombardment had prepared the ground, and the Italian outpost in the foothills crumbled quickly. In leading the Württembergers, the Rommel Detachment moved so quickly that even Sprösser found it difficult to know where it was, but the stream of prisoners that came his way gave him confidence that progress was being made. The speed was partly the result of some German inter-unit competition that Rommel had played his part in creating. Advancing on the Swabians' left flank was a sister unit in the Bavarian Infantry Brigade, a battalion of Bavarian Life Guards, which sought to be first to every objective. Led by Major Count von Bothmer, who encouraged his men to flaunt their elite status, the Life Guards consequently scorned their less fashionable comrades, prompting a piqued Rommel to make certain that his men outfought their colleagues.[63]

Carefully handled, such rivalry could be a useful stimulus to both battalions, but if mishandled it could lead to the loss of lives. The first evidence of Bothmer seeking to relegate Rommel's men to a supporting role came late on 25 October as the brigade was preparing to attack Hill 1114, the first peak of the Kolovrat Ridge line. Rommel was in no mood to accede and later wrote, 'I was not very happy because fighting in the second line did not appeal to us mountain troops at all.'[64] Having appraised Sprösser of the situation when he arrived at dawn the next morning, Rommel gained his approval to make his own independent attack. It left a furious von Bothmer a mere observer as the Rommel Detachment surprised the remainder of the brigade as well as the enemy, and burst through to take the peak. Upstaging the Bavarians delighted Rommel and further endeared him to the collection of companies that bore his name, but it laid down the gauntlet to von Bothmer, who felt humiliated.

The antipathy that grew between the Life Guards and the Mountain Battalion was born of pride, but it was fuelled by General Otto von Below, the commander of the Fourteenth Army, who had promised the *Pour le Mérite* – Germany's highest award for gallantry in combat – to the officer commanding the unit that captured Mount Matajur. Such an offer was more than enough to ensure that von

Bothmer and Rommel, in the vanguard of the attack, were amply motivated to push each other to the limits, and so on an exposed ridge in a ferocious late-October gale, both men developed the next stage of their schemes to win the prize. Rommel's plan was not to make a main assault along the ridge as the enemy would expect – that was left to the Bavarian Life Guards – but instead to climb Mount Matajur from an unexpected direction and complete the enemy's encirclement. Both attacks proceeded well initially, but as von Bothmer's men were slowed by the Italians' main defensive positions, Rommel's advance was hampered by the need to form prisoner escort parties, leaving him a mere hundred men and six machine guns with which to make his final summit assault.

Such were the numbers of surrendered enemy personnel cascading down the mountain towards Sprösser that he believed the battle had been won and sent a message to Rommel demanding that he report to battalion headquarters in person, an order he felt able to ignore because of the German Army's requirement that officers should use their own initiative as long as they acted within the framework of the senior commander's intent.[65] 'The battalion command was unaware of the tactical situation on the southern slopes of the mountain,' Rommel later wrote in justification of his decision to pursue his attack. 'There was still work to be done although, admittedly, no reinforcement was available for the foreseeable future.'[66]

Short of men, Rommel did not try to fight his way to the top, but used the kind of bold deception for which he became known: waving a white handkerchief, he simply walked towards the Italians. Thinking that such a confident act must mean the Germans had reached the position in great strength, the troops of the Salerno Brigade surrendered. Their commander was aghast, his protestations ignored by his men, and when the true number of Germans was revealed he 'sat on the roadside, surrounded by his officers, and wept with rage and shame over the refusal of the soldiers of his once proud regiment to fight'.[67] Mount Matajur had been seized by the Württemberg Mountain Battalion, and some 9,000 prisoners taken for the cost of just six dead and thirty wounded in fifty-two hours.[68] It was a magnificent achievement that revealed what a talented leader the detachment's commander had become; a worthy winner of General von Below's *Pour le Mérite*. Having fought at Rommel's side during the attack, Lieutenant Kurt Hesse later said that the events on the mountain revealed not only his 'shining courage' but also an 'inexhaustible strength and freshness [and] ability to put himself in his opponent's mind and anticipate his reactions... Danger did not seem to exist for him.'[69]

To the men of the Mountain Battalion, Erwin Rommel had become a leader to revere; courageous, skilful and caring, after his achievements in the Alps, they would follow him anywhere. In the aftermath of the battle for Mount Matajur, that meant immediately pursuing the withdrawing Italians at the head of the Alpine Corps once again. During this phase of the battle, on 7 November Rommel made an error of judgement at the Klautana Pass. Having sought to ensure that his detachment was adequately supported by machine guns, he later admitted in his memoir that he spent too long overseeing their work at the expense of personally driving the main attack forward when it became sluggish. Being a vocal advocate of the leader needing to be at the decisive point to make timely decisions and influence events, Rommel had failed to enact his own dictum and the advance was repelled. 'I was very angry about this outcome,' he wrote. 'It was the first attack I had led in the war that had failed and hours of hard work had been in vain.'[70] His officers had vacillated, and Rommel admonished them severely for their inactivity. An officer in the battalion named Hartmann later suggested that Rommel was venerated but not necessarily loved by all: 'Perhaps officers did not like him as much as the men because he always expected more of them and there were very few who could go at his pace. But he was "the best of comrades".'[71]

Censure by Rommel, however, was meant to be motivating, and the detachment did not need to wait long to redeem itself. On 9 November the Rommel Detachment arrived on the east bank of the Piave river, on the opposite side of which lay the town of Longarone, an important strategic railhead for the Italian 12th Corps and therefore likely to have been fortified. Yet rather than engaging the withdrawing Italians before Longarone as the advancing German spearhead might easily have done, Rommel allowed the enemy to enter the town with a view to encircling it. 'It is my experience', he later wrote, 'that bold decisions give the best promise of success.'[72] Sprösser supported the scheme and hastened the rest of the battalion up to the river. As the bridges into the town had been destroyed by the Italians, Rommel positioned a machine gun company on the bank opposite Longarone to fix the enemy, while the remainder of the detachment, led personally by Rommel, waded across the river a mile downstream and moved to the town in the darkness. A quick reconnaissance soon established Longarone's main exit points, but as the two companies began to establish themselves in blocking positions they were spotted and an intense firefight ensued. Sprösser had established a crucial defensive cordon facing away from the town, primarily designed to stop reinforcements reaching Longarone from the rear. Quickly overwhelmed by some 1,000 Italians from the town, the Rommel Detachment was forced from its positions, and in a frenzy of confused activity fell back to the cordon which turned around just in time to force the pursuing enemy back. With the situation stabilized by dawn, using a Rommel-like bluff Lieutenant Schöffel, one of the detachment's officers who had been taken prisoner the previous evening, informed his Italian captors that his comrades were in division strength. The Italian 1st Division defending the town – a total of 10,000 men, 200 machine guns, 18 mountain guns and all its supporting assets – consequently decided to surrender to a force that was, in reality, less than one-tenth of its strength.[73]

After his exertions at Longarone, Rommel celebrated his twenty-sixth birthday. He was still a young man, but his professional achievements over the previous three years had been exceptional. Indeed, by the time the Mountain Battalion was finally relieved on 1 January 1918, the Rommel Detachment was widely acknowledged by the chain of command to have made a decisive contribution to a raft of outstanding achievements – not just by the Württembergers but by the Bavarian Infantry Brigade and, indeed, the Alpine Corps. Before they left Italy, both Rommel and Sprösser were awarded the *Pour le Mérite* for their gallantry. However, Rommel's was not for capturing Mount Matajur. In a significant error of attribution, the medal promised by von Below had been presented to a Bavarian Regiment officer who had mistakenly reported that he was on the summit of Matajur when, in fact, he was atop a different mountain altogether. Rommel's medal was for his success at Longarone, and although hugely proud of the acknowledgement, he was furious that his detachment had been denied the recognition of their remarkable feat in taking 'the prize', and he made several unsuccessful representations to his superiors to right the wrong. Nevertheless, he returned to Germany in early 1918 a hero, the blue and gold *Pour le Mérite* hanging at his throat a symbol that he was an outstanding combat leader – a persona that Rommel was only too happy to inhabit. Unbeknown to him, however, he had led men in battle for the last time in the war.

Needing a rest after months of demanding soldiering, Rommel had every expectation of returning with his battalion to combat operations after some leave, but regretfully learned that he had instead been appointed to a staff position on the Western Front, and for the remainder of the war he served in the headquarters of LXIV Corps. Commanded by Prince Wilhelm of Urach, Count of Württemberg, 2nd Duke of Urach, the formation served in the Vosges sector Rommel knew well, with its headquarters at Colmar in Alsace. Bitterly disappointed at being taken from the men he had experienced so much with, he had to adapt to his new responsibilities in a very different military environment from that to which he had become accustomed. As a junior officer, he was given experience in a variety of sections in the months that followed, learning quickly that his role now was to advise and administer – however much his experience, personality and approach to soldiering were at odds with the role of a staff officer and the headquarters environment.

Neither the German 1918 Spring Offensive nor the Allied riposte leading to the Armistice in November fundamentally affected LXIV Corps at the southern end of the Western Front. Thus, when the Armistice was signed on 11 November, Rommel served in a formation that, although stripped of many resources, was able to march off the battlefield largely intact and so arrive back in a turbulent Germany vanquished but still full of fight. This contradiction would help define Germany in the years to come, and demand that Rommel find a role in a challenging new context.

CHAPTER FOUR

New Challenges – Leading in Peace, 1919–31

RETURNING HOME FROM the fighting fronts of the First World War was akin to the veterans of the conflict losing someone extremely close, for their relationship with the conflict had been so intense. In the weeks following the 11 November Armistice, a weary German Army began its journey back home. Their destination was a nation in the throes of a revolution. The Kaiser had already abdicated, Bavaria had declared a revolutionary government, and pro-Bolshevik demonstrations were taking place in the major cities. The troops added their discipline and training to an already explosive situation.

The victorious Allied armies, meanwhile, followed their former enemy eastwards in the wake of the agreement that they would occupy German territory west of the Rhine, forming a military buffer between the turbulent state and western Europe, but with bridgeheads across the river incorporating several major cities. The first British cavalry patrol crossed into Germany just before dawn on 1 December 1918, and duly occupied Cologne on the great river. A troop rode through the city's Domplatz in the shadow of the great cathedral, in a parade which, when reinforced with several tanks, was clearly meant as an assertion of authority. War correspondent Philip Gibbs wrote of the event: 'I do not think there were any men among us who had a sense of exultation or arrogance at this proof of victory... We gazed over the Rhine, looked round upon the Germans about us, and remembered good friends, so many of them, who had fallen on the way.'[1]

The presence of British troops in Cologne was tolerated by the city's 600,000 citizens, who feared violent disorder more than the humiliation of occupation even if it did mean registration, curfews and the city's clocks showing London time. Elsewhere, however, political violence blighted a difficult winter. In January 1919, 50,000 Communist Party supporters, the Spartacists, rebelled in Berlin, but although defeated by armed ex-soldiers organized as the Freikorps, the event sparked a wave of communist workers' councils seizing power across Germany. A tense uncertainty thus marred the spring, and by the middle of June, when a punitive peace treaty needed to be validated, the world held its breath. 'Germany has come face to face with the great problem,' wrote one British reporter covering the story, 'the acceptance or rejection of our peace terms and that she cannot look for any further extension of time in which to make up her mind.'[2]

The Treaty of Versailles was finally signed by the German delegation on 28 June 1919, and Cologne, in common with the other occupied cities, was left aghast when the Allies began to send their troops back home. Germany, it seemed, would be left to her fate.

— ¤ —

George Patton had yearned for war, but at its end he, like every other officer who sought to remain in uniform, had to make compromises. Posted back to the Light Tank School at Bourg having recuperated from his wound suffered at Cheppy, Patton continued to command a training centre but now with nothing to train for. During the remainder of autumn 1918, his behaviour became erratic, and with the adrenaline of war flushed from his veins, he wrote home in a fit of despair: 'I fear that laziness which has ever pursued me is closing in on me at last.'[3] He tried to distract himself from his insipid routine by presenting lectures to the General Staff College on tank tactics, laced heavily with personal anecdotes, and he wrote a report about the achievements of the 1st Tank Brigade which concluded that, beyond doubt, 'the value of tanks as attacking units and as a fighting arm had been demonstrated',[4] but he remained unfulfilled. Patton sought to promote himself and so bring himself to the attention of senior officers once more, but such self-aggrandisement annoyed some – including his chain of command, which received angry letters from him when he learned that he would not be awarded the Distinguished Service Cross (DSC) he coveted, for his gallantry during the Meuse-Argonne offensive. Yet it was behaviour that in many ways the system rewarded: having demanded that a fresh recommendation be submitted, in December 1918 he was awarded the DSC 'for extraordinary heroism'.[5]

Beatrice's response to her husband's good news reveals much about the sort of praise he sought. 'Georgie,' she wrote, 'you are the fulfilment of all the ideals of manliness and high courage & bravery I have always held for you, ever since I have known you.'[6] In time he would also be awarded the Distinguished Service Medal (DSM) for his service and his command of the Light Tank School, a singular tribute as only Patton and Douglas MacArthur to that point had been awarded both the DSC and the DCM. Not quite satisfied, Patton wrote to his wife in February 1919, 'I will get an M.H. [Medal of Honor] in the next war. I hope.'[7]

Part of Patton's desire for recognition was undoubtedly prompted by the uncertainty surrounding his future in a rapidly demobilizing force that would have to reinvent itself. His annual report was supportive but nuanced. 'This officer is very efficient, but youthful,' General Rockenbach opined in the first months of peace. 'He will, I believe, sober into one of highest value.'[8] Yet if his superiors hoped that Patton would soon mature, they were to be disappointed, for a complex trickiness was already deeply embedded in him. Returned home in March 1919, following an extremely brief reunion with

Beatrice after his ship had docked in Brooklyn, Patton told his war stories to the assembled pressmen and by next morning the nation was reading all about the heroic exploits of the officer.

Patton endeavoured to ease the transition to peacetime soldiering by re-establishing relationships with men of influence – including John Pershing, despite the dissolution of his relationship with Nita. He once more took command of his light tank brigade, which had been relocated to Camp Meade in Maryland, a temporary appointment before he reverted to his permanent rank of captain. While his reports continued to value his leadership and energy, his overt ambition and failure to 'appreciate the details of team work' cast doubt over his suitability as a staff officer.[9] He was under no illusion about the path to senior rank, which was paved with staff jobs in which he had to perform well if he was to be promoted. Patton's response was to endeavour to make such valuable contributions to the conceptual development of the US Army that he would become an invaluable asset.

While engaged in strategic thinking about the employment of tanks, he first met Dwight Eisenhower, a brother officer who was also pondering the future of armour. A West Point–trained officer five years younger than Patton, Eisenhower ('Ike' to his friends) was an infantryman who had nonetheless commanded a heavy tank battalion training centre at Camp Meade during the war, which he had ended as a temporary lieutenant colonel. Although his undemonstrative personality was in many ways the opposite of Patton's, the two men soon became firm friends. Describing their first meeting, which took place in March 1919, Eisenhower wrote that Patton was 'a loner, [who] did not much care what his associates thought of him' and noted his 'high, squeaking voice, quite out of keeping with his bearing'. He was also impressed by his creative thinking and energy.[10] They spent a good deal of time discussing the implications of massive defence spending cuts on the Army's development and capabilities. 'We are like people in a boat floating down the beautiful river of fictitious prosperity', Patton wrote to

Nita in October 1919, with a sense of some future calamity, 'and thinking that the moaning of the none too distant waterfall – which is going to engulf us – is but the song of the wind in the trees. We disregard the lessons of History.'[11]

Soon after, it was decided that the Army would be limited to a mere 137,000 officers and men – its size and woeful share of the defence budget set until 1936. This, it was argued, was sufficient, with the United States having adopted an isolationist policy in which the US Navy would be a priority. Consequently, six of the Army's nine fighting divisions existed only on paper and units of the other three were scattered across the country, and its personnel had to tolerate low rates of pay, substandard accommodation and low social prestige. The implications for leaders and leadership were considerable, as the Army was relegated once more to a second-rate organization whose arguments for more resources were drowned out by a population demanding peace and low taxes. It thus became critical for the future health of the institution that a handful of officers continue to stimulate the Army's heart and brain. Patton and Eisenhower were in the vanguard of this group, which over time came to include some of the greatest soldiers the United States has ever produced.

The considerable challenges faced by the Army in the face of financial retrenchment also privately affected Patton. Finding it difficult to adapt to family life again after his fighting in France, the poor behaviour that he had exhibited in Bourg earlier that year was transferred to the Patton family home at Camp Meade. His short temper got shorter, his tolerance of difference grew weaker, and his bonhomie in social settings sat uneasily alongside his jibes at Beatrice and the strictness with his children that led Ruth Ellen, his younger daughter, to call him 'an ogre'.[12] War had made George irritable and distracted, and neither tendency ever left him. He regarded himself in the mirror and saw a thickening waistline, receding hair and a man whose best years seemed to have passed. It made him melancholic and angry, and his family suffered far more than those colleagues who avoided the worst excesses of his discomfiture.

Working closely with Eisenhower, he argued that the tank should not be viewed purely as an adjunct to the infantry but that it had huge potential in an independent role, and they began a prolific period of publishing in military journals that lasted for more than two years. Some applauded their boldness and willingness to challenge, but in time the upper echelons of the Army began to view the works as subversive. Indeed, during the autumn of 1920 Eisenhower was ordered to Washington to be rebuked by the Chief of Infantry, and was even threatened with a court martial if he continued his 'sedition'. Patton had received similar admonishment, although not formally, but both heeded the warning that their prospects could be severely damaged if they continued to run against the grain of official Army thinking and traditionalists in senior leadership positions. With the Army in self-preservation mode, diminished by an impoverished military culture and with little chance of the institution embracing their ideas, the officers decided to take themselves out of the firing line. Eisenhower wrote, 'Our dream of a separate tank force was shattered.'[13]

In the summer of 1920, Patton was promoted to major and retained command of the tank brigade. He had remained loyal to armour for as long as it served his purposes, but having been effectively muzzled about its employment, he decided that the cavalry offered greater opportunity. Thus, in October, Patton returned to Fort Myer as a squadron commander in the 3rd Cavalry Regiment – the same role he had held nearly a decade earlier. Patton drew on his experiences and began to impose both his personality and standards on his men, but with ambitions to develop 'thinking soldiers'. He subsequently established the self-styled 'Patton School for Professionals' in which his officers would undertake a twelve-week 'train the trainers' course, during which he taught his leadership philosophy (in one month alone he scheduled twenty-two lectures and delivered sixteen personally) – which consistently returned to the theme of leading from the front, with even senior officers needing to be where the fighting was taking place. 'There is nothing more pathetic and futile', he explained to his officers during a talk about generalship, 'than a general who lives long to explain a defeat.'[14]

Patton moved seamlessly from the Fort Myer classroom to the dining rooms of Washington's social elite. With Beatrice on his arm, he became a regular at the most impressive events, and the Pattons reciprocated by hosting their own magnificent parties and with invitations to polo matches. But even in this company Patton retained his rather childish desire to shock and steal the limelight. Whether via profanity, vulgar jokes, inappropriate comments, personal insults or lewd activity (he was known to ostentatiously drop his trousers to show ladies his war wound), Patton was regarded as ungentlemanly, however much he considered himself eccentric. He would often justify his boldness by saying that he had led many lives as a great warrior, fighting beside the likes of Julius Caesar and Napoleon Bonaparte, and that he had been reincarnated so that he might one day lead a great army in battle. But while to some this was merely a harmless Patton affectation, others began to view him with incredulity. For a period he was banned from the home of his sister-in-law, Kay Merrill, after persistently insinuating that her husband was a coward for working in the Foreign Service rather than having fought on the Western Front, and on many occasions it was the unhappy task of Beatrice to making profuse apologies to family, friends and acquaintances upset by her husband's poor behaviour.[15]

When Patton's tour at Fort Myer came to an end in December 1922, he began the Advanced Officers' Course at the Cavalry School at Fort Riley in January 1923, completing it top of the class and with excellent reports. By September, still separated from his family, he was at Fort Leavenworth for the prestigious year-long course at the Command and General Staff School (CGSS). Careers may not have been made there, but they could certainly be broken during the highly competitive programme. Patton felt the pressure and noted, 'I doubt if I stand as high relatively as I did at Riley…[but] I think some of the others will crack – I hope so.'[16] The theory-based syllabus sought to impart specific skills to prepare students for high command, and was a means of embedding doctrine in their minds. Ten years later, Patton wrote to a friend who was about to begin the course that high marks 'depend more on technique than on INTELLIGENCE'.[17] The lack of emphasis on creative and critical thinking infuriated Patton nearly as much as the programme's emphasis on lessons designed to ensure that the US Army could refight the First World War better, rather than preparing it for something of a completely different character. While leadership and leader development was implicit in what was studied, there was an assumption that graduates would make the necessary interpretations and apply them to the senior ranks themselves. Patton graduated in the top 10 per cent of his class in June 1924 and with the endorsement of the commandant, who believed Patton to be 'one of the ablest and best officers of his grade in the service'.[18]

The summer of 1924 began well, and what with the birth of a long-awaited son the previous December, Patton was as happy as he had been since his return from war. He relaxed, spent time with his family in a rented house near the coast in Beverly, Massachusetts, and was even awarded a 'Silver Life-saving Medal of Honor' for rescuing three boys whose boat had capsized in rough seas while Patton was out sailing. Clearly valued by the Army, he was a prime contender for promotion and even, perhaps, a place at the most senior officer training school: the US Army War College. In the meantime, however, he needed to serve time on the staff, and in so doing continue his professional development in an environment to which he was not best suited. Initially he spent a short time at First Corps Area headquarters in Boston, but by spring 1925 he was settling into Schofield Barracks in Honolulu, where as a Hawaiian Division staff officer he was responsible for personnel and intelligence. The isolation of the place was offset in his eyes by the fact that the annexation of the islands by the United States at the end of the previous century had been bitterly opposed by Japan and resulted in an ongoing threat of invasion.

If he was looking for a posting that stretched him, however, he was to be disappointed, for the beguiling beauty of the island and its climate lulled Patton into a professional stupor which he had to fight lest he become the lazy, unfit officer he so despised. By the end of his first year, a report on him once again referred to the fact that he was 'better qualified for active duty than the routine of office work'.[19] He endeavoured to keep intellectually active while on the island, often thinking and writing about leadership. 'We talk a hell of a lot about tactics and such and we never get to brass tacks,' he wrote to Eisenhower in July 1926, having read the latest professional journals. 'Namely what is it that makes the Poor S.O.B. who constitutes the casualty lists fight and in what formation is he going to fight. The answer to the first [question] is Leadership [and] that to the second – I don't know.'[20] In a lecture titled 'On Leadership', delivered to the officers in Schofield Barracks, Patton expanded on his theme of motivating troops and laid out the requirements for an effective leader: 'the possession of a superiority complex'; 'a self confident combative instinct'; '[an] aura of authority' and 'a reputation for dauntless courage'.[21] Put another way, the ideal Army leader was, in his view, very much like George S. Patton.

The arrival in Honolulu of the Patton family during early 1926 provided a welcome distraction from a job that George found tiresome. His appointment in November 1926 as the headquarters' staff officer responsible for tactics, training and operations provided more of an interesting challenge, but still Patton felt unsated and his mental health suffered. The death of his father in June 1927 only exacerbated the unhappiness he had been experiencing in Hawaii, and pushed him into darkness. In common with previous bouts of unhappiness, Patton became difficult to be around, with family and now colleagues suffering from his thoughtlessness in word and deed. Criticizing the brigade's performance in a report after an exercise in November 1927, for example, his reckless language and tactless assertions were not only delivered with a sense of superiority but also undermined the commander. As Patton's biographer Martin Blumenson has written: 'For a major to "correct" a brigadier general was inadmissible.'[22] Indeed, such was the furore he caused among the senior ranks due to his insubordination, constant criticisms and patronizing tone that he was punished by being sent back into the personnel and intelligence role he so disliked.

When Patton left Honolulu in April 1928 at the end of his tour, he was forty-two years of age, still a major, and deeply concerned that his life journey had reached a cul-de-sac. His new appointment in Washington as the head of the Plans and Training Division working for the Chief of Cavalry was, again, not the best fit, but it did place him at the centre of power once more and this improved his outlook. With George's mood lightened by access to old friends, the Pattons reintegrated themselves into society and he spent lavish sums of his wife's money (and, after the death of his mother later that year, his own substantial inheritance[23]) in the pursuit of fox hunting, steeplechasing and playing polo. He also purchased a new yacht berthed on the Potomac, where he turned acquaintances into friendships, and friendships into a team of influential people who were well placed to ensure that he was well informed and that his name remained vigorous in the right circles. Meanwhile, Beatrice determined the family should put down new roots, which, she hoped, would provide stability in the years to come. Patton agreed – the recent deaths of his parents marked the end of an era – and in purchasing 'Green Meadows', a large colonial building set in superb hunting country not far from Avalon, near Boston, he hoped for a new beginning.

The Great Crash in 1929 and the onset of the Depression did not materially affect the Pattons' lifestyle, although it was the hot topic of conversation when they entertained guests at their second home, a six-bedroomed property in north-west Washington replete with nine servants and stables.[24] Henry Stimson had been appointed Secretary of State in Herbert Hoover's new administration, and Patton's old friend was a regular visitor in the 1930s. Dwight Eisenhower and his family were also welcomed, with John, his son, later recalling:

> I always held the Pattons in considerable awe, because of their obvious wealth... Silver horsemanship trophies covered a

complete wall in the living room of their quarters. Patton was a good-humoured man who loved to joke. His language was full of the purple expressions for which he later became famous. I was astonished that he not only swore profusely around ladies but also encouraged all three of his children to do the same.[25]

In the Office of the Cavalry, Patton worked diligently and began to develop some of the attributes required in such a position, not least when and how to offer an opinion and when to keep quiet. Never content with the status quo, even as a great horseman working at the beating heart of traditionalism, he tried to get the cavalry to accept change and wrote in the *Cavalry Journal* in 1930: 'If the 14th Century knight could adapt himself to gunpowder, we should have no fear of oil, grease, and motors.'[26] He made little headway with such challenging arguments, yet despite his forays into controversy his superior officer thought highly enough of Patton to grade him as 'superior' when he left the department for another period to be spent as a student, and commented that he was: 'A man of outstanding energy. A hard-worker and a great reader of military literature. Very progressive and has an extensive knowledge of various subjects. He will accomplish what he sets out to do.'[27]

Patton seemed to be in greater control of his demons than previously, and with this more positive attitude he was selected for the US Army War College, then located in the capital. He began the year-long course in September 1931 eager to impress, for it was the final part of Patton's formal military education and would make him eligible for command at the highest levels. The programme, in common with his previous Army courses, was heavily academic – sterile, even – and once again he was disappointed that command and leadership were merely subsumed into other subjects rather than being areas of study in their own right. Even so, Patton excelled at the college and was noted for both his intellect and personality. 'George had a reputation as a playboy,' classmate Bradford Chynoweth later recalled. 'He played hard, when he played. But he was a lifelong worker, dedicated to learning everything that he could about War – a tireless student of military history. In every War College assignment, whether as chairman or subordinate, he went all-out. During discussion meetings, he was a ruthless critic of outworn traditions.'[28]

Towards the end of the course, Patton produced a bold research paper in which he outlined his vision for the next war (a subject about which he had been thinking for the last dozen years), which included an exploration of the advantages possessed by smaller, more professional armies over their larger, conscript counterparts. Although a rather naive paper in retrospect, as it revealed a lack of strategic and organizational appreciation, it was described by the commandant as being a 'work of exceptional merit' and was forwarded by the War College to the War Department for its interest.[29]

Once again, his final report was 'superior' and suggested that Patton was most particularly suited to a command appointment. With such a valediction Patton could expect advancement to become a senior officer, but much to Beatrice's consternation, her husband did not just want rank, he wanted another war. Only in war, he wrote to his wife – revealing his martial alter ego – could he 'prove himself a great commander and finally fulfil his destiny'.[30]

— ◻ —

Major Bernard Montgomery transitioned from the First World War to peace with actions that showed he had a clear objective in mind: to ensure that the British Army was better prepared for the next war than it had been in 1914, and to play as large a part in that transition as he could. To do that, however, he had first to ensure that he won a place in a much smaller post-war Army that was hamstrung by the detrimental financial implications of defence planning, based on the government's premise that there would be no 'great war' for at least a decade.[31] The fact that he was selected from a panoply of talented officers to retain his commission says a great deal about the respect in which he was held.

His first post-war appointment was at the General Headquarters of the British Army of the Rhine, based in Cologne. Much of the working day was taken up with the preparation for its closure on 1 September 1919, but Montgomery also found time to tour the battlefields, and before long his deep knowledge about the fighting on the Western Front and the lessons to be drawn from it attracted an audience of junior officers and civilian visitors to the headquarters. For Montgomery, the acquisition of such military knowledge was not a luxury for an officer but an essential, and he later wrote that 'a thorough knowledge of his job, of his profession, is an absolute pre-requisite [for an officer]; and then a never-ending study to keep himself up-to-date. Not only must he be a master of his trade; he must also always be learning.'[32]

The formal development of his mind, Montgomery hoped, would take place at the Staff College, Camberley. Graduation from this august institution was essential for any ambitious officer, as it sought to prepare the brightest and best for future senior command and staff appointments.[33] Places were coveted; only sixty officers, having gained the recommendation of a suitably senior officer, were accepted for the one-year course annually. Thus, Montgomery welcomed an invitation he had received to play tennis with the Commander-in-Chief of the British Army of the Rhine, Field Marshal Sir William Robertson, in the hope of gaining his sponsorship. It worked, and in January 1920 Brevet Major Montgomery, having been selected from a strong pool of officers which included temporary brigadier generals and winners of the Distinguished Service Cross and Victoria Cross, began the course he expected would re-ignite his career.

The Staff College syllabus engaged with subjects designed to broaden the students' professional knowledge of politics, economics and history; the component parts of the British Army; the conduct of operations; and the processes and techniques required for effective staff work. Essay writing and collaborative student exercises took up a significant proportion of the working week, and in each Montgomery was so forthright in his opinions that he began to grate on students and directing staff alike. Indeed, he is reported to have said to a colleague when discussing the solution to a particular problem that 'the DS [Directing Staff] have got it all wrong. They just don't know the answers!'[34] – while in return the military instructors called Montgomery a 'bloody menace',[35] as his absence of self-awareness made his interactions with others so taxing. Indeed, during his time at Camberley the Army was given full evidence of the officer Montgomery was to become: intelligent, driven, hard-working, but also intolerant of views that did not accord with his own. Yet on leaving the Staff College, he was given no reason to change his behaviour, for he was supported by strong reports that diminished his unhelpful character traits and promoted his professionalism, and so he was well positioned for a prime appointment. In a sense, therefore, the British Army was complicit in condoning conduct that many found unappealing, and which ran deep through Montgomery's developing leadership style.

His appointment in January 1921 as brigade major to the 17th Infantry Brigade serving in Ireland was the ideal job for somebody looking to be tested in multifaceted operations. With southern Irish Catholic republicans seeking independence from Britain, Montgomery's Protestant Irish heritage and his return to the land of his family seat was bound to give the job added piquancy. He arrived to find that the nine-battalion brigade was struggling to keep order, as the Irish Republican Army (IRA) undertook a ruthless campaign that had taken the life of his cousin, Lieutenant Colonel Hugh Montgomery. As brigade major (effectively chief of staff) to the commander, Brigadier General H. W. Higginson DSO, Monty took up a familiar role but in a very different context to that of the Western Front. The work was arduous because the situation was constantly changing, accurate intelligence on the opposition was very difficult to obtain, and the Army's response was straitjacketed by strict rules of engagement. 'In many ways this war was far worse than the Great War,' he would later write in his memoirs.[36]

Higginson trusted Montgomery without reservation, impressed by his attention to detail and his work ethic, and the wider headquarters team also recognized a talented officer when they saw one, with a colleague noting, '[He] is certainly a little tiger for work, and he is also a martinet as regards punctuality.'[37] His *17th Infantry Brigade: Summary of Important Instructions* became essential reading for all officers, and was appreciated not least because it was easy to use with subjects listed alphabetically from 'Armoured Cars' to 'Wireless'.[38] However, conditions became even more unstable after the signing of the Anglo-Irish Treaty in December 1921. The aim of that agreement was to establish an Irish Free State within the year, to include all but six counties in the north to form Northern Ireland, but the outbreak of civil war made the British Army's peacekeeping task impossible to achieve. With the brigade's date of return to England in March 1922 looming, the stress began to show and Montgomery wrote to his father: 'The situation really is impossible; we have had two officers murdered in the last fortnight… I shall be heartily glad to see the last of the people and of the place.'[39]

Despite the many difficulties faced by Montgomery during his tour of duty in Ireland, he came out of it with glowing reports and valuable experience. Officers who absorbed pressure and remained effective were highly prized by the Army, and Montgomery was next appointed as brigade major in the 8th Infantry Brigade. A constituent of the elite 3rd Division (a formation that was to play a major role in his future career), it was based in Plymouth on England's south coast. His boss, Brigadier S. E. Holland, had been apprised of his subordinate's considerable abilities and particularly his passion for developing troops, and gave Monty considerable freedom of action in their training.[40] The package Montgomery created put himself at the centre of all developmental activity and the programme's delivery. It included lectures by Montgomery to the officers of the brigade on some subjects far beyond his own expertise and experience, but which he gave with such confidence that few questioned his qualifications for the task. Those who did, such as Captain David Symes, who had fought in the 1917 Battle of Cambrai and had the temerity to challenge some of his assertions during questions, came under withering attack from Montgomery, who snapped, 'Just because you were there does not mean that you are a master of the subject. If you were, I would have asked you to present this lecture.'[41] Indeed, Holland came to regret the independence he had afforded Montgomery, who began to behave as though he was the brigadier, taking decisions that were not his to take and speaking for the commander when it was inappropriate to do so. Within a year of Montgomery's arrival at 8th Brigade, therefore, Holland found an excuse to move him on. Symes, for one, was not upset, writing to his father: 'The sanctimonious Montgomery has gone. Good riddance! He made my life a misery.'[42]

Montgomery's next job, begun in May 1923 and approached with undiminished energy, was chief of staff in the 49th (West Riding) Division, a Territorial Army (TA) formation based in York and comprising part-time officers and soldiers. Its commander, Sir Charles Harington, was only too pleased for one of his few regular officers to take on the day-to-day running of the division, and before long Montgomery had become a dominating presence in the headquarters. Unlike Holland, Harington embraced Montgomery's energy and capacity for greater responsibility because he got results. Montgomery had successfully raised the morale, skills and broad fighting capabilities of the formation to a noticeable degree by the time it undertook its summer exercise in August, and he then used that two-week event to further improve the division's professionalism, transforming an average division into a good one. Its officers and men reacted positively to being regarded as professionals and treated no differently from their regular colleagues, with whom Montgomery ensured they trained while guided by his own *Tactical Notes for the use in the West Riding Area and 49th (West Riding) Division.*[43]

By the end of the year, the entire division had undergone a series of rigorous assessments to determine which areas required more attention during Montgomery's largely indoor winter training programme. It began with all officers learning how to train the men themselves, because Montgomery was convinced that unless trusted trainers had the necessary knowledge and skills there would be no longevity in what he was trying to achieve. He explained his thinking in a letter to Captain Basil Liddell Hart, a former soldier who was then forging a second career as a writer and military theorist:

> It appeared to us [in the division staff] that our units were trying to do what is not really possible; they went to the camps in the summer and tried to do collective training without having first carried out any individual instruction of the leaders… Now as you know, the underlying principle of all training is the instruction of leaders before they in turn teach their men. It was a well-known Corps Commander in France who once said: 'Teach the teachers what to teach before they teach the Tommies'… [H]e hit the nail right on the head when he said those words.[44]

Montgomery followed up his lectures on the art of instruction with practical evening classes about how to use sand tables for planning and war-gaming. He then had tables of fifteen feet by fifteen feet specially made and delivered to every drill hall for the training of the troops, and visited each location in turn to ensure that the instruction was sound. Each became a three-dimensional small-scale map, with the sand shaped into the contours of the land while coloured string denoted roads and rivers, boxes were buildings, foliage became woods, and opposing forces were represented by an array of blue and red wooden blocks. Harington saw for himself how his visionary and inspirational chief of staff had managed to successfully engage the minds of his men and leave them with an appetite for more. No longer was 49th Division regarded as the poor relation of its regular neighbours for, as Montgomery wrote to Liddell Hart in the summer of 1924: 'I always tell our Division that there is only one Army in England, and we all belong to it, whether we are Regulars, Territorials, or OTC [Officer Training Corps].'[45]

To Major Montgomery, talent was talent no matter where and in whom it resided. He was unimpressed by fashionable regiments if their surface gloss sparkled but their deeper capabilities lacked the same lustre. To facilitate improvement, Montgomery invited regular officers serving with the division to attend a course he had developed to prepare them for newly reinstated Staff College entrance examinations (TA officers could not be admitted to the Staff College at this time) and was never happier than when one of his students was awarded a place on the Camberley course. Brian Montgomery, who was himself commissioned into the Royal Warwickshire Regiment in 1923, reflected the view of many when he wrote that he believed his brother 'was at his best when helping young officers'[46] because he had the ability to light a fire in them when it came to duty, leadership and the profession of arms.

Of those Montgomery assisted during his time in York, one officer in particular stands out: Francis (Freddie) de Guingand, a lieutenant in the Royal Sussex Regiment and husband to Monty's sister, Winsome. Twenty years later the two men would develop a remarkable partnership, but even at York the mutual admiration that the two men had for each other was clear to Brian Montgomery, who was staying with his older brother and attended some of the sessions himself. 'Each undoubtedly impressed the other in a way that neither forgot,' Brian later recalled. 'Bernard, because he has the capacity, so essential in sound leadership, first of never failing to recognise real talent, and secondly of being able to isolate it to his own advantage; de Guingand, because he fell under Bernard's spell at York and, in his turn, had the capacity to recognise genius when he saw it.'[47]

While at York, Montgomery authored a series of articles on tactics in journals including the *Army Quarterly* and *The Antelope* (the Royal Warwickshire regimental magazine), as well as pamphlets for the 49th (West Riding) Division, in which he distilled his thinking into simple but practical lessons for the benefit of officers and soldiers. The results of his efforts were not difficult to find, with the chain of command noting a significant improvement in the division's morale and performances throughout 1924, and Harington magnanimously highlighted Montgomery's 'decisive contribution' to the achievement. Writing in his annual report that autumn, the general stated that Montgomery was 'an officer of very marked ability... An excellent instructor and lecturer – a student of his profession – considerably above average in professional ability and knowledge.'[48]

Montgomery left York in the spring of 1925 after nearly two years as chief of staff, having maintained the missionary zeal with which he always went about his soldiering. Returning to Shorncliffe as a company commander in the 1st Royal Warwicks, an appointment he had held ten years previously in a diminished Army that struggled to provide new opportunities for talented officers, he was determined to make his mark on his own 'military family' and show his credentials for becoming its future commanding officer. He arrived with a pre-prepared six-month company training programme, the culmination of which was scheduled to coincide with the battalion's summer exercise. His superior, the popular and charming Lieutenant Colonel C. R. Macdonald, immediately approved it, though as Montgomery set about improving his company, his brother officers began to look just like the 'idle saps' that he accused them of being. Brian Montgomery, a second lieutenant in the battalion, later recalled 'witnessing some bitter slanging matches, with few holds barred' in the officers' mess,[49] but his brother was not deterred in his plans and, critically, he had Macdonald's support. The results were soon in evidence. By the summer, Montgomery's company was becoming a well-motivated and capable team, the like of which the battalion had not seen for years.

The company's improvement was an illustration of a Montgomery leadership truth that 'soldiers will be more likely follow a leader in whose military knowledge they have confidence, rather than a man with much greater personality but with not the same obvious knowledge of his job'.[50] At first autocratic, Montgomery increasingly included his officers and NCOs in the programme as deliverers and a source of new ideas. As trust was developed, he allowed others to use their own leadership to get the results that he wanted. The *Company Training Diary* that Montgomery kept during the spring and summer of 1925 reveals carefully staged blocks of activity designed to improve skills (including a ten-day-long battlefield tour for his subalterns, conducted on bicycles[51]), culminating in mock battles, live firing training and night operations during the summer. The brigade commander was so impressed with what he observed during an exercise in which Montgomery's company co-operated variously with the Royal Artillery, the Royal Engineers and even the Royal Air Force that he selected the company as the benchmark of attainment that others had to match, and the unit that would demonstrate the brigade's accomplishments to senior officers. Some of those who had earlier felt that Montgomery's approach was disruptive reassessed their opinion. To most he remained a difficult man to like, but as one of the battalion officers later admitted: 'Underneath, as I learned, he was bloody good.'[52] By the autumn, Macdonald was rolling out the new methods across the whole battalion, with Montgomery stepping out of his company command to oversee their implementation alongside a new NCO training cadre which he was to instruct in military skills and leadership.

Recognizing his success with training techniques and programmes, the Army appointed Montgomery an instructor at the Staff College on a three-year posting, starting in January 1926 as a temporary lieutenant colonel. With his career gaining some noteworthy momentum, Montgomery was keen to influence a whole generation of officers. Always alive to exploiting potential advantageous situations, he later reflected on this time:

> At certain moments in life an opportunity is presented to each one of us: some of us are not aware of the full significance of what has happened, and the moment is lost. Others, alert and enthusiastic, seize the opportunity with both hands and turn it to good advantage; these have ambition, as every man who is worth his salt should have – not too much, but rather the determination to succeed by his own efforts and not merely stamping on other people who get in the way.[53]

Montgomery was immediately impressed by his fellow instructors, who were each responsible for a syndicate of twelve officers, running discussions after their lectures, setting work, overseeing group exercises and ensuring that expected standards were met. Each seemed to be considerably more capable than those he was taught by when a student at Camberley himself, and he was particularly taken with Colonel Alan Brooke, the Director of Studies. Brooke was a serious student of his profession whose calm demeanour, deep knowledge and clarity of thinking immediately appealed to Montgomery, who came to regard his boss as a role model and a mentor. Although retaining a superciliousness that could aggravate his students and his peers, Monty encouraged students not to seek prescribed Army solutions to problems – an instinctive desire in officers that Camberley supported – but to bring their own creative thinking to bear on an issue.[54]

By this stage in his career, Montgomery was an experienced lecturer with a reputation for confident, passionate and knowledgeable discourse on a range of military subjects. At the Staff College he refined his techniques and settled on a style that he would employ for the remainder of his life. Aware that he lacked the ability to draw in his audience with word pictures and be amusing throughout, he instead developed exceptional presentation skills – often including props such as maps and models – to get his arguments to bite. As one of his students later said, 'There was a beautiful clarity and precision to Monty's talks that few could emulate. There was no ambiguity. His message was clear, repeated and embedded. Deceptively simple, but really very clever.'[55] Those who were underprepared or revealed lazy thinking received short shrift from an instructor who constantly reminded his students of the 'critical importance of developing the mind before expecting it to function adequately in war'.[56] Yet despite his best efforts and those of his colleagues, the Staff College course did not provide its officers with the breadth of knowledge and skills they needed to fight a future European war. One of Montgomery's students, John Slessor, later reflected: 'I don't think any of us really thought in our heart of hearts that we were fitting ourselves to take leading parts in another life or death struggle.'[57]

Aged thirty-nine in the summer of 1927, Lieutenant Colonel

Montgomery was dedicated to the Army, fiercely ambitious, somewhat solitary and entirely focused on his work. Marriage, therefore, was unexpected – indeed, he had once said, 'You can't make a good soldier and a good husband'[58] – but in July that year he wed Betty Carver, having met her on a skiing holiday in Lenk, Switzerland. The widow of an officer killed at Gallipoli in 1915 and the mother of two sons, the new Mrs Montgomery understood Army life and had a brother, Percy Hobart, with a burgeoning military career himself. Artistically inclined, outgoing and charming, Betty was in many respects the opposite of her husband, but despite the odds, she managed to draw him out of his insular military world and got him to lose some of his 'military starchiness' and share his time with others. With a son, David, born in 1928, his small family provided Monty with a contentment that he hardly thought possible by the time his tour of duty at the Staff College came to an end in January 1929. 'A time of great happiness then began; it had never before seemed possible that such love and affection could exist,' he later wrote, and the staid officer found himself engaged with the world beyond the Army for the first time in years.[59]

That year hardened Montgomery's convictions that Britain would be drawn into another great European conflict. Tracking world events from a six-month secondment to the War Office, everything he heard about the Wall Street Crash and its detrimental impact on Germany made him concerned for the stability of the continent, and as German unemployment soared and the rise of the Nazis began, his apprehension deepened. As secretary to the committee tasked with revising the *Infantry Training Manual Volume II*, he saw it as a chance to shake the military out of its apathy. His challenge was to influence the conservative committee overseeing the writing of the manual, to ensure that it took account of the latest military thinking and produced something relevant to a British Army that needed modernization.

In typical fashion, Montgomery did not hold back his own views about the content of this important publication, and having roundly criticized the 1926 edition of the manual, he advocated a complete rewrite to be undertaken by himself. As mere secretary to the committee, such views were bound to antagonize its members (comprising several senior officers, including a major general who would be writing Montgomery's annual report), but after a great deal of discussion, he was awarded the task and set out to produce 'a comprehensive treatise on war for the infantry officer'.[60] When he presented his draft, the committee believed it too far removed from the 1926 manual to be fully endorsed by them. Having written to a colleague that he felt the committee 'ga-ga',[61] he agreed to revisions only to then submit his unaltered text to the War Office for publication after the committee had been disbanded. The former committee members were furious, but their one-time secretary was not concerned and later wrote, 'The book when published [in 1931] was considered excellent, especially by its author.'[62]

Many episodes in Montgomery's career gave rise to accusations that he really did not care what colleagues thought about him, but this overlooks a more complex truth: he cared deeply about how he was regarded by his brother officers, but he would not shy away from confrontation with them if he felt that honest disagreement was for the greater good. Nevertheless, many perceived his petulant behaviour (which could easily spill over into insubordination) as merely an affectation designed to grab the limelight. He felt slighted to be returning to regimental duty in 1930 as the 1st Royal Warwickshire battalion's second-in-command rather than commanding officer, and Montgomery's truculence and small-mindedness was noted by his colleagues. One junior officer later testified that Montgomery seemed determined to 'upset the battalion's harmony so that when he *did* step up, he could rebuild it and win the plaudits'.[63]

The commanding officer – the able and well-liked Clement Tomes – tolerated Montgomery's frustration, but a few firm words were exchanged between the two men to establish a good working relationship. Montgomery soon became a valuable confidant and sounding board for Tomes, whose wisdom and judgement came to be sought by all the headquarters staff. He also slipped easily into Tomes's responsibilities when there was a need for Montgomery to deputize.

Montgomery made copious notes regarding what he had learned about the command, leadership and management required at the helm of a battalion. It was time well spent, for in January 1931 he sailed from Southampton bound for Palestine, Betty following later, in the role that he had yearned for since joining the Army: Lieutenant Colonel Bernard Montgomery DSO was the new commanding officer of his regiment.

— ◻ —

The defeated Germany that Erwin Rommel returned to with his regiment at the end of 1918 was not one that befitted his sacrifices or those of his men. Political, economic and social chaos abounded in the wake of a revolution that led to bloody street fighting and an uncertainty that permeated the length and breadth of a shattered nation. The war had made men like Rommel – and now, in common with so many of his generation, he had to find his place in a traumatized country he barely recognized. To make the challenge even greater, he was no longer engaged in making life-and-death decisions; like Patton and Montgomery, he was just another officer hoping to retain his job in a much-reduced Army with an uncertain future. He watched as men from his regiment ghosted back into civilian life, returning to waiting mothers, fathers, wives and sweethearts as different men from those who'd gone to war. Most were glad to be alive, but they were also aware that the major German project to become one of the great imperial powers was over, at least for the foreseeable future.

Some took up arms again in a voluntary paramilitary force, the Freikorps, which did not necessarily fight for the new federal constitutional republic based in Weimar and its president Friedrich Ebert – reviled by many – but were motivated by right-wing political causes desirous of 'strong leadership' in the form of a conservative, autocratic government. Over half a million men served in the organization, with perhaps three times that number active informally, and they fought in direct opposition to radical left groups. This was a clash not only intellectually, in their political philosophies, but also physically in towns and cities across Germany. Having successfully defeated the Spartacists in Berlin during January 1919, for example, just two months later a general strike by workers in Berlin saw the Freikorps fighting their opponents in the streets and buildings of the capital, leading to the deaths of up to 3,000 'insurgents' with thousands more arrested.[64]

During this revolutionary upheaval, Rommel was selected for a commission in the military organization, initially called the Provisional National Defence Force (PNDF), that would eventually absorb elements of the Freikorps and further transition the nation's massive wartime army into one that served the Weimar Republic. Established during the Versailles peace negotiations in the summer of 1919, the PNDF was a vital first step in Rommel's ambition to have a military career after the war, and gave him the focus he required during the months when his unemployed and demotivated colleagues drifted on a tide of insecurity.

In the summer of 1919, appointed to command the 32nd Internal Security Company at Friedrichshafen on Lake Constance, where it was quelling civil disturbances, Rommel found the task unlike anything in his previous experience. He had been posted to the job in a chaotic situation to be a strong leader who could bring discipline to a rebellious unit; however, had he persisted with trying to lead these ratings and petty officers from the old Imperial Navy using the same techniques he had employed with the Württemberg Battalion during the war, he could well have faced a mutiny. His attempt at inspirational leadership proffered by a decorated soldier to bored sailors working for poor wages and living in squalid conditions was merely mocked. Unable to motivate them for even the most basic of military tasks, rather than getting frustrated and angry with them, Rommel instead tried to understand them better as a group and as individuals. He paid particular attention to those men of rank or reputation who were respected by the group, and over the course of several weeks, Rommel won his own respect. His ability to communicate with soldiers in a way they liked was assisted by his wickedly dry sense of humour and self-deprecating personality, which helped to create an empathy with the troops that made the company actively want to be led by him. When he said to them one day that he had always wanted to lead such excellent men – and that 'My prayers were heard because here you are!' – their cheers provided all the evidence he required that he had gained the company's loyalty.[65]

While Rommel never enjoyed the same 'hold' over these men as he had over the Rommel Detachment, his charisma and the relationship he developed with them ensured that they would follow him in even the most dangerous situations. He ordered his men to use force on their fellow Germans only as a last resort, because he believed in strict ethical parameters that he could justify to anybody who might question his decisions, but also because he had a strong aversion to fighting his own countrymen. Thus, when his men were called upon to disperse a violent crowd in Münsterhausen, Rommel successfully deployed fire hoses rather than firepower to disperse the mob, and so avoided the mass casualties that would have been created in less sensitive hands.

By 1921, the Weimar Republic had a new Army organization, the Reichswehr, limited to 100,000 officers and men by the Treaty of Versailles, with heavy weapons and a General Staff prohibited. Rommel was in significant competition to receive one of the new organization's 4,000 commissions. He succeeded because of reports of his outstanding conduct and success with the PNDF, bolstered by his wartime achievements and the personal recommendation of his regimental commander. The Reichswehr was led by the celebrated and farsighted Hans von Seeckt, whose ambition was to lay the foundations, in a force explicitly tasked with protecting Germany's borders, for an Army with world-class offensive capabilities. Dynamic leadership was critical, and skilled, motivated and agile personnel would pull the German Army out of the claustrophobic mire in which it was currently operating and onto the broad sunny uplands of the future.

How far Erwin Rommel would progress in a diminutive Army packed with other talented officers was more than just a passing concern for him, but in taking his commission he would have been aware that for himself, as for the Army and the nation, patience was essential before less restrictive times could be enjoyed. He also understood that not being a member of the specially selected and trained General Staff would be an impediment to his career. The proficiency, expertise and influence of this banned elite – the brain of the Army – remained all pervasive, because it continued to work in secret as the Truppenamt (Troop Office) and drove the German military excellence that von Seeckt demanded; for, as he said, 'the form changes, the spirit remains the same'.[66] Thus, General Staff officers would continue to be held in high esteem and enjoy special privileges and better career opportunities than the rest of the officer corps. But perhaps the new Army, Rommel hoped, would begin to eschew the traditional and outdated attitudes for something more modern and relevant to the times in which they were living – and perhaps even to the benefit of talented lower-middle-class officers like himself.[67]

Rommel's first Reichswehr posting was to Stuttgart, where in October 1920 he took command of a company in the 13th Infantry Regiment, while political and social turmoil continued to permeate all aspects of German life. The military maintained its distance from the turmoil, a resource of the government rather than an independent armed organization with its own agenda. Rommel had no personal wish to play an active part in politics, and his own conservative views – typical of his background, class and profession – remained secondary to his duties as an officer. 'Herr Rommel would happily discuss his views about the Army, tactics, leadership and all the rest', his colleague Uwe Pfaffner commented after the First World War, 'but politics – and particularly party politics – just did not interest him.'[68]

Thus Rommel observed the current of change around him, but only involved himself in it to the extent of preparing his company for its duties. He took inordinate amounts of time and energy to create a capable unit composed of well-motivated men. Although a significant portion of his senior NCOs and officers had combat experience from the war, many did not and the vast majority of the enlisted men had not served during the 1914–18 conflict. The blend of youth and experience within his company gave it an energy that Rommel sought to harness, using training to shape his troops into a self-reliant team.

This approach drew heavily on the professional, free-thinking and learning Army culture that Hans von Seeckt was busy creating. Among the methods the general used to root these values and beliefs in the Army were official publications to guide readers in critical areas. The 1921 pamphlet *Leadership and Combined Arms Combat*, for example, was suffused with a philosophy that had dominated German military thinking for the last century, but here it was given a new emphasis – namely that leaders should act in accordance with their commander's intent, using their initiative to take bold, swift and decisive action.[69] It was an approach wholly compatible with Rommel's brand of leadership.

In the four years that Rommel spent commanding his company in Stuttgart, Lucie provided a steadiness that anchored her ambitious husband's life. A man who found inactivity an anathema, Rommel used his leisure time variously to learn the violin, organize his stamp collection and mend broken pieces of household machinery. His body needed to be as active as his mind, prompting a routine of daily exercise including running, swimming, cycling, hiking and skiing, often with Lucie. For Rommel, the countryside provided the space to organize his thoughts while maintaining the level of physical conditioning he demanded of his men. He expected subordinates to participate in competitive sports, as they promoted personal dedication, enhanced teamwork and engendered a winning mentality.

The November 1923 edition of 13th Regiment's newsletter

included an enthusiastic match report about a game played by the company against a sister unit: 'Captain Rommel's men have long since produced the best football team in the Regiment, but our recent 9-0 victory over our rivals from Köln is noteworthy. It is known that Captain Rommel personally selected the team and was assisted in the preparation for the match by a professional coach… The success of the team has been the talk of the Regiment and has set a new standard.'[70] Such attention to detail, combined with his desire to win, made his company 'the stand-out unit in the Regiment'.[71]

Leaving company command in 1924 for a string of roles on the staff of 13th Regiment's II battalion, Rommel found himself once again dislocated from daily contact with the troops he adored while stuck behind a desk. These appointments challenged his self-discipline, for although keen not to waste any experience, he found the repetitiveness of the work a trial. The details of the work and the challenges Rommel faced are lost to history, but when in 1927 he was appointed to the command of a machine gun company (although ensnared at that level for over a decade) he welcomed the opportunity. He immediately developed a training programme that included leadership, tactics and fighting spirit, with each phase punctuated by lectures given by Rommel himself. These were influenced by an array of sources found in the garrison library, and indeed his own book collection. The experiences of others informed his thinking. Ernst Jünger's *Storm of Steel* was well used, for example: the famous account of a soldier who was wounded fourteen times and became the youngest recipient of the *Pour le Mérite*. Many of Rommel's talks drew on his own experiences commanding machine gun units as part of his detachment during the last war, although he used them largely to illustrate scenarios with a known outcome.

Rommel was particularly adept at capturing the imagination of his audience, creating a scene and giving it realistic details. Indeed, to prompt his memory during the summer of 1927, Rommel visited his old Italian battlefields on a motorcycle (with Lucie riding in a sidecar) to sketch the landscape and to piece together the action from his notes.

The couple trekked across the key ground at Caporetto, sometimes taking a detour to gain a new perspective, before descending to the Piave. At Longarone the locals took an interest in the inquisitive German of a certain age with a notebook and camera, but when it transpired that he was the officer who had humiliated their town in 1917, the Rommels were politely asked to leave.

Rommel's battalion commander noted in his 1929 confidential report that 'as instructor and developer of his company he has very good successes to show'.[72] His home life was enhanced in December 1928 by the birth of a son, Manfred, who Lucie largely raised while her husband pursued his career. 'He remained a serious-minded but good-tempered man of simple tastes', wrote Rommel's first biographer, Desmond Young, 'who enjoyed a quiet life and, for the rest, was wrapped up in his profession.'[73] Notwithstanding the fact that he did not particularly enjoy parties and high living, he nevertheless valued friendship, and although he could not escape all the perceptions that surrounded a decorated and highly professional officer, he was happy to show the caring side of his personality and was, according to fellow officer Uwe Pfaffner, 'a widely respected, sensitive and very kind man'.[74]

During this period, Rommel was instrumental in establishing the Württemberg Battalion Old Comrades Association. Veterans of the Rommel Detachment looked to their old commander to provide the leadership they needed to form a self-support network, and he did not disappoint them, approaching the task with all the dedication he had shown when serving with the Württembergers. Scores of old soldiers received a letter from their former officer inviting them to join the fraternity. Rommel personally organized the first meetings and enjoyed obtaining some of the missing details about his battles, but as soon as the association had a healthy membership and a regular programme of events, he was happy for former NCOs to take over the administration – and within a couple of years, his own involvement was minimal.

Appointed to a raft of worthy but relatively unchallenging jobs since his return from the war, Rommel only sensed he had been noticed when he was selected as an instructor at Major General Wilhelm List's Dresden Infantry School in October 1929. His reports and recommendations from senior officers had been uniformly strong over the years, but now, on the eve of events that were going to change world history, the Army began to recognize the officer who was described by his battalion commander as 'quiet, of sterling character, always tactful and modest in his manner'.[75] At the Infantry School, Rommel's job was to inculcate his approach to leadership into the next generation of officers, and in so doing inspire them to the selfless service to which he was devoted. 'I was never happier than when working with young soldiers,' Rommel later wrote,[76] and recognizing his impact on them, his superiors reported that he was 'inexhaustively stimulating' and an 'infectious leadership type'.[77]

Using the lessons he had recently learned from training and educating his machine gun company, his teaching sessions were absorbing, relevant and highly individualistic. List wrote in Rommel's confidential report in September 1931: 'His tactical battle lectures, in which he describes his own war experience, offer the cadets not only tactical but also a lot of ideological food for thought. They are always a delight to hear.'[78] Rommel illustrated most sessions with his models, maps, photographs and sketches. The lessons, however, were not merely opportunities for Rommel to tell his war stories, but events during which leadership challenges, tactical conundrums and the realities of war became vivid vehicles for the development of the officer cadets. 'Shed sweat, not blood,' he would say to his students,[79] making clear it was imperative that a leader make decisions informed by vital information while also listening to his instinct.

Above all, he argued, leadership was about doing the right thing: 'Be an example to your men, in your duty and in private life. Never spare yourself, and let the troops see that you don't in your endurance of fatigue and privation. Always be tactful and well-mannered and teach your subordinates to do the same. Avoid excessive sharpness or harshness of voice, which usually indicates the man who has shortcomings of his own to hide.'[80]

The way in which Rommel held his audience spellbound was the envy of many, and a report written by the senior instructor was admiring: 'He is a towering personality even in a milieu of handpicked officers... A genuine leader, inspiring and arousing cheerful confidence in others. A first-rate infantry and combat instructor, constantly making suggestions and above all building up the cadets' characters... Respected by his colleagues, worshipped by his cadets.'[81]

Yet for all his accomplishments, Rommel's self-confidence bordered on an arrogance that was soon to become an inextricable part of his persona and leadership style. Prone to eschewing alternative ideas, he was convinced that his own experience, judgement and approach to problem-solving were superior to all others – to the frustration of those who sought to influence him.

By 1931 Rommel was so well respected by the Reichswehr's leaders that List offered to make a recommendation for him to take the General Staff entrance examination. The opportunities associated with joining the influential elite were enormous, and Rommel knew that his decision would shape his future career and prospects – however, despite his lifelong instinct to take advantage of opportunities, he decided to decline the invitation. Rommel recognized that with his service record and experience, he stood a better chance at advancement into the jobs that really interested him if he remained out of the shark-infested General Staff pool. His self-awareness maintained his position as a committed and unwavering outsider.

CHAPTER FIVE

Taking Command, 1932–39

T HE GREAT DEPRESSION had not touched George S. Patton personally. His substantial wealth could be found in his substantial rented residence in Rosslyn with its magnificent stables, located just outside the gates of Fort Myer. The grand set of buildings was not just a base for the Patton family, it was a much-loved Washington home where he and Beatrice could host parties for their friends. But while the 46-year-old Army major enjoyed the company of the rich and influential, he was only too keenly aware that time was running out if his own career was to peak and his 'destiny' was to become a reality. Any opportunity to make his mark as second-in-command of the 3rd Cavalry Regiment was thus grasped and exploited to the fullest. 'The one thing I need,' Patton explained to friends over dinner in July 1932, 'is another war. Then I can become Great.'[1] Yet while friends remained patient with Patton's grand ambitions, a political grandee once asked him how he intended to reach such heights at his age. Patton never spoke to the man again. 'I don't care how important he is,' he said to Beatrice, 'the man is a fool and will not be invited back.'[2]

Patton had arrived at Fort Myer just as the weather began to warm and increasing numbers of jobless ex-First World War servicemen started to arrive in the capital. Many had driven, hitched lifts or even walked huge distances with their families, to lobby Congress for the ability to cash in the bonus certificates that had been issued to compensate each man for the difference between his earnings as a soldier and what he could have earned as a civilian. These men needed the money now, at the height of the Great Depression, and not when their certificates matured in 1945. President Herbert Hoover was sympathetic to the demands but remained intransigent, wary of significant additional spending in the middle of a depression and just before seeking re-election in November. The so-called Bonus Army therefore decided to remain in the capital, to raise the profile of their claims and to exert pressure on politicians with vocal protests outside Congress. Led by former sergeant Walter W. Waters, the 25,000-strong 'army' was organized on military lines, with no political affiliation, and was committed to peaceful protest despite its members' increasing desperation.

One of their number was Joe Angelo, the former batman who had saved Patton's life at Cheppy on the Western Front in 1918. Since then he had lost his job as a riveter and so walked 160 miles from New Jersey to Washington to join his former comrades. On his arrival, Angelo was in such dire financial straits that he asked to be buried alive, and for ten cents could be viewed breathing through a stovepipe.[3] He was one of thousands of desperate people, but Hoover and the Chief of Staff of the US Army, Douglas MacArthur, had become increasingly concerned by malicious rumours that the veterans had been infiltrated by communist agitators bent on revolutionary activity using a ready-made fighting force. Patton, too, believed the Bonus Army was 'a disgrace' and that events signalled 'the end of an era, and that the RED dawn of some terrible catastrophy [sic] is just around the corner'.[4]

The Superintendent of the DC Police, Pelham D. Glassford – a former First World War brigadier general who had retired from the Army only the previous year – did not think the group was motivated or inspired by anything other than their well-known demands, however. Extremely concerned for the welfare of the forlorn incomers who took up residence in derelict buildings along Pennsylvania Avenue and a collection of temporary shelters on the banks of the Anacostia river, he sought to keep them safe and hoped that the desolate group would prove resistant to unsavoury influences.

Although the Bonus Army's number reduced to around 5,000 over the course of the summer, Patton felt the threat remained, and he assessed the 3rd Cavalry Regiment's readiness for action soon after it had been put on standby to lend support to the civilian authorities dealing with the protestors. 'These men are on their mettle', he wrote, 'and ready for whatever comes their way. I feel at home.'[5] On 28 July 1932 he was to have the opportunity to test that opinion. That day, collective authorities led by Hoover decided that the time had come to remove the protestors from the district, and with the commander of the 3rd Cavalry absent, Patton was deputized to lead the unit.

Initially the evictions were deemed to be a police matter, but resistance led to fighting and then a riot during which two veterans were shot, one fatally. On hearing of the deteriorating situation, Hoover resolved to deploy federal troops, and Patrick Hurley, the Secretary of War, provided carefully worded instructions to MacArthur:

> You will have the United States troops proceed immediately to the scene of the disorder. Cooperate fully with the District of Columbia police force which is now in charge. Surround the affected area and clear it without delay.
>
> Turn over all prisoners to the civil authorities.
>
> In your orders insist that any women or children who may be in the affected area be accorded every consideration and kindness. Use all humanity consistent with the due execution of this order.[6]

Douglas MacArthur demanded decisive action and chose to sit on the shoulder of Brigadier General Perry L. Miles, the officer tasked with commanding the troops and completing the evictions using the 3rd Cavalry Regiment at Fort Myer. Major Dwight Eisenhower, MacArthur's extremely capable aide, said his vainglorious boss changed out of his business suit and into his uniform. Ike noted that he 'purred at the force he had ordered to be placed at his disposal'[7] and believed MacArthur's conduct that day to be totally 'inappropriate',[8] for although Miles's orders demanded restraint, Eisenhower felt that MacArthur would support whatever force achieved a decision. 'I told that dumb son-of-a-bitch not to go down there,' Eisenhower later wrote. 'I told him it was no place for the Chief of Staff.'[9]

Major George Patton paced across the road at the head of more than 200 troops under his command and their braying mounts. Behind the 3rd Cavalry Regiment, 800 infantrymen checked their equipment, and behind them six light tanks belched blue-black smoke into the summer air. The force had taken up its position without fanfare like a cartridge slipped effortlessly into a shotgun chamber. MacArthur and Patton had last worked together in the field some fourteen years before, during the operation to clear the Saint-Mihiel salient, but this was not the road to Pannes, it was Pennsylvania Avenue just south of Capitol Hill in Washington, DC, and the opposition was not the German Army but 5,000 unarmed jobless First World War veterans seeking the alleviation of their distress during the Great Depression.

The Bonus Army campaigners were initially unsure whether to clap or jeer the arrival of the uniformed men that many still so closely identified with, but by late afternoon it was clear that they were not friend but foe. Patton barked out an order and his troops unpacked their gas masks and secured them over their faces. The infantry did the same. Another snapped instruction and the cavalrymen drew their sabres and the infantry fixed their bayonets. 'For one heart-stopping minute', a protestor later wrote, 'we were rooted to the spot not believing our eyes. "They're coming at us!", someone shouted.'[10] As veterans (some with their families) began to run back down Pennsylvania Avenue, cans of tear gas were thrown by the soldiers into the crowd, causing panic, disorientation and, for some, blinding pain. A final order and, seconds later, the cavalry surged forward through the gas cloud, noisy blurs to the incapacitated but a clear vision of the state's intent to those with eyes to see what was unfolding.

Patton's horses burst through the preparatory gas cloud, with his cavalrymen using the dull edge of their sabres to strike any men within reach. The infantry followed up with their rifle butts. 'Bricks flew, sabres rose and fell with a comforting smack, and the mob ran,' Patton later wrote. 'We moved after them, occasionally meeting some resistance... Two of us charged at the gallop, and had some nice work at close range with the occupants of a truck.'[11]

Pennsylvania Avenue became the scene of some obscene brutality, which went unchecked by Miles who was firmly under MacArthur's command. The Bonus Army was hurled back towards the Anacostia, and by 22.00 its members streamed across the bridge towards 'Hooverville' – a shanty town, ironically named for the president – and Hurley sent orders for the troops to be halted. MacArthur, however, ignored them, and so the Secretary of War restated that the troops should 'desist immediately'.[12] The Chief of Staff of the US Army again disregarded instructions that had been sent to him in the name of the President, and instead gave Miles verbal orders to 'torch the shanty town'.[13] Tents, sheds, cabins, kennels, old cars, boxes, chairs and everything else were consumed by an inferno which saw scores of families run for their lives.[14]

On the following morning, 29 July, the 3rd Cavalry was marshalling the remnants of the Bonus Army camp when Patton was approached by Joe Angelo. The officer was furious, recalled colleague Lucian Truscott, who said that Patton proclaimed loudly, 'Sergeant, I do not know this man. Take him away, and under no circumstances permit him to return!'[15] He then told the assembled officers that he did in fact know the man and had been sending Angelo money for years, but was concerned at what the press would make of any such meeting so soon after the destruction of the camp if they got to hear about it. Over a decade later, Patton called the events of late July in the capital 'a most distasteful form of service', but also confessed that he 'cherished memories of a job well done'.[16] Such words exemplified Eisenhower's later belief that his friend was 'so avid for recognition as a great military commander that he will ruthlessly suppress any habit of his that will tend to jeopardize it'.[17]

The Bonus Army action was one of the few memorable episodes in Patton's two years at Fort Myer. With a routine of staff duties and occasional ceremonial outings, little in his job stimulated him and so he spent as much time as he could amusing himself playing sport and socializing. The local Cobbler Hunt proved particularly useful for making the acquaintance of senior military and political figures, some of whom he invited to sail with him on a twenty-foot cruiser he had built in his garage. Kenyon Joyce, Patton's commanding officer at Fort Myer, understood his subordinate's exasperation at his limited ability to impress in a job that failed to stretch his talents, but rated him 'superior' in 1934 and reported, 'I believe this officer could be counted on for great feats of leadership in war.'[18] Such recognition was a fillip to Patton, as was his promotion to lieutenant colonel that year; and, as always, his inner calm was reflected in a happy period in his family life, which included the marriage of his daughter Bee to Lieutenant John K. Waters. Yet Patton was reaching the limits of his tolerance for what he deemed 'undemanding soldiering',[19] and he therefore learned with dismay that his next appointment would be back in Hawaii as the division's intelligence officer.

Returning to a job he had disliked a decade earlier was not conducive to Patton's professional satisfaction nor his mental health, but his complaints fell on deaf ears and he had little option but to make the best out of the tour. Tapping into his sense of adventure, he thus took the bold decision to hire a five-man crew and, with Beatrice, sailed to Honolulu on the 53-foot yacht named *Arcturus* he had recently purchased.[20] Arriving on the island in June 1935, Patton then set about his duties with all the tact of a tormented middle-aged officer who seemed to care little for what anybody thought about him. This led to a litany of bad behaviour and poor conduct, underscored by a complete lack of self-awareness. During the summer, for example, he wrote a paper for the commanding general, Halstead Dorey, about his personal assessment of the division's manoeuvres. In it,

Patton lambasted the creativity and performance of colleagues in the formation who 'acquired information that they are either unwilling or mentally incapable of using. The result is that they try to remember rather than think.'[21] These conclusions may well have been accurate, but the way in which they were communicated was unworthy of a professional and the report was written in a supercilious style.

The report hardly endeared the ostentatious Patton to his fellow officers, who in reply questioned the judgement of an officer who drank heavily and, some said, was conducting an extramarital affair. The relationship was with 21-year-old Jean Gordon, the daughter of Beatrice's half-sister, who was staying with the Pattons and had turned his head. Whether he was endeavouring to recapture his lost youth, found the attentions of a young woman seductive or merely sought risk is unknown, but their closeness certainly threw his marriage into crisis, with grandson Robert Patton later writing in his personal history of the family: 'A powerful tension settled over the family.'[22]

While in Hawaii, Patton failed for the fourth time to secure the appointment as commandant of cadets at the US Military Academy West Point. Although it is unknown why Patton was not selected, in all probability it was because neither his personality nor leadership style were particularly well suited to the position. 'I have gained the impression that possibly the fact that I am very outspoken is held against me in some quarters', Patton wrote to Jack Pershing, 'but I do not take this criticism to heart as much as I should. Possibly the candor of a fighting soldier is not too well received in peace.'[23]

Resigned to seeing out his time with the Hawaiian Division, Patton did his job sufficiently well not to cause any further disruption to the smooth running of the headquarters. This was partly the result of the intensity of the work he did in response to Japan's grandiose ambition to secure the nation's economic future through territorial conquest – which, consequently, increased the threat to the islands. Patton studied hard to better understand Japan's strategic history and current military capabilities, a task he undertook weighed down by strong prejudices against other races and cultures. His dislike and distrust of the Japanese was a typical Patton reaction to foreigners, and it had a significant influence on his research – which, when Patton reported in June 1937, was the first to highlight the threat to Pearl Harbor.[24]

Titled *Surprise*, Patton had his 128-page document printed, bound and distributed across the division, among naval colleagues (whose defensive plans did not meet with his approval) and senior officers in the War Department. It was a significant piece of work which, even if it carried little weight among those of influence developing US strategy in the Pacific, was a siren call for enhanced military preparation. Senior officers rated him 'excellent', with the chief of staff indicating how Patton had become a reliable and esteemed officer in the headquarters by 1937. '[A]mbitious, progressive, original, professionally studious,' Brigadier General Daniel Van Voorhis wrote, 'conscientious in the performance of his duties – fine appearing – the most physically active officer I have ever known… An officer of very high value to the service.'[25] The division commander, Major General Hugh Drum, agreed, and noting a change in Patton's behaviour he testified: 'Heretofore, I have noted on this officer's Efficiency Report a weakness in "Tact". In the last year he has overcome this weakness in a satisfactory manner. Colonel Patton has those qualities so essential to a superior combat leader.'[26]

Patton may have left Hawaii in the spring of 1937 with glowing personal reports, but he remained a man in turmoil. Uncertain whether his life had meaning without having fulfilled his ambitions, he continued to worry about his legacy and whether he had achieved anything of substance. He contemplated such questions over the summer while on leave in California, cogitations which eventually took place from a hospital bed. Having taken a fall while out riding and broken his leg, Patton nearly died from an embolism and later said that he had dreamt of being prepared for Valhalla by two Viking warriors who held him aloft on a shield. 'I guess they're not ready to take me yet,' he said without a hint of sarcasm. 'I still have a job to do.'[27]

Although his recuperation and eventual recovery at Green Meadows revealed the man's tenacity, months of inactivity sent Patton into steep mental decline. Beatrice heard her husband sobbing on several occasions, and once found him beating a horse with his crutch after a failed attempt to ride it. It was a long convalescence, but despite fears that he might be medically discharged from the Army, he passed the fitness tests and in February 1938 reported to Fort Riley for his next job as executive officer of the 9th Cavalry Regiment. Again, it was an appointment that Patton had held once before, but this time he was also an instructor at the Cavalry School, which provided a welcome distraction and some solace as his health continued to improve.

His promotion to his former wartime rank of full colonel in July 1938 was a huge relief to an officer who felt that there was still a chance, if the international order continued to be challenged by Japan and Germany, that senior combat command could be his – but he needed war to break out soon. Looking to that possible future, Patton began to turn his attention to the effectiveness of the officer corps, and wrote about what was lacking in the teaching at the Cavalry School.[28] His linking argument was that Army teachers and trainers too often failed to inspire their charges, that the course content of programmes was anachronistic, and that officers lacked leader and leadership development. The impact, he said, was that officers did not think for themselves and creativity was not appreciated, and this meant that individuals with untapped potential were doing what the system encouraged and 'going through the motions'. The implications would play out badly, Patton insisted, if the US found itself at war within the next few years. He was on the verge of making a series of recommendations to improve the training at Fort Riley when, on promotion in July, he was appointed to command the 5th Cavalry Regiment at Fort Clark near Brackettville, Texas, for a short tour without his family. While a permanent appointment could be found for him, Patton luxuriated in leading men, and his professional contentment was reflected in a distinct improvement in his demeanour.

The 5th Cavalry Regiment posed considerable challenges for Patton because, should the need arise, it was to be immediately deployable. He had little time to prepare for his command's involvement in the annual Third Army summer manoeuvres, but knowing that senior leadership would be assessing the regiment's capabilities it became a priority. Having developed a short but intensive training programme including sand table exercises, tactical exercises without troops, and lectures (mostly provided by himself), Patton was dismayed to find that, when in the field, the Third Army's scheme 'absorbed the bull butting tactics of the World War' and eschewed all the latest thinking about the conduct of war.[29] It was another example of the lackadaisical attitude that he felt the US Army was taking towards modern operational methods, and it vexed him greatly. Yet before he could make his own contribution to realigning his chain of command's relationship with modern fighting techniques, he was moved on from Texas; and by December 1938 he was once again at Fort Myer as commanding officer of the 3rd Cavalry Regiment. He arrived having just achieved a 'superior' rating from Kenyon Joyce, the commander of the 1st Cavalry Division, who affirmed Patton as 'an outstanding leader', 'a cavalry officer from whom extraordinary feats might be expected in war' and qualified for promotion to brigadier general.[30]

There is little doubt that, in being brought back to Washington, George Patton was being prepared for a more senior appointment. He inferred as much and, incapable of suppressing his penchant for self-promotion, ensured that his arrival back at Fort Myer was marked by the regiment lining the road and providing him with an escort of four scout cars. This, he justified to himself, helped to create an aura that would bind him to his men. Most of his subordinates, however, felt that such affectations were neither warranted nor a good use of their time. Sergeant Dick Mills wrote to his brother: 'It was ridiculous pomp that made us wonder what kind of man Patton really was.'[31]

The 3rd Cavalry Regiment soon found out that there was more to their new boss than a taste for the theatrical, as he sought to instil 'discipline, initiative and cooperation' and create an *esprit de corps* through training. 'Troops animated by such spirit are invariably successful in peace or war,' he wrote.[32] Patton spent more time than most of those in his position observing, assessing and reporting on the officers and men who came directly under his command, and he acted as a mentor to many. Lazy officers were given no quarter by him, but those who applied themselves won his loyalty and support. He was concerned, for example, that the lacklustre report he had given a former troop commander might be misinterpreted by his new chain of command at Fort Riley. As a consequence, Patton took time to write to the officer's superior arguing that, despite the observations in his earlier assessment, the young man remained a dedicated soldier of great potential.[33] Patton bestowed similar kindnesses on many others, would always write letters of recommendation on behalf of 'the able and worthy', and would provide access to his vast network of contacts to those who, even though they may not have been the most outstanding officer, dedicated themselves to self-improvement.

By mid-1939, as Patton gradually but firmly gripped his regiment on the east coast, the world slipped towards war. With some of his contemporaries already wearing the rank of general, Patton's brief flirtation with the contentment that came from command ceased and his behaviour deteriorated swiftly once again. 'He became so tyrannical', one of Patton's biographers has written, 'that no one wanted to be around him… No one was spared his harsh tongue.'[34] Whether at home, in the office or in the field, he was temperamental and spiteful – and the inconsistency of his behaviour became a problem in itself. 'One day he would be shouting at me for some minor infraction', one of Patton's officers later recalled, 'and the next it would be all bonhomie. None of us knew which Patton was going to walk through the door and that was draining, confusing and, ultimately, demoralizing.'[35]

Nevertheless, Colonel Patton continued to get results, and his personal failings (while noted) continued to be tolerated. He was a man who had a proven ability to improve those who came under his command, and with the Army needing as many senior officers with such skills as they could find, Patton attempted to manoeuvre himself back into the view of the redoubtable George C. Marshall. The two men had remained acquaintances since their time serving together on the Western Front, and when Marshall was promoted to full general and appointed Chief of Staff of the US Army in September 1939, Patton sent him a set of sterling silver stars.

In fact, Patton was already on Marshall's mind, for in the years before taking the top job he had recorded the names of talented individuals who had come to his attention, and by the time he was pinning the four new stars on his collar that list already included Dwight Eisenhower, Omar Bradley, Walter Bedell Smith and Patton. With some amusement, therefore, Marshall observed Patton's attempts to win favour and sometimes took advantage of the situation. While his own official quarters at Fort Myer were being redecorated, for example, Marshall accepted an invitation to stay with Patton for a few days in his luxurious home. Patton had been detailing his self-promotion plan in regular letters to Beatrice at Green Meadows, but Marshall's arrival in his rooms saw him write gleefully, 'I think that if I can get my natural charm working I won't need any letters from J. P. [John Pershing] or any one else.'[36]

In the short time that Patton had to work on Marshall, he spared no effort to make an impression and prepared a variety of entertainments, including half a day sailing on his yacht. He studied the general keenly, just as he had Pershing decades earlier, and liked what he saw. Quiet in his ways and bestowed with great humility – Patton was astounded that Marshall drove himself in the evenings, rather than using the chauffeured car the Army provided – Marshall did not have to like Patton, but he felt that he could rely on his subordinate's military abilities in the right circumstances. Thus, although the general began to remove the dead wood from the senior leadership of the Army as soon as he took up his appointment (including those aged over fifty who were deemed too mentally or physically inflexible), Patton at fifty-four was to be retained. The fact that he wasn't aware of this caused him considerable anxiety, which he addressed by doing everything he could to show that his energetic and swashbuckling leadership was just what the modern US Army required.

Consequently, when the 3rd Cavalry Regiment contributed to a series of exercises during the summer of 1939 (which included the III Corps schemes in Virginia), Patton seemed to be everywhere. Exhorting his officers and men to greater efforts while executing bold, sweeping manoeuvres which caught opponents unawares, he made a huge impact on both events and their participants. In return, his commander, Brigadier General Maxwell Murray, commended Patton's performance to the War Department, writing that his 'tireless energy, prompt decision [sic], and clear grasp of the situations presented were noteworthy and I consider that his work as commander... was outstanding. I recommend this officer for early consideration for appointment to the grade of brigadier general.'[37]

When war finally broke out in Europe during September 1939 Patton's stock was high, but although he hoped for immediate promotion, he was to be disappointed. It is not known whether the decision was a ploy designed to test Patton's forbearance or merely a quirk of the inflexible Army system, but it certainly played on his mind. Just at the time when he was learning about remarkable developments across the Atlantic, Patton actually expected to find out that his services were no longer required by Marshall's Army.[38]

— ◻ —

Lieutenant Colonel Bernard Montgomery was, in January 1931, appointed as the commanding officer of his beloved 1st Battalion Royal Warwickshire Regiment. It was a critical step up the career ladder for an ambitious British Army officer, and one which combined power and responsibility for some 1,000 men on the unit's first overseas tour since the end of the First World War. Bound for Palestine, which Britain administered under a League of Nations mandate following the Army's conquest of the territory in 1917 and the subsequent collapse of the Ottoman Empire, it had an obligation towards both Jews and Arabs, who clashed frequently and violently over the future of the region. Montgomery's battalion was split into companies to undertake its peacekeeping duties, and with such a challenging task awaiting them, the new commanding officer was the talk of the battalion as it set sail for the Mediterranean.

Having determined from various sources prior to taking up his appointment that the battalion was suffering from a deficit of leadership across the ranks, on the voyage from England (and without consultation) he made a series of sweeping reforms. These included an ending of the traditional promotion process for NCOs in the unit from one based on length of service to one based on merit. At a stroke, the new commanding officer had taken a calculated risk of alienating dozens of experienced but underwhelming soldiers who had expected to be promoted in the next few years, and won the admiration of the talented. He also began the process of removing officers from roles for which their characters, skills and experience were poorly suited, and replacing them with those he deemed more appropriate. In sum, within days of Montgomery arriving as commanding officer, he had sent an unsettling shock wave through his battalion. 'Any officer or soldier with any concerns about the change currently being undertaken', he wrote in one of his first orders, 'is welcome to discuss them with me.'[39] The records do not reveal if anybody took up the offer of an interview with the formidable new colonel, but any that did would have been given short shrift. Corporal Jim Smith wrote home in October, 'The new man [Montgomery] knows his own mind. Time will tell if it all works out.'[40]

Montgomery had sought to immediately put the battalion on its mettle for good reason, as Palestine posed numerous tests, with nationalist movements seeking to promote their rival interests. The battalion's role was to ensure safety and security in the region, and was split between three locations, a company in each, with its headquarters in Jerusalem. As Montgomery was the most senior officer in the region, alongside commanding the Warwicks he was also the de facto commander of all British troops in Palestine (which included a battalion of the King's Own Royal Regiment) and acted as Military Governor of Palestine on behalf of Lieutenant General Sir John Burnett-Stuart, the general officer commanding Egypt and Palestine, who was based in Cairo. It was strenuous work, with many hours spent on the road travelling to visit various posts and headquarters to get to know his subordinates, assess their situation and, ultimately, give his orders.[41] When out of the line, unit training and instruction was given, some delivered personally by Monty, but it was always balanced with much-needed rest and entertainment. Much of the work was routine, but hostility always had to be anticipated, and Easter was a period particularly prone to violence – 'I have had troops out in the town for the last 10 days', Montgomery wrote to his mother in April, '& have escaped trouble so far'[42] – but, having searched his experience on the Western Front and Ireland for guidance, he felt confident that he had done everything in his power to prepare his men if and when violence erupted.

Though he faced a demanding year for a new commanding officer in the effective role of a brigadier general on operational duty, confidential reports about Montgomery were laudatory. Burnett-Stuart wrote, 'He is clever, energetic, ambitious, and a very gifted instructor. He has character, knowledge, and a quick grasp of military problems.'[43] Such approval was mirrored in the letters from some of those he commanded: mechanic Dennis Pease wrote in December 1931, 'The colonel is a good man. He looks after us and listens... We really needed some furniture for the mess but couldn't lay our hands on any. We told [the colonel] and a week later he arrived with all that we'd asked for. He carried some of the chairs himself. When we asked where they came from he said Don't Ask!'[44]

Montgomery had become well respected by officers and soldiers alike because he had shown himself to be capable, fair and caring. Even so, he had an eye for detail and did not hold back on his criticism when he felt the need to improve standards with the Warwickshire battalion's machine gun company commander, Captain Tom Bailey, who later reflected: 'We had the greatest respect for Monty. Mark you, there were COs I had more affection for, let's be quite honest!'[45] Burnett-Stuart also tempered Montgomery's report with a well-intentioned observation when he wrote that 'if he is to do himself full justice in the higher positions to which his gifts should entitle him he must cultivate tact, tolerance, and discretion. This is a friendly hint as I have a high opinion of his ability.'[46] Such advice, however, fell on resolutely deaf ears. Montgomery had long since determined to be the soldier, officer and leader that *he* wanted to be, and not the one his superiors expected.

The next stop on the 1st Royal Warwicks' tour under Montgomery's command began at the end of 1931 when the battalion moved to Egypt, where it became part of the garrison of the great Mediterranean port city of Alexandria. Egypt had been conquered by the British in 1882, and occupied ever since by an Army engaged in what was euphemistically termed 'colonial policing' – which included safeguarding the Suez Canal, a vital imperial link with India. For Montgomery, the fact that his battalion would not be segmented here avoided some of the morale-sapping demands placed on his men over the previous twelve months, but he was also acutely aware that Alexandria offered its own tests. Described by one officer as 'the most remarkable place. Everything was there! Racing, tennis, duck-shooting – you name it, it was there,'[47] and by a soldier as 'a place where I could look for pleasures, become lost and never return',[48] Alexandria, Monty knew, could leach away the hard-won discipline and professionalism that had been forged in Palestine. Thus, although he was now joined by Betty and David in a comfortable flat overlooking the harbour, he remained as focused as ever and was particularly keen to develop the battalion's military capabilities even at the expense of the 'parade ground sparkle'.

The Warwicks were invariably the worst-turned-out battalion in the garrison and displayed scruffy drill, but they also became the most effective fighting unit in Frederick Pile's Suez Canal Brigade. According to Brian Montgomery, his brother's superiors were well aware that 'the regiment was exceedingly well trained... by a commanding officer who was quite unusual; this adjective applied mainly to my brother's determination not necessarily to accept as sound what had always been regarded as such in the past; in short he was the very embodiment of initiative'.[49] In fact, anything that was detrimental to performance was immediately targeted by Monty, and he initiated a rumble of discontent from traditionalists in the garrison for allowing his men to attend church parade in civilian clothes so that they no longer had to spend time preparing their uniform and equipment. He also caused a sensation for establishing a clean battalion brothel in Alexandria so that his men could enjoy some 'horizontal refreshment'. If high morale and low sickness rate are an indicator, then both initiatives worked. Private Len Milford wrote home: 'Its [sic] generally agreed that the moral[e] is good. We are disiplined [sic] but train hard and have good time off. We are a happy band.'[50] Meanwhile Brigadier Pile believed the Warwicks to be 'an excellent example of a modern, well-led and hard-working battalion'.[51]

The developing tactical prowess of the 1st Royal Warwicks was rooted firmly in Montgomery's demanding training regime. His objective was simple: to create a fit, mentally agile and capable fighting unit prepared for war. Once again he looked at his battalion appointments and made the necessary adjustments to ensure that adept leaders were in place at every level to drive improvement. Those persistently revealing poor judgement, weak leadership or who failed to support the commanding officer's ambitions could expect to be removed from their appointment, for Montgomery's tolerance of failure was limited only to those willing and able to learn from their experiences.

With company training having achieved the required level of competence, the battalion was then put through its paces in desert exercises to test its stamina, teamwork and military skills. Developing his own command and leadership abilities in the process, Montgomery learned to better harness the trust and talents that resided in his officers and NCOs, allowing them to thrive in a supportive climate of his making. As he wrote a few years later: 'We must remember that if we do not trust our subordinates we will never train them. But if they know they are trusted and that they will be judged on results, the effect will be electrical. The fussy commander, who is for ever interfering in the province of his subordinates, will never train others in the art of command.'[52]

Illustrative of this was his direction that company commanders should develop their own monthly training programmes that focused on areas identified as requiring attention. Montgomery gave his officers freedom of action within his intent, but kept a watchful eye on what was being done and achieved, arriving unannounced to observe exercises and offer advice and encouragement as well as to assess performances. Captain Bailey found the whole process a revelation and recalled, 'Well, no other CO had ever done it like that… It was simply marvellous working under him',[53] although another officer believed that Montgomery merely 'allowed colleagues to make mistakes so that he could make a show when he corrected them'.[54]

Montgomery was the last man to believe that leadership was a popularity contest, but he did believe in kindness and made innumerable visits to men who were either sick or injured, and never hesitated in rewarding those who met his high standards consistently. He was especially keen to make sure that those deserving of promotion received it, that time for leave was protected, and that the battalion's good work was recognized through the provision of concert parties or other opportunities to relax with colleagues. Competitive sport was also encouraged by Montgomery, through inter-company games and, for some, the opportunity to represent the battalion in fixtures against other units. Whenever the Warwicks were pitted against another unit, Montgomery went all out for victory, saying, 'Nothing less than the thorough embarrassment of the opposition will do. We have a reputation, you know!'[55]

In preparation for one inter-battalion exercise in the desert in which he was to act as brigadier, Montgomery went to considerable lengths to bring in an officer to act as his chief of staff and thereby improve the odds of victory. That officer was Freddie de Guingand, his former student in York then serving in Cairo, whom he knew to be highly capable and hoped would bring something different to his team. It was an inspired choice as the two men presided over a rout of their opposition and gained the fulsome congratulations of General Burnett-Stuart. For his part, Montgomery noted how effortlessly de Guingand seemed to complement his own skills. It was a relationship that immediately struck Monty as being one of the most fruitful of his career, and he resolved to work with de Guingand again should the opportunity arise.

On the other hand, Montgomery felt no compunction in pushing aside any individual or organization that stood in his way, particularly those he deemed to lack common sense (and there were many). If that meant blatantly ignoring the strictures of higher headquarters and receiving a reprimand, he was willing to take his punishment. It was not uncommon, therefore, for Monty to have frictional relationships with his peers; for example, the commanders of both the Coldstream Guards and the 12th Lancers in Alexandria never forgave him for his public rebuke that, although their drill was immaculate, their attitude to soldiering 'left a great deal to be desired'.[56]

His criticisms were not exclusive to those sharing his rank, and the lieutenant colonel also gained a reputation for 'filleting the ideas of superior officers'.[57] On one notable occasion, during a division exercise in Egypt, Monty listened to a gaggle of senior officers discussing the programme for the following day, and when drawn into the conversation he immediately condemned the commanding general's plan by saying that it was all 'Nonsense!' before outlining his own concept.[58] To Burnett-Stuart's credit he accepted his subordinate's thinking, directed that it should be followed and, when events proved it to have been the correct course of action, shared the credit for its success with his team. But Montgomery was fortunate to have a general so tolerant of his attitude and language, for many would have reacted harshly to his intervention and a first-rate idea could have been dismissed purely because of the way in which it had been suggested.

A more deferential tone and carefully chosen words would, undoubtedly, have served Montgomery better on many occasions, but once again the Army gave no reason for him to fundamentally change the way in which he conducted himself. Excellent reports from his superiors continued to highlight his professionalism, knowledge, command and leadership, with Burnett-Stuart saying that he was a 'first class trainer and leader and is a man of fertile & original thought which he expresses in a most unmistakable way. He is really popular with his men who he regards and treats as if they were his children.' Brigadier Pile praised him as 'an officer of great military ability who delights in responsibility... He is definitely above the average of his rank and should attain high rank in the Army.' Any references to Monty's tendency to be arrogant – such as Pile's note that 'he can only fail to do so if a certain high-handedness which occasionally overtakes him becomes too pronounced' – were asides in otherwise-glowing appraisals.[59]

The 46-year-old Montgomery left Alexandria with his battalion on Christmas Eve 1933 bound for Poona in India, where they would once again contribute to a city garrison. He arrived knowing that it would be his last posting as commanding officer as his periodic role rotation was due soon, but also that it would make new demands on his leadership. Poona was an old outpost of the British Empire that required a garrison more adept at ceremonial activity than he believed healthy for an Army that seemed reticent in many quarters to professionalize. General Sir George Jeffreys, the commander of British Army troops in southern India, seemed to have no interest in training at all and was entirely dislocated from strategic affairs. His reaction to Montgomery's arrival and immediate establishment of a training programme and schedule of exercises is unknown, but he seems not to have interfered with his new officer with the soaring reputation. In a tactful response to being left to his own devices, Montgomery resisted criticizing Southern Command's approach to its responsibilities. Indeed, he took the opportunity to take some leave in the spring of 1934 to give himself a much-needed rest before he embarked on whatever new challenge the Army placed before him. During his six-week cruise with Betty in the Far East and Japan, his mind was never far away from military matters. When introduced to another passenger, General Hans von Seeckt – on his way to take up the role of advisor to Chiang Kai-shek, leader of the Republic of China, whose government was not only fighting a communist insurgency but also the threat of a Japanese invasion – Montgomery immediately enjoyed a series of lengthy interpreted conversations with him about the great general's ideas, his army reforms and more general military matters.[60]

While away, Montgomery received a signal regarding his next appointment: chief instructor at the Indian Staff College in Quetta, with the rank of full colonel. After battalion command, it was just the job for an officer of his abilities, and he accepted the offer without hesitation. Montgomery left Poona in May 1934 with a report from Jeffreys, who, having determined that his subordinate was 'above average', added that he was 'very strongminded and I would advise him (and this is meant as advice, *not* adverse criticism) to bear in mind the frailties of average human nature and to remember that most others have neither the same energy, nor the same ability as himself'.[61]

The three years that Montgomery spent in Quetta were extremely happy for his family, which was accommodated in an airy bungalow near the bustling town. Major General Guy Williams, the commandant of the Staff College, quickly came to appreciate his new instructor's aptitudes, as Monty once again seized the opportunity to influence both students and fellow instructors in the building of a modern Army capable of confronting European adversaries. Indeed, eighteen months after Adolf Hitler became Chancellor of Germany, Montgomery pronounced to his syndicate of students: 'You gentlemen must now get on with the business of making yourselves professionals in your chosen profession – because we only have the time it takes

Germany to become what she considers to be sufficiently re-armed.'[62] He read widely, keen to evaluate his own experiences in the light of the modern character of warfare, but Montgomery found lecturing the most useful means of refining his thinking and turning complex ideas into something digestible. 'Montgomery's erudition, knowledge and ability to bring subjects to life was a marvel,' one of his students later wrote. 'We were a long way from home, but he brought the immediacy of the challenges offered by the developing situation into stark relief. To be honest, it was all rather worrying.'[63]

The need to prepare men who, he believed, would soon enough be at the forefront of the Army's response to German initiatives prompted Montgomery to be even more tenacious with his students than he might otherwise have been. At the end of his lectures, in classrooms and even when the students were trying to relax, Montgomery would pose demanding questions and expect precise, practical responses. 'I am not a nice chap,' he remarked to his brother when discussing his techniques for putting his students under pressure. 'Quite definitely not!'[64]

At Quetta, Montgomery also refined his thinking about leadership. He cogitated about what an effective leader needed to be, and from his conclusions he later wrote: 'A leader must be the servant of a truth and he must make that truth the focus of a common purpose. He must then have the force of character necessary to inspire others to follow him with confidence.'[65] Self-confidence was the prime means of influence, Montgomery argued, and as such it was vital the leader developed confidence in others. 'Without influence a leader is worthless', he stated in one of his well-attended lectures, 'but knowing how to go about the business of influencing is not straight forward for it demands understanding of human nature – knowledge of the hopes, fears, needs, and desires of those one leads.'[66]

These were arguments that impressed General Williams, who felt that Colonel Montgomery was an excellent chief instructor and recommended his early promotion to brigadier. The War Office agreed, and on 20 February 1937 Monty received a telegram ordering him back to England in the early summer prior to taking command of an infantry brigade. In an Army not over-endowed with dynamic officers of Montgomery's calibre, it was nevertheless to its credit that the organization elevated someone who did not fit the traditional model. Just as Hitler and Mussolini were destabilizing Europe, Montgomery, it seems, was being groomed for generalship – most likely because he offered something different. Whether he had the aptitude for leadership at the highest level that matched his undoubted abilities was unknown, but the British Army seemed willing to find out.

Brigadier Bernard Montgomery took command of the 9th Infantry Brigade in August 1937. With its headquarters at Portsmouth on England's south coast, the formation was in Major General Denis Bernard's 3rd Infantry Division, and as such was part of the projected British Expeditionary Force, which would be sent overseas in the event of a war in Europe. He had no time for those content to believe that the next war would be a repeat of the last war's trench deadlock. Fully aware of how technological developments had affected the conduct of war, he was determined that his units would be able to react quickly to a fast-moving enemy.

On taking up his command, the new brigadier immediately reviewed the scheduled summer training programme and replaced several day-long schemes with four major exercises lasting three days and nights. Explaining what he was trying to achieve, Montgomery told his commanders that he intended to assess capabilities, attend to deficiencies, and impose a distinct approach on how the brigade thought and fought.[67] It was an approach that his brigade major, F. E. W. Simpson, later said was 'far removed from some of the "social" peacetime exercises then prevailing, and came as a distinct shock to some of the units subjected to it'.[68] For most, it was the first time they recognized that the brigade was being prepared for war.

Monty's 'summer campaign' (as his training programme became known) culminated in his 9th Infantry Brigade pitting its wits against a fellow 3rd Infantry Division brigade – the 7th – during August 1937, in a two-day exercise on Salisbury Plain involving some 8,000 troops and observed by the new Chief of the Imperial General Staff, General The Lord Gort, and other senior commanders from across southern England. The aim was to test the combat readiness of the division, to provide practice for its commanders and to identify lessons to be learned. Montgomery's brigade, ordered to take some high ground defended by the 7th Infantry Brigade, was victorious – with Monty having excelled in his planning and command and control of the battle. His opposing brigadier, William Platt, was furious at having lost the battle and, according to Montgomery, 'did not seem to want to see me, even to say what a good fight we had had'.[69] Both the division commander and the commander of Southern Command – Monty's former boss, Burnett-Stuart – agreed that, despite only having been in the job a few months, Brigadier Montgomery's leadership, presence, personality and grip were 'extraordinary'. Despite his recent elevation, they recommended him for promotion again to major general.[70]

While Montgomery basked in his success, however, he received news that Betty had been taken ill on returning from a holiday in Somerset with their son, David. An innocuous insect bite had become infected, leading to such devastating complications caused by septicaemia that her health went into steep decline. Betty died in her husband's arms on 19 October. The woman who had entered his life and provided it with stability, richness and happiness was suddenly ripped from him. Her funeral was one of the very few times that Montgomery lost some of his composure in public. Devastated, he wrote to Dick Carver, his stepson, after the funeral: 'But, oh Dick, it is hard to bear and I am afraid I break into tears whenever I think of her. But I must try to bear up. I have come back alone to this big empty house for good now. And I get desperately lonely and sad. I suppose in time I shall get over it, but at present it seems that I never shall,'[71] and he later wrote in his memoirs that he was 'utterly defeated'.[72] He countered the destabilizing effects of her loss in the only way he knew – by ensuring that nine-year-old David was cared for by others and then immersing himself even more deeply into his work.

Although the pain of his loss remained raw, Montgomery forged ahead with his brigade's winter training programme and produced results that superiors came to regard as the standard that all others should match. By May 1938, the 9th Infantry Brigade had a unified approach to fighting based on a set of principles that were discussed at an 'Officers' Study Week' organized by Montgomery and then applied during training. It was work that culminated in a division exercise held in the summer at which Montgomery masterminded the first tri-service amphibious assault since Gallipoli in 1915. It saw his brigade make an assault landing at Slapton Sands on the Dorset coast. The event so highlighted the weaknesses that had developed in inter-service co-operation due to years of underinvestment that generals Gort and Wavell (the new commander, Southern Command) were subsequently thrown into a frenzy of activity trying to address the situation. Montgomery had delivered a powerful, much-needed prompt for an improvement of British coastal defences shortly after Hitler had begun to flex his burgeoning military muscles with the invasion of Austria.

In October 1938, a year after Betty's death and just after the German occupation of the Sudetenland – the German-speaking area of Czechoslovakia – Montgomery was finally promoted to major general. His confidential report that autumn saw Wavell declare that Montgomery had 'one of the clearest brains we have in the higher ranks, an excellent trainer of troops, and an enthusiast in all that he does'.[73] A student of generalship,[74] Wavell also drew attention to flaws in his subordinate's personality that many previous superiors had identified, writing: 'He has some of the defects of an enthusiast, in an occasional impatience and intolerance when things cannot be done as quickly as he would like or when he meets brains less quick & clever than his own.'[75] The British Army had invited Montgomery to become part of its senior leadership team, but numerous colleagues remained unconvinced about his suitability for such organizational influence.

Nevertheless, by the end of 1938 Major General Bernard Montgomery once again was in Palestine, this time in command of the

8th Infantry Division serving in the north. It was a baptism of fire for the newly established formation, tasked with having to maintain order over an increasingly volatile population in the disputed territory, while London's eyes were fixed on Berlin. However, having been informed that he would be taking command of the 3rd Infantry Division by the autumn of 1939, Montgomery used his time in the Middle East learning how to handle more than 10,000 men before the possibility of facing the Wehrmacht. He struck up an excellent working relationship with Richard O'Connor, the 7th Infantry Division commander based in southern Palestine (and a former colleague at Camberley), and their superior, Lieutenant General Robert Haining, who was pleased to allow two such capable subordinates considerable independence. Consequently, the two division commanders developed a plan to maintain control over Palestine which, working closely with the police, was based on Montgomery's experiences in southern Ireland. It involved identifying, locating and then destroying armed gangs while gaining support of the local populace, and was extremely successful.

Montgomery travelled a great deal, maintaining a close relationship with his units and utilizing the contacts he had made while commanding the 1st Royal Warwicks several years earlier. 'His [sic] an odd little man', one private wrote home after one of Monty's unannounced sector tours, 'who chats well and is alweys [sic] smiling and having a joke… Mind you, get some thing wrong and we soon know about it.'[76]

Montgomery's aide-de-camp Captain Louis Sanderson ensured the smooth running of his schedule and invariably could be found hovering in the background of his visits and meetings, notebook in hand, scribbling down notes and especially anything that his general needed to act on. '[Monty was a] stern, dedicated, ambitious and at times ruthless, professional officer', Sanderson later wrote, but was also 'a caring, compassionate and humorous human being with an intense loyalty to all his subordinates, always provided they carried out their duties satisfactorily.'[77] Mealtimes in the headquarters mess were often jovial and chatty affairs, during which Montgomery was happy to be the butt of colleagues' jokes. Yet even at these seemingly innocent dinners, the general was working: listening, observing and taking mental notes about his colleagues. Sometimes he deliberately threw out a seemingly innocuous question to see how his subordinates reacted. It was never wise to be off one's guard when Monty was about. Through such constant and consistent attention to detail, each officer knew what was expected of him – and that included succeeding no matter what pressure they were under.

By the time he returned to England in the summer of 1939, therefore, the senior leadership of the Army had been reassured that Montgomery could work in a team and that his recent promotion had been vindicated. In late August he took command of the 3rd Infantry Division as the nation tumbled towards a new war. Within days of Montgomery arriving in his new headquarters, Hitler had unleashed his invasion of Poland; then on 3 September, as Montgomery held a meeting with his senior officers, Britain declared war on Germany.

— ▢ —

By April 1932, forty-year-old Erwin Rommel was halfway through his third year as an instructor at the Dresden Training School and, although recently promoted to the rank of major, was coming to terms with the fact that his career was hardly stellar. Even so, signs in a fragile Germany suggested a growing mood for change which might lead to the revitalization of the armed forces.[78] The Great Depression had created some 6 million unemployed, leading to increasing calls for decisive national leadership to improve the nation's fortunes. The Weimar regime was in crisis, and Rommel, a practitioner in an organization stymied by international regulation and government policy, hoped that events might eventually allow the Army to regain its prowess. It had been impossible for him to avoid the febrile political atmosphere in Germany since the end of the war, for he had personal experience of the street fighting, had spoken with angry veterans in his regiment's Old Comrades' Association, and worked in an army emasculated by the provisions of the Treaty of Versailles. Thus, although his biographers have commonly argued that 'the political turmoil that Germany had suffered largely passed the apolitical Rommel by',[79] the truth was he could not help but be affected by it and to consider the implications for the Army.

Thus, the Nazi Party's achievement in becoming the largest party in the Reichstag was not greeted with concern by the Army's officer corps, but with hope. 'Although I do not like their methods', wrote Oberst Karl Kuhn of the General Staff in his diary in November 1932, 'most of my acquaintances see developments as a good for Germany and good for the Army... Most of the soldiers seem to agree, although most seem more concerned with the implications for their pay and accommodation.'[80] The officer corps had reservations about the Nazi Party and its leadership, the tub-thumping rhetoric of Adolf Hitler feeding widespread distrust of the former First World War corporal, but many were willing to see what the Nazis could come up with to solve some chronic German problems. Berlin-based Oberstleutnant Paul Uckelman wrote in his journal that he thought Hitler 'no gentleman', and described his colleagues as 'brutes, thugs and men on the make... using vile tactics and supporting questionable policies'. Nevertheless, Uckelman also wrote that 'perhaps Hitler is the man to destroy the Communists and help revive Germany and the Army'.[81] It was a view that seems to have reflected Rommel's own thinking about the Nazis: Hitler and his party were distasteful, but they were better than the alternatives in their offer of an enticing vision to end internal crises, bolster the economy and provide a muscular nationalism that would break the Versailles shackles, reinvigorate the armed forces and redraw Germany's borders. As Rommel's biographer Ralf Georg Reuth has argued, the most influential part of the Army hoped that Hitler would become 'vanquisher of the discord that had traumatised German society since 1918'.[82]

Nothing in the military press dissuaded Rommel and others from such opinions, with the *Militär-Wochenblatt* declaring that Hitler was the man to 'rescue the Fatherland' and achieve the soldier's 'single burning desire: Military Freedom!'[83] Suddenly Hans von Seeckt's plans for military expansion could be enacted and, promoted to lieutenant colonel, Rommel was one of the officers given the opportunity to impress. In October 1933 he was appointed to command the 3rd Jäger Battalion of Colonel General Kurt von der Chevallerie's 17th Regiment.

Based in the medieval town of Goslar in the Harz mountains some 170 miles west of Berlin, the Jäger battalion command salved Rommel's yearning to get back to the leadership of soldiers. His ambition was to create a tight-knit combat-ready team with its ranks replete with capable and trusted leaders. Rommel's own role, he told his subordinates, was to provide direction for that team through dynamic and demanding leadership intolerant of standards that failed to match his own. Thus, invited by some junior officers to join them in scaling a local mountain and then skiing back down, their new commanding officer not only readily accepted but used the opportunity to send a message to his subordinates. At the end of the exhausting day, Rommel suggested the party climb the mountain for a fourth time and ski down before dark, but the young officers politely declined: the colonel had made his point that officers in a truly elite Jäger battalion needed to be supremely fit and the standard had just been set.[84]

Soon after, Rommel also established that such a light, mobile and agile unit also needed to excel in stalking, skirmishing and marksmanship – skills in which he was also highly proficient. He consequently used the unforgiving terrain offered by the Harz mountains as a training area in which the battalion's capabilities could be developed. On the slopes, ridges and exposed summits he looked to make both exemplary leaders and loyal followers, men who would understand the need for co-operation across the unit, who embraced the opportunity to take bold decisions and were confident in imposing themselves on an enemy until victory had been achieved. Gradually, the battalion learned to be more resilient, to trust each other and to be proud of what they had achieved together. By the end of Rommel's first year in command of his Jäger battalion, it was regarded by Chevallerie as the 'finest' in his regiment largely due to its 'outstanding' commander.[85]

Rommel distilled his approach into a 76-page Army booklet published in 1934 as *Gefechts-Aufgaben für Zug und Kompanie* (Combat Tasks for Platoon and Company).[86] It contained no ground-breaking theories, but was clearly written by somebody with considerable fighting experience and reflected the way Rommel perceived leadership as the basis for all tactical success: emphasizing the importance of wisdom and good judgement in effective decision-making, allied with excellent communication. Rommel had written a treatise on the need for junior officers to be knowledgeable, bold and decisive because, to him, there was 'nothing like victory to sustain fighting spirit and confidence in a leader'.[87]

The years that Rommel spent in command of the Jäger battalion were among the happiest of his career,[88] and while he went about his work at Goslar, Hitler concentrated on securing himself a robust power base. On 30 June 1934, in what became known as the 'Night of the Long Knives', the brown-shirted Sturmabteilung (SA) – the Nazis' ambitious paramilitary wing – was purged and debilitated. It was an event that helped to quell the Army's fear that its role was being undermined by an armed Nazi faction, and encouraged the Army not to react to Hitler's merging of the chancellorship with the presidency later that summer. Thus, by August 1934, when Hitler demanded that all members of the German armed forces swear an oath of personal allegiance to himself as Supreme Commander, the Army found itself without any space in which to manoeuvre. It was a serious dilution of the military's independence, but few failed to comply. Rommel readily took the new oath, and soon after his unit was ordered to provide the guard of honour when Hitler visited Goslar for a thanksgiving ceremony. However, as the proud commander of an excellent battalion, Rommel stubbornly refused to have his men stand behind a line of the Nazis' own Schutzstaffel (SS) security personnel,[89] and having argued his case to SS Reichsführer Heinrich Himmler and propaganda minister Joseph Goebbels, the SS men were removed from view. Photographs taken that day show a serious-looking Rommel, in his officer's cap and dress uniform replete with medals, walking beside Hitler during an inspection of the Jäger battalion. The sight of Erwin Rommel accompanying the Führer was a vision of the future, even if what passed between the two men that sunny autumn afternoon in 1934 was cursory.

By the time Lieutenant Colonel Rommel left Goslar and the command of his beloved battalion in September 1935, his stock had risen at a propitious time as this coincided with the establishment of a new conscript Army – a constituent part of Hitler's unified armed forces (Wehrmacht) – and rearmament, both in defiance of the Treaty of Versailles. His next posting was as a senior instructor at the Potsdam Kriegsschule, the cradle of German militarism – a prestige appointment as it involved the moulding of the Army's next generation of junior officers. Rommel tackled his responsibilities with his usual relish and success, but now more than at any other time in his career he became aware of being sneered at by General Staff–trained officers who treated him with some disdain. Although not regretting the decision he had taken to decline the invitation to take the selection examination that was the gateway to the elite group, Rommel never lost his irritation at feeling marginalized by its members. His testiness on the subject sometimes spilled over into his teaching, during which he was known to deride officers of the General Staff with quips about them knowing 'all the theory but little about practical soldiering' and being better suited to 'sitting on their well-honed arses rather than engaging in real combat'.[90] Rommel inevitably focused his teaching on *real* combat. He continued to have no time for the abstract, rote learning or stock directing-staff solutions, and was keener than ever to encourage independent thinking. When a student started to quote a long-dead military authority on a subject, the colonel would snap, 'I don't want to hear what Clausewitz thinks, tell me what *you* think!'[91]

Despite encouragement from colleagues, Rommel was not interested in schmoozing with senior officers or attending parties to meet persons of influence; essentially a quiet man with modest tastes, he was content that his outputs be the main factor on which he should be judged, and he showed little concern for what others thought about him. Nevertheless, most regarded Rommel favourably because they admired the way he was always true to his values. These attributes recommended him for a temporary attachment to Hitler's escort for the annual Nazi Nuremberg rally in September 1936. It was a brief engagement for which Rommel received Hitler's personal thanks, but afterwards he made no attempt to gain more of the Führer's attention and simply got on with his instructing at Potsdam and a new writing project.

Since returning from war in 1918, Rommel had collected diaries, letters, official papers and the recollections of colleagues to assist him in the development of his teaching content. While an instructor at Potsdam, however, he realized that his growing archive and associated lecture notes provided him with enough material to prepare a book based on his combat experiences that might be of interest to some serving soldiers and, perhaps, some veterans. *Infantry Attacks*, eventually produced by a small publishing company in 1937,[92] was a highly readable volume that combined carefully crafted tactical 'Observations' with outstanding insights into fighting at the sharp end. While the book did not gloss over Rommel's part in the events he described, its tone was not heroic and his narrative continually emphasized the importance of teamwork, comradeship and the realities of war. The challenge of leadership was one of the strongest themes running through the book, and although Rommel never distilled the subject down to a series of principles, his approach to being a leader, including his style and techniques, were revealed in some detail.

Initially selling in modest quantities to soldiers intent on self-improvement, within just a few months sales of *Infantry Attacks* grew substantially as the German public began to purchase copies. The book inadvertently tapped into a national *Zeitgeist*, revealing how 'superior forces could be overcome by energetic leadership, ruthlessness, self-sacrifice and heroism. It was the new [Nazi] regime which had now created the conditions under which these qualities would be both valued and encouraged.'[93] The success of the book stunned nobody more than Rommel, who had hoped that perhaps a few hundred copies would be sold; when it began to sell in the tens of thousands he found himself the recipient of admiring letters from generals, soldiers – new and old – and German people across the nation.[94] Although Rommel later claimed that Adolf Hitler had read his book, perhaps given to him by his adjutant Nicolaus von Below (a former student of Rommel's at Dresden), there is no evidence that this was the case. What does seem likely, however, is that the success of *Infantry Attacks*, combined with his previous excellent service to Hitler, were influential in getting the newly promoted full colonel added to a list of 'competent front-line officers who had no previous general staff experience' for special assignments in the wake of the *Anschluss*, the annexation of German-speaking Austria, which was also Hitler's homeland, in March 1938.[95] The Führer sought respected outliers who had proved themselves in combat, and Rommel fitted the bill supremely well.

Nevertheless, because Rommel was unwilling to compromise, far less be bullied by anybody, he proved a handful. In October 1938, for example, he had to be removed from a part-time role as Army liaison officer with the Hitler Youth after he clashed with its leader, the smooth Baldur von Schirach. Having learned that the organization wished to instil some military discipline into the ranks of its 5.5 million male teenagers, Rommel argued strongly against the idea – saying that unless discipline was accompanied by the development of character and leadership then unthinking martinets would be produced.[96] The two stubborn men would not be moved from their positions, and Rommel lost the job; however, in a show of support to a new military favourite, Hitler immediately had him appointed as temporary commander of his personal escort battalion for the German occupation of the Czech Sudetenland.

And so began a relationship between Hitler and Rommel that was based on mutual respect even if they did not agree on all matters of political and military policy. At first, the officer felt privileged to have been selected for this role and to be given the honour of personally serving a remarkable leader, but having been in Hitler's company this was replaced by a deep admiration for the man. Enthralled by bearing witness to historic events, Rommel drank in the experience and took the opportunity to study Hitler closely, paying particular attention to how he got people to do his bidding and noting that he 'always acted by intuition, never by reason'.[97] He was also impressed by Hitler's powers of communication, which went far beyond the formal speeches that he had heard on the wireless or on newsreels, and became absorbed by the nuances of Hitler's language, his tone and the way in which he subtly worked individuals and deployed flattery. Rommel noted that 'the great man' had an ability to hold the attention of a sizeable audience and always offered everybody listening something that satisfied their needs. A proud Colonel Rommel, therefore, received from Hitler an autographed photograph of himself mounted in a silver frame on his return from Czechoslovakia. It was a sign of the Führer's deep respect for an officer with whom he had seemed to find a bond.

In becoming the commandant of the prestigious Wiener Neustadt Kriegsschule in Austria at the end of 1938, Rommel took a significant step towards the most senior ranks of the German Army. The school was the most modern and progressive military institution of its type in Europe, and his selection to lead it, endorsed by the head of the Army and chosen from a highly competitive field (largely consisting of General Staff officers), filled him with confidence. 'He was ambitious, he hungered for responsibility', wrote Reuth in his biography of Rommel, 'and felt flattered by the choice and was grateful for the trust placed in him.'[98] His superiors had received nothing but glowing reports about Rommel from those working with him; the commandant at Potsdam wrote of his 'crystal clear character' and described him as 'selfless, unassuming and modest… popular with his comrades and highly respected by his subordinates'.[99] At Wiener Neustadt, Rommel did his utmost to ensure that the course was what he had long believed military education should be: practical, inspiring and discursive. Only then, he judged, could the school produce the free-thinking leaders of character that the modern German Army required.

While his lectures were a tour de force – many based on episodes from his celebrated book – Rommel also made sure he had a role to play in practical assignments. One student, Ralf Haas, wrote to his girlfriend during February 1939 about how unrelentingly challenging the Wiener Neustadt programme was: 'The instructors are very demanding and continually ask us to think about situations in a real war. This is most difficult as we do not have the experience… but Oberst Rommel is very clever at providing scenarios based, I think on his own experiences. He talks in a measured but intense manner and brings lessons to life… He is captivating.'[100]

Rommel strode the corridors of the school purposefully every day and was well known to all staff and students. He slipped into teaching sessions unannounced, arrived on exercises in the middle of the night, and whenever he had the opportunity he probed students (and instructors) with questions. There was nothing that Rommel did not know about what was happening in the Kriegsschule. Ralf Hass noted, for example, that one of his instructors consistently lost the attention of the class, and before long senior instructors were sitting in on his sessions before meeting with the officer at the conclusion of his lectures. There was no improvement until one evening Haas witnessed Rommel 'providing after-hours tuition' to the man. 'After a short time', wrote Haas, 'our lessons became very much better. The commandant, it seems, had quietly worked his magic. It was appreciated by all – not least our instructor, I think!'[101]

Rommel's impact at the Kriegsschule was significant, for within six months he had established a vibrant culture that was supported by a team of competent instructors willing to challenge convention in their classes and who were adept at getting the best out of their students. As commandant, Rommel also ensured that a deputy was prepared in detail to stand in for him when he was not present physically at the school. Thus, when he was called away from Wiener Neustadt on a temporary assignment, this time as commander of the Führer's headquarters during the occupation of the remainder of Czechoslovakia in March 1939, there was a seamless handover. Hitler and Rommel, meanwhile, quickly re-established a close working relationship marked by mutual trust. Indeed, in urging Hitler to drive in an open car under his personal protection to Prague (Hradčany) Castle, the president's country seat situated on a dominating hilltop, the colonel was offering advice contrary to that provided by the melee of risk-averse generals also in attendance. 'You have no other choice,' Rommel is reported to have said to Hitler, having recognized the propaganda value of a visit to the site. 'For you, my Führer, there is only the path into the heart of the country, into the capital, and up to the Castle of Prague.'[102] Newsreels and photographs of Hitler driving up to the castle with Rommel were seen around the world. It was an important moment in their developing relationship, for Hitler saw in Rommel an officer who understood intuitively what he was trying to achieve, and who was willing to take responsibility for the associated risks in delivering a desired outcome. It was leadership of the highest quality, and so different from the echelons of colleagues who seemed more concerned with avoiding failure than seizing opportunities.[103]

On his return to the Kriegsschule in the spring of 1939, Rommel enjoyed his work for several months but was ultimately delighted when on 23 August he was informed that he had been assigned to command Hitler's headquarters (*Führerhauptquartier*) with responsibility for security, at the rank of major general. Seven years previously Rommel had been a major, his career progressing painfully slowly, but now in the new Germany and championed by Hitler, the Swabian had found that his talents were admired and recognized. The usually restrained Rommel was filled with a great sense of achievement, and on 1 September, in a letter to Lucie written in the wake of Hitler's famous speech on the declaration of war on

Poland, said, 'Isn't it wonderful that we have this man?'[104] Two days later, Rommel's men took up their positions aboard Hitler's mobile command train, the *Führersonderzug*, as it rumbled out of Berlin heading east to Poland. The spartan conditions of Hitler's private car, the *Führerwagen*, and his insistence that he eat a 'soldier's ration' were not lost on Rommel, who found that he was gaining more insights into leadership at the highest level every day.[105] In particular, he was inspired by being offered an opportunity to contribute to some of the Führer's evening situation conferences, making him feel a valued part of a trusted team.[106]

Rommel also enjoyed numerous informal conversations with Hitler as they travelled around Poland – some about their First World War experiences – and was occasionally seated next to him at the dinner table. Whenever Hitler ventured from the train, Rommel and his team of elite SS guards, motorcyclists and armed reconnaissance vehicles were never far away. '[I]t seemed to give him pleasure to be under fire,'[107] Rommel later wrote in veneration of Hitler's desire to see the front line, but he allowed nobody to increase the danger that Hitler was exposed to. On one occasion he found it necessary to publicly remonstrate Martin Bormann, Hitler's uncouth and dangerous private secretary, when the man's car tried to fall into line behind Hitler's on the way to the conquered port of Gdingen. Rommel stopped the vehicle and rebuked Bormann, saying: 'I am the commander of the Führer's Headquarters. This is no kindergarten excursion. You will do as I say.'[108] The infuriated Bormann screamed at Rommel's back as the officer walked slowly to his car and drove off. The 'Führer's General', as he was becoming known, would allow nobody to come between himself and the conduct of his duty.

When Poland eventually fell at the end of September, Rommel – his reputation burnished by another outstanding performance – remained with the *Führerhauptquartier* after Hitler was safely ensconced back in Berlin. However, as soon as he learned of Hitler's intention to invade the West when the necessary preparations had been made, he sensed an opportunity. Although a significant portion of the Wehrmacht's senior leadership were horrified at the prospect of another campaign so soon after Poland,[109] Rommel's only concern was that he be selected for combat once again – and, ideally, in command of one of the new armoured divisions.

CHAPTER SIX

A New War, 1940–41

IN JANUARY 1940, while Germany, Britain and France continued to prepare for the next campaigning season in their 'Phoney War' – as the early months of the war, during which there were no major hostilities, were known – George Patton grilled all his contacts for clues about whether the United States would join the conflict. As commander of the 3rd Cavalry Regiment at Fort Myer, he was well placed to read the mood-music emanating from Washington, and all he learned was that, even though President Franklin D. Roosevelt sympathized with the Allies' plight, a strong isolationist sentiment remained in the nation. Despite the ongoing conditioning of the American people for eventual involvement, there would be no rush to war. 'It looks like I'll just have to wait,' he wrote to a colleague, 'I feel drawn toward war... The task now is to get the army ready. We have work to do if we are not going to arrive [in Europe] and be good for nothing but digging trenches.'[1]

Despite his fervent desire to fight again, Patton felt that, at fifty-four years old, his age was against him. He knew that George Marshall was carrying out an audit of his senior officers and assessing their aptitude for the physical and mental rigours of war, but what he did not know was that, although dozens of his peers had been pushed towards retirement, he had already been selected as a future combat commander. Marshall saw in the feisty Patton not only the ostentatious cavalryman who repelled some but also a bold, energetic leader and fighter who could drive change and achieve the desired outcome.

Patton took pains to project the image of a mature and experienced officer who had retained his currency by engaging fully with new military developments and, in particular, with armour. In becoming an umpire for Third Army manoeuvres in Georgia and Louisiana during the spring of 1940, therefore, Patton played a significant role in one of the major US Army events of the year and displayed his knowledge of armoured doctrine, equipment and command. After years living in the shadow of technological change for the sake of his personal advancement in the cavalry, Patton now stepped forward to become one of tank warfare's foremost advocates, convinced that his 'grab the enemy by the nose and kick him in the pants'[2] style was ideally suited to them. Indeed, by the time Third Army manoeuvres had been completed, the success of the panzer divisions in the German victory over France and the Low Countries had reinforced his fervour for the machines. Consequently, Patton and a group of like-minded senior officers recommended to the War Department that the US Army create an independent armoured force, and Marshall agreed.

The nucleus of the Armored Force (which would shortly become a corps consisting of two armoured divisions, each with two brigades) was formed in July 1940 under Major General Adna R. Chaffee, who came from command of the impressive 7th Cavalry Brigade, at that time the Army's only mechanized force. Patton immediately offered his services to Chaffee and received a reply that he was being considered for one of the armoured brigades. 'I think it is a job which you could do to the queen's taste', Chaffee wrote, 'and I need just such a man of your experience in command... We have an enormous job in front of us to get this thing organized, trained, and going in a minimum of time... I shall always be happy to know that you are around in any capacity where there is fighting to be done.'[3]

Patton was delighted, and his 'superior' rating improved his chances of clinching the appointment along with a laudatory confidential report from his brigadier stating that 'through his personal leadership [Patton] builds a high esprit in his command. He is well fitted for higher command in peace or war.'[4] Suddenly Patton's experience, hard work and willingness to serve looked as though they would pay dividends, and his prize in August was command of the 2nd Armored Brigade – part of the 2nd Armored Division, which was commanded by an old friend, Charles L. Scott, at Fort Benning. 'I thought it would be just the sort of thing you would like most to do at the moment,' George Marshall wrote to Patton. 'Also, I felt that no one could do that particular job better.'[5] Patton was also pleased to learn that two old friends had been appointed to positions of influence that could prove useful to him: Henry L. Stimson as Secretary of War and General Lesley McNair as chief of staff of General Headquarters (GHQ), which was tasked with creating a 630,000-man reservoir of manpower and to oversee all training.[6]

Taking command of a newborn brigade, Patton realized, was a huge leadership challenge, for it had no history, a limited identity and indistinct standards, but he relished the opportunity to build a first-class fighting organization from scratch. He had created something from nothing before, at Bourg in 1917, and led a brigade in combat the following year, and since then his knowledge, skills and techniques had only improved. He awaited the arrival of his 350 officers, 5,500 soldiers, 383 tanks, 202 armoured cars and 24 105-mm howitzers,[7] and as each man and piece of equipment arrived Patton began to forge them into well-led teams and left no doubt as to who commanded the brigade. There are precious few occasions in a military career when an officer is given the opportunity to start something completely new, but having been provided with a fresh canvas Patton was keen to express himself and take this last chance to deliver himself to the greatness he had long believed was his destiny.

With Patton reunited with Beatrice at Fort Benning after a protracted period during which she had been living at Green Meadows and he wherever his responsibilities took him, their relationship was rekindled. 'I hope some day you may forgive me', he wrote to

Beatrice just before her arrival, in reference to his past poor behaviour and personal transgressions, 'but I will be damned if I see why you should. I love you anyhow.'[8] She did forgive him, although long since recognizing that she would never change her husband's domineering character.

The late summer of 1940 was a dizzying period, topped off that autumn by Patton's promotion to the rank of brigadier general after more than three decades of service. 'At last', Patton wrote to Stimson, 'I can begin to make a difference.'[9] But just as at Bourg, he found his patience severely tested by a labyrinthine bureaucracy that seemed intent on stopping him doing his job rather than supporting him in it. To make the situation even more trying, he found that too many of his officers were failing to show the leadership excellence he demanded. Patton could not abide men in positions of responsibility who complained incessantly and used excuses, as they undermined the spirit of the men, but he commanded a clutch of them. As soon as he became aware of such individuals he reasserted his standards to them, and if they were not met, he facilitated the officers' removal as he had at the Bourg Light Tank School, where his 'driving presence and personal intervention in every detail of tank operations and training had spelled the difference'.[10]

The brigade soon learned that Patton's eyes and ears were everywhere, for by using a network of trusted individuals to supply him with regular situation reports to supplement the information he gleaned from his own tireless schedule of visits, he knew his brigade well despite it being spread over Fort Benning's nearly 300 square miles. The first indication that any unit would often have that Brigadier General Patton was about to arrive among them was the sound of an obnoxious blaring steamboat siren that he'd had fitted to both his staff car and a light tank. It was a stunt that led to some rolling their eyes, but to Patton it was an outward expression of his personality and leadership that had worked in the past; he would not change. The 2nd Armored Brigade was very much Patton's brigade, and although some may not have liked its commander's dominance, few could deny that he created a stronger *esprit de corps* than found elsewhere. 'Every one of us knows Patton by name, his silhouette, his voice and his bark!' wrote Major Larry Hind to his sister in the early autumn of 1940. 'We know what he wants to achieve and our role in it. Everything is made very clear and although his presence can send a chill through the men, he is also quick with a smile and kind words for good work.'[11]

Central to Patton's focus during the early months of the 2nd Armored Brigade's existence was his impressing on his subordinates the importance of discipline. Success in modern warfare, he argued, demanded far more than the production of well-turned-out automatons, but that did not mean that discipline was not the best foundation on which to build smart soldiers who could be relied on to use their initiative. Thus, while he was creating an obedient body of men through his NCOs, supported by his officers, those same officers were undergoing their own training and education so that they were better equipped to lead with boldness, courage and practical creative thinking. Patton personally lectured his officers on Monday mornings on a variety of military subjects, and in so doing drove their collective development and established himself as such an authority on the art of warfare that it justified his bombast.[12] Subjects included 'Great Leaders in History', 'Tactics from Ancient Greece' and 'The Recent German Invasion of Poland' (a lecture that he took a week to write and memorize), all of which were enlivened by Patton's colourful language and resonated with his audience via carefully crafted practical lessons.[13] During an exposition about Roman legions, for example, he stressed that when Julius Caesar 'committed them to battle against the Gauls, it was not necessary to give them orders, for they knew what to do and how to do it'. He explained that this is what he was endeavouring to achieve with the 2nd Armored Brigade, and ended his lecture by saying, 'I know that we shall attain it and when we do, may God have mercy on our enemies; they will need it.'[14]

By the end of the year, the progress that Patton had made with his brigade was impressive. From a seed he had managed to create a fighting outfit, so when in November 1940 Scott took over all command of the armoured corps from a sick Chaffee (who succumbed to cancer the following summer), Patton became his natural successor to command the 2nd Armored Division. He slipped into role without a glance backwards, merely scaling up the work he had been doing with his brigade. He immediately enjoyed the ability he had to express himself on an even larger canvas, although he found it a challenge to give up the 'face-to-face leadership' that he had always enjoyed in his career to this point. He now had to learn to trust others to provide expertise, interpret his orders and make decisions. This was not easy, as Patton was never happier than when he was doing what he called 'gettin' your hands dirty leadership, leading in person and not from behind a desk',[15] but now his responsibilities demanded that he ruthlessly prioritize his time. 'We have to ensure that the general allows his commanders to get on with their jobs', wrote Captain 'Duke' Ellis, one of Patton's training staff, 'although he is always fussing about this and that. The staff try to guide him to the areas that he needs to be, but it is like trying to marshal an unruly child. It's one hell of a job because he wants to be everywhere and involved in everything.'[16]

Patton was gradually weaned off constant personal intervention by colleagues and was mentored by Scott, who urged his division commander to look up to the priorities of his corps commander as well as down into his brigades. Within a few months he had asserted himself on his brigades, overseen a rigorous late-winter training programme and set about creating a division identity. This was most obviously illustrated by the red, white, blue and yellow stripes that Patton had painted around the turret of his command tank, and a new (and rather cluttered) triangular division badge that he designed himself and which sought to depict the formation's mobility and firepower.[17] Patton also gave the division the 'Hell on Wheels' sobriquet, but as an adherent of the way in which the German Army had used its main armoured effort the previous year as a psychological weapon rather than a battering ram, he explained to his senior officers:

'You can kill more soldiers by scaring them to death from behind with a lot of noise than you can by attacking them from the front.'[18]

The commander of the formation's reconnaissance battalion, Major Isaac D. White, later said that:

> General Patton was really the person who instilled the division with great pride in itself and developed a great spirit, as well as a great deal of aggressiveness which characterized the division throughout its entire service. He inspired everybody with the idea that when you have gone just as far as you can go you can still go a little bit further. He also I think instilled the division with the idea that no mission was too difficult to accomplish... You might not have loved him but you respected him and admired him and you wanted to put out for him.[19]

The respect to which White alludes was born, despite Patton's bravado and unremitting sense of self, from the deep concern he had for the welfare of those he led. 'I can promise,' Patton announced at an address to the division, 'that I shall never ask any man to undergo risks which I, myself, do not incur.'[20] That may have concerned some who knew something of Patton's style, but it was rooted in his fervent desire to repay loyalty with loyalty and to never stint on efforts to care for his men. Because of his pomposity, however, some could never believe that Patton really cared for anybody other than himself. The image that Patton wanted to project was that of a brave, no-nonsense, inspirational leader who spoke the language of the soldier and was revered by his subordinates; yet his grand entrances, profanity and behaviour repelled some who were frustrated by the way Patton seemed to believe rules that applied to others did not apply to himself.

Thus, despite a number of officers having been disciplined by their superiors for speeding in Fort Benning, Patton ordered his driver to pay no attention to the limits, and when a military policeman flagged down his car and sought to detain Patton, an argument ensued during which the general became abusive. When the incident came before the senior officer at Fort Benning, Major General

Lloyd R. Fredendall, Patton was reprimanded and told to make a full and unreserved apology to the corporal, which he did in a gracious and sincere manner.[21] Typically, any challenge to Patton's behaviour or beliefs by a subordinate received a tempestuous response, which reflected his belief that authority was vested only in rank. His temper and frightening ability to bawl out a subordinate had won him the epithet 'Old Blood and Guts', and although it helped enhance the persona he had developed, it indicated a side of his personality that was to undermine his career in the years to come.

Despite the sometimes-questionable techniques and behaviours he exhibited in command of 2nd Armored Division, Patton indisputably put every ounce of energy he had into creating a highly capable formation with a formidable reputation. Meanwhile, US mobilization gathered pace, including the institution of the Selective Training and Service Act in September 1940 – the first peacetime draft in the nation's history – for all men aged 21–45, which massively increased those undertaking basic military training by the end of the year. By then the Army's strength was 620,000, and it was to approach 1.5 million six months later, with some heading to the armoured formations.[22] Before they arrived, Patton had put his division through an intense training programme through the late autumn, and followed it with an exercise in mid-December 1940 involving the 6,500 troops, 1,100 vehicles and 125 operational tanks that had been delivered to the division. Consisting largely of M2 light and medium tanks, but including some M1 Combat Cars, these machines were originally designed and built at the Rock Island Arsenal in Illinois but were soon to be produced by the new Detroit Arsenal Tank Plant. Engineers scrutinized the armour's reliability throughout the division's 270-mile advance from Fort Benning to Panama City in Florida and back again, which tested the formation's ability to move fast while retaining structure and momentum.[23] The event, which had also been designed as part of Patton's 2nd Armored Division promotional campaign, had been carefully routed along public roads and with aircraft flying overhead so that it might attract considerable public interest. 'Patton's Push', as *The West Georgian* newspaper called it, successfully drew huge crowds onto the streets to watch the impressive-looking force as it passed through several large towns,[24] and its progress was charted over the two-week exercise by the local and national press. The *Washington Sunday Star* gave Patton a glowing review as a 'picturesque and dashing officer' and explained: 'His men swear by him… [He is] a hard-riding, hard-hitting "fightin' man" of the old school, with a mind to absorb and improve on new military ideas.'[25]

In early January 1941, with the division back in Fort Benning, the lessons of the exercise were pored over by headquarters staff, and a report written that was to be used as the basis for 2nd Armored Division's spring training plan. The areas identified for improvement included 'logistics and supply', 'maintenance', 'communication' and 'coordination', with the role of the leaders and leadership highlighted in each.[26] With his division having found its feet, Patton determined that 1941 would be the year in which the formation prepared for war. 'The year was a rush of activity for us all,' one tanker later said. 'New men continued to be trained. New equipment arrived, including the tanks. We worked on our own jobs, and then worked with others to improve. Patton was all about improvement. We tanks spent a lot of time with the infantry, engineers and the artillery. There was always something new to learn and we began to realize what a great potential we had. Patton was always pulling the strings. He knew what he wanted and we wanted to deliver.'[27]

By 1941, Patton's division had become an organization that visitors, the press and the public wanted to see and hear about, and one the Army could hold up as an exemplar of a new dawn in US fighting power. This was recognized by Patton's superiors and not least by General Scott, who rated him 'superior' and reported in March: 'In the event of war, I would recommend this officer to command an armored corps… This officer renders willing and generous support to the plans of his superior grades regardless of his personal views in the matter. Of 90 general officers of his grade that are personally known to me, I would give him number 3 on the list. Further remarks: An extremely energetic ambitious officer and a natural and highly capable leader.'[28]

Shortly after, Patton was promoted to major general and given permanent command of the division. His joy at the developments can be inferred by the flurry of letters of thanks he wrote to a variety of supportive individuals, including to Marshall ('I deeply appreciate the honor you have done me'[29]) and to Stimson ('When war comes I promise that you will not be ashamed of me'[30]). Patton had at last attained a rank to which he had always aspired, and that was a huge motivation for him.

A month after unit training in April, the 12,000-man-strong 2nd Armored Division joined the Second Army's corps level in Tennessee, with Patton determined to show off his formation's talents. In a speech before they took to the field, he told his assembled troops that they were an integral part of 'the most powerful organization ever devised by the mind of men'. Then, using a football metaphor, he explained that the division was 'that element of the team which carried out the running plays. We straight-arm, and go around, and dodge, and go around... One of the greatest qualities, which we have is the ability to produce in our enemy the fear of the unknown. Therefore, we must always keep moving, do not sit down, do not say "I have done enough," keep on, see what else you can do to raise the devil with the enemy.'[31] He probed the detail when he gathered his officers together for their own personal briefing, and issued a warning: 'I wish to assure all officers and all men,' he said, speaking slowly and pausing occasionally for effect, 'that I shall never criticize them or go back on them for having done too much but that I shall certainly relieve them if they do nothing. You must keep moving.'[32]

During the first engagement of the exercise, the 2nd Armored Division's performance was barely adequate, with Patton criticized by his chain of command for a lack of operational grip. This riled him for the remainder of his time in Tennessee. His own performance during the next phase of the exercise was much improved, however, with his division undertaking a night-time attack that ended the next morning with the capture of the opposition's general and his headquarters staff. Emboldened by that success – and knowing that McNair was observing during the third phase of the exercise – Patton used tactics akin to those employed by Rommel in May the previous year in France, and having outmanoeuvred his opponent, forced its surrender in a fraction of the time assigned to him. Then, during the last contest, Patton triumphed again, deftly combining boldness and aggression with speed and surprise to outflank the defenders opposing him before cutting their lines of communication and, once more way ahead of time, taking his objective.

The capture of the town of Tullahoma capped an outstanding exercise for Patton and his division, with Scott and McNair describing his performance as 'exceptional', although they made a point of criticizing him for leaving his command post at critical times when he could have asserted his will using radio communication. Privately, Patton disagreed, as he continued to feel that personal leadership at the decisive point could often prove vital, but overall he was gratified by the positive reaction of his superiors. Indeed, the reports received by Marshall detailing the 2nd Armored Division's accomplishments and Patton's role in them reinforced his view that Patton would be supremely well suited for formation combat command in war. He was also not displeased that the officer was doing such a good job in garnering interest and support for the US Army among the American people. Patton's latest publicity coup was an appearance on the cover of *Life* magazine (a magazine then read by 10 per cent of the population[33]) in early July 1941. The photograph, carefully curated by Patton, depicted him standing in the striped turret of his command tank wearing his 'war face', the 2nd Armored Division patch prominent on his uniform. The article, titled 'Armored Force', included quotes from the general and was heavily illustrated with photographs of the division during the Second Army manoeuvres.

The training of Patton's formation during the summer of 1941 climaxed in the 'Louisiana Maneuvers' in August, during which the

Second Army took on the Third Army in Louisiana.[34] By that time, Hitler's panzers were pressing deep into the Soviet Union, the progress of which Patton followed with increasing amazement (although ultimately with increasing incredulity, as they stalled outside Moscow later in the year). By comparison the scheme in which the 2nd Armored Division participated was small, but with some 400,000 participants in twenty-seven divisions it was the largest event of its kind ever held in the United States, and a defining moment in the development of the Army's capabilities after twenty years of neglect.

In his preliminary briefings, Patton again asserted that his officers needed to be agile, decisive, bold and ruthless. 'If you do your part as leaders,' he told them, 'the men of the 2d Armored Division will make it utterly irresistible in manoeuvres or in war.'[35] In the days that followed, Scott's I Armored Corps was put through its paces for the first time as a formation in its own right, and with support provided by some 1,000 aircraft its command and control was forcefully tested. Observed by Marshall and other senior officers, Patton felt as though he was participating in a final audition for a major appointment for wartime command, and he rose to the challenge admirably. With his division leading the corps in a creative 400-mile advance that outflanked, out-thought and dislocated a paralysed enemy, Patton's performance was critical to the corps' victory. He passed on his thanks to his hard-working division in his own idiosyncratic way at an address on 25 October: 'I further wish to congratulate all of you,' he said, 'and particularly myself, on being members of such a division; and it is my fond belief that we will get better and better.'[36]

The division did not have to wait long before its next opportunity to show its adeptness, in another major exercise with the I Armored Corps. It took place in mid-November, just weeks before the Japanese attack on Pearl Harbor, with the First Army's 300,000-man-strong advance across the Carolinas providing a stern test for all involved, once again observed by Marshall and the Army's senior leadership team. On the first day, the 2nd Armored Division's reconnaissance battalion captured the First Army commander (who had to be released by umpires so that the exercise could continue), and thereafter Patton pushed every man in every unit hard, determined to take them to the edge of their physical and mental endurance in an attempt to break the opposition's ability to respond effectively. He supported their efforts personally when the need arose, and at one point joined a junior officer to solve a fuel resupply problem that threatened the momentum his division had gained.

Stepping back only as far as he needed in order to achieve a full picture of battle, Patton's developing maturity as a commander impressed his superiors. His leadership remained assertive but he had learned to trust his subordinates, and they returned that trust with a string of outstanding performances. Overall, the division had gone beyond just being combat-ready; it was rapidly reaching the point at which it could be tested against a real enemy. Marshall, for one, viewed Patton as difficult to command but too good to waste. He therefore advised his new Chief of Armored Forces, Jacob L. Devers, to 'keep a tight rope round his neck' but also 'give him an armored corps when one becomes available'.[37]

— ◻ —

Major General Bernard Montgomery had very little time to prepare the 3rd Infantry Division before it left for France as part of the ten-division British Expeditionary Force in the mid-autumn of 1939. He believed the vast majority of the British Army 'totally unfit to fight a first-class war on the continent of Europe',[38] but worked tirelessly in the few weeks before its deployment across the English Channel to improve its confidence and capability. Montgomery's previous success in such work had been influential in his appointment, but his corps commander, Alan Brooke, was under no illusions as to how disruptive his subordinate could be in his efforts to get results. Nevertheless, their mutual admiration helped to create a strong bond, and they shared similar views on many aspects of military affairs, including a low opinion of the commander of the BEF, Lord

Gort, whom Monty later said was 'unfitted for the job – and we senior officers all knew it'.[39]

Brooke's II Corps arrived in France during mid-October 1939, initially consisting of the 4th Infantry Division alongside the 3rd Infantry Division, with orders to take up a position between French formations on the border with Belgium, in a sector just south of Lille. French general Maurice Gamelin commanded the combined Allied forces, convinced that the Germans would advance, as they had in 1914, via Brussels, the only invasion route conceivable with the supposedly 'impregnable Maginot Line' providing protection along the common border with Germany. Thus, as daylight hours shortened and the weather worsened, the cream of two armies watched and waited. As his two divisions dug in, Brooke became increasingly uneasy not only that the Allies had ceded the military initiative to Germany, but that inactivity during a northern European winter would significantly undermine his formation's morale. 'I am not happy about our general attitude', he wrote in his diary, 'we are facing war in a half hearted way… I feel that the Germans would have been tackling the situation very differently.'[40]

Montgomery was similarly anxious, but his division – based around the town of Lesquin – was afforded no opportunity to fall into the sort of stuporous malaise that affected other Allied formations, because he introduced a demanding training programme. His ambition was to do what he had been unable to do in England, and prepare his division for war while ensuring that its personnel remained active in body and mind. He based the training scenarios on what he knew about the enemy and its capabilities, which is why they included a fighting withdrawal as well as an advance to contact. Every military grouping trained – from section (or equivalent) right up to the full formation – for, at Montgomery's insistence, four full-division exercises were to be conducted before the next spring. One battalion staff officer later recalled: 'The exercises were a carefully thought through attempt to raise us from a mediocre organisation to an elite. At the time we viewed them as unnecessary, but looking back they were an obvious use of the time we had available and we never regretted a minute of them.'[41]

The first division exercise took place in early November, an opportunity for an assessment of where improvements could be made, and the brigades and battalions then used this as the basis for their own training plans. One senior infantry NCO asserted: 'General Montgomery keeps us on our toes. The officers said, "The general would not like this, and he would not like that." We knew who the general was all right and we all upped our game to keep him sweet.'[42]

Monty soon became a familiar figure to everybody in his 'large and demanding divisional family'.[43] His visits to units were well received by most, who appreciated chatting with the general in small groups (although Monty often pointed to a single man and pulled him away for a confidential discussion, much to the discomfort of his superiors) and enjoyed his addresses, during which he deployed his impish humour and always thanked the men for their efforts. 'The personal relationship between a [leader] and his soldiers', Montgomery later wrote, 'is and has always been one of the most potent single factors in war,'[44] and he did everything in his powers to strengthen that relationship and the individual's attachment to the formation. Mirroring Patton, he had each man sew onto his right sleeve a new 3rd Infantry Division badge he had designed (a black triangle with a red triangle at its centre), with instructions to remember their place in a 'team of teams'. In time, their commander hoped, these men would not only fight for each other, they would also fight for 'General Monty'.

The 3rd Infantry Division increasingly assumed a new identity, as Montgomery encouraged his units to regard themselves as superior to their peers because they worked harder and were better led. Peter Carington, a subaltern in one of the division's two elite battalions of Grenadier Guards, was one among many who thought that Monty established 'a new esprit de corps [and] a long overdue professionalism',[45] but Montgomery could also be tactless, and one occasion nearly lost him his job. In November 1939, as the damp and cold began to test the morale of the Allied troops on the French border waiting for the German invasion, Monty was informed that incidents of venereal disease were escalating rapidly throughout his 3rd Division. His response was immediate and took the form of a division order which, although seeking to ensure that his men remained healthy, completely failed to consider the sensitivities surrounding his formation's sexual behaviour. 'My view', Montgomery wrote in the order, 'is that if a man wants to have a woman, let him do so by all means: but he must use his common sense and the necessary precautions against infection – otherwise he becomes a casualty by his own neglect, and this is helping the enemy.'[46] The document disgusted the Right Reverend John Coghlan, the senior chaplain at GHQ, who demanded that Commander-in-Chief Gort take action against Montgomery for his 'moral infirmity' and said he was determined to take the issue to London if he did not get satisfaction.[47]

Montgomery's immediate superior, Alan Brooke, stepped into the maelstrom to avoid his best division commander from being sent back to England in disgrace just as the German invasion was looming. Using all the diplomacy he could muster, Brooke told Gort that he would admonish his misguided subordinate and warn him about his future conduct. With the dressing-down of Montgomery duly delivered, Brooke wrote in his diary: 'I think it ought to have done him good. It is a great pity that he spoils his very high military ability by a mad desire to talk or write nonsense.'[48] It was a check on Monty's high-handedness and not the first of his career. He would later write, 'I have no doubt I deserved all I got',[49] having learned 'that it is better to remain silent on such occasions and take all that comes to you'.[50] Throughout his career, Montgomery rarely wasted energy fretting over the decisions he had made; they were in the past. It was an approach born of his determination to always be moving forward – to always do whatever was necessary to create success, no matter who was upset by it. It made him a devastating leader, but a poor follower and the most difficult general in the British Army.

His order concerning the prevention of venereal disease reveals just how naive Montgomery could be in the face of the military's prudishness, and yet he shrugged off the admonishments for this and other displays of misconduct (usually caused by his confrontations with those in higher headquarters whom he saw as exceeding their authority by blocking some of his plans) because he was convinced that only he knew what was best for the 3rd Infantry Division. GHQ's criticisms were balanced by the realization that, while other formations in the BEF (and the wider Allied forces) were suffering from weakening morale as winter set in, by contrast the 3rd Infantry Division had a robust spirit that was the envy of many – largely because of Montgomery's efforts to keep his units active and improving.

The progress made by the formation was amply illustrated during its second exercise, held during a particularly dank and gloomy period in mid-December. Over four days, Monty's men rehearsed their part in a new Gamelin plan which required an Allied advance into mid-Belgium once the Germans invaded, but although revealing good co-ordination, according to Montgomery 'there was plenty of room for improvement in communication and leadership'.[51] A 'wash-up' conference held with his officers just before Christmas provided a new set of training priorities for the division over the remainder of the winter, and while the units attended to them, Montgomery took the opportunity to make changes in his headquarters. Having concluded that the staff was too large and unwieldy for the sort of operations the division was likely to fight, he slimmed it down. With the assistance of Lieutenant Colonel 'Marino' Brown, his chief of staff, Montgomery pared the headquarters to the essentials, and in so doing demanded more of those who remained (which was never well received) but created efficiencies that dramatically improved its reaction time.

The third of Montgomery's division exercises was run in early March 1940, and using his experiences of 1914 as a guide, he sought to practise the highly technical business of withdrawal while maintaining contact with the enemy. Brooke described it as 'an excellent exercise...

real useful'.[52] And with the spring weather making an enemy invasion ever more likely, the 3rd Infantry Division ran a fourth exercise in late March. Thus, by the time the temperatures drew away from freezing, Monty's had become an admirable fighting formation, while the 4th Infantry Division had conducted only a single division exercise, and the recent addition to II Corps, the 50th Infantry Division, was still orientating itself.

Even then there was more work to be done, for in April Montgomery finally began to remove those officers he assessed as hindering progress, writing to Brooke: 'I consider that in a front-line fighting Division it is necessary to have commanders who have character and personality that will inspire confidence in others.'[53] He sent a memorandum to his brigadiers and commanding officers which asserted that 'when the real test comes it is leadership that is going to pull us through... Our British soldiers are capable of anything if they are well led.' He requested they report the names of any officers who failed as leaders, promising ominously, 'I will do the rest.'[54] A slew of sackings followed, with replacement officer Lieutenant Colonel Brian Horrocks recalling that he knew of Monty because he had been 'probably the most discussed general in the British Army before the war... [and] was not a popular figure'.[55]

When the German invasion of the West began on 10 May 1940, the plan for the Allies to move into mid-Belgium to take up defensive positions along the Dyle river was enacted, and the 3rd Infantry Division led the II Corps advance. Going into combat again, Montgomery approached the challenge with the confidence of an officer confronted with the much-anticipated puzzle that he had been preparing himself to solve for over twenty years.[56] He greeted the order to advance in the relaxed and professional manner that his staff and subordinate commanders had witnessed during exercises: there were no histrionics, no great speeches, for every man in his division knew what they had to do and they followed their general's lead willingly.

The vanguard of the division arrived at the Dyle on the second day of the campaign, and Montgomery used great tact to get the commander of a weak Belgian formation already *in situ* at Louvain to fall back into support. It was a vital sector specially selected for the 3rd Infantry Division, as it protected the main communication route to the capital Brussels, just fifteen miles to the west, and so could expect a strong German attack. Montgomery toured the front in his usual fashion, encouraging his men as they arrived over the next two days – and as they watched the shattered Belgian border units withdrawing through the British positions with the Germans not far behind. 'They could provide little news, they had no officers with them,' Lieutenant Guy Courage remembered of the troops fresh from battle with the Germans, 'they were disorganised and demoralised… We drew our own conclusions and anxiously awaited the coming Hun.'[57]

The enemy finally arrived outside Louvain on 15 May, and immediately attempted to break through the 3rd Infantry Division in a series of uncompromising assaults. Now, in the formation's first engagement, all the hard work it had done over the previous months began to pay dividends, for its leaders were magnificent and the men stuck to their tasks well despite the enemy's ferocious onslaught. Yet although Montgomery's men held their sector of the line with admirable skill, less able divisions elsewhere began to crack, and with every passing hour Marino Brown was relaying messages to his boss that a general withdrawal was imminent. The Allies, it seemed, had fallen into a German trap. While the main part of Gamelin's force had been pinned in mid-Belgium by one German Army Group, a second, consisting of the enemy's rapidly moving main armoured effort, was outflanking them to the south. Even as the 3rd Infantry Division was fending off attacks at Louvain, German panzers were rushing to the Channel coast in an attempt to encircle the cream of the Allied forces. The audacious German plan had been brilliantly executed, leaving Brooke to note in his diary on 15 May: 'The BEF is therefore likely to have both flanks turned and will have a very unpleasant time in extricating itself out of its current position.'[58] What followed was, in Montgomery's words, 'a real shocker of a campaign',[59] but it was also a stage on which his leadership could shine.

When a withdrawal was announced by Gamelin on 16 May, Brooke issued his orders to Montgomery (which, he noted, were accepted 'full of confidence that he would bring off this rather difficult move with complete success'[60]) and a new phase of the campaign began. Three days later, the 3rd Infantry Division was in a new position west of Brussels at one of the BEF's 'phase lines' on the Escaut river. Private Eddie Wood recalled: 'As we began to fall back, we did so with trust in our officers and took heart from the fact we had a general of Monty's quality. We knew that he was doing everything he could to get us out of a big mess and it allowed us to concentrate on our jobs. He helped us and we helped him – that's the way it worked.'[61] The 3rd Infantry Division's self-belief helped the entire formation fight through the next two extraordinarily demanding weeks, as the BEF fell back towards the Channel ports more than 100 miles to the west.

Throughout a series of dangerous, complex and exhausting manoeuvres, Montgomery's leadership was exceptional. He soon fell into a daily routine that was founded on Marino's understanding of Montgomery's intent, because he was empowered to take decisions on the general's behalf when required. With Monty spending much of the day away from headquarters visiting his units, this proved to be a highly effective way of operating as it allowed him the freedom to lead and command the division rather than become tied down by the many demands at headquarters. Having spent the morning and early afternoon touring the division – during which time he was kept updated about significant developments by radio – Montgomery would return to his headquarters at around 16.00 to chair a conference with his staff, receive briefings, make decisions and issue orders. After dinner with colleagues, a time that Montgomery encouraged to be a brief period of relaxation, he retired to bed at around 22.00 with strict instructions 'never to be disturbed except in a crisis'.[62] He had selected and trained his key personnel for war, and expected them to do what was necessary while he took the rest he required to sustain himself over a long and stressful period.

The risk of not getting enough rest, and in trying to do too much for too long due to the inability of the commander to relinquish control, had been a potential issue that Montgomery had worked hard to avoid since taking command. Others had not, and having subsequently become physically and mentally exhausted during the fighting they were prone to increasingly erratic decision-making. One such man was the commander of I Corps, Lieutenant General Michael Barker, who suffered a nervous collapse but remained at the helm of his formation until it reached the Dunkirk beaches.

The challenges faced by the officers and men of the BEF to keep each other alive, organized, motivated and fighting in the front line were immense, and a few revealed themselves to be leaders of the highest calibre. Brooke was among those who excelled under pressure in France, and he observed that the desperate situation in which II Corps found itself acted as a 'stimulus' to Monty, because it 'thrilled him and put the sharpest edges on his military ability'.[63] Thus, after 20 May, when the leading German armour reached the Channel coast and so completed its encirclement, the 3rd Infantry Division became the BEF's lynchpin as the Allied units were squeezed into a shrinking pocket by a German force pressing from all sides. 'Nothing but a miracle can save the BEF now', Brooke wrote in his diary on 23 May, 'and the end cannot be very far off,' but through a measured withdrawal to beaches around Dunkirk there remained the slim chance of a Royal Navy evacuation – and with it, the hope of salvaging a portion of the Allied forces from disaster. The first British troops were plucked from the coast on 27 May while the 3rd Infantry Division, having crossed back into France, was still fighting forty miles south-east of the embarkation points at Roubaix (near Lille), on the lower right flank of a bulging Allied line. Montgomery's task was to lead all the BEF units in that line out of danger and into new defensive positions to the north. On the night of 27–28 May, he began a series of complex and hazardous moves in close proximity to the enemy. Brooke later wrote: 'It was a task that might well have shaken the stoutest hearts, but for Monty it might just have been a glorious picnic!… There is no doubt that one of Monty's strong points is his boundless confidence in himself. He was priceless on this occasion, and I thanked Heaven to have a Commander of his calibre to undertake this march.'[64]

The 3rd Infantry Division subsequently successfully established an anchor point for a shallower and more defensible line just north of Ypres, without which the entire front may have collapsed and the ongoing evacuations would soon have been forced to cease. It was a period of great uncertainty for the division, but there was no panic; intelligence officer Kit Dawnay reflected the attitude of many when he later explained, 'I don't think I had any great worries. I was supremely confident in Monty. He gave one a tremendous feeling of confidence.'[65]

The final phase of the BEF's campaign began with the capitulation of the Belgians on 28 May, causing a fifteen-mile gap to suddenly open up on the 3rd Infantry Division's left flank to the coast. Montgomery filled this with his division's gunners (hastily issued with rifles) and engineers, along with a variety of French units. He retained an energy precious few other formation commanders could match, and retained his ability to assert his will on events and even seize the initiative when he could. '[He was] always the same,' remembered Brian Horrocks, 'confident, almost cocky you might say, cheerful and apparently quite fresh. He was convinced that he was the best divisional commander in the British Army and that we were the best division. By the time we had reached Dunkirk I had come to the same conclusion!'[66]

The admiration and respect that Brooke himself had for his subordinate was underlined on 30 May, the day on which the 3rd Infantry Division fell back to the town of Furnes, less than five miles from the coast and critical to the defensive perimeter forming around Dunkirk. Having been ordered back to England to take charge of developing a new British force, *Brooke handed command of II Corps to Montgomery* knowing that he would not be fazed by the new responsibility. Just a few hours later, the new corps commander was offering advice to the Commander-in-Chief. Having attended a GHQ conference during which the plan to evacuate II Corps the next day was outlined, Montgomery took Gort to one side and 'speaking plainly' said that he was not happy at having to rely on I Corps' support while it was still commanded by the struggling Barker. Despite being only a temporary corps commander, Montgomery went further still and recommended that Barker be replaced by Harold Alexander, a division commander in I Corps whom he trusted without reservation. Gort agreed and the change was made, thus enabling Montgomery to focus on his corps without having to make allowances for the erratic Barker.

II Corps began to disengage from the enemy on 31 May, and in carefully co-ordinated phases its three divisions moved back to their allotted embarkation points and began to board a variety of vessels. By the evening, as the last of his men congregated on the promenade and with enemy shells bursting nearby, Montgomery personally directed his men towards Dunkirk harbour, from where the last tranche of his troops would be loaded onto ships. At one point Monty's aide-de-camp Charles Sweeney, standing at his boss's side, was knocked to the ground by a shell splinter which struck his head. Immediately going to his assistance Monty helped Sweeney to his feet, and when it was clear that the wound was superficial, the general, replete in a beret, delivered Sweeney a mock rebuke for not wearing a helmet.

Not until the early hours of 1 June did Montgomery conduct a final sweep of the environs, personally calling out in the darkness for any more II Corps troops, and at 03.30 he finally left French soil. Alexander had done a superb job protecting the formation's evacuation, and I Corps itself – the last of the BEF – left Dunkirk the following evening. By the time the Germans finally overran the area on the morning of 4 June, some 338,226 Allied troops had been evacuated. It was to become a critical event in the outcome of the Second World War.[67]

Montgomery and Brooke were among the few to emerge from the sad affair with their reputations enhanced. Sadly, Monty's faithful chief of staff, Marino Brown, was killed during the latter stages of the withdrawal delivering a message one evening to Brooke

– most probably shot by a nervous sentry in the dark at II Corps headquarters.[68] The strategic situation for Britain was now bleak. Isolated and vulnerable to a German invasion – which the RAF and Royal Navy eventually held off during an anxious summer in the Battle of Britain – the British Army was now in need of rebuilding. It was a task for which Montgomery was admirably qualified, and so he was appointed to the command of V Corps with the rank of acting lieutenant general.

The formation was responsible for protecting the central section of England's southern coastline, a likely invasion sector, and comprised two infantry divisions and a regiment of medium artillery. Although Montgomery had no faith in his immediate superior, Claude Auchinleck, his predecessor as V Corps commander who had been elevated to Southern Command ('I cannot recall that we ever agreed on anything,' Montgomery later wrote[69]), he could at least rely on Alan Brooke who had recently been appointed Commander-in-Chief, Home Command Forces. Brooke always tried to save Montgomery from himself and so, realizing that his new corps commander disliked Auchinleck so vehemently, wrote to him: 'I have backed you strongly and shall go on doing so and only ask you not to let me down by doing anything silly.'[70] Brooke had known Montgomery long enough, however, to recognize that such a request was unlikely to dissuade Monty from speaking his mind.

While Montgomery avoided pointless confrontation with Auchinleck, he still unceremoniously replaced a significant number of his predecessor's appointees at headquarters with his own hand-picked staff. A new, stiff broom had begun to sweep with vigour, and it would not stop until the formation was free of the detritus that Monty argued, with increasing anger, it had accumulated. He was the agent of change and was self-confident in it, and though Auchinleck disagreed that such deep change was required due to recent 'poor stewardship', Monty stuck to his task. The capabilities of the two divisions in his corps were, he said, 'poor', and he felt that the existing plan for a broad static defence on the beaches with concentrated mobile counter-attacks further inland was 'inept'.[71] Whenever Auchinleck directed Montgomery to do something with which his subordinate did not agree, he found that V Corps headquarters always had an excuse ready for its lack of implementation. Brooke once again had to step in to protect Montgomery from Auchinleck's wrath as he became incensed by Monty's 'huge appetite for self-importance and vanity' and increasingly frustrated by his disregard for orders (which bordered on insubordination) and the amount of time it was taking to manage his slippery subordinate.[72]

As senior leadership disagreements played themselves out during the autumn of 1940, Monty, established in his headquarters at Longford Castle near Salisbury in Wiltshire, forged ahead with his corps' training plan. Unit and division exercises culminated in the first corps scheme in October, which opened with an 'Operations of War' study week for all division, brigade and battalion commanders. Brooke felt Montgomery had delivered a training model that should be adopted by others, but Auchinleck was less sanguine: 'No coughing, no smoking, runs before breakfast – aspiring and made me feel quite inadequate. But I doubt if runs before breakfast really produce battle-winners, of necessity.'[73]

The runs referred to by Auchinleck had been introduced for all ranks and were poorly received by some, including a rather rotund colonel who made it plain that he'd die if he took part. Montgomery replied simply that if he was to expire, 'it would be better to do it now, as he could be replaced easily and smoothly… I preferred him to do the run and die.'[74] The general then banned wives and families from entering the officially designated corps area so that there were no distractions while on duty. 'To be frank', Captain Roger Stillwell later wrote, 'we all thought Monty was a complete nuisance but what we did not realise – and he did – was how much work we needed to do if we were ever to send the Germans back into the English Channel if they ever invaded.'[75]

Gradually, improvements were made. Montgomery's task was made considerably easier when he managed to get one of his less able formations replaced by his old 3rd Infantry Division, and even more so when Auchinleck was replaced at Southern Command by Harold Alexander. Thus, by December 1940, when Montgomery held a full-scale V Corps exercise (which included an armoured division, the Army's new parachute forces and RAF close-support aircraft), he felt at liberty to be as creative as he wanted. In an article titled 'The New British Army: A Cooperative Attack', *The Times* described the events as 'the most ambitious exercise in the field that has ever taken place in this country' and reported that shock troops even seized Alan Brooke and chauffeur at gunpoint while their attention was diverted.[76] Montgomery was jubilant at the acclaim his exercise received. While his self-promoting extravagances may have been unpalatable to many, few questioned his contribution to the work that was being done the length and breadth of the United Kingdom to improve the Army's capabilities. An overseas command looked increasingly likely as Britain's imperial possessions were threatened.

The Italian invasion of Egypt in September 1940 had threatened the Suez Canal and raised the prospect of another significant British military defeat, but Richard O'Connor's remarkable riposte in December resulted in the enemy being ousted from Egypt and then pushed back deep into Libya before surrendering in early February. It made military sense, therefore, to send a significant force to strengthen the defence of Egypt, and Monty's name was prominent among those discussed as likely candidates to command it. He wanted the position, but in the spring of 1941 Montgomery learned he was to remain in England. The rapidly promoted 53-year-old lieutenant general, the wise Alan Brooke had decided, would benefit from another year with a corps at home before being put forward for a senior combat command overseas; and so at the end of April, Montgomery was appointed to command XII Corps. The three-division-strong formation was tasked with the defence of the eastern sector of England's south coast, also in the likely German invasion zone, and had its headquarters in Tunbridge Wells.

However, the threat of the enemy crossing the Channel significantly diminished in early summer when Germany invaded the Soviet Union. At the same time, the threat to Egypt increased after an offensive by Erwin Rommel – an opponent Montgomery had recently learned about after Rommel's exploits in France – retook much of the Libyan territory lost earlier in the year. Monty ensured that he was kept fully abreast of developments in North Africa, but his daily focus remained on XII Corps, which he sought to transform through his usual process: setting a vision, forging a professional culture, gaining the support of his officers and men, creating capable teams and establishing trust. 'So the ideas and the doctrine of war, and training for war, which began as far west as Dorset,' Montgomery later wrote, reflecting on his time in England after Dunkirk, 'gradually spread along the south of England to the mouth of the Thames.'[77] Ably assisted by his new chief of staff, Brigadier Frank Simpson, whom he had brought across from his previous headquarters, Monty ensured that XII Corps was, as he put it, 'knocked into shape'.[78] Brian Horrocks – who, with the esteemed general as his patron, had risen rapidly since the campaign in Belgium and France and now commanded Monty's 44th Infantry Division – later wrote: 'I was unprepared for his astonishing activity... It was as though atomic bombs were exploding all over this rural corner of Britain.'[79]

Exercise 'Binge', a XII Corps initiative held in June 1941, was Montgomery's first opportunity to assess his new command, and its initial mediocre performance concerned him. Gathering his officers together, Montgomery asserted: 'We cannot afford to be complacent about our mistakes. Let us be quite frank about it and see what went wrong. Let us put it right; and we can be thankful we have time to do it.'[80] They left the auditorium determined to do better. 'We were confident,' recalled Major Donny McDonald. 'We could have been gloomy, but Montgomery was a man who never revealed a problem without already having thought of a solution and so we felt encouraged!'[81] Everywhere he went, Montgomery looked to instil confidence that people could do more and do it more effectively.

The same was even true of the civilian audiences Monty addressed during the summer and autumn of 1941 as he tried to raise morale in those who also had a vital part to play in the war effort. 'I didn't know who this odd little man was that came into our factory one day but we were told it was a General Montgomery,' said tin packer Ethel Graves from Maidstone. 'I thought, "Oh no, not more lame words from some sort of official," but there was something in what he said and he had a kind smile. As I say, a funny little man, but I did not forget him or his name.'[82]

After a second XII Corps exercise took place in August which involved both seaborne and airborne landings and revealed an improvement in the overall performance of the divisions, the formation took part in the Army's autumn manoeuvres. The brainchild of Alan Brooke, Exercise 'Bumper' was held in East Anglia over four days and pitted Eastern Command against Southern Command with Montgomery acting as umpire. Supported by the RAF and the Royal Navy, the focus of the event was to develop closer co-operation between ground, air and maritime forces. It was complex but successful in that it thoroughly tested those involved and provided a host of lessons. The debrief day, led by Brooke and Montgomery, was held at the Staff College, Camberley, on 10 October and was attended by 270 officers. Colonel Ian Milton later wrote that it was 'the most scintillating final conference I ever attended. The two men were hand in glove, perfect foils for each other and on top form. We were left in no two minds about where there was room for improvement, and they were absolutely right. It was a tour de force.'[83]

The conclusions drawn from the exercise were to form the basis for much of home defence training for the next year. By that time, Alan Brooke had been appointed Chief of the Imperial General Staff and was fully engaged with matters of strategic imperative, but Montgomery, though having been given responsibility for the new South Eastern Command, seemed more interested in taking the lessons from 'Bumper' and using them to fashion a force that could be sent overseas to attack. Consequently, Monty insisted on referring to his new command as the 'South Eastern Army'. It consisted of XII Corps and a new Canadian Corps commanded by the indomitable Henry Crerar, a fiercely ambitious and independently minded officer who refused to be browbeaten by anybody. He did not hide his dislike, for example, of what he perceived to be Montgomery's egotism, and nor was it uncommon for Crerar to evade his superior's orders if he did not like them. This was a new 'international' leadership challenge for Monty, and one he could not afford to foul up as he stood on the cusp of an overseas command appointment.

— ◻ —

Major General Erwin Rommel's appointment in February 1940 as commander of the powerful 7th Panzer Division, one of the Wehrmacht's ten elite formations, was Hitler's gift to a loyal and highly capable officer. Based at Bad Godesberg on the Rhine river, near Bonn, it was the appointment he had wanted – one in which he could turn his bold, instinctive, mobile approach to combat into something that could have a significant impact during the German invasion of the West. The final plan for that offensive had been sanctioned by Hitler just days after Rommel took command of his new formation, and as part of Army Group A the division would be part of the main manoeuvre force tasked with outflanking the Allied forces in Belgium and France.

The race was now on for Rommel to learn all he could about his specialist division, a concern to subordinates who understood that he had never commanded armoured forces before, far less a complicated all-arms outfit like the 7th Panzer Division. He read the reports of its actions in the recent campaign in Poland, analysed the personnel reports of his key subordinates and, assisted by his staff, learned all he could about the formation's strengths and weaknesses. He then made a tour of his units, talking to officers and men, discussing their requirements and making an assessment of their fighting spirit. After a month of learning and assessing, Rommel unveiled his plan to prepare the division for its next mission and, in particular, to redefine what its personnel believed a bold and fast-moving panzer division was capable of achieving.

Rommel's approach to the leadership challenge of winning the trust of his combat formation on the eve of battle was not to destabilize the division through great change – although one battalion commander was soon relieved from his duties – but to promote practical excellence. He had little ability to shape the division's training programme in the time available, but he could bring his desire to see speed and momentum created through leaders' swift, audacious decision-making and aggression. Soon everybody in the 14,000-man division knew Rommel by sight and, through their unit commanders, what he expected of them. '[B]risk, incisive, intolerant of slackness or infirmity of purpose, inventive, questioning, essentially business-like, enormously energetic', one of Rommel's biographers wrote of him. 'He had always been impatient of others, whatever their rank, who failed to meet his own standards, and with the authority of a divisional commander his impatience was fortified... Rommel was by instinct a humane man, but his kindness never extended to toleration of inadequacy.'[84]

On a corps exercise in March which saw the 7th and 5th Panzer Divisions use the Moselle to practise their river crossings, Rommel made sure that he was personally located where he could make a difference with his leadership. Arriving in his command tank he would, as one engineer explained 'dismount, find out where the seat of all the action was, and exhort greater efforts while ensuring that everybody knew that, in that place, the battle would either be won or lost. If necessary he would help unloading a truck, or even wade into the water, and then suddenly he would be gone, off to do the same somewhere else. He was a real dynamo.'[85] At this time Hermann Hoth, the corps commander, began to recognize just what a talent he had in Rommel, but also how difficult he might be to command and control on operations.

The night before the invasion of France and Belgium, Rommel wrote to Lucie: 'We're packing up at last. Let's hope not in vain.

You'll get all the news for the next few days from the papers. Don't worry yourself. Everything will go alright.'[86] The newspapers were well placed to ensure that Mrs Rommel could track her husband's progress, for with Rommel shaping up to be the sort of charismatic leader that the German people could love, Hitler had personally directed Joseph Goebbels's Propaganda Ministry to attach a junior staff officer as well as the editor of the Nazi newspaper *Der Stürmer* to the 7th Panzer Division. Rommel himself was not averse to the notion and provided full co-operation to the men whose job it was to give him and his division national publicity.

When the offensive began on 10 May and Army Group B advanced into Belgium to fix the most capable part of the Allied forces mid-country, Gerd von Rundstedt's Army Group A began its advance through the densely wooded Ardennes region to the south in preparation for its breakthrough. Not until his panzer divisions arrived at the Meuse river, however, did they face potentially decisive military challenges. A 7th Panzer Division detachment reached the great water obstacle after dark on 12 May and began to seek out potential crossing points. The competitive Rommel, voice already sore from shouting orders and desperately tired due to lack of sleep, demanded a crossing the next morning, and by midnight preparations were under way for assault crossings at two points. The attack across the 100-yard stretch of water began at dawn on 13 May, with Rommel observing the assault made by his 6th Rifle Regiment through binoculars. He later described what he saw as 'none too pleasant', for French fire ripped into the flotilla of small craft and Rommel rushed down to the waterfront to shout directions over the din of battle.

Gradually, enough men reached the opposite bank to start an attack on the enemy defences and, confident they would prevail, Rommel left the site to see how his second assault was progressing. When he arrived, he found the 7th Rifle Regiment being subjected to withering enemy fire, and the bank on which he was standing was deluged with mortar and artillery rounds. Hauptmann

Hans-Joachim Schraepler, Rommel's aide-de-camp, was hit by shell splinters and Rommel was lucky to escape unharmed, but he did not run for cover. His operations officer, Major Otto Heidkämper, found this difficult to countenance, for not only was the division's leader in harm's way, he was also out of immediate contact with his headquarters.[87] Heidkämper believed that the tactical issues his commander was involving himself in were not the general's business, whereas Rommel, convinced that his presence was required to ensure that tactical success could be turned into operational victory, was even content to take command of 2nd Battalion for a short time after its commander had been wounded. Only after the 7th Rifle Regiment began to clamber up the west bank, did Rommel, 'shouting like a sergeant-major where necessary', finally return to his command tank for an update on the division's situation.[88] An hour later the general received confirmation that his two assaults had been successful, that footholds had been established on the opposite bank and the enemy was withdrawing.

Having ensured that plans were progressed for the next phase of the operation over the Meuse, Rommel left his headquarters group and went down to the river to oversee the construction of pontoon bridges, across which the division would feed the heavy weaponry required to consolidate the bridgeheads. For the time being, this was the decisive point of the division's attack and nothing else would distract him. It was therefore no surprise to the troops that their general was bustling around giving orders, or up to his waist in the water lending a hand to the engineers – the sort of activity their exercises had led them to expect from their general. Rommel was still on the riverbank when the first bridge was complete on the morning of 14 May, and his command tank was among the first vehicles to use the crossing. On the west bank, he located himself in a position where the ground opened up before him, and from there began to co-ordinate operations to enlarge the German lodgement and so create the launch pad for the next phase of operations: the advance to the Channel coast.

Determined to seize the initiative and give the enemy little time to muster a decisive counter-attack, Rommel struck out well before the entirety of his division had crossed the Meuse. His attack on 15 May was ferocious and used the tanks of his own division's 25th Panzer Regiment to smash through the developing French concentration and race forward, while those of the 5th Panzer Division's 31st Panzer Regiment, which Rommel had gained permission to bring under his command, 'mopped up'. Advancing at forty miles an hour while the battle was still raging to his rear, Rommel rode with the lead tanks where he could order artillery or dive-bomber support within minutes.[89] Following in the armour's dusty wake were the 7th Panzer Division's lorried infantry and artillery, primed to push forward when required to clear stubborn resistance. As it was, however, the armour was free to drive on unmolested, the speed and unexpectedness of its attack etched on the bewildered faces of a fractured enemy that included some French army motorcyclists who 'were so shaken at suddenly finding themselves in a German column that they drove their machines into a ditch and were in no position to put up a fight'.[90]

Only in the days following the crossing of the Meuse did the Allies recognize their vulnerable situation and, in particular, that their exposed southern flank was being used as a fifty-mile-wide highway for Army Group A's advance. The 7th Panzer Division formed the right wing of that German front, pushing hard and fast across the French border before then rolling through an unfinished extension of the French defences on the evening of 16 May. 'The flat countryside lay spread out around us under the cold light of the moon,' Rommel later wrote. 'We were through the Maginot Line! It was hardly conceivable… [We]were driving deep into enemy territory. It was not just a beautiful dream. It was reality.'[91] Awash with possibilities after this nocturnal success and feeling invincible, the 7th Panzer Division commander ordered his men to push on, and in so doing signally ignored orders that had stated 'No breakthrough!'[92] due to the fear that the formation was pushing too far ahead of the main body of the Army Group and thus rendering itself vulnerable to the enemy.

This was typical of a German Army not quite as confident in the potential of such opportunistic advances as history would suggest, for not only were the methods used by the panzer forces not formalized, there was not even an agreed plan for the advance to the Channel coast.[93] Bold officers like Rommel, who were willing to push the German fighting machine to the limits of its tolerance during this remarkable period of armoured exploitation, ultimately created an *ex post facto* validation of such methods, but at the time they exasperated higher headquarters. 'The officers of a panzer division', Rommel later wrote, 'must learn to think and act independently within the framework of the general plan and not wait until they receive orders.'[94]

Anxious to avoid contact with superior headquarters during this unauthorized advance, Rommel was later to plead that radio failure was behind his lack of communication. Consequently, the division that was often impossible to locate, and even more difficult to direct, became known as the 'Ghost Division'. Hitler later dubbed this period of the campaign Rommel's 'private offensive',[95] and, indeed, his brashness had created a rapier-like advance that managed to stupefy enemy and superiors alike. Sometimes the mere presence of his vehicles was enough to encourage a mass surrender, although one French lieutenant colonel's eyes 'glowed with hate and impotent fury' and, having disobeyed his captor's orders three times, Rommel had him shot.[96]

Nevertheless, even Rommel recognized that by the time the 7th Panzer Division's spearhead group had reached the hills east of Le Cateau in the early morning of 17 May, it was imperative to stop to draw breath, restore communications and reorganize. The formation had carved a massive hole deep into enemy territory, but at the headquarters of Army Group A, von Rundstedt was in the perplexing position of not knowing whether to congratulate the commander of the 7th Panzer Division or reprimand him.

Although Rommel's instinct was to apply unrelenting pressure on the enemy, having been checked by both Hoth and von Rundstedt he was obliged to proceed with more caution. Thus, when on the morning of 20 May men of General Heinz Guderian's armoured corps arrived on the Channel coast, Rommel's formation was still approaching Arras. Although frustrating, the care with which the 7th Panzer Division skirted around the south of the city the following day was judicious, for that afternoon Rommel's men faced what was, perhaps, the most significant Allied counter-attack unleashed against Army Group A. Although events revealed that the relatively small combined tank-infantry force with which the BEF struck was no match for the 7th Panzer Division, the fighting was hard. During the battle Rommel was in the thick of the action, establishing a defensive line of guns with his aide-de-camp Lieutenant Joachim Most and personally directing their fire onto the approaching British armour. During this particularly dangerous activity Most fell mortally wounded at Rommel's side. 'Blood gushed from his mouth,' Rommel wrote, '[he] was beyond help and died before he could be carried into cover beside the gun position. The death of this brave man, a magnificent soldier, touched me deeply.'[97] This British 'jab' could easily have cost Rommel his life, and having inflicted 400 casualties on the 7th Panzer Division and damaging or destroying a dozen tanks and scores of vehicles, it caused considerable alarm in higher headquarters.

This was precisely the type of enemy attack against von Rundstedt's flank, the Army high command (OKH) argued, that could destroy everything to date – and a nervous Hitler agreed. Therefore, senior leadership anxiously tracked Army Group A as it continued to wend its way towards the coast, concerned that the vast gap between the panzer divisions and the standard German infantry division following on foot could be exploited by the enemy. It was a legitimate concern, but what the OKH did not know was that the Allies had no ability to mount any such operation, for they had no strategic reserve and, moreover, were in such shock that their forces were in survival mode.

When the 7th Panzer Division returned to its advance, Rommel was personally unconcerned about the brief confrontation at Arras. 'I'm fine in every way,' he wrote to Lucie after a few hours' sleep on 23 May. 'My division has had a blazing success... Now the hunt is up against 60 encircled British, French and Belgian divisions. Don't worry about me. As I see it the war in France may be over in a fortnight.'[98]

A few days later, the attentive Schraepler, having recovered from his wounds, sent his own note to Frau Rommel. In it, he informed Lucie that Rommel had been awarded the Knight's Cross, saying, 'nobody has deserved it more than your husband' and adding, poignantly, that at that moment the general was 'up with the tanks again'.[99] By this time, the two German Army Groups (supported by the Luftwaffe) had just began to apply the *coup de grâce* to the encircled Allied divisions, but only after a three-day lull ordered by Hitler to allow the infantry time to catch up with the armour. It was a pause the enemy used to good effect, for by the time it ended on 27 May, Allied formations had consolidated their defensive perimeter around Dunkirk and evacuations from the port and its adjacent beaches were proceeding apace.

With troops from Britain, France and Belgium limping back to England defeated, the first chapter of the campaign in the West had ended, but Rommel was already preparing for his role in what followed. A visit by Hitler to the front on 3 June saw him pay Rommel considerable attention, and was a ringing endorsement of a general of whom he remained especially fond. Some of the 7th Panzer Division commander's superiors felt that Hitler's blandishments were worth little, and others had a professional disdain for all the attention he was generating, but none could deny that Rommel was a supremely successful armoured division commander. It was no surprise, therefore, that Rommel's formation was given a major role in the next stage of the offensive, which began on 5 June and saw Hoth's corps (now part of Army Group B) delivering the main attack across the Somme river north of Paris, before conducting a breakout running parallel to the

Channel coast. 'We're off again to-day,' Rommel wrote to Lucie on 4 June. 'The six days' rest has done a lot of good and helped us to get our equipment more or less back into shape. The new move won't be so very difficult... Would you cut out all the newspaper articles about me, please? I've no time to read at the moment, but it will be fun to look at them later.'[100]

The corps was immediately successful, and while other formations initially struggled against tenacious defences, Rommel's forced its way through and advanced eight miles across open countryside on the first day with its commander in the vanguard. With the Allied line broken, there was little more to stop the panzers advancing other than the roads filled with fleeing civilians and weaponless French troops. They reached the Seine in the early hours of 9 June and then paused to wait for bridging materials to be brought forward to facilitate a crossing.

During this wait, Rommel was informed that a large force consisting of the French 9th Corps and the majority of the British 51st (Highland) Infantry Division (which had been serving in the Maginot Line but had been withdrawn and thrust into the rapidly developing defensive line) was tumbling back along the Channel coast from the Somme. Having stalked his prey, by 12 June Rommel's tank and reconnaissance units had successfully surrounded the wretched force as it sought evacuation from St Valéry. Then, having deceived it with a display of firepower of such magnitude that it was suggestive of a German force far larger than was actually in position, he obtained its surrender. The bag of 46,000 prisoners included twelve British and French generals, one of whom admitted, 'You are too fast, much too fast for us. That's all there is to it!'[101] In an image captured in the St Valéry market square by one of the 7th Panzer Division's photographers, a clutch of grim Allied senior officers chat impassively while the diminutive Rommel stands in the foreground wearing a broad grin. 'Wonderful moments,' he wrote to Lucie.[102]

Having given his division a much-appreciated break on the French coast – 'Men fell out of their vehicles and onto the warm grass', wrote one corporal, 'I slept for four hours and then we went for a swim. We felt blessed'[103] – Rommel assessed his units' situation reports and, having received orders from Hoth, planned the division's next move with his staff. France was in the process of being overrun, and now the only issue was how much of its territory would be occupied before it capitulated. Paris fell on 14 June, and four days later the 5th Panzer Division reached the Atlantic coast at Brest, with the 7th Panzer Division seizing the vital port of Cherbourg in Normandy on 19 June after two days' shelling, having completed a 155-mile advance from the Seine in a single day. 'The only real constraints on our advance were the wear and tear on our vehicles,' tank driver Paul Henkelmann later wrote. 'The mobile workshops were kept extremely busy, but the weather was good and we knew that the end of the campaign was in sight. I personally felt that we had just won the war.'[104]

When the French surrender finally came on 25 June, the entire northern portion of the country was in German hands with an only nominally independent regime established in the south. France had been crushed. German boldness, despite its stuttering at senior levels at times, had been rewarded with victory over France, Belgium and the Netherlands in just six weeks, and the BEF had only just survived the experience. In a stroke, the stinging memories of 1918 had been wiped away, and within a few weeks Goebbels had created a narrative that told of the Führer having masterminded one of the greatest victories in military history.

Rommel's role in the success was significant, and particularly remarkable considering his recent arrival at the 7th Panzer Division. His achievements had cost just 2,624 casualties (682 killed, 1,646 wounded and 296 missing)[105] – First World War battles had consumed more men in minutes – and the troops appreciated that. Hoth's campaign report was generous to his subordinate, although in saying that Rommel 'explored new paths in the command of Panzer divisions' he could well have been making a point about the officer's unreliable followership.[106] The German propaganda machine, however, was far less subtle in its opinion of Rommel, with the weekly newspaper *Das Reich* proclaiming him 'the soldier for our time' and 'a gallant hero of the Reich'.[107] The Swabian general – strong, successful, invincible – had caught the imagination of the German people, and it was therefore logical that he feature prominently in the propaganda film *Sieg im Western* (Victory in the West), which was shot during the late summer in 1940 on battlefield locations and released several months later. The newspapers' coverage and then the film made Rommel into a military star, a darling of the Nazi propaganda machine and an established Hitler favourite. The senior Army leadership was inevitably scornful of the attentions lavished on one officer, but the 7th Panzer Division could not have been happier. 'What a remarkable man,' wrote Paul Henkelmann, 'we took him to our soldierly hearts not only because of our victories, but because we admired him in the same way that he admired us.'[108] Even sceptical Major Heidkämper in headquarters had come to appreciate Rommel's talents, and bent himself to the general's requirements. He was, Heidkämper admitted, 'irresistible'.[109]

After leave, refits and lesson-learning conferences, during the autumn the 7th Panzer Division made refinements to its organization and then, from its base in Bordeaux, began a training programme. Rommel oversaw the process from beginning to end, his staff and commanders now entirely confident in their ability to translate his intent into actions. 'We are working hard again,' wrote Corporal Luis Althaus in his diary in mid-October, 'we are to become more efficient in everything we do... There also need to be some tactical improvements.'[110]

As the headquarters scheduled demanding exercises for the autumn, Rommel took increasing interest in North Africa, where an Italian force commanded by Marshal Rodolfo Graziani had invaded Egypt. Italy had run to Germany's side during the summer, when it had become clear that victory in the West was assured, and by September was undertaking its own offensive. Initial success, however, was soon followed by the unedifying Axis spectacle of Lieutenant General Richard O'Connor's British Western Desert Force first repelling the Italian attack and then sending the enemy scuttling back across Cyrenaica, the northern coastal part of Libya, before forcing its capitulation in early February 1941. It was a major setback for Axis ambitions, and a strategic blow, but Italy continued to occupy most of Libya and thus retained a base from which further operations could be launched against British strategic interests, particularly the Suez Canal. As a consequence, Hitler sent reinforcements to Tripoli which included the Deutsches Afrika Korps (DAK), and Lieutenant General Rommel was selected by Hitler to command it.

Rommel's rapid elevation to corps command was due entirely to Hitler's influence and his continued appreciation of an 'unbelievably tough commander who led his Panzer division in France like a reconnaissance party and advanced to the Channel coast without regard for danger or physical exhaustion'.[111] Although subordinated to General Italo Gariboldi's Supreme Command North Africa on his arrival in the theatre in mid-February 1941, Rommel immediately recognized the potential of being the senior German formation commander in North Africa, with orders simply to stabilize the situation and then to prepare an attack. Although his priority was to shore up the front and protect Tripoli, his real ambition was to launch a major new offensive into Egypt. The Italian high command was circumspect about the German senior officer, who was soon making his presence felt with his disparaging comments about Italian Army capability and how it could have lost so much ground so quickly. Gariboldi thus found it necessary to remind Rommel that North Africa was Italy's theatre, and provided not only his superior officer, but also the majority of troops and the homeland ports from which Axis troops in North Africa were supplied.

Rommel, however, was not cowed; he would be his own man, and while happy to go through the charade of deference to his Italian superior, would not feel constrained by an ally's authority. Thus, by the early spring, with a firm grasp of what he wanted to achieve and how the Afrika Korps would achieve it, Rommel advanced his plans. Travelling to visit, lead and assess his formations (elements of which were still arriving in Libya), Rommel also spent time with his staff developing plans for his new offensive. 'A lot to do,' he wrote to Lucie. 'Can't leave here for the moment as I couldn't be answerable for my absence. Too much depends on my own person and my driving power.'[112] By mid-March, having been encouraged by intelligence that O'Connor's British force was vulnerable due to overstretch and a centralized command that, as in France, hindered agility, Rommel established a forward headquarters at Sirte on the Libyan coast and made his final preparations. Authorization for his attack came from Gariboldi, but it was strictly limited to retaking the port of Benghazi some 350 miles away, even though Rommel personally saw no good reason why he should be artificially bound if opportunities existed to push further.

Rommel's plan relied on surprise to wrong-foot the enemy, followed by mobile operations to exploit the situation that had been created. 'One of the first lessons I had drawn from my experience of motorised warfare', he later wrote, 'was that speed of manoeuvre in operations and quick reactions in command are decisive. Troops must be able to carry out operations at top speed and in complete co-ordination. To be satisfied with norms is fatal. One must constantly demand and strive for maximum performance, for the side which makes the greater effort is the faster – and the faster wins the battle.'[113]

The initial attack on the British defences at El Agheila was launched on 24 March 1941 by Johannes Streich's 5th Light Division supported by two Italian divisions. It took a little over a week to create the breakthrough allowing Rommel to send a portion of his force to Benghazi, but a far larger force – expressly against Gariboldi's orders – raced across Cyrenaica to create an encirclement. One major later recalled, 'I remember a briefing by my commanding officer in which Rommel's name was mentioned several times. Even at this early stage in the desert campaign, I felt that Rommel was sitting on my shoulder watching everything I did.'[114] Throughout the attack, the DAK's energetic commander did not do as others in his position would have done and remain with his headquarters, but instead applied his leadership where it was most required. This was Rommel's supreme skill: recognizing during complex and often fast-moving battles where he would have the greatest impact. He used his Storch light aircraft to monitor events in real time and often acted as the eyes of a division, but he also took the opportunity to send messages to his commanders, with one receiving the threat 'If you do not move on at once, I shall come down! Rommel.'[115]

No matter where he was physically located during operations, his aim was always to ensure the maintenance of an irresistible momentum to his attack and so diminish the enemy's ability to react. Yet as the DAK advanced, not only did the British recognize that they had been outflanked, Gariboldi also realized that he had been outmanoeuvred. Both were caught in a trap and were furious at having been so elegantly duped. 'I took the risk against all orders and instructions because the opportunity seemed favourable,' Rommel wrote home on 3 August. 'The British are falling all over each other to get away. Our casualties are small. Booty cannot be estimated yet. You can understand why I can't sleep for happiness.'[116]

With the British in chaos, and sensing a rout, Rommel exploited his advantage and advanced towards the vital Allied port of Tobruk, causing a flurry of panic in London and Cairo. 'His headlong advance is almost enough to make one anxious,' wrote Goebbels in his diary on 15 April. 'But Rommel is not only bold; he is also thoughtful, and a stubborn Swabian into the bargain.'[117] Tobruk, however, was not going to be relinquished by the British without a struggle, and with its fortress defences strengthened rapidly by General Archibald Wavell, the British theatre commander, the scene was set for a monumental clash of arms. Having sent part of his force to create an entry point in the British defences on the Egyptian border in mid-April, Rommel's extended DAK (which was still being supplied from Tripoli) began besieging British and Australian troops at Tobruk.

This was just the sort of protracted, resource-heavy, set-piece battle that Rommel had always sought to avoid and to which he was ill suited in both temperament and method. The situation that

Gariboldi and the OKH had feared was now being played out: Rommel's overstretched and split force had become dangerously exposed due to his naked ambition and, moreover, Axis strategy had been hijacked by an operational commander. His career hanging on the outcome of the brash advance, Rommel knew that he had to inspire his troops to victory despite the harsh terrain, exacting climate and a well-set enemy. Fighting conditions were poor and resources were scant, but he reached into his experience of what could be achieved from the most unpromising situations. 'We are standing at the door of a great and important success,' he wrote in a general order in late April 1941. 'Your efforts will see us push it open and view the greater glories beyond.'[118] It was to be a long and hard spring of combat demanding great sacrifice, but this time the Afrika Korps became its own motivation, its members wanting to fight harder and longer for their comrades and for their commander. Rommel had become revered by his subordinates not just because they wanted to be associated with battlefield success, but because they felt close to their commander. As one DAK solider explained, 'Rommel was one of us, a German soldier with dust on his boots and dirt under his nails. He was the sort of general we all would have wanted to be. He was the type of general we wanted. He was *our* general.'[119]

Rommel had always been a demanding but considerate leader, but although this was no contrivance on his part he did give a carefully studied performance. He wanted to be seen sharing the discomforts of his men, eating soldiers' rations, wearing only issue clothing, and sleeping in the open (although Schraepler did successfully encourage Rommel to use a small Italian caravan to save him from the penetrating cold that caused him painful joint stiffness). The German press carried stories of his frugal living and, of course, how he could most often be found with his men in the front line, where he came under attack by enemy aircraft and patrols with alarming regularity. Such stories were frequently accompanied by heroic photographs of Rommel pointing out across the desert, or in the middle of giving orders into a radio transmitter, the goggles strapped to his general's cap coated in thick desert dust. Rommel understood the power an image could have and rarely let an opportunity pass by if he saw a camera being pointed in his direction. As aide Heinz Werner Schmidt later wrote, 'I noticed that he often deliberately fell into a pose that would make the photographer's task easier and more effective.'[120]

Having been conceived by Goebbels in early 1940, the 'Rommel Legend' was born in early 1941 and matured throughout that year. But what the majority of the DAK did not see, far less the German people, was the Erwin Rommel who by May had become frustrated by his failure to force the capitulation of Tobruk. His plans to invade Egypt were impossible due to the threat Tobruk would pose in his rear, and the battle that continued around its walls was taking up valuable resources and time. The situation caused Rommel's stubbornness, sharp temper and intolerance to surface, and they did him no credit and only exacerbated his chronic and debilitating stomach disorder. To some this was the real Erwin Rommel, beneath the gloss of his public persona – a bully who in the words of Harald Kuhn, a company commander in one of Rommel's panzer regiments, 'used his authority in an unfair, shameful manner [and] demoted responsible men who dared to raise their voices'.[121]

He could indeed be callous and quick to remove those who failed him, such as Colonel Walter Neumann-Silkow, the commander of the 5th Panzer Regiment, who refused an order to attack and was subsequently court-martialled. Yet Rommel could also be extremely generous, particularly to those who made mistakes while trying to act positively, and he was generally forgiving of those who failed trying. He had no tolerance, however, for subordinates who could not judge risk and reward, and thus admonished General Johannes Streich, the commander of the DAK's 5th Light Division, for being too willing to protect the lives of his men in the fulfilment of his missions. Streich is reported to have replied, 'Actually, greater praise could not be given to a divisional commander.'[122]

During the battle for Tobruk, when Rommel's usually consistent behaviour took a significant dip, Walther von Brauchitsch, Commander-in-Chief of the German Army, began to receive complaints about him from senior colleagues. In a message sent to Rommel, von Brauchitsch said that, while he understood the conditions 'required toughness in leadership', he asked him to reconsider whether the 'harsh criticism' of proven officers was necessary and suggested that an 'instructive conversation carried on in a fraternal spirit without any edge to it would be more likely to accomplish the aim'.[123] Streich was nonetheless sacked, and Rommel replied to von Brauchitsch that his former division was prospering under the 'intelligent and firm leadership of its new commander'.[124]

Rommel ignored the advice to withdraw from the Egyptian border offered by General Friedrich Paulus, the OKH chief of operations who had been sent to report back on the situation in North Africa; while in Berlin, General Franz Halder, the chief of the General Staff, wrote that Rommel 'storms around all day long with his formations strewn all over the place' and even referred to him as 'insane'.[125] The situation was tense, for with the invasion of the Soviet Union just weeks away, the Army's senior leadership had little option but to leave Rommel and the DAK to their fate. Nevertheless, Hitler showed his faith in Rommel's enterprise by promoting him to General der Panzertruppe and to the command of the new Panzer Group Afrika, which comprised the three-division DAK plus two Italian corps.

Rommel's hand had been strengthened, but the senior leadership of the Army remained exasperated by North Africa. The very idea of a new resource hungry offensive that would leach off their main effort in the East was so concerning that the OKH sent him a chief of staff with instructions to curb his ambitions and to send regular reports back to Berlin. As soon as Major General Alfred Gause arrived, Rommel was dubious about the loyalty of a man he needed to trust implicitly, but it was a tribute to the professionalism of both that before long they developed an unbreakable bond.[126] Indeed, Gause led the headquarters of Panzer Group Afrika so successfully that Rommel's ideas for an offensive were quickly translated into plans, and plans into action. But the British struck first.

On 18 November 1941, just days before Panzer Group Afrika was to launch its offensive, the new British theatre commander, Claude Auchinleck, unleashed Operation Crusader from Egypt. The aim was for Alan Cunningham's Eighth Army to retake Tobruk and push the Axis forces back into Libya. Although the surprise of a scything British XXX Corps advance across the desert towards Tobruk took place while immense pressure was delivered against the German force on the Egyptian border, the assurance of Rommel's response saw the enemy contained. Indeed, after a frenetic period of action, by 23 November he felt secure enough to inform Lucie: 'The battle seems to have passed its crisis. I'm very well, in good humour and full of confidence. Two hundred enemy tanks shot up so far. Our fronts have held.'[127]

The OKH demanded a phased withdrawal, but Rommel, sensing an opportunity with the enemy having wandered far from its lair, personally led the 15th and 21st Panzer Divisions towards the Egyptian border to cut XXX Corps' lines of communication. It was an outrageously imprudent move, and a mistake by Rommel – who overestimated the ability to sustain his own operations and underestimated the enemy's ability to break free of the Axis's loose noose. The Allies managed to relieve Tobruk on 28 November and Panzer Group Afrika then had to undertake the withdrawal that the OKH had ordered in the first place, and faced the ignominy of retracing their tracks over Cyrenaica while the British pursued them remorselessly. By Christmas Day, Rommel was back in El Agheila, the very place from where he had begun his offensive with the DAK nine months earlier.

With the withdrawal over, Auchinleck sought to reinforce the cushion he had created between the enemy and the Egyptian border, and Rommel ruminated on his options. The OKH had been content to put the North African campaign into suspended animation during the invasion of the Soviet Union, and was even more convinced that, with that campaign continuing into 1942 and the implications of the United States having entered the war in December, Libya needed to be held but nothing more. Rommel disagreed; he would badger for more resources, prepare a major offensive for the spring of 1942 and gain a great victory in North Africa before any strategic impediment restrained him.

George S. Patton Jr in Virginia Military Institution uniform, 1903.

Erwin Rommel as a cadet, Danzig, 1910.

Bernard Montgomery (2nd row, with ball), the captain of St Paul's School rugby 1st XV, 1906.

George Patton and Beatrice Ayer
wedding portrait, 1910.

Captain Bernard Montgomery
while serving as brigade major with
104th Brigade in early 1917.

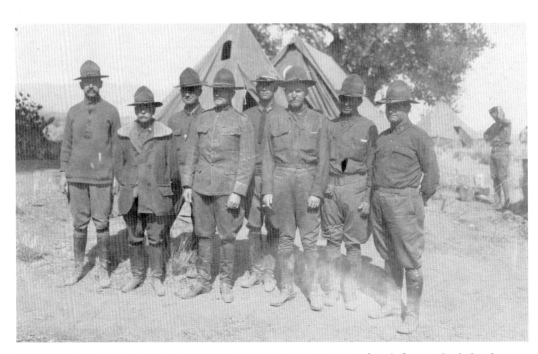

US field headquarters in Mexico, 1916. Lieutenant George Patton is fourth from right, behind
the left shoulder of General John J. Pershing.

Oberleutnant Erwin Rommel while on the Italian Front in 1917.

Lieutenant Colonel George Patton, commander of 1st Tank Brigade, posing before a French Renault FT light tank, summer 1918.

Lieutenant Colonel Bernard Montgomery while commanding officer of 1st Battalion, Royal Warwickshire Regiment, c.1931.

George Patton and General Billy Mitchell, the 'father of the US Air Force', at the Virginia fox hunt in Middleburg, c.1935.

Major General George Patton, proudly displaying his 2nd Armored Division's 'Hell On Wheels' insignia on his left breast, during the Louisiana Maneuvers in late summer 1941.

Adolf Hitler leads a review party of Major Erwin Rommel's Jäger Battalion at Goslar in late September 1934. Rommel wears a peaked cap at the rear of the group, keeping a close eye on his men.

A carefully composed photograph depicting a self-assured Major General Erwin Rommel in the market square of St Valéry, northern France, in June 1940, his 7th Panzer Division having just helped to surround over 40,000 British and French prisoners.

Lieutenant General Bernard Montgomery in North Africa, 1942. He is wearing his bush hat decorated with the badges of units serving under him, keen to develop a relationship with his regiments and to be regarded as a personality with his troops and the press.

Generalleutnant Erwin Rommel (right) inspecting his Afrika Korps troops with Italian Italo Garibaldi, Governor-General of Libya, March 1941.

General der Panzertruppe Rommel with the 15th Panzer Division between Tobruk and Sidi Omar, Libya, November 1941.

Lieutenant General Sir Bernard Montgomery posing in the Grant tank that he used as a prop when being photographed during the Battle of El Alamein, 5 November 1942. His preferred mode of transport on the battlefield was an Armoured Command Vehicle.

President Franklin D. Roosevelt with Major General George Patton, affixing the Congressional Medal of Honor upon Brigadier General William Wilbur in the presence of General George C. Marshall during the Casablanca Conference, January 1943.

Lieutenant General George Patton in North Africa, March 1943.

Hitler congratulates the 51-year-old ailing Rommel on the officer's promotion to field marshal in the Reich's Chancellery, Berlin, September 1943.

General Sir Bernard Montgomery examines a map of Sicily with Lieutenant General George Patton at the Royal Palace, Palermo, Sicily, 28 July 1943.

Three commanders meet to discuss the push on Messina: Major General Troy Middleton, commander of 45th Division, Lieutenant General Omar Bradley (centre), commander of II Corps, and Lieutenant General George Patton.

Generals Montgomery and Patton 'grin and grip' at Palermo airfield, 28 July 1943.

Montgomery meets with General Sir Harold Alexander, commander of 15th Army Group, at an advance airfield in Sicily, July 1943.

Rommel with his chief of staff, Fritz Bayerlein, in North Africa.

Lieutenant General Patton flanked by his chief of staff, Brigadier General Hobart R. Gay (on left) and deputy chief of staff Brigadier General Paul D. Harkins in Germany, March 1945.

Montgomery's loyal and hard-working chief of staff, Brigadier General Sir Francis de Guingand, outside his boss's caravan in Tripoli, Libya, January 1943.

Having returned from the Italian front a few weeks' earlier, General Sir Bernard Montgomery joined fellow Allied commanders in London for a planning conference on 2 January 1944. L–R front: Air Chief Marshal Arthur Tedder, General Dwight D. Eisenhower, Montgomery; L–R back: Lieutenant General Omar Bradley, Admiral Sir Bertram Ramsay, Air Chief Marshal Sir Trafford Leigh-Mallory, Lieutenant General W. Bedell Smith.

Generalfeldmarschall Rommel and officers inspecting beach defences in Normandy, France, April 1944.

Rommel inspecting German 21st Panzer Division, Normandy, 30 May 1944.

Montgomery speaking to Allied correspondents at his Tac HQ in Normandy, 11 June 1944.

Montgomery playing with his two puppies, 'Hitler' and 'Rommel', at his Tac HQ in Blay, Normandy, 6 July 1944.

King George VI inspects US Fifth Army troops with their commander, Lieutenant General Mark Clark, in Italy, July 1944.

Montgomery and Patton share a joke in Normandy on 7 July 1944. Omar Bradley looks on.

Patton and Bradley flank Eisenhower in Bastogne, late December 1944, soon after its relief.

Among the 'dragon's teeth' of the Siegfried Line near Aachen, Germany, 30 March 1945. L–R: Field Marshal Sir Alan Brooke, Montgomery, Prime Minister Winston Churchill, US General William H. Simpson.

Portrait of Generaloberst Erwin Rommel taken on 6 June 1942, Knight's Cross and Pour le Mérite hanging around his neck.

Rommel with his family at home in Herrlingen on 5 June 1944, the day before his wife's 50th birthday. L–R: Manfred Rommel, Lucie Rommel, Erwin Rommel, family friend Hildegard Kirchen and Lucie's sister, Helene.

State funeral of Generalfeldmarschall Erwin Rommel in Ulm, 18 October 1944.

Churchill, Montgomery and Alan Brooke take lunch on the banks of the Rhine, 26 March 1945, shortly after the river had been crossed by 21st Army Group in Operation Plunder.

Montgomery and Prince Bernhardt of the Netherlands (on left of group) inspect the Arab stallion previously owned by Rommel, 2 August 1945.

Montgomery with President Harry S. Truman on a visit to the White House, 11 September 1946.

CHAPTER SEVEN

Three in North Africa, 1942–43

E RWIN ROMMEL'S REPUTATION had been dealt a significant blow at the end of 1941. The Axis withdrawal across Cyrenaica proved a humiliation to Berlin, the commander of Panzer Group Afrika and the men he led. Nevertheless, the possibility of redemption was never far from Rommel's mind, and he was convinced that it would come by manoeuvring through the Western Desert, crossing the Egyptian border and advancing to the Suez Canal. The first step towards the fulfilment of such a grandiose aim was for the newly promoted Colonel General Erwin Rommel (at fifty, the youngest Wehrmacht officer in the rank) to exploit the vulnerabilities of an overstretched British Eighth Army with a limited attack from El Agheila.

The ever-insistent Rommel demanded a huge effort from his subordinates to prepare for the operation before the enemy regained its poise. 'Rommel was not an easy man to serve,' said Friedrich von Mellenthin, a one-time Afrika Korps staff officer who later rose to become a general himself. 'He spared those around him as little as he spared himself. An iron constitution and nerves of steel were needed to work with Rommel, but I must emphasise that… once he was convinced of the efficiency and loyalty of those in his immediate entourage, he never had a harsh word for them.'[1]

The Axis attack began on 21 January 1942, and General Neil Ritchie's Eighth Army was undone by the guile and unremitting violence with which Panzer Group Afrika went about its business. 'I wonder what you have to say about the counter-attack we started at 08.30 yesterday?' Rommel wrote to Lucie. 'Our opponents are getting out as though they'd been stung. Prospects are good for the next few days.'[2] By the last week of January, by which time Rommel's formation had been redesignated 'Panzer Army Afrika', Ritchie's formations were stumbling back across Libya, amazed that their enemy could regenerate such fighting power so quickly, but after Benghazi had fallen to him on 29 January, Rommel had little option but to suspend his attack. Without further preparation his force would soon run out of vital supplies, and so with the British digging in at Gazala, plans were made to restart the offensive in the spring after a renewed effort to secure the necessary resources.

Rommel was once again the pride of the Goebbels propaganda machine at a time when the Germany military had little to boast about, and he was awarded the highly prestigious Knight's Cross of the Iron Cross with Oak Leaves and Swords for his latest achievement. 'Rommel continues to be the pronounced favourite even of the enemy news service,' Goebbels wrote in his diary. 'He has succeeded in becoming a real phantom general.'[3] Winston Churchill, keen to create the impression that the recent setback in Libya had not been caused by just any general, contributed to the growing aura surrounding Rommel by calling him an 'extraordinary bold and clever opponent, a great field commander'.[4] The British press reacted by providing various insights into the Eighth Army's charismatic nemesis; *The Times* published a lead article about the German general and the *Observer* a biographical sketch, although most newspapers merely offered a few superlatives about his command and leadership abilities.

Such was the laudatory coverage being given to Rommel that Claude Auchinleck, the British commander in the Middle East, felt compelled to issue a circular to his commanders which insisted: 'I require you all to use all available means to get rid of the perception once and for all that Rommel represents something more than a normal general… The main issue is to ensure that Rommel is not always referred to when we mean the enemy.'[5] Yet there was a pathetic futility in any ambition to diminish Rommel's reputation by order, and the attempt to do so, Churchill felt, was the unhelpful symptom of a despondency that Auchinleck was propagating.

Rommel chuckled when he learned that he was the focus of so much attention, but was quietly delighted, saying, 'I seem to have come from nowhere and made quite a stir!'[6] He was particularly pleased that articles focused on his work ethic, which by the spring of 1942 had not diminished despite the chronic discomfort that he was suffering due to his still-undiagnosed stomach condition. Colleagues sought to decrease his burden, but he almost always refused such assistance. On 6 April, for example, while plans were developing for Panzer Army Afrika's renewed offensive, Rommel struck out into the desert having been informed that the British could be on the verge of delivering an attack of their own. Accompanied by a single tank, the general was in the midst of conducting his personal assessment when his small party came under long-range enemy shellfire. One round landed so close to his car that he was peppered with shell fragments, and one large splinter ripped through his coat and jacket. 'All it left was a multi-coloured bruise the size of a plate,' he wrote to Lucie. 'It was finally stopped by my trousers. The luck of the devil!'[7]

He had seen no evidence of any enemy movement on his reconnaissance, largely because the British remained incapable of striking back. Even as spring matured, the Eighth Army focused more on the preparation of its defences (to Churchill's astonishment) rather than launching a weak spoiling attack to wrong-foot the enemy's own preparations. The Axis offensive was finally reignited on 26 May, and with such power that one Eighth Army unit reported, 'Enemy tank columns moving towards us. It looks as if it's the whole damned Afrika Korps!' followed by two words that were designed to underline the urgency of the situation: 'Rommel leading!'[8]

Although the image of the general leading this armoured advance in person is fanciful, there were nevertheless times when Rommel could not help himself and became immersed in tactical affairs. On 28 May 1942, with the simple order 'Follow me!' he personally led panzer division supply columns along a route he had scouted from the air. His desire to create an agile organization that could react quickly to his will and enemy initiatives stood in stark contrast to the plodding centralized command that continued to dominate the British Army and was central to the Eighth Army's defeat at Gazala – which, by 15 June, had sent it scuttling back into Egypt. 'The battle has been won and the enemy is breaking up,' Rommel wrote to his wife about what became known as the 'Gazala Gallop'. 'I needn't tell you how delighted I am.'[9]

Panzer Army Afrika surged on, and although drained after three weeks of fighting, proceeded to force the surrender of the 32,000-man Tobruk garrison on midsummer's day. It was a totemic prize that shocked London, but so delighted Hitler that he promoted Rommel to the rank of general field marshal. The issue of having enough resources to sustain a further attack east into Egypt had yet to be resolved, but with the border so close Rommel did not vacillate and announced to his troops in a written message: 'Soldiers of the Panzerarmee Afrika! Now for the complete destruction of the enemy. We will not rest until we have shattered the last remnants of the British Eighth Army. During the days to come, I shall call on you for one more great effort to bring us to this final goal. ROMMEL.'[10]

The relentlessness of the German offensive at the height of summer stunned the British, but having swept across the border at the end of June and seized the coastal town of Mersa Matruh, the Panzer Army Afrika was then held back by the fortifications at El Alamein, a narrow bottleneck of good ground between the coast and the Qattara Depression. A concerted effort to force the position in July was resisted by the Eighth Army – since the previous month, personally commanded by Auchinleck – with Rommel later admitting: '[I had] brought the strength of my Army to the point of exhaustion.'[11] Indeed, in a personal manifestation of the fatigue that gripped Panzer Army Afrika, the general then fell ill when his painful stomach complaint returned. Forced to admit that on the cusp of a major victory his formation needed time to rest, regroup and be resupplied, he was nevertheless concerned that he had not been able to reach the Suez Canal in one extended operation – and, with the British still in Cairo, that his opportunity to create a surprise strategic victory in 1942 had been lost. He hoped to take to the offensive again within a couple of months, but much depended on the ongoing struggle to convince Berlin to assign him even a fraction of the resources that he required, and on the British remaining on the defensive.

In the weeks that followed, Rommel argued his cause tirelessly, but with the campaign in the East now into its second year and on an expanding front without any sign that the Soviets would soon collapse, his persistence merely angered the Oberkommando der Wehrmacht (OKW), the German armed forces high command. What is more, he learned in August that the Eighth Army had appointed another new commander, Bernard Montgomery, and that Monty's efforts to harden the formation's resolve had met with some immediate success. Concerned by the development and the likely corollary that Montgomery had been brought in to lead a new offensive, Rommel resolved to strike again himself at the end of August. His aim was to exploit a weak spot that had been noted in the enemy's defences in the southern sector and then, turning north, strike out towards the Alam el Halfa ridge to create an envelopment of the Eighth Army. Just before the battle began at nightfall on 30 August, commanders read a message from Rommel to the men of Panzer Army Afrika: 'Today our Army sets out once more to attack and destroy the enemy, this time for keeps. I expect every soldier in my army to do his utmost in these decisive days!'[12]

The British, however, had the advantage from the start, for Montgomery had access to a weapon that provided him with information not only about where and when the Panzer Army's offensive was going to be launched, but in what strength and the objectives it sought. The Ultra signals intelligence, obtained from having broken high-level encrypted enemy communications, allowed the British to prepare for Rommel's offensive in a way that was unthinkable without such detailed information, and this allowed Montgomery to draw his enemy into a trap.[13] Panzer Army Afrika lived to fight another day, but by 5 September it had suffered a defeat that marked a watershed moment in the North African campaign, for in Rommel's own words, 'With the failure of this offensive our last chance of gaining the Suez Canal had gone.'[14]

There was little that Panzer Army Afrika could now do but prepare itself for an Eighth Army onslaught in the autumn, and knowing what a demanding experience that would be, Rommel oversaw the development of a defensive plan. By the end of summer 1942 his monumental efforts to retake Cyrenaica from the British and push its Eighth Army across the Egyptian border had been completed, but at significant costs to its architect's health. On 23 September, Rommel returned to Germany to rest. The general was fatigued, his stomach complaint had flared up again and, suffering from a panoply of other ailments promoted by eighteen months of strain in the desert, he was advised to rest. He intended to return to the front well before any British attack, leaving his deputy, General Georg Stumme, to provide him with regular updates and, in the worst-case scenario, to contact him immediately if the British attacked before he was back in command.

Before returning to his family home, however, he made a stopover in Berlin to provide a situation report to Hitler, argue for more resources, receive his field marshal's baton, and give a speech. Still not fifty-one years old, he was the youngest field marshal in the Wehrmacht and remained 'the Führer's General', a fact that Goebbels sought to exploit at an international press conference before the Third Reich's senior leaders and thousands of their carefully selected followers at the Berlin Sportpalast, a cavernous indoor arena used by the Nazis for grand speeches and rallies. Rommel, it was hoped, would rouse all those listening in the hall as well as the millions tuning in around the country on the wireless sets.

Following an animated but distinctly tedious speech by Hitler, Rommel took the stage. His tanned face looked tired, but as soon as he began to speak his audience recognized that the man needed no histrionics to make his points – for although his cool, calm words were simply spoken, they were delivered with a beguiling authority. He talked about his approach to leadership and explained that every leader should be at the right place at the right time, to make the difficult decisions that could change the outcome of events. If, as a military leader, that meant placing oneself in personal danger to be influential, then so be it, because 'duty', as Rommel explained, 'demands self-sacrifice'. His words prompted much head-nodding from Nazi Party officials, who looked out over the 14,000-strong audience and found them enthralled. 'Today we stand 100 kilometres from Alexandria and Cairo, and have the gates of Egypt in hand, and with the intent to act!' Rommel announced. Cheers immediately reverberated around the auditorium, for few who heard the field marshal's words that day had any reason to believed that he would not be victorious.[15]

When Rommel finally returned to Lucie and Manfred, both could see his exertions etched in the deep lines that had appeared on his bronzed face and were deeply concerned for his well-being.[16] Yet although doctors had insisted that the field marshal rest and reduce stress, he was unable to remove himself completely from his weighty responsibilities and was often on the telephone or to be found absorbed in piles of military papers. 'With one part of me I rejoice at the prospect of getting out of here and seeing both of you again,' Rommel had written to Lucie from North Africa just before his departure. 'With another part of me I dread the difficulties of this campaign if I can't be here myself.'[17]

He continued to work, sometimes for several hours a day, and therefore his medical progress was not as rapid as his doctors had hoped, and he was still nowhere near full health when the telephone rang on the morning of 24 October: the British were attacking at El Alamein, he was told – a thousand guns of the British artillery had been pummelling their positions, infantry were swarming forward to clear a path for their tanks, and General Stumme, who was later found dead from a heart attack having come under fire during a visit to the front, was initially reported as missing. Leaving for the front the next day, Rommel found his acute stomach pains returning even before he landed in Egypt, and by the time he arrived at his headquarters for a briefing he was in considerable discomfort. His first instruction was for a signal to be sent to all units and, therefore, unknowingly to the British: 'I have taken command of the army again. Rommel.'[18]

To many, the field marshal's return was a great stimulus, and not just because of his military abilities but because the troops felt confident that this 'soldier's soldier' would not let them down. 'I remember the sense of relief when we heard that Rommel was back with us,' Captain Horst Wack later said. 'We felt that he gave us an advantage just by his presence.'[19] What this meant in practice was Rommel's utter determination not to allow El Alamein to be the graveyard of his Panzer Army. While doing all he could to fight Montgomery to a standstill and break the Eighth Army's will, he would withdraw if necessary rather than indulge in futile gestures of defiance. Before then, he sought stoicism from his formations in the face of the Eighth Army's grinding operations, which continued unremittingly day and night. Before the first week was over, Rommel wrote to Lucie: 'At night I lie with my eyes wide open unable to sleep, for the load that is on my shoulders. In the day I'm dead tired.'[20]

Some of that load was self-inflicted, because even though he remained weakened through illness, his style demanded that Rommel give himself entirely to leading, and he relied on others far less than he should have. On 31 October, therefore, having received intelligence that British tanks had reached the coast road, the field marshal drove immediately to the location to personally organize a counter-attack. Whether his presence was essential or not is a moot point, but it is invidious to criticize Rommel for leading as he always had. Indeed, he had been rewarded for the past success of such behaviour, and the field marshal felt compelled to 'see and feel' a situation rather than basing his decisions on 'falsehoods, half-truths and assumptions'.[21] He did not need to be at the front, however, to be convinced by reports received by his headquarters on 1 November that the Axis line was cracking, and by nightfall the following day the complicated process of saving his formation had begun.

It was a considerable act of moral courage on Rommel's part for he issued the withdrawal order without authorization from the OKW, which was subsequently furious at what it regarded as an act of insubordination. Hitler signalled immediately: 'In the situation in which you find yourself there can be no other thought but to stand fast and throw every gun and every man into battle... As to your troops, you can show them no other road than that to victory or death.'[22] With a direct order from the Führer not to cede ground, Rommel was immediately placed in a more difficult position, but although he initially reversed his withdrawal order – 'The Führer must be a complete lunatic,' he was heard to say[23] – he reissued it on the afternoon of 4 November. It was a fait accompli – a challenge to which the OKW could have responded by sacking the errant field marshal – but, it seemed, Rommel still had enough credit with Hitler not to suffer that fate. And, in any case, nobody else was as qualified as the current commander to lead Panzer Army Afrika in their present predicament.

There followed weeks of pursuit of Panzer Army Afrika by the Eighth Army, with Rommel leading his staff and commanders in the complex task of facilitating a phased withdrawal so that none of the force was overrun. Tobruk was evacuated on 12 November, followed soon after by Gazala, Derna and Benghazi – the Axis forces under great pressure from Montgomery's mobile units and close support aircraft. Rommel wrote to Lucie on 13 November, 'The end will not be long for we're being simply crushed by the enemy superiority,'[24] but although this was a tortuously demanding period requiring a supreme effort to retain order and discipline, Panzer Army Afrika continued to survive. The strategic situation, however, remained dire – for even while Rommel's force was shunted out of Cyrenaica, Anglo-American landings further west along the North African coast had created bridgeheads in both Morocco and Algeria, and the Allied forces were beginning to turn east. As such, the jaws of an Allied vice were closing on the Axis forces and attempting to crush them in Tunisia.

'We had lost the decisive battle of the African campaign,' Rommel later wrote, blaming Berlin's lack of support for his endeavours.[25] However, many senior officers in Berlin believed the field marshal's naked ambition had caused the situation – and then, moreover, provided the Allies with an opportunity to compound his mistakes. The question facing the OKW at the end of 1942, therefore, was whether to prepare to evacuate all Axis forces from North Africa, or to reinforce them with resources that were also desperately required on the Eastern Front.

While this significant strategic dilemma was considered, Panzer Army Afrika merely sought to survive, and was perhaps the greatest leadership challenge of Rommel's career in what one soldier described as 'a living hell of improvisation'.[26] Not until late November, when the Panzer Army reached the relatively secure position at El Agheila – the place from which it had begun its great offensive towards Egypt at the beginning of the year – did Rommel order a brief operational pause so that his force could rest and reorganize before continuing its withdrawal. The OKW, however, was pressing for him not to undertake a temporary halt, but to make a stand. The situation was 'an horrendous strategic mess',[27] and with the Eighth Army just to the east at Mersa Brega and keen to attend to its own logistic frailties before pressing on, Rommel knew that this was the only opportunity he would get to attempt to convince Hitler to see that there was only one logical military solution to the North African problem: to evacuate the Axis forces from the theatre.

Travelling to the Führer's Rastenburg headquarters in East Prussia after a series of arguments not only with the OKW but also with Field Marshal Albert Kesselring (the Commander-in-Chief of the

Southern Theatre) and the Italian senior leadership, who feared that an evacuation would lead to an Allied invasion of their homeland, the mood was tense. To make matters worse, the situation on the Eastern Front was precarious, with the summer offensive having failed and the German Sixth Army in the midst of being surrounded at Stalingrad.

Rommel found Hitler in an agitated state. Unresponsive to logical argument, he raged at the field marshal about his withdrawal order at El Alamein, the inability of Panzer Army Afrika to do anything but fall back, and how the officer's actions had caused a strategic emergency. Heinz Linge, Hitler's orderly, wrote that Rommel's demeanour was like that of a 'drowned poodle',[28] and although Hitler did offer a mumbled apology shortly after, the field marshal knew exactly where he stood. The campaign in North Africa would continue with General Hans-Jürgen von Arnim's Fifth Panzer Army being fed through the port of Tunis to hold northern Tunisia – with Hitler even holding on to the hope that a major Axis counter-attack would force the Allies back. The Führer, it seemed to Rommel, was more willing to find resources to reinforce defeat than properly prepare for the enemy's next strategic move.

Rommel returned to Libya on 2 December a chastened and disappointed man, but he had won an agreement that his force could withdraw 250 miles west to Buerat, further shortening his lines of supply and offering better protection against an outflanking movement by the Eighth Army. Here Montgomery was held from the last days of December 1942 to mid-January 1943, before Rommel's divisions were forced to withdraw as far back as the defensive positions at Mareth, across the Tunisian border, in early February. 'I simply can't tell you how hard it is for me to undergo this retreat and all that goes with it,' Rommel wrote to his wife. 'Day and night I'm tormented by the thought that things might go really wrong here in Africa. I'm so depressed that I can hardly do my work... I shall hold on here as long as I can.'[29] The extra troops and hardware that he had been promised by the OKW to replace some of his losses had still not arrived, and with the Eighth Army applying unremitting pressure from the east and the Anglo-American forces crossing the Tunisian border from the west and threatening his lines of communication, Rommel could only see disaster looming.

In reaction, the field marshal split his force, and having left the Italian portion of Panzer Army Afrika to man the Mareth defences, he personally led a DAK assault group north to attack the threat developing to his rear, where US II Corps was looking to push through to the coast. In a throwback to his time in France nearly three years earlier, he rode with an armoured division, this time the 10th Panzer Division (whose head of operations was Lieutenant Colonel Claus von Stauffenberg), a return to the sort of combat leadership he enjoyed most. One of his aides, Captain Alfred-Ingemar Berndt, subsequently wrote to Lucie of Rommel: 'It was wonderful to see the joy of his troops during the last few days, as he drove along their columns. And when, in the middle of the attack, he appeared among [the 10th Panzer Division] right up with the leading infantry scouts in front of the tank spearheads, and lay in the mud among the men under artillery fire in his old way, how their eyes lit up. What other commander has such a wealth of trust to draw upon.'[30]

The DAK counter-attack was a success, and the first major engagement between Axis and American forces in North Africa ended with Lloyd Fredendall's US II Corps not only stopped, but being pushed back fifty miles through the Kasserine Pass and out the other side. It was also to be Rommel's last victory of the campaign, and one that was to see Fredendall replaced by George S. Patton at the helm of the battered corps. Although on 23 February the cantankerous German officer was made commander of the new Army Group Afrika, which unified all ground forces in Tunisia under him, just two weeks later Hitler recalled Rommel to Germany to 'improve his health'.[31] The field marshal was never to return to the theatre where he had cemented his reputation as an outstanding commander. And his professional future had never been more uncertain.

Rommel's relationship with Hitler had cooled over the winter of 1942–43, and with the strategic situation in North Africa looking doomed to end in an Axis disaster, there remained a problem about what to do with the famous field marshal. Some in the OKW wanted him sent to the Eastern Front, a leveller for any commander, but as Goebbels noted, a 'military authority such as Rommel cannot be created at will and again disposed of at will'.[32] What would become of him, however, was barely discussed during the short spell he spent with Hitler at the 'Werwolf' headquarters in central Ukraine before returning to Germany. The unpalatable news from all fronts made for a strained atmosphere in the claustrophobic complex of bunkers, but there was eventually an attempt at a form of reconciliation by Hitler, who paid Rommel various compliments and decorated him with the highest order of the Iron Cross, the very rare Knight's Cross with Oak Leaves, Swords and Diamonds.

Even so, nothing that Hitler said made Rommel feel confident that he was being considered for another command appointment, and back in Germany he became convinced that his most productive days of the war were in the past. Initially admitted to hospital for a battery of tests and treatments, he then returned home to recuperate. A poor patient who could not abide being idle despite his doctors' demands that only complete rest would alleviate his symptoms, he used much of his time writing a highly subjective account of the North African campaign. The memory of certain episodes did little to reduce the stress that he was meant to avoid, but his medically enforced exile did settle his symptoms while also giving Hitler time in which to plan the rehabilitation of an officer – and a man – for whom he still had high regard. Thus, in mid-May 1943, shortly after the Axis surrender in Tunisia from which he had been cleverly disassociated, it was announced to the German people that Rommel had spent the last two months in convalescence and, shortly after, that he had a temporary appointment as the Führer's 'resident field marshal', advising on military matters in his headquarters. Being at Hitler's side once again was indeed a privileged position, and one that his critics among senior officers and party officials disliked due to the influence he might have, but it gave Rommel hope for the first time in many months that he could still make a valuable contribution to Germany's perilous military situation.

While Rommel was acting as Hitler's military consultant in mid-1943, he was also tasked with planning the defence of Italy against an Allied invasion which, as Mussolini had long feared, was regarded as an inevitable consequence of defeat in North Africa. The Allies were expected to invade Sicily first before then crossing to the mainland, and it was the field marshal's job, supported by a small staff based in the barracks at Berchtesgaden in the Bavarian Alps (near Hitler's 'Berghof' home), to make their task as difficult as possible. There was little that they could do to keep Sicily from falling to the Allies, but they could make it a slog for the attackers, thus creating time for the development of defensive lines across central Italy under Kesselring's supervision.

Rommel also anticipated the possibility of an Italian capitulation as plots against Mussolini developed. Having enjoyed an unusual degree of independence in combat for so long, he was now challenged by needing to consult, co-operate and compromise more than at any time since his promotion to general nearly four years earlier. 'Rommel sat at the head of a long shining table, his face impassive as he listened to the senior officers arguing over one thing or another', Captain Lothar Homan wrote of a meeting he attended in June 1943, 'and when he had heard enough said, "Gentleman, I thank you for your contribution, but I have decided…" and gave his decision. He listened but was keen to move on. I have to admit to being aware that the more junior attendees seemed more than a little terrified by him.'[33]

Routine business was always dealt with by Rommel in an abrupt manner, but he spent more time deliberating complex operational issues that were placed before what Homan called 'Rommel's inner sanctum', comprising trusted personnel and subject experts. With this group the field marshal encouraged unfettered and honest discussion that would inform his decision-making. He knew that it was important work, but those closest to Rommel understood that he found it unrewarding even if it was a test that he had to pass if he were ever to be given command again.

The Allied invasion of Sicily in early July 1943, together with the pivotal German defeat on the Eastern Front at Kursk the same month, deepened Germany's strategic woes. A malaise that had engulfed the senior officers since the fall of Stalingrad in February now deepened, with only the most fanatical, optimistic or inept believing that the situation could be recovered by either the application of Hitler's strategic 'genius' or greater effort by the armed forces. Such men did exist in the Führer's headquarters, and so when Rommel was asked on a visit to Rastenburg why he was there, he replied, 'I am here for a sunray cure. I am soaking up the sun and faith!'[34] Having always had little time for naysayers and those who seemed to luxuriate in a negative mindset, it seems Rommel fell under Hitler's spell again during the summer of 1943, despite personal evidence of the man's fallibility. 'The extraordinary strength which the Führer exudes,' he wrote to Lucie in August, 'his unflustered confidence, the foresighted assessment of the situation… have made it very plain in these days that we are all poor souls in comparison to the Führer.'[35]

The reward for his loyalty was command of Army Group B, the formation based in northern Italy. After the overthrow of Mussolini on 25 July by his own Grand Council, and his subsequent arrest by Italian authorities, Rommel's Army Group B was formally tasked with disarming the Italians just as soon as the government capitulated. Taking up his position on 16 August at his headquarters on Lake Garda, he co-ordinated his activity closely with the ever-optimistic Kesselring, who was busy to the south constructing bands of defences across the country, from the Mediterranean coast to the Adriatic, while refuting the very notion that the Italians would surrender. What soon became clear to Rommel was that Kesselring's own firm ideas about how Italy should be defended differed from his own. While the commander of Army Group B was convinced that southern Italy should be forsaken and all assets concentrated in the north of the country to create an immovable blocking force that could not be outflanked, Kesselring was equally sure that his defences could hold the Allies until at least the spring of 1944, thus enabling the retention of Rome and keeping Allied airfields at an advantageous distance from the Reich. The victor of this strategic disagreement would logically become the commander of all troops in Italy to ensure unity of purpose, but although initially confident that he would be awarded the role, Rommel was shocked to find that Hitler was being swayed by Kesselring's confidence.

Having successfully taken Sicily in concert with Patton's US Seventh Army, the invasion of the Italian mainland by Montgomery's British Eighth Army at Reggio di Calabria on 3 September was not a surprise to the German leadership; however, Italy's surrender just a few days later had been less widely anticipated. Thus, as British forces swarmed over the 'toe and heel' of southern Italy and Mark Clark's US Fifth Army arrived in the Bay of Salerno near Naples on 9 September (Patton's command having been mothballed), Rommel's eight-division Army Group B sought to disarm the Italian armed forces. With few formations in the south to stall the two Allied incursions – although Clark's force was initially checked before it was established – Rommel and Kesselring could ultimately do little but watch as the enemy armies linked up, the Fifth Army on the left and the Eighth Army on the right (Montgomery writing in his diary about Rommel, 'I look forward to taking on my old opponent again'[36]), and began their advance north towards the German defensive lines. They attained some impressive forward momentum during the early weeks of fine, dry weather, but when the autumn rains began the terrain became more challenging and General Heinrich von Vietinghoff's Tenth Army managed to slow their progress.

When the Allies began to flounder in the first lines of Kesselring's impressive defensive system in late September, Hitler made his strategic decision: southern Italy *would* be held. It was a blow to Rommel, but one he anticipated, for he knew all about Hitler's disdain for withdrawal and it became increasingly clear that any decision about the defence of Italy would come too late for anything other than the adoption of Kesselring's plan. German troops would, therefore, defend the rivers and mountains south of the Italian capital and withstand the Allies' onslaught for as long as they could. How long depended on more variables than the Army Group B staff could accurately predict, for with the Soviets producing a series of powerful offensives in the East and the prospect of the Western Allies launching a cross-Channel invasion by late spring 1944, the situation in Italy was merely one factor in Germany's rapidly evolving strategic catastrophe.

On 21 November, Kesselring's successful efforts to slow the Allied attack were rewarded by Hitler with his appointment as commander of all German forces in Italy and the title Commander-in-Chief Southwest. 'Events have proved Rommel wrong', Hitler remarked to colleagues after a slew of gloomy reports from the commander of Army Group B, 'and I have been justified in my decision to leave Field Marshal Kesselring there, whom I have seen as an incredible political idealist, but also as a military optimist, and it is my opinion that military leadership without optimism is not possible.'[37] Rommel's military judgement had been questioned and found to be wanting, but not so disastrously that he was left to stagnate in northern Italy while important work needed to be done elsewhere. Indeed, two weeks earlier, Rommel had been appointed General Inspector of the Western Defences, with the headquarters of Army Group B to assist him. His job was to examine Germany's Atlantic invasion defences (stretching 1,700 miles from the North Sea coast in Denmark, along the English Channel and down France's Atlantic coast to Spain) and to make recommendations for their improvement. It was a monumental task confirmed by a dossier which highlighted massive gaps in the defences, unfinished construction, and a front manned by poorly motivated troops lacking leadership and vital resources. The invasion, Rommel was told, would most likely occur during the period from late April to early June 1944. Thus, with barely five months available before the Allied storm was predicted to break, Rommel set to work.

— □ —

By January 1942 the 100,000-man-strong South Eastern Command was feeling the full force of Bernard Montgomery's positive energy as its commander. Speaking with a Canadian Corps officer during a study week in early January, he said, 'Our worst enemy is "defensive mentality". We have got to develop the offensive spirit in our officers and men' – and excellent leadership, he argued, was the answer.[38] Throughout the long, cold winter of 1941–42, Montgomery stalked unit training sessions to assess troop motivation – or, as he put it, 'to see if they had the light of battle in their eyes'.[39] Then, in the spring, he used division and corps exercises to review the extent to which that training had contributed to formation fighting capabilities, and demanded improvement where he identified weakness. The process culminated in a twelve-day Exercise 'Tiger' in May 1942, which concluded with a conference held in the Tonbridge Odeon Cinema for his 2,000 officers.

Brian Horrocks, the commander of the 44th (Home Counties) Infantry Division, later described Monty's hold over his audience as he gave his verdict that day and elucidated on the lessons he had drawn from the event:

> 'Sit down, gentlemen,' he would say in a sharp, nasal voice. 'Thirty seconds for coughing – then no more coughing at all.' And the curious thing was that we didn't cough.
>
> Then, perhaps for as long as two hours, he would keep us spellbound as he described all the salient points of the exercise. I have held many similar conferences myself and have always tried to follow the Monty technique, though… I could never hope to acquire Monty's power of mass hypnosis.[40]

Although Montgomery was not a great orator, audiences listened to him because, as one junior officer described it, 'he oozed professionalism and calm control'.[41] Indeed, Major General Dwight Eisenhower – soon to become commander of the US Army's European Theater of Operations – was so impressed with what he saw of Monty during an exercise that he noted in his diary: 'General Montgomery is a very able, dynamic type of army commander. I personally think that the only thing he needs is a strong immediate commander. He loves the limelight; but in seeking it, it is possible that he does so only because of the effect upon his own soldiers, who are certainly devoted to him. I have great confidence in him as a combat commander. He is intelligent, a good talker, and has a flare for showmanship.'[42]

Eisenhower was not the only man of influence that Montgomery had impressed, for having already been identified as a future combat commander by Alan Brooke, he was being associated with an appointment in North Africa by the summer of 1942. The theatre needed a dynamic presence, and Monty was the obvious choice if the decision was to make a change of leader.

Winston Churchill later referred to 'a long succession of military misfortunes and defeats'[43] when describing British setbacks in North Africa in 1942, and at the time he was anxious about the threat they posed to Egypt, the Suez Canal and, therefore, British access to her eastern Empire. Claude Auchinleck, the Commander-in-Chief, Middle East who had taken personal command of the British and Commonwealth troops that comprised the Eighth Army in late June, when it withdrew back to El Alamein (the last defensive position before Cairo), was capable, but deemed by Churchill and Brooke to be poorly suited to the task of reversing the situation. In a flurry of appointment changes that coincided with Axis encroachment onto Egyptian soil, General Sir Harold Alexander replaced Auchinleck as theatre commander (with Monty eventually becoming Commander-in Chief of the Indian Army), and on 15 August, Montgomery was appointed to lead Eighth Army,[44] the formation's fourth commander in twelve months. He was greeted in the desert by the commander of the 2nd New Zealand Division, Bernard Freyberg, with a question: 'Africa is the graveyard of generals. How long do you think you will last?'[45] Monty's answer is not known, but on his flight from England he had committed to paper for the first time his 'command philosophy', which he believed would be the foundation for success.

He later explained that the philosophy could be summarized in a single word: 'leadership'.[46] In applying it, Monty would first tour his new domain to evaluate his formations and their commanders, then make the requisite changes, before finally winning the hearts and minds of his subordinates. It was an approach that had worked well for him in the past, and now, as he was to later reflect, 'The work and experience of many years were about to be put to the test.'[47]

Within days of his arrival in Egypt, Montgomery had begun to surround himself with a trusted team. One of the first he brought in was Freddie de Guingand as his chief of staff. He wanted de Guingand because, as he later explained: 'I [needed] someone to help me, a man with a quick and clear brain, who would accept responsibility, and who would work out the details and leave me free to concentrate on the major issues – in fact, a Chief of Staff who could handle all the details and intricate staff side of the business and leave me free to command.'[48] De Guingand would lead the Eighth Army staff while acting as the commander's advisor, confidant and deputy. He and Monty quickly rekindled their excellent working relationship, and it was clear that de Guingand's personality and skills complemented his own.[49]

His chief of staff's frank report about the state of the headquarters prompted Montgomery to move it from an oppressive and fly-infested inland location to a far more comfortable site by the sea, which had the impact of immediately improving morale and the HQ's effectiveness.[50] Although leaving de Guingand to take responsibility for the daily running of the headquarters, Montgomery made a point of getting to know each man in the headquarters team well and committed himself to the same with his sixty most senior officers. He introduced himself to them on 13 August and said that old contingencies to fall back had been cancelled and would be replaced by plans for an offensive to push the Axis forces out of North Africa. 'Together we will gain the confidence of this great Army and go forward to final victory in Africa,' he said to his engrossed audience. 'Let us have a new atmosphere... We will stand and fight *here*. If we can't stay here alive, then let us stay here dead. I want to impress on everyone that the bad times are over... I ask you to give me your confidence and to have faith that what I have said will come to pass. There is much work to be done... The great point to remember is that we are going to finish with this chap Rommel once and for all.'[51] It was an impressive performance which left the officers inspired and, in de Guingand's words: 'We all went to bed that night with a new hope in our hearts.'[52]

In the wake of his address, countless visits to his formations and assessments of his subordinates, Montgomery undertook to remove those officers whom he felt either lacked leadership or the willingness to support his ambitions.[53] Having replaced six senior officers with colleagues he knew and trusted – including Brian Horrocks, who took command of XIII Corps – Montgomery knew that he had created a reliable conduit for his influence and so tightened his grip. 'Orders no longer formed "the base for discussion"', he later asserted, 'but for action.'[54]

The energy and change of mindset that Monty engendered among his officers soon percolated down to the troops, who began talking in animated fashion about their new general. One Middlesex infantryman, Sergeant Ron Davies, felt that the general's arrival marked a step change from what had gone before. 'I was under no illusions from the CO that the men were to understand that there was a new sheriff in town,' Davies recalled. 'Monty's messages were read to the men and provided great reassurance that the tide was about to turn... We wanted a general with fire in his belly and he seemed to have that. We rallied around him and for the first time in months we felt that we had a future.'[55]

Montgomery knew, however, that fighting troops' relationship with their general was fickle, and that it was vital for a new commander to lead his men to success on the battlefield if his efforts to raise morale and fighting spirit had any hope of being sustained. Montgomery's attention was therefore split between preparing the Eighth Army psychologically for renewed combat, attending to its physical needs with the build-up of vital resources, and providing for it conceptually with an appropriate plan. In each of these areas he was assisted by intelligence reports – including Ultra decrypts of high-level German codes, which provided him with a deep insight into the enemy's strength and intentions. They told the Eighth Army to expect an enemy attack from the south towards the Alam el Halfa ridge; using that information, Montgomery devised exercises that rehearsed his intention to lure the enemy into 'gaps' deliberately created in the defences that would lead Rommel's forces into killing zones replete with minefields, dug-in armour, massed artillery and infantry.

Panzer Army Afrika attacked on 30 August, just two weeks after Montgomery had taken over as commander of the Eighth Army, and when woken with the news by de Guingand he had such faith in his preparations and subordinates that he merely muttered, 'Excellent, excellent,' and went back to sleep.[56] The following morning the general strode into the headquarters at his normal hour to receive a situation report, and having reassured himself that everything was under control, left for the front. One senior NCO later recalled Montgomery's arrival at the 4th Light Armoured Brigade headquarters: 'Although we were in the eye of the storm, the general arrived all smiles and saying, "The battle is proceeding exactly as I expected. Rommel will soon be turning back, do not fear!" I didn't know what to think, but I couldn't fault the man's confidence.'[57] His conviction rippled through Eighth Army, and when Rommel was forced into a withdrawal on 2 September, it felt like Monty was keeping his promise to the troops. Having had its self-assurance gradually drained by Panzer Army Afrika's advance over recent months, the Eighth Army was suddenly revitalized by a battle which revealed not only that Rommel was fallible, but that their new commander was a man worthy of their respect.

Churchill, moreover, was delighted: the victory of Alam el Halfa was an early vindication of the command changes that he had authorized, and a firm foundation for a riposte that would push Panzer Army Afrika back into Cyrenaica. Montgomery, however, was not temperamentally inclined to what he called 'unwarranted acts of rashness';[58] a methodical officer, he sought to develop an overwhelming superiority of resources before launching an Eighth Army offensive in a set-piece battle in which 'complete victory was assured'.[59] Using Brooke to rebuff the unwarranted interventions in the operational sphere by the prime minister, Montgomery developed a plan to 'destroy' the enemy opposing the Eighth Army in the autumn.[60]

Over the next seven weeks, the Eighth Army's programme of skills, drills and exercises were devised personally by Montgomery. He placed a high priority on leadership, and made notes about individuals, units and formations in a 'little black book' when either observing training personally or from the reports he demanded of subordinates.[61] As a consequence, he promoted some officers who impressed him as leaders, but replaced numerous senior officers who did not: the X Corps commander was replaced by Herbert Lumsden, an officer who had been recommended to the Eighth Army, while XXX Corps was taken over by one of Monty's former Staff College students, Oliver Leese. New commanders were also found for the 7th Armoured Division (the 'Desert Rats') and the 51st (Highland) Division, along with several brigades. Once he had the officers he wanted in position and they had been inducted into the 'Montgomery Way', the Eighth Army commander saw no need for micromanagement as long as they understood that his orders must be followed at all costs. As Brigadier Sidney Kirkham, a gunnery expert, later explained: '[Montgomery] told me I was responsible. As far as he was concerned there was no more to be said, He was satisfied that I would do the job – why therefore waste time discussing it?… There are very few people who have that faith! Quite extraordinary from my point of view.'[62]

Such faith helped to create a strong bond between Monty and his officers, but it was through the leadership of those officers that a reciprocal trust with his troops was established. Thus, by the early autumn of 1942 the slight, rather scruffy officer in his non-regulation shapeless sweater, corduroy trousers and baggy beret (bearing his general's badge as well as that of the Royal Tank Regiment) never missed an opportunity to address them directly. He spoke most often from the hood of a jeep, his message clear, caring and delivered with humour. Montgomery could be rather evangelical at times, prompting one officer to remark, 'I see that the Almighty, from being "in support", is now firmly "under command"!'[63] but the troops enjoyed hearing from him and it was unusual for him not to be cheered when he had finished speaking. The Eighth Army wanted to be led, and now, it seemed, they had found a leader they would follow willingly.

With the Eighth Army's strength and projected capability growing daily to nearly 220,000 men, more than 1,000 tanks and almost 900 artillery pieces,[64] 23 October was set as the date for the new offensive at El Alamein, with Ultra providing its commander with information about Panzer Army Afrika's order of battle, logistic situation and defensive plans. On the morning of battle, a personal message from General Montgomery was read to each of his units:

> When I assumed command of Eighth Army I said that the mandate was to destroy ROMMEL and his Army, and that it would be done as soon as we were ready. We are ready NOW. The battle which is now about to begin will be one of the decisive battles of history. It will be the turning point of the war. The eyes of the whole world will be on us, watching anxiously which way the battle will swing. We can give them the answer at once, 'It will swing our way.'[65]

By that time, Montgomery had taken up residency in his Tactical (TAC) headquarters close to X and XXX Corps, by the sea. Consisting of thirty-eight vehicles in total, the general was insistent on a very modest allocation for his own use: one caravan for his sleeping quarters, another for his map room and a third for his office, replete with a portrait of Rommel to better 'understand the character of the man who was a demi-god to his own army'.[66] He most often used an armoured command vehicle for moving around the front line,[67] and with his TAC headquarters so close, Monty never wasted time travelling to and from main headquarters some forty miles behind the front line. He also liked to remain close to corps headquarters in case there was a need to confer personally with his commanders.

Such a requirement occurred early in the battle. On the first day the X Corps' armour began to stall after XXX Corps infantry had taken the tactically vital Miteiriya Ridge, and so Montgomery acted on his belief that Herbert Lumsden's divisions 'required galvanising into action, and wanted determined leadership', and sent them an order that they *must* advance. He was therefore angered to be woken in the early hours of 25 October to be informed that X Corps' armour remained immobile.[68] At an immediate conference of his corps commanders in his map room lorry, Montgomery was told by a sheepish Lumsden that the commander of the 10th Armoured Division, Alexander Gatehouse, had ignored his orders to advance. Montgomery's response was uncompromising: he would remove any commander who failed to follow orders or failed in his duty of leadership. He then personally issued orders to X and XXX Corps.[69] Within four hours the armour was moving forward and a satisfied Monty was free to write in his diary: 'It was a good thing I was firm with LUMSDEN and GATEHOUSE last night', because his plan was back on schedule and a warning shot had been fired across the bows of anybody who believed that they knew better than the Eighth Army's commander.[70]

Throughout the remainder of the battle at El Alamein, Montgomery's presence, control and coolness under pressure were fundamental to the developing success. The failure of the enemy's counter-attacks, seen off by an Eighth Army with a new tenacity, was testament to what Monty had achieved since taking command just ten weeks earlier. 'Our mindset had changed,' infantry captain John Robinson remarked. 'Rather than being concerned about what needed to be done, we were keen to fight and re-establish our lost reputation. That doesn't mean we were blasé or without fear, but for the first time that I can remember, we fought as one great team. That word *team* is important. It gave us strength. It allowed us to endure and then to succeed.'[71]

The new Eighth Army doggedness was in great evidence during its attempts to break in to the enemy's defences, and also in their 'crumbling' operations once breaches had been made. Montgomery retained his usual self-assurance throughout and radiated a confidence to all, which one staff officer in the 51st (Highland) Infantry Division described as 'intoxicating, affirming and inspiring'.[72] However, when on 2 November Rommel began to withdraw, Montgomery acted pragmatically. A natural desire to seek the destruction of the enemy's armour in the short term had to be tempered by the abilities of his formations and logistics, and, of course, Rommel's ability to strike back. It was not in Montgomery's nature to take undue risks, particularly having suffered over 13,500 casualties, and with scores of his tanks having been destroyed and hundreds requiring repair, the Eighth Army's remaining armour was not 'let off the leash' but made to advance 'at heel'.

By allowing Panzer Army Afrika to withdraw and thus survive to fight another day, Montgomery's performance in early November may be seen as illustrating a characteristic lack of boldness. Yet one can argue with equal legitimacy that Montgomery's judiciousness revealed a pragmatism that few generals could match. The debate regarding Montgomery's generalship is unlikely to conclude in a consensus, but what is undeniable is that the Second Battle of El Alamein made a significant contribution to a change in Allied strategic fortunes. Winston Churchill wept when he heard the news of the Eighth Army's success, and in ordering church bells to be rung across the kingdom, marked an event that he hoped would prove to be a new beginning. Soon after, the successful landings of Anglo-American troops in western North Africa gave him reason to believe that his confidence had not been misplaced, and with news reaching London that Hitler's operations in the Soviet Union had suffered a significant reverse, the prime minister was convinced that autumn 1943 was a turning point in the war.

In the wake of El Alamein, Bernard Montgomery was knighted, elevated to the rank of full general and became the national hero that a melancholic Britain had been yearning for. However, the general's stock remained wholly dependent on his ability to turn a battlefield accomplishment into something of lasting strategic consequence. And so, recognizing that there was space for his portrait to be hung in the hall of failed British desert generals, Montgomery carefully choreographed the Eighth Army's advance westwards.

By 11 November, the vanguard of Montgomery's formation had crossed the border into Libya, and soon after Tobruk, the symbol of so many British hopes and fears, fell for the last time in the war. The achievement was marked by a message sent to all those serving under Montgomery's command, congratulating them on their 'very fine performance' and ending with a final encouragement: 'On with the task, and good hunting to you all.'[73] Towns and cities along the Cyrenaican coast were soon occupied by Monty's men, in some cases just minutes after the enemy had left. 'I found a hot pot of German coffee still steaming on a stove,' wrote one armoured corps driver. 'It was disgusting and so we made some tea in a little china pot I had brought with me from Surrey.'[74] Gazala was taken, then Derna, and on 20 November, Benghazi was seized and work started on making the destroyed port operational once more.

The logistical needs of the Eighth Army were never far from the minds of the headquarters staff, and with the worsening weather, Montgomery needed to be sure of his supplies as he looked to play his part in the final destruction of the Axis forces in North Africa. He was in no rush, therefore, to 'bounce' the strong defensive position that his enemy had been preparing before El Agheila, and instead waited until the Eighth Army was well set before attacking on 11 December.

The battle proved to be another significant Eighth Army success, and affirmed to subordinates and superiors alike that Montgomery could facilitate the destruction of Panzer Army Afrika, in concert with the Allied forces advancing from the west. The team of senior Eighth Army commanders that had fought at El Alamein, however, were not necessarily those in whom Montgomery retained his faith. Lumsden and Gatehouse were both sacked having been found 'wilting under strain',[75] and the general kept a close eye on all his formation commanders, ready to replace any who failed him.

Montgomery would not allow the Eighth Army to rest on its laurels as the advance continued. On Christmas Day 1942 the formation entered Sirte (some 1,200 miles from its start point in Egypt), and on 23 January 1943 marched into Tripoli, the capital of Libya and the last major objective before the Tunisian border. In Tripoli, the Eighth Army paused to reopen the port, take on supplies, and for the first time since El Alamein, revel a little in its success. When Churchill visited the city on 4 February, newsmen captured the first British victory parade of the war. Alan Brooke stood next to the prime minister as Montgomery's troops marched past, and later wrote: 'For the first time I was beginning to live through the thrill of those first successes that were now rendering ultimate victory possible.'[76]

While eschewing gratuitous publicity, Montgomery featured prominently in the newsreels and press coverage, knocking Rommel off the front pages and taking the opportunity to impress on the British public what the Eighth Army was capable of. Indeed, Monty began to regard himself as some sort of military messiah, and as such sought to spread his doctrine and lessons to as many as possible. Having dispatched his liaison officers to England to teach his approach and methods to various formations, Montgomery then ran study week for his officers in mid-February, with an open invitation for those serving with other armies to attend and so profit from the general's wisdom. George S. Patton was the only US officer delegate but was impressed by Monty, whom he described as 'small, very alert, wonderfully conceited, and the best soldier – or so it seems – I have met in this war'.[77] Monty's diary noted the meeting but merely recorded that Patton was 'an old man of about 60'.[78] It was a characteristically cutting observation by an officer whose shallow pool of humility was gradually evaporating in the North African sun.

Not until early March 1943 did the Eighth Army make its next concerted move to the west as, crossing the Tunisian border, it advanced 100 miles to approach the Mareth Line. It was a formidable obstacle that actually consisted of two defensive lines which were covered by artillery, protected by barbed wire and other obstacles, and with a main line boasting concrete strongpoints replete with machine guns and anti-tank weapons. The campaign's denouement was expected in Tunisia, for although Hitler was reinforcing North Africa with the Fifth Panzer Army, converging Allied forces were looking to encircle their enemy along the coast plain south of Tunis by the spring. The Mareth defences were the last before Montgomery could swing his force north towards Tunis.

Although he had given the Americans a bloody nose at the Kasserine Pass in late February, Rommel knew that Allied fighting power would ultimately prove irresistible. His spoiling attack against the Eighth Army at Medenine on 6 March was to be his last action in North Africa before returning to Germany on health grounds. It was violent, but did little to upset Montgomery's Ultra intelligence-informed plans to break the Mareth Line in what was to be the Eighth Army's greatest concentration of force since El Alamein.

The battle opened on 19 March and the Eighth Army took a week to create a breakthrough, but the Italian First Army barely escaped encirclement having been pinned by a frontal infantry assault while British armour undertook an outflanking manoeuvre, and Montgomery had another success. As the general led his troops along Tunisia's eastern coast, against which the Axis forces were now trapped, Monty was riding the crest of popular acclaim which even saw his face adorn the promotional poster for the Oscar-winning propaganda film *Desert Victory* – 'The full-length feature story of the rout of Rommel in Africa by the British 8th Army… With the most thrilling scenes ever taken under fire!' – released in March 1943 as the fighting in Tunisia reached its climax.[79]

His troops were rightly proud to be associated with their accomplishments, and they recognized the role that their commander had played in their renaissance. When he arrived for a show that he had put on for them in Tripoli, the audience chanted, 'We want

Monty! We want Monty!' as he took his seat and when he left it. 'It was a remarkable thing for the British troops to do for a general,' noted Brian Horrocks.[80] Even more, those same men jostled to catch a glimpse of Montgomery whether he was on a visit or even just speeding past in his staff car. This adoration, rooted as it was in a string of accomplishments over the previous six months, was translated on the battlefield into a magnificent confidence and a desire to remain unbeaten. 'We will not stop, or let up, till Tunis has been captured', Montgomery told an expectant Eighth Army, 'and the enemy has either given up the struggle or been pushed into the sea.'[81] The fall of Gabès in early April opened the final phase of the formation's North African campaign, which was to last just five weeks. In a co-ordinated advance with Anglo-American forces coming from western and north-western Tunisia, the Eighth Army helped to roll the Axis forces back to Tunis where, on 13 May, they surrendered.

After the breaking of the Mareth Line, Montgomery was informed that he had been selected as a commander for the invasion of Sicily, to be known as 'Operation Husky'. It was to be conducted as soon after the fall of Tunisia as practicable. Under the auspices of Harold Alexander's new 15th Army Group, the British Eighth Army and Patton's US Seventh Army were charged with seizing the island so that it could be used as a base for an invasion of the Italian mainland. It was a strategy executed by Lieutenant General Dwight Eisenhower's Allied Force Headquarters, which had held responsibility for the entire Mediterranean theatre since Operation Torch, the Allied invasion of French North Africa in November 1942. A strong leader with compelling organizational skills and the talent to navigate sensitive relationships, Eisenhower had only spent a few months in London as the general commanding the new European Theater of Operations when he was given a second job as the commander for Torch, with the rapidly promoted Mark Clark as his deputy.[82] Both men oversaw the refining of the complex inter-Allied land, sea and air planning for the Sicily invasion that had begun months before Montgomery received news of his appointment.

On seeing what was being proposed, however, the British officer liked neither the dilution of the two armies over wide areas nor the fact that there was no obvious main effort, despite the Eighth Army's experience and recent accomplishments. He determined to have the plan changed, but with no authority to do so looked instead to exploit what he perceived to be a weakness in the chain of command. Although a long-time admirer of Alexander, Montgomery did not believe he had the attributes required for a multinational Army Group commander and he felt he could manipulate his old colleague. Montgomery liked Eisenhower personally, but after meeting him wrote to Alan Brooke, 'I can say, quite definitely, that he knows nothing whatever about how to make war or to fight battles; he should be kept right away from all that business if we want to win this war.'[83] Montgomery therefore felt that both men had to be brought under his influence if the campaign was to be fought effectively, while his fellow commander in Husky, George Patton, would just have to take a back seat.

The tussle that was to develop specifically between Montgomery and Patton was the inevitable consequence of two strong-minded and ambitious generals from either side of the Atlantic who craved independence. Operation Husky was regarded by both men as an audition for the cross-Channel invasion that was projected for the following year, which both believed to be the 'main event' as it would involve fighting the main enemy on the Western Allies' critical front. Montgomery, however, had already raised questions in Eisenhower's mind about his suitability for a North-West Europe command due to some recent unreasonable behaviour. After the Eighth Army had taken the Tunisian coastal town of Sfax on 10 April, for example, Montgomery had embarrassed Walter Bedell Smith, Eisenhower's chief of staff who, several weeks earlier, had made a light-hearted remark to Montgomery that he would give 'anything' for a rapid exploitation of the Mareth Line breach. Having done so, Montgomery demanded his prize: a US Boeing B-17 'Flying Fortress' heavy bomber and air crew for his personal use for the remainder of the war – an outrageous request considering its value to the war effort. Smith initially thought

Monty was joking, but having recognized he was in earnest, had to find him an aircraft. An aircraft was found by Eisenhower which Monty used for his personal transport, until it crash-landed during the summer in Sicily.[84] Brooke later called Montgomery's demand for 'his present' an act of 'crass stupidity' and said that it 'laid the foundations of distrust and dislike which remained with Eisenhower during the rest of the war'.[85]

Montgomery's proprietorial authority over Sicily was rooted in his belief that he was the outstanding combat commander in the theatre, and as such he would only support the chain of command where his superiors did nothing to interfere in his own ambitions. Thus, the British officer went straight to Eisenhower with his new plan for Operation Husky without even informing Alexander, far less gaining his approval. In Monty's new scheme, the Allied landing forces were no longer dangerously dispersed but concentrated in two adjacent landing areas: the Eighth Army south of Syracuse on the east coast, and the Seventh Army in the Gulf of Gela on the southern coast. With there being no decision about the exploitation phase until the invasion force had been firmly established on the island, Monty pre-positioned the Eighth Army in the most favourable ground to advance rapidly to Messina, the north-eastern port from which the Axis defenders would be evacuated to the Italian mainland just two miles distant.

The new plan was readily accepted by Eisenhower, who believed it to be superior having listened to Montgomery's arguments, but it was to the chagrin of Alexander who now recognized that he could not rely on his subordinate's loyalty and knew that Montgomery already had a powerful patron in Brooke, the Chief of the Imperial General Staff (CIGS). Brooke, however, was under no illusion about Montgomery's foibles, and noted in his diary in June that the commander of the Eighth Army was a 'difficult mixture to handle, brilliant commander in action and trainer of men but liable to commit untold errors in lack of tact, lack of appreciation of other people's outlook. It is distressing the Americans do not like him... He wants guiding and watching continually and I do not think Alex is sufficiently strong and rough with him.'[86] Monty had challenged Alexander, refusing to be hamstrung by somebody he regarded as being ineffective as an Army Group leader, and in these complicated circumstances he moved in to fill the 'leadership vacuum'.[87]

The politics of higher command increasingly occupied Montgomery's thoughts, but they never replaced his responsibility towards the Eighth Army. 'By the end of the [North African] campaign', Montgomery wrote in his memoirs, 'I believe they would have done anything I asked; they felt we were all partners in the battle and that they themselves "belonged," and mattered. They gave me their complete confidence. What more can any commander want? My only fear was that I myself might fail these magnificent men.'[88] Such words raise the question about the ways in which Montgomery thought he might 'fail' his men, but it is doubtful he considered his own hubris a possibility. As such, he attended to the fighting capabilities of his command rather than moderating his own behaviours, which he deemed vital to his influence. The result was an entrenchment of a belief that his approach to war-fighting and his leadership style were not only appropriate but necessary, and he tackled the campaign in Sicily like just any other military puzzle that he had previously solved.

Operation Husky began on the night of 9–10 July 1943 and saw the Eighth Army establish itself in the south-eastern portion of the island with notable speed before Montgomery then struck inland. Using his two corps, the general attempted to encircle a large portion of the Italian Sixth Army (which included a German panzer and a *Panzergrenadier* division) and so clear the way for a rapid advance northwards. Alexander subsequently deemed Montgomery's attack as the main effort, just as the Eighth Army commander had anticipated, with the Americans playing a subsidiary role protecting the British left flank and rear. Yet by 15 July, neither Patton nor the enemy had shown any willingness to accommodate. Patton prepared to make his own mark in the campaign, and the Italian Sixth Army withdrew from the Eighth Army's pincers to better defensive terrain. With operational command having been taken up by German general Hans Hube, the Axis forces sought to hold the Allies for as long as possible so that defences on the Italian mainland could be completed. The result was that while the British Eighth Army was drawn into stagnant and attritional fighting in the east of the island, the US Seventh Army was authorized to clear the west, which gave Patton the opportunity to steal the headlines in a dash to the north coast to capture Palermo, the Sicilian capital, on 22 July and, potentially, move east to reach Messina before Montgomery. As Captain Leo Ross in XXX Corps headquarters later recalled, his commander, Oliver Leese, 'took the brunt of Monty's ire on more than one occasion',[89] for although outwardly calm and always collected, Montgomery disliked coming second – and particularly to US forces, which he had broadly criticized for being 'naïve and poorly led' in North Africa.[90]

In the wicked heat and dust of a Sicilian summer, and with two more German divisions sent to the island as reinforcements, Montgomery reached back into his knowledge of how to fight geographically constrained operations. His approach was typically methodical: building up resources on narrow fronts and then 'biting and holding' small handfuls of territory, rather than bold advances that would stretch his lines of communication in complex terrain. Reinforcing his strong leadership and the need for his subordinates to demonstrate the same, Monty himself went to even greater lengths than usual to get out to his formations and inspire his troops. His trademark confidence was never in short supply, and nor were his attempts to put a smile on the faces of his troops. He regarded 'the simple act of a good laugh [as] a tonic that should be encouraged whenever the situation allows',[91] and Monty himself was always praising the troops for their sense of the ridiculous. Years later, he would regale colleagues with the story of being driven to the front in his staff car in Sicily, and passing a lorry whose stark-naked driver leant out of his cab and raised his silk top hat in a mark of respect. 'I just roared with laughter,' Monty later wrote. 'However, while I was not particular about dress so long as the soldiers fought well and we won our battles, I at once decided there were limits,' and he subsequently issued the only order of his career about dress, which stated: 'Top hats will not be worn in the Eighth Army.'[92]

The morale of the troops remained high, but Montgomery knew it would suffer a blow if they remained static for too long. Thus, as soon as Patton's Seventh Army began to progress along the north coast, Monty encouraged Alexander to convene a meeting to discuss the next phase of the campaign. The conference took place on 25 July, and here Monty and Patton agreed, before the arrival of their delayed boss, that while the Seventh Army sought to turn the German flank, the Eighth Army would continue its slow advance in the hope that unremitting pressure would cause the front to crack open. The plan was presented as a fait accompli by the British officer to Alexander when he finally arrived, and in such an overbearing manner that Patton wrote, 'I thought Monty was ill bred both to Alexander and me.'[93]

All three commanders recognized that Montgomery would never give up hope of reaching Messina first, despite the Seventh Army's seemingly advantageous position; and, indeed, he hoped that American advances might relieve pressure on the Eighth Army and so facilitate its own breakout. He nearly got his wish, for Patton's push along the northern coast rendered the Axis position in north-east Sicily untenable, prompting first a withdrawal and then, commencing on 11 August, an evacuation. Seventh Army units arrived in Messina five days later, just hours ahead of Montgomery's men.[94] Although piqued by the turn of events, Montgomery was satisfied by the outcome, and in any case he had to prepare to lead the Eighth Army across the straits to Reggio di Calabria on 3 September in the first phase of the invasion of mainland Italy.

The Italian campaign did not excite Montgomery in the same way as it did the men who believed in the efficacy of a Mediterranean strategy, and so it was to be endured while preparations were made for the cross-Channel invasion of France. The next four months were, according to Brian Montgomery, 'possibly the most frustrating for him of all the war years',[95] as Monty battled the enemy and the terrain, despite never being fully convinced about what he was supposed to be achieving.[96] Was his aim, he complained, to chew up the enemy in a resource-heavy slog, or to take ground? If the latter, to what end? The Allies had 'embarked on a major campaign on the continent of Europe', Montgomery wrote, 'without having any clear idea – or plan – as to how they would develop the operations and fight the land battle' – and for this he blamed Alexander and Eisenhower.[97]

On the day that Monty's troops first set foot on the mainland, the Italians surrendered, the conditions having been accepted by the nation's new prime minister – with the agreement publicized on 8 September, the day before Mark Clark's Fifth Army landed at Salerno. With Montgomery's force having cleared the southern extremities of Italy, the British and American armies linked up on 20 September and an Allied front was created across the Italian peninsula. Monty's force was to advance up the eastern side of the country (Adriatic coast) while Clark progressed on the western side (Mediterranean coast). But while the Fifth Army had a clear path to Rome, Montgomery did not. His was a role that one British artillery officer, Lieutenant Colonel Edwin James, called 'the big push to nowhere', as he began to haul his regiment's guns against the grain of a merciless countryside in rapidly deteriorating conditions.[98] The weather, terrain and a series of defensive lines constructed under the direction of the very able German commander in southern Italy, Field Marshal Albert Kesselring, combined to ensure that the Allies had no option but to become embroiled in a slogging match.

By 7 October, both Allied armies had become fully entangled in an exhausting cobweb of obstacles which did nothing to convince Montgomery that the costly and demoralizing 'side show' in Italy was worth the effort it demanded. His divisions were in extreme discomfort, with increasing numbers becoming non-battle casualties due to the damp and cold, and the performance of his formations took a sharp decline. Even his own visits to his troops eventually became impossible due to the time that it took to get anywhere on roads blocked with his own vehicles, across rivers lacking adequate bridges, and through a terrain that frequently degenerated into an impassable mire. His commanders did all they could to motivate their men, but casualties were heavy and the unremitting grind of operations that measured effectiveness in yards was not conducive to success. Those senior officers that needed a break from the strain were sent on leave to regain their strength. Lieutenant General Oliver Leese, for example, was dispatched to Syria for a break. 'You would not think it', Monty wrote to Brooke of the XXX Corps commander, 'but he is of a nervous disposition and temperament and there have been times when his staff have found him very difficult. This continuous fighting is a great strain for a Corps Commander... A good 2 to 3 weeks will put him quite O.K. He is a very valuable officer and has done splendidly as a Corps Comd in my Army – he is easily the best I have.'[99]

If there was an answer to the challenges of static warfare, Montgomery knew from his time in the trenches of the First World War that it lay with the leadership of junior officers and their senior NCOs. Orders directing all formations to spend time developing these men in study weeks and through ad hoc lectures were issued, and Montgomery wanted to know what each division had planned. Indeed, the general personally contributed to as many programmes as he could, but largely saved his time for the education of senior officers. 'I do concentrate on teaching my Generals', he wrote, 'and I am certain one has got to do so.'[100] With so many senior officers lacking any training in the art of generalship, it was up to the victor of El Alamein to step in to make up the deficit with lectures covering various themes relating to the 'command and leadership of higher formations',[101] including the art of influence, leading remotely, communication and what he called 'Understanding the Human Condition'.[102] Improved leadership among the generals, Montgomery argued, would percolate down through the ranks and eventually benefit all.[103] It was one part of his wider attempt to make sure that the Eighth Army, although stuck in the Italian quagmire, remained a vibrant, thinking, learning organization – and if nothing else, it made current and future generals reconsider the benefits of self-improvement even when on operations.

In early December, the Allies were grappling with the Gustav Line – defended by General Heinrich von Vietinghoff's Tenth Army – which ran across the peninsular sixty-five miles south of Rome and incorporated the dominating hilltop abbey of Monte Cassino in Clark's sector. As he made plans to tackle his part of the German defences, however, Montgomery received the news about appointments for the cross-Channel invasion. Operation Overlord, he already knew, would see Eisenhower reprise his role as Supreme Commander in western Europe, but the choice of British Commander-in-Chief was between Alexander and Montgomery. The former had worked closely with Eisenhower, and in so doing had revealed all the political skills required for such a role – but, as Brooke pointed out, he lacked the leadership skills and fighting credentials required for this undertaking. Montgomery therefore was rewarded with the appointment as commander of the British 21st Army Group, and, moreover, as land forces commander for the opening phase of the invasion. 'This is a very fine job', Monty wrote in his diary with considerable understatement, 'and it will be about the biggest thing I have ever had to handle.'[104] He did not want to stay in Italy a day longer than was necessary.

With his troops having failed to make a clean breakthrough of the Gustav Line in its latest offensive, Montgomery suspended all further offensive action for the remainder of the winter and packed his bags as Clark prepared to continue his attack with the US Fifth Army, which failed to create a breakthrough until mid-May 1944. In an emotionally charged farewell address to his headquarters staff and senior commanders on 23 December, Monty thanked everybody for their efforts, saying, 'You have made this Army what it is. You have made its name a household word all over the world. Therefore, you must uphold its good name and its traditions.'[105]

Freddie de Guingand was impressed that Monty had managed to hit just the right notes with his talk on leaving the Eighth Army, just as he had when taking command sixteen months earlier, and later wrote: 'There were no great feats of oratory and no false note. It was exactly right and I found it intensely moving.'[106] The general received a heartfelt round of applause at the completion of his address, and then, having shaken the hand of each commander, left the building to take up new responsibilities for one of the greatest events in world history.

— □ —

When George S. Patton took command of I Armored Corps at Fort Benning, Georgia, in mid-January 1942, his childhood dream of becoming a general in combat became significantly more likely. Starting as he meant to go on, he made a grand entrance to the camp on his first day, having arranged for his gleaming staff car to be escorted by a dozen motorcycle outriders and several truckloads of troops following two tanks. The headquarters staff tumbled outside from their offices believing that the sound of blaring horns must signify a fire, but instead found a sergeant major barking instructions at them to form ranks for an address by the new commanding general. In his speech, Patton explained that their job was to prepare the corps for war and so: 'As officers we must give leadership in becoming tough, physically and mentally.'[107] He spoke about discipline, duty and courage before concluding with the announcement of a task: in thirty minutes, every man in the headquarters would run a mile in full kit – and complete it in under fifteen minutes. Several officers subsequently submitted transfer requests, but those who stayed participated in a period of organizational transformation that they would remember for the rest of their lives.

As the weeks passed and the corps became used to the energetic Patton and the fact that he seemed to be a news story wherever he went – *Life* published a second article about him in February – signs of a growing *esprit de corps* began to be seen across the formation. Patton seemed to galvanize the men – and, like him or loathe him, the troops knew what he stood for and the standards they had to meet. He delivered an address to every regiment under his command and made it abundantly clear that, if they obeyed orders, worked hard and did their duty, they would find him 'a kindly and compassionate man', but if they did not – and here he deliberately snarled – they would come to regard him 'as the meanest SOB in the US Army'.[108] He reinforced that message whenever he could across the vast Fort Benning camp, and purchased speakers from his own funds that were erected in every one of the corps' main communal areas. Although they were initially used to broadcast music and news to the men for their enjoyment, he soon had a microphone installed in his office and would often interrupt the schedule with an announcement which began 'This is General Patton!'[109]

During the first three weeks of his command, Patton oversaw thirteen major tactical exercises to assess capabilities and to 'show every single man that there is nowhere to hide in a corps commanded by General Patton'.[110] He prowled across the training ground, observing, issuing directions, directing dawn attacks, lambasting forlorn lieutenants, joking with squads of soldiers and helping one bewildered crew shift its bogged truck. He demanded that all exercise scenarios be as realistic as possible and, aware the corps was likely to fight in North Africa, established the 18,000-square-mile Desert Training Center (known as 'Little Libya') in south-eastern California, where over half a million US troops were eventually exposed to harsh desert conditions. Patton commanded the centre from March to July 1942, with his I Armored Corps the first to be put through its paces on the rugged terrain to better understand the challenges of desert warfare, and to refine operational methods and tactical acumen.

Patton's desire to lead in combat again was undiminished (he even wrote to the head of the War Department's personnel board, 'I wish to God that we would start killing somebody, somewhere soon, and trust that if we do, you will use your best influence to see that I can take a hand in the killing'[111]), and his delight was unbounded when he was informed in early summer that he had been appointed Western

Task Force commander for the invasion of North Africa, then held by Vichy France. The tri-service Operation Torch was to be overseen by Eisenhower as the theatre's Supreme Commander working from Gibraltar, with Patton's 35,000-strong force landing in Morocco while other Anglo-American divisions assaulted beaches further east, in Algeria. The objective was for the Torch forces to advance east while Montgomery's Eighth Army advanced west through Libya, aiming to crush the withdrawing Axis forces in Tunisia.

Patton bade farewell to his corps in late July 1942 – expressing his fervent desire that he would see it 'kicking the enemy "in the ass" some place soon'[112] – and headed to Washington, where the planning for the Western Task Force invasion had already begun. On arrival, he established a headquarters filled with officers he knew and trusted, making Brigadier General Geoffrey Keyes his deputy and taking the talented Colonel Hobart R. 'Hap' Gay from I Armored Corps as his chief of staff. Patton, Keyes and Gay acted as a well-balanced triumvirate working to common standards. Any man that failed to meet their requirements was immediately replaced, with one staff officer later opining, 'You either knew your job, or you didn't. If you didn't, or if you were the cause of any friction in the Headquarters, you were quickly and quietly gotten rid of… But if you knew your job you were allowed to perform it in your own way… Results were all that counted.'[113] Patton did shout and throw his weight around when something went wrong or was not done to his satisfaction, but Gay was always there to ensure that any damage was contained and Keyes was good at mopping up. It did lead to some disgruntled members of headquarters staff, but if they could not work with the commander's personality then they too were replaced.

Patton found it difficult to control his inner feelings, and sometimes that revealed itself in a show of indignation towards someone or an impassioned speech to his troops. Indeed, just before the Western Task Force's 2nd Armored Division embarked for its voyage across the Atlantic in October, Patton addressed them with tears in his eyes. At the conclusion of his speech, recalled the formation's commander,

Ernest Harmon: 'The Division stood up spontaneously and cheered and cheered again.'[114] However, gathering together his commanders just before heading for North Africa himself, Patton used different tactics and, wearing his 'war-face', said in conclusion to a long speech about their responsibilities: 'If you don't succeed, I don't want to see you alive.'[115]

Aboard the *Augusta*, the flagship of the Western Task Force, Patton had plenty of time to ruminate on the coming campaign, his role and his fate. 'I can't decide logically if I am a man of destiny or a lucky fool, but I think I am destined,' he wrote in his diary on 3 November. 'I feel that my claim to greatness hangs on an ability to lead and inspire.'[116] Five days later, despite his elevated rank, Patton was one of the first senior officers to set foot on Moroccan soil. Arriving soon after the first wave, and despite incoming French fire, he patrolled the beach shouting directions to his troops. Finding one frightened man lying in the foetal position, he acted instinctively: 'I kicked him in the arse with all my might and he jumped right up and went to work.'[117]

Ultimately the opposition proved fragile – disappointingly so for a general who had hoped to distinguish himself – and when the French surrendered on 11 November, Patton wondered whether his one opportunity had ended before it had properly begun. His dissatisfaction was only deepened by orders from Eisenhower to remain in Morocco to conduct diplomacy with the nation's leaders, while his troops trained and built a logistic base there. The Central and Eastern Task Forces, meanwhile, would prepare an early advance on Tunisia from Algeria. The whole show, it seemed, was being run by the British after all, for Lieutenant General Kenneth Anderson commanded the advancing First Army (albeit initially consisting of a single division as other formations were still to arrive), while General Harold Alexander, commander of the new 18th Army Group, was de facto land commander.

Patton blamed Eisenhower for not doing more to protect US interests and for being overly deferential to the British. The fact that Patton did not keep such views to himself (particularly when Anderson's advance began to struggle) earned him a reprimand from the Supreme Commander at a sensitive time in the development of the Anglo-American alliance. He was subsequently requested to be on his best behaviour during the Allied strategic conference held in Casablanca during January 1943, at which the sociable Patton was tasked with entertaining senior politicians and generals. The event was a success and Patton a gracious host, although the British looked askance at his self-promoting tales, vulgarity and assertion that his ambition was to die on the battlefield. Alan Brooke was not impressed, writing in a note to his diary after the war: '[H]is swashbuckling personality exceeded my expectation. I did not form any high opinion of him, nor had I any reason to alter this view at any later date. A dashing, courageous, wild and unbalanced leader, good for operations requiring thrust and push but at a loss in any operation requiring skill and judgement.'[118]

By the end of January 1943, Anderson's First Army had been unable to create the decisive breakthrough to Tunis despite the arrival of increasing numbers of his formations and the addition of a new French corps. Eisenhower also placed Major General Lloyd Fredendall's US II Corps under his command, but since it was fighting through the Western Dorsal mountains it made Anderson's front 200 miles long and stymied by poor communications. Fredendall's inexperienced formation subsequently suffered a humiliating defeat by Rommel's DAK at the Kasserine Pass (19–24 February), which precipitated Fredendall's dismissal and the appointment of Patton as his temporary replacement. Taking command of a formation in the middle of a campaign, and particularly in the wake of a significant failure, was a leadership challenge that Patton had never previously faced and would have been a significant test of any commander's talents, but he was determined to raise the corps' confidence, morale and fighting spirit.

Having first put measures in place to deal with the lack of discipline he had identified, he used his new deputy, Major General

Omar Bradley, to enforce them. It was typical of Patton's leadership to focus first on his men's duty to obey orders, and Bradley later wrote that throughout the war Patton was 'unmercifully hard on his men, demanding the utmost in military efficiency and bearing. Most of them respected but despised him.'[119] Indeed, Patton demanded that all commanders find new ways of motivating their troops, and insisted that all junior officers lead from the front – although without first putting in any support for men who were in dire need of more training and guidance. Nevertheless, believing that the best cure for inexperience was experience, Patton sought the first opportunity to get his formation back in battle. Some of the theatre's senior leadership thought it might not be ready, but learning in late February that the British Eighth Army would soon be mounting an offensive on the Mareth Line, twenty miles to the south-east, the general looked to draw the enemy's reserve and, perhaps, even cut its lines of communication. In a message to his corps before the attack began in mid-March, Patton said: 'We must utterly defeat the enemy… Of course we are willing to die but that is not enough. We must be eager to kill, to inflict on the enemy – the hated enemy – wounds, death, and destruction. If we die killing, well and good, but if we fight hard enough, viciously enough, we will kill and live. Live to return to our family and our girls as conquering heroes – men of Mars.'[120]

During the subsequent advance Patton was often seen in the vanguard riding in a new scout car through enemy bombardments, minefields and firefights. As he hoped, 'Crazy Patton' became the talk of the corps. Before long, not a single II Corps officer could ever argue that Patton was asking his troops to do something that he himself would not do, while millions across the United States learned from radio broadcasts that Patton was 'a hard-hitting, fast-thinking American hero', and as such just the sort of courageous gunslinger hero that many found so attractive.[121]

Patton also had a sensitive side that those who worked closely with him knew. Units returning from battle could expect kind words from the general if he was nearby and particularly if they had taken casualties, whom he would then visit in hospital. Patton would also become reflective when passing dead US troops, never forgetting his part in their demise, and he wept openly over the body of his aide, Captain Richard Jenson, when he was killed in an enemy dive-bomber attack.

Yet such was his complexity that if he thought his troops had failed to show enough courage, he could be vindictive. Indeed, one junior officer recalled a furious Patton standing among the dead, yelling at troops engaged in a firefight in Tunisia: '"Move, move, move! Take that goddam hill or die trying!" – and he meant it. He wanted dead heroes, not live cowards.'[122] Above all else, Patton sought military success, and he believed that casualties were a necessary and unavoidable by-product of fighting. He was not cavalier with the lives of others, but he had little time for those who were not willing to sacrifice themselves for their comrades, for the US Army and for himself. He was thus frustrated by the failure of his corps to push through to the Mediterranean coast and cut Panzer Army Afrika's lines of communication, however unrealistic this was in the wake of the Kasserine Pass debacle. Nevertheless, he did not hesitate in attending to those issues that he believed had contributed to his formation's failure to take more ground.

First, he sacked Major General Orlando Ward, the popular commander of 1st Armored Division, for his lack of drive and leadership – a decision that left him in bad odour with its officers – and then he became embroiled in an unseemly argument with British Air Vice Marshal Arthur Coningham, the commander of Allied tactical air forces in North Africa, whom he accused of having failed to adequately support US II Corps – and, by implication, of having caused the death of Jenson. It made for a messy end to his tenure as commander before handing over to Bradley in April, a month before the Axis surrender, but Patton felt that he had done what was necessary to put the corps 'back on course'.[123] Marshall agreed, writing in a note of congratulation: 'You did a fine job and further strengthened our confidence in your leadership',[124] while Eisenhower complimented Patton on his 'outstanding example of leadership' and informed him that he would lead the US Seventh Army in the invasion of Sicily.[125] Having had a mixed experience since landing in Morocco, Patton was thrilled to be given the responsibility of an army in such an important operation, and he immediately joined the Husky planning team.

Previously critical of the fact that the British were the senior partner in North Africa, Patton was dismayed to learn that, despite Eisenhower's role as Supreme Allied Commander, the British again dominated operations in the Mediterranean. In particular he felt that Bernard Montgomery was acting as if he was Army Group commander rather than his countryman Harold Alexander, and he blamed Eisenhower for not being firm enough with America's ally. 'The trouble is we lack leaders with sufficient strength of character,' Patton wrote in his diary, echoing Montgomery's own beliefs. 'As I gain in experience, I do not think more of myself but less of others. Men, even so-called great men, are wonderfully weak and timid. They are too damned polite. War is very simple, direct and ruthless. It takes a simple, direct, and ruthless man to wage war.'[126] Thus, while he did not disagree with the essence of Montgomery's amended plan, he was concerned that his army – initially a single corps to Montgomery's two corps – was being set up for a secondary role in the advance to the port of Messina.

Despite Patton's protestations, Eisenhower approved the revised plan, thus leaving the commander of the Seventh Army with little option but to take advantage of whatever opportunities arose on the island in the weeks to come. Patton's preparations for the invasion placed great emphasis on the importance of leadership excellence, and he wrote in a letter of instruction to his subordinate commanders on 5 June: 'Officers must assert themselves by example and by voice.'[127] His example of that during a beach landing rehearsal, however, reminded the observing Marshall and Eisenhower that Patton's behaviour was not always as they hoped, for they observed him berating a struggling infantryman in the most appalling manner. Eisenhower's subsequent appraisal of Patton stated: '[He is a] shrewd soldier who believes in showmanship to such an extent that he is almost flamboyant. He talks too much and too quickly and sometimes creates a very bad impression. Moreover, I fear that he is not always a good example to subordinates, who may be guided by only his surface actions without understanding the deep sense of duty, courage, and service that make up his real personality.'[128]

Senior officers had consistently pointed out similar flaws, but Patton was not going to change his style nor his personality this late in his career, for he led instinctively and authentically. Indeed, writing to Beatrice about his success as a leader, he said, 'The funny thing is that I don't know how I do it.'[129] This statement was at best a half-truth, because Patton thought carefully about how to project himself in certain situations, and particularly so when he addressed troops formally, as he did in late June when he gave a speech to each of his divisions. Standing ramrod-straight and immaculately dressed before 45th Division on one such occasion, he spoke words that he had toiled over for days and inhabited the character that he felt would resonate best with his audience: 'Battle is the most magnificent competition in which a human being can indulge. It brings out all that is best; it removes all that is base. All men are afraid in battle. The coward is the one who lets his fear overcome his sense of duty… In this next fight, you are entering the greatest sporting competition of all times… for the greatest prize of all. Victory.'[130] Not for the first time in such circumstances, Patton's 'lip quivered' during his delivery and 'a tear rolled down his cheek' as he spoke. His audience was mesmerized, and cheered as he left the stage.[131]

On the morning of 10 July, just hours after the invasion of Sicily had begun, Patton waded ashore at Gela to the clatter of press camera shutters while shells exploded just thirty yards away. With the famous images captured, he then made a conscious effort to allow his subordinates to fight the tactical battle while he supported them by looking after their operational interests. Before long, however, Patton got restless and, unable to contain himself, left his headquarters to stroll along the beach. There he stood during an enemy strafing, confirming to himself that he was no coward. Coming across a group of prostrate troops, as he later wrote, he 'continued to walk up and down and soon shamed them into getting up'.[132]

In the days that followed, the Seventh Army had no difficulty in establishing itself on the island and, having learned on 12 July that the Eighth Army's advance would be the main effort, Patton began to look for those operational opportunities that would take him out of Montgomery's shadow. Five days later, with the main body of the enemy ranged before Montgomery withdrawing to better defensive ground, Patton made his move and, with Alexander's authorization, used Geoffrey Keyes's new Provisional Corps to clear the western portion of the island while US II Corps advanced to the north coast. Patton had emphasized to Alexander that these new Seventh Army operations might well help dilute the opposition faced by Montgomery, as they would demand a reorientation of the enemy's defensive efforts, but Alexander was astute enough to recognize that his subordinate wanted to get to Messina first. 'Monty is trying to steal the show', George wrote to Beatrice, having begun his advance, 'and with the assistance of Devine [sic] Destiny [Eisenhower] may do so but to date we have captured three times as many men as our cousins… If I succeed, Attilia will have to take a back seat.'[133]

While Montgomery's force fought through complex terrain and fixed the enemy in position, Keyes's corps soon occupied the entire north-western corner of the island. On 23 July, the day after Palermo had fallen, Patton entered the Sicilian capital city just like one of the conquering heroes he had learned about as a child, and he posed for the press cameras wearing an expression of defiance and promising further victories. Indeed, his Seventh Army was now well placed to strike out for Messina, and so on 25 July Alexander's two army commanders agreed that while the Eighth Army continued to attack, the Seventh Army would seek to advance around the enemy's coastal flank in the expectation that the front would fragment – thereby creating opportunities for a final push through to Messina.

During this critical phase of the campaign, however, Patton's behaviour became so shameful that it nearly ended his career. On 3 August, as the general was making his way to II Corps head-quarters to be awarded a second Distinguished Service Cross for his 'extraordinary heroism' at Gela on 11 July, he stopped at the 15th Evacuation Hospital to visit its patients. There he met battle-stressed Private Charles H. Kuhl, an infantryman from 1st Division, who told the general, 'I guess I can't take it.'[134] Patton's rage at the soldier was uncontrolled: he first slapped Kuhl across the face with his glove and then manhandled him out of the tent. That evening, a still-seething Patton wrote in his diary that such men should be 'tried for cowardice and shot'. A week later, Patton verbally abused another mentally fragile soldier, Private Paul G. Bennett, calling him a 'goddamned coward' who was a 'disgrace to the Army'. To the sound of the bewildered man's sobbing, Patton grabbed Bennett, and snarling that he should be 'lined up against the wall and shot', slapped him and then pulled his pistol from its holster, threatening to do the deed himself. News of the incidents soon spread through the Seventh Army, but although of great interest to the press, nothing was published out of respect to Eisenhower and the implications for the war effort. Instead, a group of journalists presented the Supreme Commander with all the evidence they had obtained on the events, and a veiled threat that if it was not acted upon, the story would come out.

This was just the sort of storm that Eisenhower knew Patton was capable of precipitating, and a scandal in the middle of a campaign was an unwelcome distraction that nobody benefited from except the enemy. He immediately censured Patton for his 'brutality' and 'uncontrollable temper' while warning him that the episode had cause to 'raise serious doubt in my mind as to your future usefulness'.[135] A contrite Patton replied in a typically theatrical manner: 'I am at a loss to find words with which to express my chagrin and grief at having given you, a man to whom I owe everything and for whom I would gladly lay down my life, cause for displeasure with me.'[136] He subsequently apologized in person to the soldiers he had abused and the hospital staff who had witnessed the events, before then touring his formation to express regret to his troops personally. It was a particularly humiliating experience for all concerned, but based on what his troops knew of their general, few believed his sincerity. The 1st Infantry Division listened quietly to the general's words, but despite a rousing finale, US II Corps' chief of intelligence reported, 'Not a man applauded and the division was dismissed. It faded away in silence to the great embarrassment of its commander and the total chagrin of Patton.'[137] The brash prince's coronet had slipped and, to some, it looked so ridiculous that its wearer could no longer be taken seriously. Patton had lost the two vital elements that all effective leaders require: the trust and respect of his followers.

Omar Bradley was one of those who had always been somewhat dubious about Patton's character, and the slapping incidents merely underlined his concerns about Patton's suitability for such high command. He later wrote, 'I was horrified. Even for George Patton it was excessive conduct.'[138] Yet Patton seemed determined to show that recent events had not thrown him off his stride, and he seemed keener than ever to beat the Eighth Army to Messina. The result, in Bradley's opinion, prompted decisions that were totally inappropriate considering the determined resistance the Seventh Army was facing. For example, when Lucian Truscott, the outstanding commander of the 3rd Infantry Division, made it clear that he was not willing to sacrifice the lives of his men unnecessarily and so postponed an attack, Patton stormed into his headquarters and raged, 'Goddammit, Lucian, what's the matter with you? Are you afraid to fight?'[139] As if it was not enough having to fight a cornered and desperate enemy, the Seventh Army's corps and division commanders felt they were also now having to fight their commander's unbridled ambition.

Even so, mercilessly driven by Patton, by the evening of 16 August – with the Axis evacuation completed – a 3rd Division patrol arrived in the ruins of Messina just ten miles ahead of their British counterparts.

But even in victory, and most likely because of it, Patton made a decision that left his subordinates shaking their heads in disbelief. Despite the fact that the town was under accurate enemy shellfire from the Italian mainland, the Seventh Army commander insisted on making a triumphant entrance; and the next day, having ensured that the press were in place to capture the moment, he led an exposed convoy into Messina. The casualties taken when the occupants of the third vehicle in the party were hit by shell fragments during the unnecessary event appalled Bradley, as did the final sentence of Patton's order of the day, which announced to his exhausted troops at the end of a campaign in which he had suffered nearly 9,000 casualties: 'I certainly love war.'[140] There was no congratulatory communication to Patton from Eisenhower, and Bradley later wrote, 'We learned how not to behave from Patton's Seventh Army.'[141]

Patton was in purdah, self-induced and painful. Although having achieved a great deal militarily in Sicily, his future in the developing Allied campaign was in serious doubt even as preparations were being made to invade Italy. Having learned that Montgomery's Eighth Army would land first on the mainland in early September, he was particularly hurt to find out that it would be followed shortly after by the Fifth Army commanded by Eisenhower's former deputy – the young, rapidly promoted and intensely ambitious Mark Clark. Patton had never rated the officer he had called 'too damned slick',[142] and was not entirely surprised when Clark ran into some initial difficulties establishing his force at Salerno during the invasion. Nonetheless, the young lieutenant general was in the thick of the action while Patton, approaching his fifty-eighth birthday, remained in Sicily. As the Italian campaign developed during the autumn, the Seventh Army was gradually stripped of its assets en route to disbandment and its commander remained exiled by Eisenhower and Marshall, a situation challenging for Patton's mental health – and particularly so when he learned that Bradley had been appointed to command the US First Army for next year's cross-Channel invasion.

Before leaving the theatre for England, Bradley went to say farewell to Patton and found him in a poor state, later writing, 'This great proud warrior, my former boss, had been brought to his knees.'[143] Patton was being made to pay for his mistakes, and he knew it, but that only made him more desperate not to end his career before having the opportunity to rehabilitate himself in Operation Overlord. He was also keen to revive his rivalry with the commander of the Eighth Army, and wrote acerbically in his diary, '[T]he British are deliberately trying to build Monty as the hero of the war. That is why they are not too fond of me… I know I can outfight the little fart any time.'[144]

Patton had little option but to use the skill for patience that he had developed at other points in his career, and wait until he heard his fate from the chain of command. His endurance was not made any easier when in November the story of his misdemeanours in Sicily was leaked to the press and prompted calls for his dismissal from the outraged American populace and their politicians. And yet Patton was not sacked, because he was paying penance, during which time the Army's leadership decided that although severely flawed, he was a commander of such talent that the US Army might well need him in the forthcoming campaign in western Europe. He did not know that, however, and a few days after his birthday the morose and underemployed general wrote, 'I have seldom passed a more miserable day. I have absolutely nothing to do and hours of time in which to do it. From commanding 240,000 men, I now have less than 5,000.'[145]

The confirmation of Eisenhower's own appointment in early December as Supreme Commander for the great invasion raised Patton's hopes that he might learn something about his future soon, but no word came, and by the time Montgomery left Italy for his Overlord command just before Christmas in 1943, it occurred to Patton that if he was given another appointment, it would be 'as a subordinate to both Monty and Brad'.[146] He spent a wretched New Year in Sicily, pacing, scowling and sniping at colleagues, having convinced himself that his next orders would be to return home to the United States, not as a hero but in disgrace. But then, without warning, he received his reprieve: Eisenhower wished to meet with him in London. There was, it seemed, to be one last adventure after all.

CHAPTER EIGHT

Three in North-West Europe, 1944–45

BERNARD MONTGOMERY returned to England in early January 1944 delighted at having not only been appointed as commander of the 21st Army Group for Operation Overlord but also Allied land force commander for the opening phase of the campaign in Normandy. The invasion plan had been under development for several months, but just as he had prior to Operation Husky, he rejected it. 'I must have more in the initial punch,' Montgomery explained to Churchill, and with Eisenhower's agreement he ordered an increase to the landing frontage and an improvement in logistical arrangements, to ensure that a lodgement could be adequately sustained and, if possible, expanded.[1] While the revisions were being made, he settled into his new headquarters located at his old school, St Paul's in London, and took the headmaster's study for his own office.

As far as Montgomery was concerned, he had to make up for the fact that the Supreme Commander had no talent for campaign fighting, and be especially careful to ensure that he caught everything that was dropped by the chain of command. Brooke agreed with Montgomery's assessment of Eisenhower and was unimpressed with the American's performance in the Mediterranean theatre, noting in his diary that he 'has got absolutely no strategical outlook and is really totally unfit for the post he holds from an operational point of view'. He also said that Eisenhower made up for the deficit 'by the way he works for good cooperation between allies'.[2] The Eisenhower-Montgomery relationship was, as a consequence, a complex one, and although the two men could work well together when they played to their strengths, few senior Allied leaders failed to recognize the likelihood of significant friction between the two men during a long and demanding campaign.

Montgomery's attention to the details of the Overlord plan was typical of the officer. With responsibility for the largest amphibious assault in the history of warfare, he was only too aware of the great risks involved in the endeavour. While content to allow planners the space to operationalize his intent, he was nonetheless fastidious in his expectation that his intent was realized in a practical way. The initial landing, supported by the Royal Navy and RAF, was to be on a fifty-mile front and consist of three airborne and five infantry divisions from the United States, Britain and Canada. Thirty more divisions, 16 million tons of supplies, 137,000 vehicles, 4,217 armoured fighting vehicles and 3,500 guns were to follow to fight the Battle of Normandy, and then, when the enemy was sufficiently weakened, break out.[3]

The enormity of the challenge facing the whole planning team was like nothing any of them had previously experienced. Captain Brian Metcalfe, a British Second Army logistics staff officer later testified: 'There were nights when I could hardly sleep. The long hours, the endless list of tasks and various other issues playing on my mind. Goodness only knows how Monty managed to drop off at night.'[4] But the general slept well, keeping his regular routine and using his time not to meddle in tactical details but to attend to the bigger picture. This included the handling of Winston Churchill who, having been First Sea Lord during the disastrous assault at Gallipoli in 1915, could not stop himself from interfering in Monty's business. The general politely rebuked the prime minister every time he tried to become too involved, and on one occasion made his position very clear by saying, 'I understand, sir, that you want to discuss with my staff the proportion of soldiers to vehicles landing on the beaches in the first flights. I cannot allow you to do so. My staff advise me and I give the final decision; they then do what I tell them.'[5]

With little time to 'shape' those individuals who would be working under his command, in time-honoured fashion Montgomery engaged (where possible) those he already respected and trusted to fill key 21st Army Group positions. Miles Dempsey, an extremely loyal and capable officer who had led an Eighth Army corps in North Africa, Sicily and Italy, was, for example, given command of the British Second Army, while former subordinates Guy Simonds, Harry Bucknall and Brian Horrocks were all appointed to corps command. Monty also brought loyal, trusted and capable staff officers with him from the Eighth Army, including chief of staff Freddie de Guingand, intelligence head Bill Williams, head of plans Charles Richardson, head of operations R. F. K. Belchem and military assistant Kit Dawnay. He also managed to get two of his favourite formations transferred from the Eighth Army to his new command. The 7th Armoured and 51st (Highland) Divisions, along with his hand-picked personnel, were to provide an important continuity in Monty's fighting machine, and all were used to align the 21st Army Group to his methods and thinking.

As he later wrote: 'My own team at 21 Army Group is quite first-class. I can say definitely that if I had not brought my own team of senior officers back with me from Italy, I could not have done the business and got ready for the Overlord operation. It was essential to have practical knowledge on the job, with officers who know the battle end of the business.'[6] Those senior officers, in command and on the staff, who had not previously served under Montgomery were subsequently schooled in the Montgomery way of warfare in the weeks following their appointments, because 'there was no reason to tinker with a victorious formula'.[7]

Through the messages endlessly passed on by Monty and his acolytes at conferences, meetings and in pamphlets and notes, every officer in the 21st Army Group was left in no two minds about what the boss wanted, what he valued, what he expected and that they should transmit his will to their soldiers. Notes from one of Montgomery's lectures to his senior commanders provide an insight into what he had learned and expected his subordinates to benefit from, and included his strong belief that 'it is all a great study of human nature; you have certain human material at your disposal and what you can make of it will depend on yourself'.[8] Even though the US forces were under his command, Montgomery sensibly left Omar Bradley and his First Army commanders to their own devices, because he recognized that they were in a far better position to offer their troops what they required. This was appreciated by the Americans, and Bradley was impressed with Montgomery's leadership. 'Psychologically, the choice of Montgomery as British commander for the Overlord assault came as a stimulant for us all,' he later wrote. 'For the thin, bony, ascetic face that stared from an unmilitary turtle-neck sweater had, in little over a year, become a symbol of victory in the eyes of the Allied world. Nothing becomes a general more than success in battle.'[9]

Montgomery's reputation was formidable, but he still made it his business to address every major British, Canadian and American formation and show that, as he described it, 'I had absolute confidence in them, and I hoped they could feel the same about me.'[10] Using *Rapier*, a four-carriage train which provided him with accommodation, a mess and an office, Montgomery tore around the British Isles spreading the faith. In one ten-day period he spoke to the troops of seven different divisions in three different corps, often arriving deliberately late to build the tension. He later wrote of such visits, 'I had parades of about 5,000 men each, walked through the ranks, and then got up on a jeep and got the men round and addressed them. My general theme was – the war has gone on long enough; together we will see it through and finish it off; it can be done, and we will do it.'[11] His words were fervent, rousing and reassuring. Their lives, Monty's troops learned, were his priority, and as their commander he was determined they would all 'see this thing through'.[12] After he had finished speaking, the general would inspect a preselected group of the assembled troops and exchange a few words with some – often those wearing an Africa Star ribbon – before gathering them round him for an informal chat.

The British troops were generally impressed by a visit from Monty and could recall the event decades later, while those from the other side of the Atlantic were far more cynical about being lectured at by a British officer. Although he spoke their language he seemed, as one GI later said, 'to have come from a different planet'.[13] Soon recognizing that cultural differences demanded a change of tactics, Monty subsequently spent much of his time when addressing American troops trying to break down barriers, talking about 'one team, comrades in arms, with shared values and outstanding fighting abilities engaged in a common enterprise'.[14] The fact that some massed US troops did not give Montgomery their attention until he yelled at them, and that some officers felt that his words 'belittled them',[15] was inevitable, but few were scornful of his attempt to inspire them as the day of reckoning moved closer. As one US officer noted in his diary after a visit, 'Montgomery's confidence is his strongest asset and despite his odd appearance and accent, he gets his message across well.'[16]

As the weeks passed and winter gave way to spring, improved weather allowed for more intense training. When Montgomery found fault, sloppiness or obstruction anywhere in the massive Allied invasion organization, he was merciless in his reaction, leading Brooke to write that, although his man was making good military progress, he was 'equally successful in making enemies as far as I can see! I have to spend a great deal of my time soothing off some of these troubles.'[17] It was as well that Brooke was attentive, for by the first major briefing on the Overlord plan, which took place on 7 April at St Paul's School, most of the attendees were feeling the pressure of the impending endeavour. At the conference Montgomery used a large map laid out on the floor to reveal every phase of the invasion with 'rare skill', according to Bradley, because he gave every commander a very clear sense of his role. A final briefing orchestrated by Montgomery at the same location on 15 May was an even larger affair, with the King, senior politicians, the chiefs of staff and scores of generals listening intently to Eisenhower, Montgomery and then to each senior commander. With the invasion likely to be launched in a matter of weeks, the mood was serious, and although Monty endeavoured to inject some humour into the proceedings while displaying his characteristic confidence, one attendee called the event 'a justifiably dour affair considering the gravity of what we were about to undertake'.[18]

Over the coming weeks the 21st Army Group's staff pored over the lessons identified by the training and exercise reports they had collated, and having analysed them, shared their findings. Montgomery, meanwhile, attended to his combat leadership teams. Having actively encouraged his subordinates to identify those who revealed chronic leadership weaknesses, Montgomery then undertook the time-consuming process of personally interviewing every British officer in the assault wave down to the rank of lieutenant colonel. He immediately removed any individual he found to be lacking in leadership and anybody who failed to reveal confidence in themselves or their team. The result was that when the invasion force gathered in southern England in late May, Montgomery was as confident as he could be that it had the right men in the right place at the right time.

On 5 June 1944, Rome fell to Mark Clark's US Fifth Army – a great prize despite Italy's now massively diminished strategic importance – and the Western Allies made their final preparations for the invasion of France the following day. Montgomery sent a message aimed at every man:

> The time has come to deal the enemy a terrific blow... To us is given the honour of striking a blow for freedom which will live in history... We have a great and a righteous cause. Let us pray that 'The Lord Mighty in Battle' will go forth with our armies, and that His special providence will aid us in the struggle. I want every soldier to know that I have complete confidence in the successful

outcome of the operations that we are now about to begin. With stout hearts, and with enthusiasm for the contest, let us go forward to victory.[19]

Montgomery would once more be pitting his wits against his old adversary Erwin Rommel, a general he had great respect for and enjoyed the challenge of fighting. 'I have never before had to face up to a Field Marshal in battle', he had written to his brother while in North Africa, 'and I thoroughly enjoyed it.'[20]

The success of the Allied assault on the French coast during 6 June, notwithstanding the particularly heavy casualties taken by the US First Army on Omaha Beach, was beyond even the most optimistic expectations of the Allies' senior leadership. It was, however, merely the first phase of the campaign, which had first to secure Normandy before it could think about pushing east. To do this, the Allies had to overpower the Germans by seizing critical locations, applying devastating ground and air firepower, and breaking the will of the 80,000-strong German Seventh Army. Although Rommel's Army Group B contained many ill-equipped second-rate formations, it had the advantage of defending complex, mobility-resistant terrain that it knew well. Nevertheless, the Allies made a good start by landing 156,000 troops on the first day alone, a number that had risen to 326,000 six days later, along with 54,000 vehicles and some 104,000 tons of supplies.[21] Air supremacy, meanwhile, provided flexible, mobile firepower that was devastating against enemy concentrations, and also severely undermined German reinforcement and resupply.

Yet despite the mass of men and firepower that the Allies landed in Normandy, the fact that the British failed to take the city of Caen on 6 June as Montgomery had planned denied them an important road hub and provided the Germans with a vital anchor point for their defences. Although Montgomery later argued that, in fact, his plan had always been to use Caen as a lure to pin the Germans, thus allowing the US First Army forces the opportunity to create a breakthrough, there is no doubt that on balance the failure to seize the city relegated the 21st Army Group's contribution to the Battle of Normandy to a series of casualty-heavy attempts to wear down the enemy.

Having come ashore on 8 June, Montgomery established himself at his TAC headquarters close to the front – the epicentre of his command in Normandy – with de Guingand's main headquarters not due to arrive until the Normandy lodgement had been expanded in mid-August. The general's caravans were in the centre of the forty-vehicle encampment, which moved twice before settling in late June at the village of Blay (just inside the US sector), where it remained for the rest of the battle. Accompanied by three aides-de-camp and two puppies – a cocker spaniel named 'Rommel' and a Jack Russell named 'Hitler' – Montgomery soon established a daily working routine that consisted of meetings and visits until mid-afternoon, conferences with his staff into the evening, a simple dinner with colleagues and then early retirement to bed. There was little space in Montgomery's day to relax, hence him prioritizing getting enough sleep no matter what the operational situation.

To his immense frustration, his headquarters became a magnet for senior visitors, including King George VI, Winston Churchill, Alan Brooke and Charles de Gaulle. He acted as host with such ill-disguised irritation that one visiting officer described him as 'verging on rude – no, actually, he was bloody rude – and extremely discourteous!'[22] Even so, everybody who came into Montgomery's orbit was subjected to his absolute conviction that everything was going to plan, that the German defences were crumbling and that he had created such a happy situation.

The slogging match that developed after the initial landings was one that the land forces commander was confident of winning, even if it was not the most edifying military spectacle. The continued failure to take Caen, however, led to criticisms of his excessive caution among senior American officers and produced a rash of sackings by Montgomery including several brigade commanders and even the commanders of his 'favourite' 7th Armoured and 51st (Highland)

Divisions, which had invariably been in the thick of the action. Montgomery wrote that Rommel was proving a 'stubborn and worthy opponent once more',[23] but was well aware that his admiration for a skilled opponent meant little unless he was defeated soon, for Rommel's tenacious defence was creating cracks in the resilience of those troops on whom Montgomery relied most. The fact that a significant proportion of those relieved from their duties had very probably reached the limits of their physical and mental endurance after their exertions in North Africa and the Mediterranean had not been anticipated by Montgomery, who seemed not to understand why the performance of these tired formations dipped significantly during this period. As one Scottish captain explained about his division, 'The over-reliance on us took the gloss off our previously close relationship with Montgomery',[24] and as the attritional battle continued it became clear that the overstretched general just could not lever his leadership in the same way as he had in previous campaigns.

When Caen finally fell on 21 July after several weeks of exhausting Anglo-Canadian attacks and the close attentions of RAF bombers, it proved to be just the turning point in the battle that the senior leadership had hoped. Happily, four days later the US First Army won itself a position from which to launch Operation Cobra, its armoured breakout, after a protracted struggle through the close *bocage* countryside. Allied attacks since D-Day had produced a four-to-one superiority and significant advantages in hardware, supplies and morale which could now be exploited. Montgomery recognized that as the Americans took the lead in this new phase of the fighting, it signalled a decisive point in that nation's journey to becoming the senior military partner in the North-West Europe campaign. The development significantly undermined his own argument to remain as the Allied land forces commander beyond the completion of the Battle of Normandy, which his cautious approach to fighting and the lacklustre performance by the 21st Army Group did little to counter.

The issue of Montgomery's trustworthiness had also recently been raised at the Supreme Headquarters Allied Expeditionary Force

(SHAEF), where some felt that it had been misled about the objectives of Operation Goodwood (18–20 July). Although Eisenhower and Bradley had been led by Montgomery to believe that this major British attack east of Caen would plunge twenty-five miles south to Falaise and so provide a distraction from the US breakout to the west, in reality it was far more limited and petered out long before it could have the impact expected. Montgomery's disingenuousness so riled SHAEF that Brooke even found it necessary to make an offer to Eisenhower that he would travel to Normandy and 'assist him in handling Monty'.[25] The offer was declined but the damage was done, and the much-anticipated friction between Montgomery and Eisenhower began to bite. 'My God', wrote Brooke in a diary entry dated 27 July, 'what psychological complications war leads to!'[26]

Operation Cobra made little progress from its narrow launch point during the first week, but on 1 August the dam of German resistance finally broke, and banked-up US armoured division formations flooded out into the French countryside. That same day, Omar Bradley effectively became Montgomery's equal as he took command of the newly operational US 12th Army Group – consisting of the First Army, then commanded by Courtney Hodges, and the Third Army, commanded by George S. Patton. Despite his significant flaws, Patton had been appointed by Eisenhower to provide the bold leadership of armoured forces that the Allies required during this phase of the campaign. This planned organizational development would add new impetus to the Allied offensive, and was soon tested by an opportunity that arose in mid-August to surround the enemy's Fifth and Seventh Panzer Armies in an operation co-ordinated with the 21st Army Group.

Although the US Third Army raced forward to successfully complete its responsibilities, Patton reminding his officers of one of his (and Napoleon's) favourite sayings – 'De l'audace, encore de l'audace, et toujours de l'audace!' ('Audacity, more audacity, and ever more audacity') – the British attack stuttered, and some 50,000 German troops managed to escape the encirclement before it was finally sealed on 21 August. Nevertheless, the Battle of the Falaise Pocket was the death knell of the German Army in Normandy, since perhaps another 50,000 were successfully captured along with vast quantities of equipment. Yet Montgomery's troops had once again struggled to deliver what looked like a wholly achievable contribution to Allied operations, and the British commander was left making excuses about why his subordinate commanders had failed to show the required boldness and drive.

As a result, when the new phase of the campaign began and his TAC HQ moved to the village of Proussy, twenty miles west of Falaise, Montgomery faced a cluster of significant leadership challenges that would severely test the celebrated officer. Chief among them was adjusting to Eisenhower taking over as land forces commander, for Montgomery had little respect for his abilities in that area and so found it difficult to follow him. Thus, as the 21st Army Group raced across western Europe behind a fleeing enemy in operations that were pregnant with opportunity, Montgomery made it entirely clear that he believed the Allies were lacking a sensible strategy.

By 26 August, the day after US troops liberated Paris, the Allies had created a bridgehead over the Seine and were poised to push the 200-mile-long front towards the German border. The 21st Army Group operated on the Allied left flank, with the 12th Army Group on its right and with the prospect of General Jacob L. Devers's 6th Army Group (comprising the US Seventh Army and French First Army) taking up a position on the right flank, having pushed north after its successful invasion of southern France earlier in the month. Eisenhower based his 'broad front' strategy around these three Army Groups – a strategy that Monty referred to as 'a wasteful and languid approach'.[27]

Eisenhower's front sought to maintain a consistent pressure on the enemy while avoiding the military vulnerability that the prioritization of a single formation would create. He was also keen to ensure Allied harmony during the advance east – which, he believed, would be impossible if any one of the formations was prioritized, because with precious supplies still being brought forward from Normandy until another port could be opened, the others would need to be halted. To Montgomery, however, the thinking was flawed and he told Eisenhower so:

> I said that if he adopted a broad front strategy, with the whole line advancing and everyone fighting all the time, the advance would inevitably peter out, the Germans would be given time to recover and the war would go on all through the winter and well into 1945. I also said that he, as Supreme Commander, must sit on a very lofty perch in order to be able to take a detached view of the whole intricate problem... Someone must run the land battle for him.[28]

Monty was somewhat consoled that on the day he lost land forces command, he was promoted to the rank of field marshal (an elevation that Churchill felt 'would mark the approval of the British people for the *British* effort that had led to the defeat of the Germans in France through the medium of Montgomery's leadership'[29]). But he still felt slighted by circumstances. Knowing this, Brooke – who had himself been promoted to field marshal in January – wrote to Monty: 'I should like at this moment of your triumph to offer you one more word of advice. Don't let success go to your head & remember the value of humility.'[30] Montgomery and humility, however, were to become increasing strangers.

With the British Second Army having covered up to sixty miles a day in the previous week, Brussels fell to its Guards Armoured Division on 3 September and Montgomery's idea for a narrow-fronted thrust by his Second Army began to mature. Indeed, so distracted was he by the immediate possibilities of cracking open the front, that he made a significant error of judgement in failing to give precedence to the opening of Antwerp port to help ease the Allies' logistic frailties. Instead, at a meeting in the Supreme Commander's Mitchell B-25 on a Brussels airfield a week after the fall of the Belgian capital, Montgomery pitched Eisenhower the concept that was to become Operation Market Garden. The offensive, he explained, would exploit the enemy's recent disorganization and see the Second Army's XXX Corps, with supply priority, advance through the Netherlands with the support of the First Allied Airborne Army, and cross the Lower Rhine at Arnhem. From that position, the field marshal contended, his force would be well placed to encircle the enemy's industrial heartland, the Ruhr, and advance across Germany's northern plains to Berlin.

For someone with such a strong reputation for caution, it was a remarkably bold idea. In reality, however, often de Guingand was the one who urged more caution when his commander explained some of his more audacious initiatives, and when Market Garden was proposed, de Guingand was in England on sick leave. Thus Monty had no check on his daring and highly complex proposal before it reached Eisenhower, and the Supreme Commander had to decide whether he was willing to advantage Montgomery at the expense of Bradley's 12th Army Group. His authorization of the plan, a temporary suspension of his strategy in order to give Montgomery the supplies he required, was justified in his own mind for its potential to capture a useful crossing point over a major water obstacle and unhinge the front in a way that was advantageous to all.

A delighted Montgomery looked past the strictly temporary primacy that Eisenhower had given the 21st Army Group, writing to Brooke: 'So we have gained a great victory. I feel somewhat exhausted by it all but hope we shall now win the war reasonably quickly.'[31] Bradley, however, thought that Market Garden should never have been supported, and although he would have jumped at the opportunity to receive temporary supply supremacy for his own formations, believed that the operation was rooted in little more than self-interest. 'Monty's plan sprung from his megalomania,' the American general later wrote. 'He would not cease in his efforts to gain personal command of all the land forces and reap all the personal glory from our victory.'[32]

As it turned out, Operation Market Garden (17–25 September) did not achieve its main objective of getting the British Second

Army across the Lower Rhine at Arnhem, and even if it was a worthy endeavour that erased some powerful formations from the German order of battle, it was regarded by the Americans as a costly failure that Eisenhower should never have supported. Montgomery had been indulged and, once again, had failed to deliver. It was an outcome that, like every operational failure he presided over, wore away a little more of the respect that the 21st Army Group (and the Americans) had for his military talents. The implications for his leadership were, therefore, profound. As the Allies reverted back to their broad front during the darkening days of autumn, Allied intelligence suggested that the Germans had regained much of their lost poise along their western border. Like his American colleagues, the field marshal thus faced leading his troops in a demanding slog through another northern European winter.

In such circumstances, Montgomery felt under no obligation to support SHAEF's strategy, and during October he made a string of stinging criticisms about the Supreme Commander's approach, which only further undermined his reputation in the eyes of senior colleagues and were only (temporarily) ended by an Eisenhower rebuke. 'You will hear no more on the subject of command from me,' Montgomery replied to his boss. 'I have given you my views and you have given your answer… That ends the matter and I and all of us up here will weigh in one hundred per cent to do what you want.' He signed the letter 'Your very devoted and loyal subordinate MONTY'.[33]

Having commanded the British officer for so long, Eisenhower knew that he was not a reliable follower and by this time may have wished that Alexander had been given the senior British command for Overlord rather than the obstinate Monty. However, knowing the esteem in which the victor of El Alamein was held in Britain and the political sensitivities surrounding his management, Ike had long since realized he needed to both placate and control Montgomery.

The character of the operations in which the Allies were to engage over the most difficult campaigning months of the year was illustrated by the 21st Army Group's attempt to finally open the port of Antwerp. It took far longer than expected due to tenacious German defence of Antwerp's protective estuary and cost Monty's formation 13,000 casualties (half of them Canadian).[34] The first Allied shipping convoy did not unload there until 29 November, and Montgomery later admitted that his failure to open Antwerp earlier was 'a bad mistake on my part'.[35] He also failed to recognize the true impact that the gruelling campaign was having on the performance of his formations. Some, including XXX Corps, had been fighting since North Africa and were consequentially mentally fatigued, and as Market Garden progressed, they showed signs of drained motivation and faded morale. There were similar difficulties across the 21st Army Group, with infantry divisions having averaged 7,500 casualties since D-Day (40 per cent of each division) and losses being increasingly difficult to replace (with largely inexperienced troops) as the well of British manpower dried up.[36]

Only in late autumn did Montgomery make a new and concerted effort to re-engage with his troops to raise them out of what he feared could become a deep malaise. Major Laurence Wright had been wounded in Normandy and was still walking with a pronounced limp when he joined the staff of 130th Brigade in early November. Several days after his arrival, the brigade commander announced at a conference that Montgomery had issued a reminder to all divisions that 'we all had a responsibility to maintain the fighting spirit of our men and that he would be arriving in a few days to "check it was being done"'.[37] During the visit Wright was pulled to one side by Montgomery and quizzed about morale. Having informed the field marshal that the lack of some basic equipment and clothing made their lives more difficult than they needed to be, he was delighted to be informed twenty-four hours later that a convoy of trucks containing everything he had requested was making its way to the formation, 'with the compliments of Field Marshal Montgomery'.[38]

Montgomery also insisted that the 21st Army Group was supplied with adequate cold-weather clothing, that troops were given leave from the front and that entertainment was provided to help make the long hours of darkness more bearable. During those gloomy evenings Montgomery once again began to agitate about strategy – unable, it seems, to remain Eisenhower's 'loyal subordinate' for long. With the Allies yet to cross the German border and facing a motivated enemy protected by both the Rhine and the Siegfried Line defences, he wrote to Brooke: 'If we go drifting along as at present we are merely playing into enemy hands, and the war will go on indefinitely.'[39] He restated his feelings at a commanders' conference in Maastricht on 7 December, held to specifically discuss strategy. While Bradley advocated advances either side of the Ardennes, aligning with Eisenhower's broad front, Montgomery instead sought a concerted push on the Ruhr, which would advance his own ambitions. According to Bradley, he 'refused to admit that there was any merit to anybody else's views except his own'.[40]

Nevertheless, Eisenhower – recently promoted to five-star general and so no longer nominally outranked by Montgomery – authorized limited offensives by Bradley using his First and Third Armies to move up to the Rhine, and in doing so hoped to create a position from which to undertake a major new offensive in the spring. Just days later, however, on 16 December 1944, Allied plans were rendered obsolete when Hitler launched a counter-attack through the Ardennes. This surprise offensive sought to achieve what had barely been considered a possibility by Allied intelligence: a major armoured offensive consisting of some 400,000 troops and over 1,400 armoured fighting vehicles pushing through inhospitable terrain on a fifty-mile front in the middle of winter.[41] Hitler's ambition was to retake Brussels followed by the port of Antwerp, creating a physical split in the 12th Army Group and a political crisis in the high command. The offensive was to become the major battle of the campaign during the winter, and one of the most remarkable of the entire war.

The stoicism of the American troops facing the onslaught in the most diabolical conditions was a tribute to the US Army, its tactical leaders, and the superb reaction of senior commanders. Led by Eisenhower – who realized quickly that, within reasonable limits, the attack could be allowed to run its course without threat to any objective of strategic importance, and would render an overstretched enemy vulnerable to counter-attack – the Allied reaction was calm and considered. Despite Montgomery's criticisms of the Supreme Commander's abilities, the soundness of Eisenhower's thinking was soon borne out by events which saw the German force unable to exploit its initial penetration, leaving Patton's Third Army to deliver a stunning relieving riposte.

Montgomery's role in the Allied response was important rather than decisive. In taking temporary command of the US First and Ninth Armies on 20 December, after their communication with the Third Army and Bradley's 12th Army Group headquarters was severed, he stabilized the northern front and rushed British formations into a blocking line along the Meuse river. The German offensive stalled before the obstacle was reached, but as part of a wider Allied effort Monty's quick and efficient action helped to ensure that the threat was contained.

However, Montgomery showed incredible insensitivity even as the 'Battle of the Bulge' was being fought, claiming that the German blow would never have been landed had he been land forces commander. Eisenhower's rage at such a pronouncement while American lives were being lost was so great that he prepared a draft of a letter to the Joint Chiefs of Staff in Washington explaining why Montgomery should be sacked. 'It looks to me as if Monty, with his usual tact, has been rubbing into Ike the results of not having listened to Monty's advice! Too much of "I told you so" to assist in creating the required friendly relations between them,'[42] Alan Brooke wrote in his diary at the end of December. Having learned from de Guingand about Eisenhower's letter, a 'very distressed' Montgomery once again found it necessary to write a letter of apology to the Supreme Commander and signed it, without a hint of irony, 'Your very devoted subordinate, Monty'.[43] Eisenhower never sent his letter about Montgomery to Washington, his initial outrage having subsided and the political implications of his potential actions trumping his desire for justice.

In such circumstances, it was all the more galling for Eisenhower to learn that the field marshal had held a press conference at his TAC headquarters located in Villa Magda, a grand house in the eastern Belgian town of Zonhoven, and given the impression that his intervention in the battle had been decisive. The Americans were still regaining their poise; the shock German offensive had carved deep into the 12th Army Group, but aided by General Patton's bold riposte – which drove hard and fast into their southern flank to relieve Bastogne – they had subsequently made an impressive recovery. British involvement in the outcome had not been decisive or even particularly significant, but in talking to the press about the battle Montgomery was not only seeking to give the impression of his being a guiding hand in the Allied response, he was also making another bid to be reinstalled as land forces commander. He addressed the assembled reporters wearing a new beret arrangement with his general's badge now accompanied by the winged insignia of the Parachute Regiment. In what several participants later described as a rather dull event, Montgomery proceeded to praise the American soldier, saying earnestly, 'I want to take this opportunity to pay a public tribute to him. He is a brave fighting man, steady under fire, and with a tenacity in battle which stamps the first-class soldier.' He also underlined his loyalty to Dwight Eisenhower: 'Let me tell you that the captain of our team is General Eisenhower,' Montgomery enthused. 'I am absolutely devoted to Ike. We are the greatest of friends.'[44]

Yet, although the field marshal said nothing particularly controversial, his patronizing tone and the clear desire to promote himself led his chief of intelligence, Brigadier Bill Williams, to label the event 'disastrous', for in failing to take account of obvious sensitivities surrounding US losses, 'the presentation [was] quite appalling'.[45] Once again, Montgomery's sparkling egotism had been revealed in all its embarrassing gaudiness. The consequences were not insignificant, for the German propaganda machine latched on to the story and wasted no time in intensifying the storm around

Montgomery's generalship, which subsequently fed US anger. 'Eisenhower told me that the anger of his generals was such', Winston Churchill wrote to his military assistant, 'that he would hardly dare to order any of them to serve under Montgomery.'[46]

That Montgomery's poorly considered, ill-mannered and high-handed behaviour was not allowed to fundamentally unsettle the campaign was due to some excellent leadership by Eisenhower. In the final analysis – with spring on the horizon, logistical stability regained and the Germans under growing pressure in the West while being ravaged in the East – Montgomery's infelicities had to be tolerated by SHAEF lest they become an adverse distraction. As it was, the Allied Army Groups were each preparing for operations to close in on the Rhine, and they began on 8 February 1945 when the 21st Army Group (with the US Ninth Army still under its temporary command) enacted a pincer movement towards the river, and by 10 March had gained its west bank. Progress was being made, albeit slowly and at the expense of heavy casualties.

The simmering antipathy between Montgomery and Eisenhower continued to concern Brooke. Having breakfasted with the American in London during the 21st Army Group's advance to the Rhine, he wrote in his diary that the Supreme Commander's 'relations with Monty are quite insoluble', and he was perturbed that Eisenhower only saw 'the worst side of Monty and cannot appreciate the better side. Things are running smoothly for the present, but this cannot last and I foresee trouble ahead before long.'[47]

Indeed, although the US armies were not scheduled to cross the Rhine until after Montgomery had launched his own meticulous set-piece crossing of the river, Bradley, frustrated that the laborious Brit was again being given the opportunity to make the first historic crossing of the Rhine, encouraged his commanders to close in on the river and establish themselves on the east bank before Monty 'even [had] an oar in the water'.[48] As a consequence, Courtney Hodges's men were the first to cross the Rhine on 7 March using an intact bridge at Remagen, and then two weeks later – and still before Montgomery had launched his complex airborne-amphibious operation – Third Army troops crossed in boats at Oppenheim. Bradley was so gratified that he sent Patton a signal congratulating him on his achievement, which, he noted, had been accomplished 'without the benefit of aerial bombardments, ground smoke, artillery preparation and airborne assistance'.[49]

Monty did nothing in the face of these developments other than suggest that, as usual, he had benefited his American colleagues by drawing the enemy to the threat posed by his preparations. In aiming not just to 'bounce the Rhine' but to do so in a manner that would not squander lives unnecessarily, Montgomery believed that he was fighting in a manner appropriate to the manpower crisis that was biting deeply into the 21st Army Group's resources. Endeavouring to motivate his men on 23 March, the eve of his Rhine crossing, the field marshal invited them all to play their part in the final phase of the campaign:

> The complete and decisive defeat of the Germans is certain; there is no possibility of doubt on this matter. 21 Army Group will now cross the Rhine. The enemy possibly thinks he is safe behind the great river obstacle... but we will show the enemy that he is far from safe behind it... Over the Rhine, then, let us go. And good hunting to you all on the other side. May 'The Lord mighty in battle' give us victory in this our latest undertaking, as He has done in all our battles since we landed in Normandy on D-Day.[50]

As expected, the power of his Operation Varsity-Plunder so overwhelmed the defenders that criticisms were immediately made of Montgomery's unnecessary caution. Such reproaches were not without merit, particularly from an American perspective, but Montgomery's Army Group was British, and artillery officer Raymond Wilkins spoke for many when he said that although the operation was 'a typical Monty sledgehammer to crack a nut... we were all grateful that at this stage in the war no unnecessary risks were being taken and that, ultimately, was because Monty was looking after us'.[51]

With both the 21st and 12th Army Groups well established and expanding bridgeheads east of the Rhine by the last week of March, the final phase of Eisenhower's broad-fronted strategy could be executed by his armies as they advanced east. There would be no British or American dash to the finishing line, but a measured Allied advance that was choreographed to ensure that the link-up with the Soviet Red Army, approaching from the opposite direction, was swift but non-confrontational. Thus, although Montgomery typically sought to manoeuvre into a position from which he could capture Berlin, Eisenhower stood firmly against this, not only seeing problems with the British taking such a prestigious objective but also that the German capital would not fall without a protracted and bloody fight. Montgomery was not the only man infuriated by Eisenhower's subsequent agreement with the Soviets (authorized by the new US president, Harry S. Truman, shortly after Franklin Roosevelt's death, and supported by General Marshall) to leave the German capital to the Red Army. Churchill was furious that the opportunity to send a strong political message to the world had been missed. 'Berlin was the prime and true objective of the Anglo-American armies,' the British prime minister proclaimed,[52] while Montgomery later opined that the Americans had failed to understand 'that it was of little avail to win the war strategically if we lost it politically'.[53] Berlin was, in Montgomery's words, 'off the menu',[54] but elsewhere there was the need for haste. While the final movement of the Western Allies into Germany was to be restrained to avoid a clash with the Soviets, it could not afford to tarry lest the Soviets overrun the agreed demarcation lines.

Although Montgomery referred to the strategy east of the Rhine as 'a dog's breakfast',[55] he was entirely clear what the 21st Army Group had to achieve, and his main priority was to stop the Red Army from advancing to the Danish border and denying the West access to the Baltic Sea. It was an objective that he sought to achieve with the least possible loss of life – soldiers and civilians – in consideration of the imminent ending of the war in Europe. To this end, Colonel

Peter Duke, an officer who described his duties as 'conducting public relations with the German people on behalf of British Second Army', was present at a meeting at which Montgomery said: 'Preservation of life is essential in these final weeks. We must be aware at all times that civilians – the people of our enemy – are present on the battlefield for we will soon be occupying their homeland. This is not the time for revenge, but it is time for good British soldiering.'[56]

The final weeks of the war in Europe were among the most grim and difficult that Montgomery and the 21st Army Group had experienced since landing on mainland Europe ten months earlier. During April, the cruellest of months, both the 6th and 12th Army Groups had commenced operations that projected them eastwards into central Germany, while the US Ninth Army, fighting under Montgomery's command for the last time, successfully encircled 317,000 troops and twenty-four generals in the Ruhr Pocket. The 21st Army Group, meanwhile, struck out north. As the First Canadian Army set about clearing those areas of the Netherlands still in German hands and making a sweep of Lower Saxony, the British Second Army began its advance across the north German plain. Miles Dempsey's leading divisions pushed hard for the Baltic, the armour leaving areas of resistance to the infantry following so that the armoured formations could maintain their momentum. British forces crossed the Elbe river on 29 April, four days after US troops first linked up with the Red Army and the day before Adolf Hitler committed suicide in his Berlin bunker.

The city of Lübeck on the Baltic coast fell to British troops just hours before the arrival of the Red Army on 2 May, and Hamburg followed twenty-four hours later. The battle for Hamburg, Germany's second-largest city, lasted five days – during which XII Corps fought a mix of Volkssturm national militia, Wehrmacht troops from the First Parachute Army, SS units, Hitler Youth, sailors, and anybody else either willing or able to fight for the Third Reich in its dying days. 'It was a sad, bloody affair,' recalled Corporal David Kirkmore, a tank driver in the 7th Armoured Division, 'the old and the young, the fanatics and the bewildered all contributing to a nightmarish melee that everybody knew was for little in the last days of the war.'[57] Nevertheless, the success allowed Montgomery to write to Brooke, 'All's well that ends well and the whole of the Schleswig peninsula and Denmark is now effectively sealed off and we shall keep it so.'[58]

On 3 May, as the 21st Army Group began to consolidate its newly won positions, a four-man OKW delegation authorized by Hitler's successor as head of state, Admiral Karl Dönitz, arrived at Montgomery's TAC headquarters on a hill at Häcklingen on Lüneburg Heath. After leaving them standing in the cold under a fluttering Union flag for just enough time to feel uncomfortable, Montgomery emerged from a tent and the German party saluted. 'It was a great moment,' the field marshal later wrote, 'I knew the Germans had come to surrender and that the war was over.'[59] Having detailed his exacting terms for the unconditional surrender of German forces in the Netherlands, north-west Germany and Denmark, together with all naval vessels in those areas, Montgomery was forceful with the two admirals and general. 'If you do not agree to... the surrender', he told them, 'then I will go on with the war and I will be delighted to do so. All your soldiers and civilians may be killed.'[60] Having been given time to consult with the OKW, the representatives returned the following evening for a signing ceremony witnessed by military officials and members of the media.

The deed done, Montgomery retired to his caravan and wrote to his senior commanders with the news that an armistice would come into effect at 08.00 the following day. The field marshal then drafted a final message to the officers and men of the 21st Army Group. His words reflected the great journey they had all been on, the many pronounced sacrifices they had made and the 'great joy and thankfulness' that they had been spared to witness final victory. Although sounding a note of warning that 'great problems lie ahead; the world will not recover quickly from the upheaval that has taken place; there is much work for each of us', he ended with his thanks to all. 'It has been a privilege and an honour to command this great British Empire team in Western Europe', he explained. 'Few commanders can have had such loyal service as you have given me… Let us now win the peace.'[61] Joining his colleagues at a simple but celebratory dinner, even the abstemious Montgomery was persuaded to drink a glass of champagne, but he soon left his colleagues to enjoy the party, preferring to retire to bed at his usual time.

The final German Instrument of Surrender was signed by representatives from both sides at Karlshorst in Berlin on the evening of 8 May 1945. By this time Montgomery was in a reflective mood, knowing that the events, decisions and relationships of the previous year would soon come under critical scrutiny, and he ended his war diary with a predictably pointed entry: 'When I review the campaign as a whole I am amazed at the mistakes we made. The Supreme Commander had no firm idea as to how to conduct the war and was "blown about by the wind" all over the place… the staff at SHAEF were completely out of their depth all the time. The point to understand is if we had run the show properly the war could have been finished by Christmas 1944. The blame for this must rest with the Americans.'[62]

Very rarely admitting an error of judgement, never doubting his value as commander and always believing that he was master of the battlefield, Montgomery ended his war as he began it: with an overwhelming sense of his own worth and a limited tolerance for views that did not accord with his own.

— □ —

On 3 November 1943, Führer's Directive No. 51 stated that the strategic situation had changed and that 'the threat from the East remains, but an even greater danger looms in the West: the Anglo-American landing!'[63] Shortly after, Erwin Rommel and the headquarters of Army Group B were doing their utmost to ensure that this invasion never achieved a foothold on mainland Europe. The field marshal began consulting with a variety of experts to better understand the coastal defensive situation. One of those interviewed personally by Rommel was Major Wolf Hansen, a staff officer specializing in engineering who had served in a variety of formations on the coast for three years. 'We discussed aspects of the Allied beach obstacle clearance,' Hansen later recalled. 'The field marshal impressed me with his knowledge and complimented me on the meticulousness of a report I had prepared for him... I liked Rommel and it was clear that colleagues respected him, but I also learned that he was difficult to work for. Very demanding.'[64]

While his staff continued their talks with various authorities in the field of defensive works, Rommel began his visits to the coastline and by Christmas had inspected those in Denmark. He was not impressed but neither was he unduly concerned, because his military instinct, supported by intelligence, told him that the invasion would not come across the North Sea but the English Channel. Thus, having established his headquarters in a comfortable Fontainebleau chateau, he attended a series of meetings with his boss in Paris.

Field Marshal Gerd von Rundstedt, the master strategist and Commander-in-Chief West, despised the Nazis, though he felt officers should avoid politics. He distrusted Rommel largely because of his background, rapid rise and intimacy with Hitler. He also remembered him as the general who had caused him so much grief during the invasion of France four years earlier, when as Army Group commander he had struggled to control Rommel, then commanding the 7th Panzer Division. The feeling was mutual. Rommel did not like the opulence of the Army Group West headquarters at the George V hotel near the Champs-Élysées and he found the conservative, traditional 68-year-old Prussian nobleman just the sort of officer he had spent much of his career trying to avoid. But while the initial relationship between the two men was frosty, they soon came to admire the other's professionalism and both agreed that Germany's strategic situation was nothing short of disastrous.

Joined by Lieutenant General Alfred Gause as his chief of staff, thus continuing an almost-unbroken working relationship which stretched back to North Africa in 1941, along with representatives from the Luftwaffe and the Navy, Rommel inspected the Atlantic Wall along the Channel coast during January 1944 and identified innumerable weaknesses. They included too few pillboxes, inadequate fields of anti-personnel and anti-tank mines, the lack of an armoured reserve, poor leadership and serious deficiencies of fighting spirit. The field marshal made it his priority to tackle each, and principally in the sectors that had been identified as most likely to receive the invasion: either side of the Somme, or in the Pas-de-Calais sector. Rommel also expected the invasion to be led not by Montgomery, the man he said 'never made a serious strategic mistake', but by the man he considered to have contributed 'the most astonishing achievement of mobile warfare' during the past year, George Patton.[65]

Defended by General Hans von Salmuth's seventeen-division-strong Fifteenth Army, these areas were accessed by the shortest route across the Channel and connected by a good road network to the Ruhr, Germany's industrial centre. It was where Rommel himself would have landed if he were the Allied commander, and having put himself in the enemy's position he decided that the invasion had to be defeated before the enemy had created a viable beachhead. 'If we cannot get at the enemy immediately after he lands we will never be able to make another move, because of his vastly superior air forces,' Rommel announced at a conference of senior officers. 'If we are not able to repulse the enemy at sea or throw him off the mainland in the first forty-eight hours, then the invasion will have succeeded, and the war will have been lost.'[66]

With the Allies likely to have overwhelming air superiority, he argued, it was essential that panzer divisions be clustered as close to the probable invasion beaches as possible. The alternative – a large concentration of armour held further back and mobilized en masse when the invasion began – would become a prime target for Allied fighter bombers and also take too long to arrive at the decisive point. Von Rundstedt disagreed, arguing that the enemy's aerial artillery had been overestimated, and as such he was an advocate of ten panzer divisions being held in depth. It was an important issue, but one that was left unresolved for the time being, as Rommel rolled out his plan to improve the Atlantic defences. One of his first decisions was to direct his head of military construction, General Wilhelm Meise, to attend to the most obvious deficiencies in defences designed to slow the enemy's attempt to get off the beaches – both obstacles on the shoreline and heavily armed strongpoints.

Meanwhile, Rommel created a list of those formations defending the critical beaches and determined to imbue them with greater fighting spirit. Many, he felt, had become 'fat and lazy' in body and mind – having led comfortable lives as occupiers away from the fighting fronts – and needed some discipline and training.[67] He had no truck with anybody who failed to fulfil his intent, including von Salmuth, with whom he had furious rows because Rommel found the general was picking and choosing which orders to follow and on a time scale that did not meet the requirements of the emergency. Although the field marshal had himself evaded orders from his chain of command on many occasions over the previous four years, he was brutal to those who did not follow his directions to the letter. Nevertheless, he wrote to his fifteen-year-old son Manfred, who was soon to join the youth section of the Luftwaffe: 'You'll have to learn to obey the orders of your superiors without answering back. Often there'll be orders that don't suit you, or that you don't get the point of. Obey without question.'[68]

By mid-January 1944, Commander-in-Chief West and the General Inspector of the Western Defences had established a good working relationship based on mutual trust, and von Rundstedt recommended that Hitler give Rommel operational command of Army Group B (which incorporated the Fifteenth and Seventh Armies). Thus granted this greater authority, the field marshal continued his tour of the defences. What he found did not fill him with confidence, and in Friedrich Dollmann, the Seventh Army commander (and an officer who had not seen action since 1918), he identified the personification of infectious indolence. 'The job's being very frustrating,' Rommel wrote to Lucie on 26 January, after his latest tangle with Berlin over his request for more fighter aircraft. 'Time and again one comes up against bureaucratic and ossified individuals who resist everything new and progressive. But we'll manage it all the same.'[69]

Rommel drove improvements hard, and by late winter his efforts were rewarded with more beach obstacles, more extensive minefields, hundreds of pillboxes, and troops improving their defensive skills. One of Dollmann's corps commanders, Erich Marcks, a one-legged veteran of the Eastern Front, was comforted that somebody was finally taking control of the situation, and wrote to his son: '[Rommel's] very frank and earnest. He's not just a flash-in-the-pan; he's a real warlord. It's a good thing that [Hitler] thinks a lot of him, for all his bluntness, and gives him these important jobs.'[70] The commander of Army Group B was an inspiration to those who recognized that the situation was grave and that their lives – and those of their men – might very well depend on doing exactly what he demanded.

In February the Army Group B headquarters relocated to a chateau at La Roche-Guyon, north-west of Paris, to be closer to the Channel coast, and here Rommel fell into a demanding routine. Leaving his headquarters no later than 06.00 (and often as early as 04.00), having already conducted a breakfast meeting with his chief of staff, Rommel would travel around his command for most of the day, returning only in the evening for conferences, a simple supper with colleagues and a walk in the grounds before retiring to bed. The little time that Rommel carved out for himself, he liked to share with Elbo, his dachshund puppy, whom he took for walks in the woods, but he never fully relaxed, his mind always turning over ideas and seeking solutions to the myriad complex problems that he faced every day. Goebbels wondered how long Rommel could keep up such a pace with his chronic poor health, writing in his diary: 'He must be a broken man due to the extended time in Africa. But one cannot let this fact become public because Rommel is, after all, the war idol of the Germans.'[71] The propagandist's concerns were well founded, for despite Rommel's outward vivacity he remained exhausted from his exertions in the desert and in great discomfort from his stomach ailments. He did his utmost to hide both from his staff, but they all knew that their commander needed more assistance than he would ever dream of requesting, and did what they could to ease his burdens despite an increased tetchiness which sometimes made him a difficult man to care for.

By early spring 1944, a frenzy of activity gripped Army Group B as its commanders, energized by Rommel's insistence that the war in the West would be decided within months by them, refined their preparations. In March, Hitler assigned eight panzer divisions and two panzer grenadier divisions to Panzer Group West (later renamed the Fifth Panzer Army). This armoured formation would act as von Rundstedt's armoured reserve, and its commander, Leo Geyr von Schweppenburg, agreed with him that the entire force should be concentrated away from the coast, near Paris. Despite several arguments with von Schweppenburg, Rommel could not change his mind and Hitler needed to broker a compromise: the force would be split, with some divisions being held in deep reserve while the remainder were located near the coast. Neither, however, could be committed without the Führer's express permission. Both camps recognized that this could hardly have been a worse decision, but now their hands were tied and the headquarters of Army Group B had to alter its plans to accommodate this new development.

Around the same time as these important events, Rommel found it necessary to find a new chief of staff even though Alfred Gause remained an outstanding staff officer. The reason for his replacement seems to have emanated from a trivial domestic issue hundreds of miles away. The Gauses had been living in the Rommel family home in Herrlingen, a suburb of Ulm in southern Germany, after their own had been bombed. Lucie, however, found it increasingly difficult to live in the same house as Frau Gause and demanded they leave. The result was not just that the Gauses had to find somewhere else to live but, remarkably, that Alfred was removed as Rommel's trusted and highly capable chief of staff. His replacement, the scholarly Lieutenant

General Dr Hans Speidel, was handpicked by the field marshal. A fellow Swabian who was known to Rommel – having served with him in the Württemberger Regiment during the First World War – he was regarded as a methodical, calm and efficient officer, and the two men struck up an excellent working relationship. 'He makes a good fresh impression,' Rommel wrote.[72] Indeed, Speidel had hardly had time to receive all his briefings and get to grips with the running of a new headquarters before the Allied invasion was expected.

Despite deep concerns in the Army Group B headquarters about its formation's ability to withstand the coming onslaught, by early May Rommel was adopting a public-facing confidence for German newsreels that gave the Reich hope. Marianne Weiss, serving with the Luftwaffe in Italy, recalled: 'Erwin Rommel was a beacon of hope. I first remember him as a great hero in the desert, but it was in France before the invasion that we listened most closely to his words. We trusted him at a time when our faith in others was faltering.'[73] Those 'others' included senior military figures who believed that Hitler was leading Germany to disaster and that the only hope was to decapitate the Nazi regime.

Indeed on 27 May, the day on which Rommel received praise from Hitler for his accomplishments with Army Group B, Speidel attended a meeting with conspirators in Germany whose concerns about the Nazi regime had become so acute that they were willing to risk their lives – and those of their loved ones – to become involved in a plot to assassinate Hitler. The extent to which Rommel knew about their plans is not known, but it is unlikely he was aware that he was being suggested by the conspirators as the officer with universal appeal who might be capable of leading the nation to peace. No evidence exists that Rommel was in any meaningful way involved in the conspiracy, and even if he had been tempted to investigate the fringes of the group, he had clearly committed all his energies to the defence of the Channel coast.

The stress he worked under was immense and his body reacted badly to it, but he looked forward to seeing his family for one last time before the invasion; and thus on 5 June, encouraged by von Rundstedt's assessment that conditions were not conducive for an Allied invasion, Rommel travelled back to Germany to celebrate Lucie's fiftieth birthday. Consequently, just as Rommel had been in Germany when Montgomery launched his attack at El Alamein on 23 October 1942, so the commander who prided himself on being at the decisive point at the critical time was away from his headquarters when the Allies launched their cross-Channel invasion on 6 June 1944.

The arrival of Dwight Eisenhower's force on and over the Normandy coast was a surprise to much of the German senior military leadership, which had remained convinced that the main invasion force would land in the Pas-de-Calais sector. It was a military judgement reinforced by a brilliant Allied deception campaign, which included the creation of a fictitious formation called the 'First US Army Group', based in southern England and commanded by George Patton. Airborne troops had been dropped during the night, and began to secure the flanks of a bridgehead initially consisting of five beaches that were subsequently assaulted during the following morning under the cover of intense close air support and naval gunfire. Von Rundstedt sought to obtain the authorization he required from the OKW to launch his armoured reserve towards the invasion area, but Hitler was asleep. Rommel, meanwhile, had been contacted before dawn by Speidel, who relayed to him reports about parachutists landing north-east of Caen and north of Carentan, and he was convinced that such operations were unlikely to be part of a feint. The field marshal asked to be updated during the morning once the broader strategic situation had been assessed; several hours later he was informed about the beach assaults.

Within minutes of learning the news, Rommel began the 500-mile journey back to his headquarters, which had to be taken by car due to Allied aerial dominance and only made him more anxious about what he would be told when he got there. He hoped that the armour was moving towards the beaches, but in fact only the 120-tank-strong 21st Panzer Division, located near Caen, had mounted a counter-attack that day – and even then, it missed an early opportunity to make an impact because the complicated arrangements surrounding its authority to move had stymied its commander. But Rommel knew that a single panzer division would never be enough to stop the Allies from establishing themselves in Normandy, and so it was on Dollman's static Seventh Army and, specifically, three infantry divisions that so much depended. However, having been subjugated by the invader's naval and aerial firepower, the defenders struggled to do much more than hold the line.

By the time Rommel arrived back at La Roche-Guyon at 22.30 that evening, some 155,000 Allied troops were ashore and the British had made particularly good progress with a bridgehead twenty miles wide and up to six miles deep – although, importantly, not including the city of Caen. According to one artillery commander present at Rommel's headquarters when he bustled through the door, the field marshal's return was a relief, and he noted soon after: 'He's very calm and collected. Grim-faced, as to be expected.'[74] He immediately went into conference with Speidel and his senior staff, and within minutes fresh orders were being transmitted to his commanders.

Over the next week, as the Allies looked to enlarge their Normandy bridgehead and so create space for their massive invasion force, Army Group B came under remorseless pressure. The impact of the German armoured counter-attack when it was finally unleashed was, as Rommel had predicted, severely undermined by Allied air power. Indeed, on 10 June, Panzer Group West's headquarters – located at La Caine, twelve miles south-west of Caen – was attacked by the RAF's Second Tactical Air Force, working from Ultra intelligence which had revealed that the formation was preparing for an attack. The raid killed eighteen staff officers, wounded von Schweppenburg and forced the cancellation of its already-belated contribution to undermine Allied lodgements. That same day, Rommel wrote in his diary, 'Our operations in Normandy are tremendously hampered, and in some places even rendered impossible, by the following factors' – and then listed the enemy's air power, naval gunfire support, superior

American weaponry and the insertion of so many airborne forces.[75] With his reserves deployed, ammunition low, casualties mounting and innumerable holes in the line to fill, Rommel feared that his ability to contain the enemy was weakening and implored his subordinate commanders to hold their positions until they became untenable. His complete immersion in battle details left the field marshal with precious little time to stand back and provide the sort of considered senior-level decision-making that other Army Group commanders worked hard to ensure they had time to prioritize.

His British adversary Bernard Montgomery, for example, had a regimented routine, a TAC headquarters and teams of liaison officers that allowed him to remain in touch with the fighting while also being remote from it. Rommel, on the other hand, spent hours travelling between his headquarters and the front, often unable to see the bigger picture and making himself vulnerable to Allied aircraft. When he arrived at his headquarters he was invariably informed that his request to the OKW for reinforcements had been declined – Hitler even suggesting that his 'wonder weapons' would soon push the Allies back into the sea[76] – or that another air strike had devastated a convoy or fatally undermined an attempt to retrieve vital lost ground.

Seventh Army dispatch rider Daniel Vasel often saw the devastation wrought by Allied aircraft, and on several occasions was targeted himself. On one day in mid-June, he found the field marshal's staff car pulled off the road and sheltering under trees on the edge of a wood:

> I had to deliver a message to a senior officer accompanying Rommel and found the party surveying the ground behind our line. I announced myself and handed the message over and while the general was reading it the field marshal and I passed a few words. 'Be careful on the road,' he said and pointed to the sky, 'we were spotted and they'll be back.' He looked me in the eye, placed a hand briefly on my shoulder, and then returned to his conversation. That touch sustained me for the rest of a difficult day. Rommel had that ability.[77]

Rommel knew that a touch of his hand, a kindly word or, indeed, a sharp rebuke could motivate his troops; it was one of the reasons that his leadership style continued to rely on his presence long after his responsibilities should have precluded prolonged contact with his subordinates in the field. As in 1940, he ghosted around the battlefield to see his divisions, often accompanied by the corps commanders. Speidel noted that the field marshal 'knew how to keep the right balance between praise and criticism'[78] and said that he 'ceaselessly exerted his remarkable powers of leadership on the soldiers'.[79]

By 12 June, the individual Allied beachheads had been unified into a single and impressive entity, and Rommel knew that it was only a matter of time before Normandy became untenable. The Allies had won the first phase of the battle; the Americans were threatening to seal the base of the Cotentin peninsula prior to advancing north to take Cherbourg as a main supply port, while British attention on Caen demanded constant vigilance and was soaking up huge resources. Rommel and von Rundstedt consequently met with Hitler and Alfred Jodl, the OKW's chief of operations, on the morning of 17 June during the Führer's only visit to his field headquarters (*Führerhauptquartier*), which had been constructed at Margival, near Soissons, for his use during the planned invasion of Britain.

The two field marshals found Hitler 'sitting hunched upon a stool'; he looked pale and exhausted, and fidgeted constantly with his spectacles as the officers received 'a curt and frosty greeting'.[80] After a brief introduction, von Rundstedt handed over to Rommel who spoke frankly about the situation in Normandy, saying 'that the struggle was hopeless against such tremendous superiority in the air, at sea, and on land' and that they needed reinforcements and the freedom of action to fight the battle as they saw fit.[81] Endeavouring to hold on to the port of Cherbourg, he argued, was a waste of troops, and he advised that the front line be withdrawn out of the range of Allied naval gunfire. Hitler did not accept either the situation report or Rommel's assessment that giving ground was a solution to anything. Pacing the room, he began one of his long, rambling monologues, blaming treachery, poor generalship and cowardice for the precarious situation in which Germany had found herself, and reasserted his faith in another new wonder weapon: the V-2 rocket, the first long-range guided ballistic missile, which he expected would bring Britain to her knees.

Rommel was unimpressed with the rhetoric that he had heard so many times before, and particularly so when, sooner or later, his troops would be overrun by the enemy. He waited for the stenographers to be dismissed before offering a riposte, and in so doing hinted heavily that the best course of action would be to make peace with the West and carry on the fight in the East.[82] The officer was given short shrift by Hitler, who was enraged by such talk and asserted his demand for loyalty and fanatical resistance – and, pointedly, that his field marshals leave the politics to the politicians. The meeting at Margival was, Speidel later noted, 'highly destructive in its military, political, and psychological consequences'.[83]

Two weeks after Rommel's meeting with Hitler, Army Group B's situation had deteriorated. By the end of June, German armoured forces had been frittered away in local counter-attacks, the attritional fighting had thinned the defensive line even further and a despairing Dollmann had taken his own life after the fall of Cherbourg. Summoned to Berchtesgaden for another conference with Hitler on 29 June, Rommel and von Rundstedt undertook the 600-mile drive to the Führer's Bavarian eyrie without any confidence that it was worth the time away from their responsibilities. They were unsurprised on their arrival, therefore, to have to listen to another Hitler rant, this time fuelled by the recent launch of a massive Soviet offensive in the East that was in the process of destroying an entire Army Group. When Hitler finished, Rommel gave his report: the front in the West was on the verge of collapse and, as a consequence, he recommended a strategic withdrawal to avoid calamitous losses and, ideally, the commencement of exploratory peace talks with the Western Allies. Hitler seethed and once again reminded the field marshal that it was his job to 'deal only with the military situation in the west, nothing else'.[84] Not dissuaded, Rommel again pressed for the consideration of peace talks, but Hitler only hissed, 'Field Marshal, I think you had better leave the room.'[85] There would be no talk of a negotiation in the Führer's presence, only of ultimate victory or death trying. On the long return journey back to Paris, while their conversation is unknown, it would have been entirely natural if von Rundstedt and Rommel had contemplated what would happen if Hitler was removed from power.

A few days after the Berchtesgaden meeting, von Rundstedt was sacked – a scapegoat for the situation in Normandy and a warning to Rommel. He was replaced by Günther von Kluge, a former Eastern Front Army Group commander who had been directed by the OKW to keep a close eye on Rommel, as his fame, independent spirit and gloomy outlook had raised concerns about his loyalty. The commander of Army Group B took an instant dislike to the man, who tried to clip his wings through an assertion of authority that he barely possessed. The OKW's disquiet about Rommel was, however, well founded. The field marshal's respect for Hitler was broken, his loyalty to the Supreme Commander challenged by the strategic nightmare in which Germany had found herself and the Führer's unwillingness to take his professional military advice.

Speidel knew this and made attempts to encourage his commander into the conspiratorial ring of which he was a member, but found that Rommel wanted no part in any plot. Rommel was not a simple soldier, but he had no political ambitions and was no traitor. Thus, the plan that would see Colonel Claus von Stauffenberg and others attempt to assassinate Hitler on 20 July at the Wolf's Lair headquarters in Prussia was progressed without the field marshal's involvement – and, ultimately, was enacted while Rommel was fighting for his life in hospital.

On the afternoon of 17 July Rommel had just completed a meeting with Sepp Dietrich at his I SS Panzer Corps headquarters in Saint-Pierre-sur-Dives when his Horch staff car was spotted and attacked by Allied fighter-bombers on the Livarot–Vimoutiers road.

The field marshal was riding in the front passenger seat with a map in his lap, as was his habit, when the attack was launched. Hellmuth Lang, Rommel's aide who was in the back of the vehicle alongside two other staff officers, later recalled: 'The left-hand side of the car was hit by the first burst... Marshal Rommel was wounded in the face by broken glass and received a blow on the left temple and cheekbone which caused a triple fracture of the skull and made him lose consciousness immediately.'[86] His injuries had been sustained when the car skidded and turned over into a ditch, throwing Rommel out and leaving him unconscious and near death. Rommel owed his survival to the outstanding critical care he received at a Luftwaffe hospital thirty miles from the incident site, followed by specialist treatment at a hospital near Saint-Germain on the outskirts of Paris. During the next week, Rommel struggled to remain conscious for long, but on 24 July he managed to write to Lucie. In that letter he referred to the failed attempt on Hitler's life, doubtless concerned about prying eyes reading his words: 'We must thank God that it passed off as well as it did.'[87]

The investigation that followed the latest failure to murder Hitler soon saw the prime conspirators rounded up, including von Stauffenberg, and shot.[88] The Gestapo then hunted down those associated with the plotters and this led to the arrest of thousands – of whom 4,980 were summarily executed.[89] Rommel was implicated even while recuperating in hospital, as interrogators extracted names from desperate prisoners; his association with known conspirators, his advocacy of peace, and his occasional flippant comments about the regime all made him the object of deep suspicion. News of Rommel's injuries had been suppressed for fear of the impact that it was likely to have on German (and Allied) morale, but with leaks about his condition circulating on 1 August, the visibly weak field marshal was paraded before the cameras, a totem of resilience, even while the Gestapo sought to expose his apparent treachery.

In mid-August, as the deadly maelstrom of retribution was meted out to his colleagues, the field marshal was allowed home to

Herrlingen to continue his slow recovery with Lucie and Manfred, who was given special leave to be with his father. Still suffering from blinding headaches and feeling feeble, Rommel accepted visitors who kept him abreast of the latest war news, with Speidel visiting when he could. He tried to put a brave face on his health and circumstances, saying to his soldier-servant, 'Well, Loistl, so long as one isn't carrying one's head under one's arm things aren't too bad!'[90] but he guessed that he was being watched and that before long the Gestapo's net would close around him. Rommel was an officer of interest because of his prominence, his natural attraction to those who knew that a strong leader would be needed for the Army if Hitler was assassinated, his recent difficult relationship with Hitler, and his belief that the war was lost.

Speidel was arrested on 7 September,[91] when his relationship with the plotters came to light, and he was questioned about Rommel after the field marshal's name was mentioned by General Carl-Heinrich von Stülpnagel – leader of the conspirators in France – while under torture. But it was Rommel's connection with Günther von Kluge that offered his accusers an opportunity to make a great deal out of very little. Hitler was deeply saddened that 'his general' had been implicated, but although he was willing to be more sensitive to the consequences for his family, he expected Rommel to suffer the same fate as the other conspirators. Any execution, however, would have to be carefully choreographed, for the famous field marshal retained the deep respect and admiration of millions in Germany.

Rommel sensed that agents of the state were closing around him, encouraged by all those in Berlin who resented him as a popular figure and a single-minded officer who had benefited from access to Hitler. He would not give up without a fight for himself nor, moreover, for those who had remained loyal to him. Indeed, Rommel wrote to Hitler on 1 October outlining his fractious relationship with von Kluge, but noting that he was perplexed by Speidel's arrest – referring to his colleague as an 'outstandingly efficient and diligent Chief of Staff'. The letter concluded with a reassertion of Rommel's own personal devotion to his duty. 'One thought only possesses me constantly', he wrote pointedly, 'to fight and win for your new Germany.'[92] Nevertheless, on 7 October he was called to attend an important conference in Berlin, which Rommel knew was evidence that he had lost his final battle. 'I'm not that much of a fool,' he said in response to his summons. 'I'd never get to Berlin alive.'[93] He thus looked to put his affairs in order with the assistance of his most trusted aide-de-camp, Hermann Aldinger, and prepared for a visit by emissaries from Berlin.

Several days passed without incident, but on 14 October two senior officers from the Army Personnel Branch arrived at Rommel's home. Generals Wilhelm Burgdorf and Ernst Maisel informed Rommel that they had been sent by Field Marshal Wilhelm Keitel, head of the OKW, on Hitler's orders because of evidence that implicated him in the plot on the Führer's life. He had two options: a trial by the People's Court, a kangaroo court which would inevitably end in execution and may well have harmful implications for Lucie and Manfred, or to take his own life with the guarantee of a state funeral and no recriminations against his family, who would be provided for after his death.[94] The decision was not a difficult one. Having said an emotional farewell to his family, Rommel left with the two generals in their car. Minutes later, the field marshal took a cyanide capsule and was dead.

Rommel had been true to himself until the very end: pragmatic, courageous and resolute – but his spirit had been broken. Signals and letters of condolence from senior figures in Berlin soon began to arrive for Lucie. Hitler, who took Rommel's suicide as evidence that he was guilty, wrote: 'Accept my sincerest sympathy for the heavy loss you have suffered with the death of your husband. The name Field Marshal Rommel will be for ever linked with the heroic battles in North Africa.'[95] But she read them with disdain, for she had been told by her husband that he'd had nothing to do with the assassination plot, and knowing the character of the man better than anybody, she believed him without reservation. 'I would like to once again establish that my husband did not participate in the preparations and execution of 20.07.1944', Lucie later wrote to an acquaintance, 'because as a soldier he rejected taking such a path. My husband had forever honestly represented his opinions, his intentions and his plans to the highest levels, and the leadership did not find this comfortable. During his entire career he was always a soldier and never a politician.'[96]

The field marshal, it was reported, had succumbed to his car crash injuries, and a state funeral took place on 18 October 1944 in Ulm on Hitler's decree, to help protect Rommel's reputation. It was filmed to be shown in cinemas. Rommel's coffin, bedecked with his field marshal's baton, steel helmet and decorations, was escorted by troops from all three services in a grand parade which ended at the Rathaus, where senior military and civil dignitaries had gathered for the service. Hitler was represented by von Rundstedt, who delivered an oration written by the Propaganda Ministry which described the achievements of 'a great soldierly leader'[97] and, with decreasing accuracy, spoke of Rommel's affinity with National Socialism. Rommel's 'heart belonged to the Führer', von Rundstedt stated blandly.[98]

After he lay Hitler's large wreath, a nineteen-gun salute was fired by an artillery battery which reverberated across Ulm. It marked the end of the grand funeral that Lucie was not alone in believing her husband deserved, but in the circumstances was merely a tortuous charade founded on his murder. Never wavering in her support of her man, Lucie later wrote of those dark mid-October days: 'Thus ended the life of a man who had devoted his entire self to the service of his country.'[99]

— ¤ —

Arriving in wet and gloomy London from Sicily in late January 1944 for a meeting with Dwight Eisenhower, George Patton was buoyant. Since September he had been left unpicked while the Operation Overlord team formed up, but now he hoped – expected, even – to join his colleagues. His old friend put the shamed officer out his misery quickly: he would command the US Third Army in Omar Bradley's 12th Army Group. Although he would not be involved in the initial assault – or, indeed, for much of the Battle of Normandy – Patton's talents as an aggressive commander of armour would be required once the Battle of Normandy had been won. He had approximately four months to train and prepare his new army for battle, while also acting as the personal focus for Allied deception plans as 'commander' of the fictitious First US Army Group (FUSAG).

Several months after it had been established and the Germans became aware of its existence, Patton had been selected by Eisenhower to command the invented formation – partly because his role in the coming invasion was to lead the US armoured breakout from Normandy and thus he was relatively free to devote time to the ruse. More particularly, Allied intelligence had revealed that Patton was the general the Germans feared most and, therefore, was the man they expected to lead the invasion's main landing strike force.[100] The aim of FUSAG, as part of Operation Quicksilver, was to anchor the main German defensive force in the Pas-de-Calais sector by providing the enemy with all the indications they would expect prior to a force landing there, and so divert attention away from Normandy to the south-west. After months in Sicily doing nothing and feeling that he was going nowhere, the prospect of getting back into combat immediately revitalized the cantankerous 58-year-old.

Taking command of the Third Army as a new formation was not unfamiliar to Patton. 'As far as I can remember', he wrote in his diary on 26 January, 'this is my twenty-seventh start from zero since entering the US Army. Each time I have made a success of it, and this must be the biggest.'[101] Having established his headquarters near the city of Manchester in England's industrial north-west, the re-energized officer was soon venturing out to visit his troops. At one address to around 1,000 new arrivals, Patton said, with his new English bull terrier, Willie, standing statue-like at his heel: 'I can assure you that the Third United States Army will be the greatest army in American history. We shall be in Berlin ahead of anyone else.'[102] The general had lost none of his powers to inspire his men, with one of his staff officers recalling, '[T]hat towering figure impeccably attired froze you in place and electrified the very air.'[103]

Such talks were variations on the themes of duty, courage and the glory of victory that he had emphasized prior to the invasion of Sicily, but while his wild claims and profanity visibly enthused some, officers in particular were left feeling uncomfortable and wondering whether this man who had been so recently vilified by the US people was anything more than an obnoxious bigot. Nevertheless, as infantry Captain Michael Wilson later admitted, 'We soon learned that all the histrionics were for the men and before long his training and leadership pointed us all in the right direction. Patton was an actor – and not a very good one in my opinion – but he delivered his lines, struck a pose and men followed him.'[104]

Having begun to introduce himself to the troops, Patton undertook changes to the headquarters staff he had inherited – and replaced many with men that he had previously served with in the US Seventh Army. He had hoped to procure the services of Hap Gay as chief of staff, but his request was declined by Eisenhower as he did not believe the officer had the sort of uncompromising qualities the Army would require in the forthcoming campaign. As a consequence, Patton reluctantly transferred Hugh Gaffey into the post from command of the 2nd Armored Division, and, as a consolation, made Gay the deputy. The three men were to become a powerful team, a well-balanced combination of an experienced fighting general and skilful staff officers who understood combat command and could create a stimulating culture, which, it became evident, was based on Patton's dictum: 'Never tell people *how* to do things. Tell them *what* to do and they will surprise you with their ingenuity.'[105]

With the processes established that would allow his headquarters to become the Third Army's brain, Patton sought to influence his commanders as they began to build the organization's muscle. On 6 March he issued his first letter of instruction to higher-echelon officers 'in the principles of command combat procedure, and administration which obtain to this Army' and which was studded with recommendations: 'lead in person'; 'visit the front daily... to observe, not to meddle'; 'praise is more valuable than blame'; and 'see with your own eyes and be seen by your troops'.[106] He followed his own advice and made regular visits to corps and division headquarters for conferences with his senior officers, after which he took the opportunity to address troops from a truck specially fitted with loudspeakers for just such 'impromptu' occasions. By the end of March, Patton was writing to Beatrice: 'I have just finished "inspiring" [the troops]... I reassured them as to their futures. I told then I was just as much their father and as deeply concerned for their welfare as [their previous commander] had been... Things are shaping up pretty well now but I wish we had more of the killer instinct in our men.'[107]

Patton had been making a good impression on the chain of command – with reassuring reports submitted by assessors to Eisenhower's office that the Third Army was making 'excellent progress'[108] – when, out of the blue, the accident-prone general made another career-threatening error of judgement. The 'Knutsford Incident', as it became known, occurred on 25 April 1944, when Patton made an unofficial talk at the opening of a GI club during which, in a speech that foolishly strayed from the matter at hand, discussed the Allies but failed to mention the Soviet Union. It was a relatively minor error, but the US press was keen on any Patton story and it caused a brief but intense storm, with the *Washington Post* opining in the wake of his behaviour in Sicily that the general's words 'revealed glaring defects in him as a leader of men'.[109] Eisenhower was livid that Patton had made himself visible and vulnerable at a time when his whereabouts were being carefully choreographed, and wrote to him: 'I am thoroughly weary of your failure to control your tongue and have begun to doubt your all-round judgment, so essential in high military position.'[110] Admonished personally by his boss on 1 May and with the threat of dismissal hanging over him, Patton had to wait another two days before learning that he was not going to be sent back home in disgrace. It was made clear, however, that he had been delivered his 'final warning', and he was banned from making public comments without his words having first been vetted by Eisenhower.

Patton had let himself down once again and needed to mend his ways, but he also had a very strong sense that he could not. 'There are apparently two types of successful soldiers,' he wrote to his son, who was then an officer cadet at West Point. 'Those who get on by being unobtrusive and those who get on by being obtrusive. I am of the latter type and seem to be rare and unpopular; but it is my method. One has to choose a system and stick to it. People who are not themselves are nobody.'[111] Nevertheless, determined to stay out of trouble, the general focused on the steady improvement of the Third Army and gradually learned more about the role his formation was to play in France.

In mid-May, Patton attended the final invasion conference for senior commanders run by Montgomery in London, where he listened as a variety of senior officers took the audience through each unfolding part of the plan. Although not called on to speak as he would not become involved until the breakout phase, he was inspired by what he heard and, knowing that the invasion was imminent, returned north to address the massed divisions of the Third Army before it went to war. As a band played rousing music, Patton walked through an Honor Guard and, wearing his 'war face', began a speech that was laced with all his usual motifs. 'Americans have never lost and will never lose a war,' he said, 'for the very thought of losing is hateful to an American.' He went on to describe the US Army as consisting of 'the best men in the world' while emphasizing that 'every single man in the Army plays a vital role'. He concluded: 'We will win this war, but we will win it only by fighting and showing guts,' and with that his audience clapped, cheered, and returned to their barracks under no illusion about what was expected of them.[112]

When the invasion began in early June, Patton remained in England, where he proved to be a poor spectator. He told anybody willing to listen – and even those who were not – how he would fight the break-in battles more effectively, and wrote in his diary on 9 June: 'Time drags terribly.'[113] Not until 6 July, after a month of fighting, did Patton finally accompany the vanguard of his army across the English Channel to Normandy, where they would begin their final preparations before going into battle. As Bradley struggled to forge a path through the dense *bocage* countryside, Patton opined that his Third Army would 'break through in three days'[114] and was critical of those who fought a battle that revealed 'no progress, but only casualties'.[115]

In the last week of July, the grinding attrition finally created the opportunity for which Montgomery, Bradley and Patton had been waiting, and on 25 July, five days of fighting began in Operation Cobra west of Saint-Lô, creating the opening for an armoured breakout. Patton's Third Army became operational on 1 August, with Courtney Hodges taking over the First Army from Bradley, who himself was promoted to the command of the 12th Army Group. In keeping with the original Normandy plan, Patton's formations were directed to liberate Brittany while further efforts were made by the First Army to broaden the breach in the enemy's line. At last, Patton was in the saddle again, and he whipped his three corps hard, being keen to impress on his commanders that 'flanks are something for the enemy to worry about, not us'[116] as he sought to disorientate and dislocate the enemy. Sweeping through Brittany, admirably supported by XIX Tactical Air Command, his army liberated Rennes on 4 August and Brest was reached three days later (although it took until 19 September before the garrison there finally surrendered).

Before long, Bradley's situation map of the Atlantic coast was a mass of seething Third Army arrows, and although on occasion his headquarters lost track of exactly where each division was, that was because Patton's own staff had only a vague idea about their locations. Patton was unperturbed, however, and wrote to his friend Kenyon Joyce: 'We are having the loveliest battles you ever saw. It is a typical cavalry action in which, to quote the words of the old story,

"The soldier went out and charged in all directions at the same time, with a pistol in one hand, and a sabre in the other."[117] Although the Third Army's broad and fast territorial gains led to subsequent criticisms of Patton's command and control, the officer himself was content that his intent was being fulfilled and, as such, the enemy's cohesion in Brittany was being so undermined that it could never be reconstituted. Nonetheless, neither he nor any of his subordinates could fully reconcile why they were fighting in the extreme west of France while the main body of the enemy lay to the east, but Bradley had given his orders and Patton followed them assiduously.

Events moved quickly, however, and when it became clear on 8 August that the enemy's entire position in Normandy was collapsing, Bradley directed that Patton's main effort should shift east in preparation for a massed Allied breakout towards the German border. Patton was in his element. While his XX Corps plunged further south to the Loire river, his two other formations, VIII and XV Corps, swung east in line with Bradley's new orders. The great war of movement and destruction was very much to Patton's taste. Indeed, at one point, having walked down a road pitted with craters, burning vehicles and burned corpses, he turned to his aide-de-camp Charles R. Codman and said, 'Just look at that, Codman. Could anything be more magnificent?'[118]

With every mile taken and every town and village secured, Patton become more elated and the US press became more interested in the colourful general's achievements. In the wake of the slapping incidents in Sicily, the *Washington Star* remarked on 12 August that these events were evidence 'vindicating a man who may be short on diplomacy but whose qualities as a fighting officer are beyond dispute'.[119] Stories abounded about the eccentric officer, with one report saying that the general had sat in a deckchair during an enemy bombing raid and shouted obscenities at the Luftwaffe, while another applauded his courage for advancing with the troops into action. 'If you want an army to fight and risk death', Patton said, 'you've got to get up there and lead it. An army is like spaghetti. You can't push a piece of spaghetti, you've got to pull it.'[120] It was just the sort of heroic leadership that captured the imagination of the American population, and the troops of the Third Army could bask in the light of Patton's reflected glory.

By 13 August, the Third Army was at the Loire river in the south, while in the east it had taken Le Mans in a front-line bulging effort that looked to reach the Seine. 'In exactly two weeks', he wrote excitedly (but inaccurately) in his diary, 'Third Army has advanced further and faster than any army in the history of war... I am happy and elated.'[121] Such was the success of his formations in their advance parallel to the Normandy coast, that with the enemy pinned north of them by a combination of the US First Army and the British 21st Army Group, a pocket had been created around the ancient town of Falaise, containing both the German Seventh and Fifth Panzer Armies. A fortuitous opportunity had arisen, which with the necessary drive could result in hundreds of thousands of enemy troops and their equipment being surrounded. Montgomery's Canadians attacked south, while Patton's XV Corps advanced north with the object of meeting at Argentan and thereby sealing the last remaining route out of the Allied trap.

Although the Third Army reached its objective the First Canadian Army did not, and while Patton was keen to continue his advance to occupy the untaken ground, Bradley forbade him – fearing fratricide as friendly forces closed in from opposite directions. The result was a fifteen-mile-wide gap through which tens of thousands of enemy troops poured, until the Polish 1st Armoured Division finally snapped it shut. By 21 August around 50,000 German troops had been trapped, but Patton believed it could have been far more had Montgomery completed the task assigned to him and Bradley been less risk-adverse. Had he been Supreme Commander, Patton wrote in his diary, the missed opportunity would never have been allowed to happen.[122]

The Battle of the Falaise Pocket could have been a more significant Allied victory but, nonetheless, it did herald the disintegration of the German resistance in Normandy and immediately led to a change in the operational character of the campaign, as a mass Allied pursuit of the fleeing enemy began. During this phase, Eisenhower's force advanced dozens of miles each day, with Paris falling on 25 August – by which time the Third Army had reached Troyes on the Seine, 100 miles south-east of the capital. Patton had observed the advance from the L-4 two-seater Piper Cub aircraft which he used to travel between his dispersed formations; he very much enjoyed being able to land on rough grassy fields to speak with commanders. Although he tried not to interfere with operations, as he was determined to give his subordinates the ability to fulfil his orders (which eschewed prescriptive detail and so never took up more than half a side of typed foolscap) as they saw fit, he would intervene to admonish officers not showing enough drive or to provide support if they were encountering difficulties.

Generally, however, Patton was surprised at the time he had on his hands, and wrote to his brother-in-law Frederick Ayer on 1 September: 'When you get to command... 450,000 you have a surprising amount of time on your hands because it is physically impossible to be at the front all the time... What I usually do is go up to the front every second day except when things are tight, in which case I go up every day. I find that people get used to you if they see too much of you.'[123]

If he thought the campaign would remain as mobile as it had for the previous five weeks, however, he was soon to be disappointed. With orders to advance into the Lorraine region of eastern France before crossing the German border and tackling the Siegfried Line defences, the Third Army would have anticipated some hard fighting as conditions deteriorated in the autumn. Eisenhower made it clear to Bradley that in such circumstances the Third Army commander needed to be kept under control and not be allowed to 'try and fight the Germans on his own'.[124] Thus, Bradley asserted to his commanders that they were fighting as part of a team aligned to the Supreme Commander's broad-fronted strategy and that everything they did had to be in that context. As such, by September, at which time the enemy's withdrawal from France was coming to an end, the 12th Army Group were in line: Hodges's First Army on the left (adjoining Monty's 21st Army Group); William Simpson's newly arrived US Ninth Army in the centre; and Patton's Third Army on his right (adjacent to Devers's 6th Army Group, which had advanced from the south of France).

Despite the co-ordination, one of the great challenges associated with Eisenhower's favoured method of advancing began to cause problems along the front, for it required roughly equitable resources to be supplied to all three Army Groups, from the North Sea down to the Swiss border. To the Americans' huge frustration, Montgomery's Second Army was given supply priority for the duration of Operation Market Garden in mid-September. Patton, of course, wanted his own supply priority and told one correspondent in characteristic manner, 'If Ike stops holding Monty's hand and gives me the supplies, I'll go through the Siegfried Line like shit through a goose.'[125]

The Third Army had every reason to feel aggrieved considering the British failure to achieve its stated objective and take a crossing over the Lower Rhine. Having been forced to continue its advance with just one-tenth of the supplies that it had previously enjoyed, the Third Army lost momentum and the Germans quickly consolidated their position. Even after his supplies were restored, they were just not enough for Patton's force to make a significant impact. He made protestations through the chain of command but to no avail, prompting his legendary comment to a supportive Bradley: 'I'll shoot the next man who brings me food. Give us gasoline; we can eat our belts.'[126] Having been on his best behaviour over the previous five months, Patton's frustration was palpable as the Third Army confronted a better-organized enemy defending advantageous terrain in deteriorating weather. His advance having slowed to a crawl in Lorraine during the autumn – the fortified city of Metz stubbornly withstanding everything that was thrown at it – Patton reverted to his usual cranky and independently minded self. 'To hell with Hodges and Monty,' he shouted at Bradley. 'We'll win your goddam war if you'll keep Third Army going!'[127]

The battle to 'keep Third Army going' took many forms, and thus while the quest for fuel, ammunition and other combat necessities thoroughly occupied his staff officers, Patton also demanded that they were adequately supplied with rations, cigarettes, cold-weather clothing and entertaining diversions from their daily routine. Consequently, when Metz finally fell on 22 November, Patton ensured that the opportunity to celebrate was not missed and distributed the 50,000 cases of champagne captured there across his army. It was a small but welcome gesture, and with winter approaching the general knew that sustaining morale would be a priority task for all his leaders in conditions that, as one of his Californian officers suggested, were 'hardly conducive to taking a short walk, far less fighting a determined enemy day after day'.[128]

Thus, while his subordinate commanders did all they could to ensure that fighting spirit was maintained in the dark months before them, Patton endeavoured to bring a little of his own razzamatazz to the business of leadership. Stories subsequently raced through the Third Army again about the general turning up at the front during enemy bombardments and shaking his fist towards the enemy's guns even as shells exploded all around. 'I saw him once in November,' recalled Private First Class Jimmy Stark. 'I was someplace being patched up after being hit during an artillery bombardment. It was still going when the general arrived and a shell landed close by covering him in dirt. I remember that he did not dive for cover, he just carried on walking but then, although covered in mud, he walked around a small puddle so that he didn't get his shining boots wet.'[129] It was just the sort of anecdote that brought a smile and a shake of the head to the men of the Third Army, and Patton knew that his performances – an exaggerated version of himself – were appreciated.

Always ready to praise men verbally for their efforts, to make a field promotion, or even to dip into a box of medals and pin a Distinguished Service Cross on a deserving soldier, Patton remained alive to any opportunity to reward his soldiers because he fervently believed that 'the glory and magnitude of their achievements have a great influence on morale'.[130] Such acts were wholly in line with Patton's personality and brassy approach to leadership, with radio operator Corporal James Stark saying 'my pals were envious that I had a story to tell about Patton while they had nothing. I was asked to repeat it time and again.'[131]

Patton did what he felt was required to maintain or raise fighting effectiveness, and while rewarding his men played a significant part in that, he was also willing to punish those who failed to live up to the values and standards of the US Army. In his formation, Patton declared, any soldier found guilty of rape would be hanged, any man who showed cowardice before the enemy would be shot and any officer whose leadership or judgement was impaired would be sacked.[132] Thus, when it was brought to his attention in late November that the commander of the 4th Armored Division, Major General John Wood, had failed in his mission due to a lack of aggression and then been insubordinate, Patton – despite his personal liking of the officer and Wood's past success – immediately sacked him. His replacement was Hugh Gaffey, thus allowing Hap Gay to become Patton's chief of staff once more.

On 1 December, the Third Army finally cleared Lorraine and crossed the border into Germany. It was a significant psychological boost to an organization that had taken over 50,000 casualties in the abrasive fighting over the past three months[133] – although, as Patton stressed at every opportunity, the task of breaching the Siegfried Line in winter was a significant new challenge. In a letter to his daughter Ruth Ellen, he said, 'If we get through we will materially shorten the war – there is no *if* about getting through; I am sure we will.'[134] Yet before he could get more than a small part of his army across the Saar and make the final advance towards the German positions, the Allies were struck by a wholly unexpected counter-offensive. Opening on 16 December, it was focused against the single First Army corps in the Ardennes and was situated on the Patton's left flank, after the Ninth Army had been moved north to support the right flank of Montgomery's force. The Third Army's proximity to the German main effort meant that it would have an important role to play in the Allied reaction, and indeed the Battle of the Bulge was destined to provide one of the best illustrations in his long career of what Patton's leadership could achieve.

The surprise, power and violence of the German offensive through inhospitable terrain, after a series of major strategic reversals, initially rocked the Allies. The Fifth and Sixth Panzer Armies made significant headway in their attempt to advance to the Meuse, with Patton writing in his diary on 17 December: 'The German attack is on a wide front and moving fast.'[135] He was impressed, but noticed that the offensive was vulnerable on its flanks and was also doubtful that the enemy would be able to sustain its early momentum due to the terrain and weather, and their combined impact on logistics. After, Hodges's 106th Infantry Division had been overrun and the front line distended in a manner that suggested an imminent breakthrough, and even before a meeting called by Eisenhower to discuss a response with his senior commanders, Patton had developed plans that could be operationalized as soon as the Supreme Commander made clear his intent. Having started to establish new fuel depots and dumps for supplies, issue new mapping, reconnoitre new roads and lay new communications wires, he also re-orientated his divisions 90 degrees north to face the southern flank of the developing German salient, and once in position, awaited further orders.

At the subsequent conference held in Verdun on 19 December,[136] SHAEF's chief of intelligence outlined the current situation before Eisenhower gave his reaction. 'The present situation is to be regarded as one of opportunity for us and not of disaster,' he said. 'There will be only cheerful faces at this table.'[137] Having already identified potential prospects, Patton retorted in characteristically gung-ho fashion: 'Hell, let's have the guts to let the bastards go all the way to Paris. Then, we'll really cut 'em off and chew 'em up.'[138]

Unperturbed, Eisenhower outlined his plan. Montgomery was to bring the First and Ninth Armies under his command to create a hard 'north shoulder' to contain the German offensive, while sending his own XXX Corps to create a blocking line on the Meuse. Patton, meanwhile, was to counter-attack with at least six divisions from the south by cutting into the enemy flank, and then relieve US troops besieged by German units just across the border in Bastogne, a vital road hub in complex terrain where few paved roads existed and through which the Fifth Panzer Army could expand its attack towards the Meuse and beyond. Unaware of Patton's vital preparations, Eisenhower believed that the Third Army commander's claim that three of his divisions could be on the move within forty-eight hours was little more than Patton bravado. At the conclusion of the summit, Patton transmitted a message to Gay which included the pre-arranged code word for the execution of the plan that best suited the fulfilment of Eisenhower's intent. Patton was centre-stage, faced with an exigent task and in his element.

Patton established his forward headquarters twenty miles south of Bastogne.[139] He then visited the headquarters of each of the counter-attacking formations before they plunged into the whirlpool of combat. On 21 December he wrote to Beatrice, 'Yesterday I again earned my pay. I visited seven divisions and regrouped the Army alone... Destiny sent for me in a hurry when things got tight. Perhaps God saved me for this effort.'[140] At each formation he outlined the plan, transmitting his confidence – and excitement – that they would succeed in their missions. The following day, just sixty-six hours after his meeting with Eisenhower and colleagues in Verdun, three divisions of Patton's III Corps began their advance across a twenty-mile front. He drove man and machine harder than ever before, as he believed hard-won momentum was vital to the success of his endeavour, but arduous terrain, fresh snowfall and a determined enemy conspired against rapid progress, and with Allied air power grounded due to the bad weather, the attack failed to get to Bastogne by Christmas Eve as had been planned. Yet Patton was not dejected, and instead called a press conference. Correspondent Larry Newman wrote in admiration of what then occurred: 'In the midst of the battle – perhaps the most desperate a US Army has ever had to fight... Patton strode into the

room, smiling, confident, the atmosphere changed within seconds…
[and said] "This is the end of the beginning. We've been battling our
brains out trying to get the Hun out in the open. Now he is out. And
with the help of God we'll finish him off this time – and for good.'"[141]

The general's robustness despite his huge responsibility was
impressive, and he even managed to inject some humour into
proceedings, a style he adopted to raise spirits wherever he went.
While giving an order to a field commander, for example, he noticed
a Red Cross nurse listening nearby, and said with a broad smile and a
wink belying the pressure he was under, 'You have had the privilege of
hearing the greatest general in Europe make a decision.'[142] Once again
Patton moved from unit to unit conveying a paternal pride in troops,
who took strength from the fact that 'the general had bothered to visit
their little sector of hell'.[143]

The tenacity of the III Corps' riposte as it fought towards
Bastogne on Christmas Day was in keeping with that shown by the
101st Airborne Division and the collection of other units that had
fought so valiantly to deny the enemy its critical objective. Patton
had created a capable and resilient organization with 'the habit of
obeying in a tight place',[144] and on 26 December, the day after the
German push reached its culminating point short of the Meuse,
the ever-reliable 4th Armored Division broke through to relieve
the town. 'Now the enemy must dance to our tune, not we to his,'
Patton wrote to Beatrice a few days later, and added: 'This is my
biggest battle.'[145]

Although the fighting in the Ardennes spilled over into the first
weeks of 1945, two weeks after three panzer divisions began their
withdrawal on 3 January, the former bulge had been reduced to a
shallow curve in the front line. In the final analysis, although US
losses during the German offensive were nearly 90,000 (of which
half were suffered by Patton's Third Army) and over 730 armoured
fighting vehicles,[146] the similar level of losses suffered by the Germans
was strategically far more debilitating. Patton's own contribution to
that success was not underestimated by Bradley, who later wrote that

his 'generalship during this difficult maneuver was magnificent'.[147] Patton knew it. The Battle of the Bulge was his finest hour, and he wrote of the experience to his son, George: 'Leadership… is the thing that wins battles. I have it – but I'll be damned if I can define it. Probably it consists in knowing what you want to do and then doing it and getting mad if any one steps in the way. Self-confidence and leadership are twin brothers.'[148]

The general's reputation among both his troops and his peers was enhanced by his work in the Ardennes, and the press were keen to make him a hero. Patton was quick to point out that his contributions to the Third Army's accomplishments were as nothing compared to those of his men – and he meant it – but those closest to him knew that his personal contribution to the outcome was enormous. 'A General Officer who will invariably assume the responsibility for failure, whether he deserves it or not', a reflective Patton wrote two years later, 'and invariably gives the credit for success to others, whether they deserve it or not, will achieve outstanding success.'[149] Yet while the commander of the Third Army actively sought to share success with his troops, Bernard Montgomery tried to take personal credit for having had a decisive hand in the affair. Even before the British officer's unsolicitous comments during his Zonhoven press conference, Patton's diary was full of vitriol towards Montgomery, but after it he became one of the agitators for Monty's censure by SHAEF – and, for once, Eisenhower shared his outrage.

The directed pause in the 12th Army Group's offensive action in February 1945 while Montgomery advanced to the Rhine was partly on account of the weather, but more specifically for it to rest and reorganize after the exertions of winter. As soon as conditions were right, however, Eisenhower was determined to recommence his 'slow but sure' strategy to see his troops through the Siegfried Line and over the Rhine. Patton did not like the lack of boldness any better in early 1945 than he had earlier in the campaign, and having decided to deviate from the plan, he wrote on 6 February to Frederick Ayer: 'I am taking one of the longest chances of my chancy career; in fact, almost disobeying orders in order to attack, my theory being that if I win, nobody will say anything, and I am sure I will win.'[150]

As Montgomery's formations were slogging through the Reichswald to the north, Patton tested Bradley's patience by pulling on the leash that all recognized was there to check his wild inclinations rather than change the ingrained behaviour of a general whose boldness had been so lauded. The Third Army attacked the hilly, river-festooned and densely forested Eifel sector, which had been incorporated into the Siegfried Line. Once again, in vile weather, Patton's formations made painfully slow progress in a series of actions that tested the resilience of everybody concerned, and ultimately checked his desire to make a bold drive eastwards. It subsequently took all of February to pass through the region – an area roughly the size of the county of Norfolk and only slightly larger than Rhode Island – at the cost of another 63,000 casualties (of which one-third were non-battle casualties).[151] Irritable and stressed after his efforts for so long without a break, Patton managed two days' leave in Paris during mid-February, but he would not take one day more despite the advice of Gay and others, given the approaching challenge of crossing the Rhine.

When Hodge's US First Army managed to utilize an intact Ludendorff railway bridge at Remagen to achieve the first Allied crossing of the river on 7 March, Patton later said, 'We were quite happy over it, but just a little envious.'[152] He immediately set himself the task of getting his own troops on the east bank before Montgomery's huge multinational airborne-amphibious set-piece battle had an opportunity to dominate the headlines.

Despite the arrival of the 4th Armored Division's vanguard on the river south of Mainz, there was no intact bridge for it to use and so there it waited – until the Third Army reached the river across its front and an assault could be undertaken. This finally took place on the night of 22–23 March, when Patton sent 5th Division across the river in small assault craft from the outskirts of Oppenheim, soon carving out a bridgehead on the opposite bank. The success came just hours before Montgomery began his own massive attack across the

Rhine, which encouraged Patton to call Bradley and say, 'For God's sake tell the world we are across. I want the world to know Third Army made it before Monty.'[153] The next day, as a mark of contempt for the enemy, Patton was photographed urinating in the river from one of his newly constructed pontoon bridges.

With the combined challenges of winter, the Siegfried Line, the Rhineland and the Rhine crossing now behind him, Patton's mood seemed to improve with every mile that his army pushed deeper into Germany. As the general said to an officer during a visit in early April: 'Firm ground, daylight and what passes for weather in this country will make us unstoppable. The Germans are all but beat!'[154]

Patton was not the only one whose spirits were buoyed by recent achievements; the morale of his men also began to improve as their uniforms started to dry and they could feel the sun on their backs once more. The imminent end to the campaign became a topic of conversation in a way that it had not been just a few weeks earlier. 'With the Rhine behind us', recalled 5th Infantry Division engineer Donald Swann, 'we could begin to think more about home, not as a dream-like place but a place that we'd see again, where our families and girlfriends were waiting for us. We didn't want to be heroes. We just wanted to get home.'[155]

Back in the United States, the families and friends of the men serving in the Third Army knew all about their general – his popularity was reaching new heights, with his portrait having adorned the cover of *Life* in mid-January and then *Time* in early April. Patton had been rehabilitated in the eyes of the press; his fall from grace and subsequent recovery became a story in itself. Venerated by his troops and cherished by the American public, Patton seemed once again entrusted to carry the hopes of the nation into battle. The general felt that responsibility keenly, and as the weeks passed he became more focused than ever on playing his part to ensure that the Third Army's sacrifices were not diluted by the rapidly advancing Red Army, and thereby a regime which he had always regarded as sinister and despotic. Although he had little option but to abide by the agreement that Berlin would be a Soviet objective, he was motivated to advance as far as possible in the time remaining, to ensure that the United States was not regarded as a 'push over' by Stalin.

Patton had proved himself trustworthy over recent months – a refreshing revelation to the chain of command. Characteristically, however, in the wake of his success the errant general once again revealed his fallibility. At the end of March, he became fixated on intelligence that an Allied officer prisoner-of-war camp, Oflag XIII-B – located at Hammelburg on the Main river – might hold his daughter Beatrice's husband, Lieutenant Colonel John K. Waters, who had been captured in Tunisia two years earlier. In an abuse of his position and power, Patton decided to launch a rescue mission using a task force from the 4th Armored Division to liberate the camp. The risk involved in a column advancing fifty miles behind enemy lines without a clear sense of what they could find when they arrived at the camp was not lost on either Manton Eddy, the corps commander, or William M. Hoge, the commander of the division. Both believed it to be a reckless escapade, but Patton insisted, during a visit to XII Corps headquarters on the morning of 26 March, that the operation must be mounted.

Named 'Task Force Baum' after its commander, 24-year-old Captain Abraham Baum, the force consisted of 314 troops accompanied by sixteen tanks, three 105-mm self-propelled guns, twenty-eight half-tracks and ten other vehicles. Setting out after dark on 26 March, their attempt to break through German lines was a protracted affair, but having managed to advance into open country, the column was then spotted by a German aircraft as it approached the objective.[156] Only half of Baum's force reached the camp to crash through the gates on the afternoon of 27 March, but although resistance was light, John K. Waters was shot in the lower back during the confusion and there were far more prisoners than the diminished force could hope to carry on their return journey. In their weakened state, after months of eating unhealthy German camp food, most decided to remain where they were, including the wounded Waters, leaving Baum to extract his team as German units began to surround them. The raid was a disaster. Just thirty-two men and none of the vehicles managed to fight their way back to American lines by 29 March, with many having been taken prisoner – including the injured Baum – and taken back to the camp.[157] The mission had achieved nothing other than a graphic illustration of another lapse in Patton's judgement.

The camp was liberated nine days later, as part of Eddy's rolling operations, and visiting Baum in hospital Patton awarded him the Distinguished Service Cross. 'He sat on my bed', Baum later recalled, 'and started talking about anything to evade [discussing] the task force. I was thinking, do I rock the boat? This is the best general we have, the one I'd want leading me in war – though I wouldn't want him to marry my sister. Finally I said, "How's my unit doing?" I gave him an out. He said, "Well, 4th Armored Division moved forward 75 miles with little resistance because of the raid." He felt very good about that.'[158] At a subsequent press conference, Patton denied knowing that Waters was being held at the camp and said that he mounted the raid having received intelligence that prisoners were being murdered there, but Eddy and Hoge knew the truth and both Eisenhower and Bradley guessed it. 'I took Patton's hide off,' the Supreme Commander later wrote, but Bradley admitted: 'I did not rebuke him for it. Failure itself was George's own worst reprimand.'[159]

Patton's latest misdemeanour did attract some press interest, but circumstances rather than the intervention of Eisenhower and Marshall defused the developing situation on this occasion. First, the death of American president Franklin Roosevelt on 12 April temporarily consumed the news agenda. When the front pages once again focused on war news, the battle for Berlin, the advancing Allied armies and the horrors of the Nazi regime provided the copy. Indeed, on the day that Roosevelt died, and while tensions still ran high over the raid, Eisenhower, Bradley and Patton visited the Ohrdruf concentration camp near the town of Gotha in Thuringia, which had been liberated by the Third Army a week earlier.

The three officers were appalled by what they witnessed that day, with Eisenhower writing to Marshall, 'The things I saw beggar description', and Patton noting that it was 'one of the most appalling sights I have ever seen'.[160] Such scenes were so powerful, so tangibly demonstrable of why the United States had been fighting Nazi Germany, that members of Congress and the press were permitted to visit the camps. In Britain, *The Guardian* newspaper reported the Third Army's role in the liberation, noting that on 11 April at Buchenwald it 'brought release to the 21,000 inmates at this resort of starvation, torture, hangings, and shootings',[161] while in Utah *The Sunday Herald Carried A Gruesome Photograph Of Eisenhower* watching 'concentration camp inmates re-enact ways of torture used by the Nazis'.[162] Yet Patton sought to ensure that the Third Army remained focused. 'We have still have a job to do', he wrote on 25 April, in reply to a letter he had received from the mother of one of his soldiers, 'but I am confident that our discipline – with God's support – will deliver us victory.'[163]

Events were moving fast all along the Allied line during the second week of April. German towns and villages were falling to Eisenhower's armies so quickly that SHAEF had to give direction to advance with caution due to fears of an unintentional clash with Red Army troops. For the Third Army this meant that, having taken both Weimar and Jena by 13 April, its VIII Corps was ordered to halt just before Chemnitz, south of Leipzig. On its right flank, however, Patton's XII Corps was ordered to advance alongside Devers's Sixth Army, which had been tasked with clearing southern Germany before crossing into Austria. Shortly after, SHAEF directed all three Third Army Corps to re-orientate, and with the Czech border on their left flank, begin their advance south-east on 19 April.

Days earlier Patton had received the news that he had been promoted to full general. Like in Montgomery's relationship with the high command, despite his failings and misdemeanours Patton's peccadillos were overlooked in view of his wider achievements and the acclaim he enjoyed on the home front, and so he was rewarded once more. Thus, with a fourth star on his collar and a new badge made for his jeep, Patton led his now 540,000-man, eighteen-division-strong Third Army safe in the knowledge that he had achieved the rank after which he had long hankered before the end of the war in Europe – and despite the recent furore over the Hammelburg debacle. As they advanced, he directed that his troops remain alert but also, after years of endeavouring to develop a fighting hatred of the enemy in his commands, to show compassion to soldiers and civilians alike. In what became known as the 'Third Army War Memorial Project', Patton's units fired warning shots to announce their approach on towns and villages as an encouragement to surrender. 'The object of this', Patton explained, 'was to let the inhabitants have something to show future generations of Germans by way of proof that the Third Army had passed that way.'[164]

The town of Passau, on the border with Austria, benefited from this policy. A place of rich historic and cultural value, it surrendered without a fight on 3 May, just three days after a former resident, Adolf Hitler, had committed suicide. News of events in Berlin made it likely that the war had just days to run, and so on 4 May Eisenhower directed that the Third Army's VII Corps should cross the Czechoslovakia border and take as much ground as possible – though stopping short of Prague, which had been allocated as another Red Army objective. Two days later, the advance had taken the corps' spearhead to Pilsen, just fifty-five miles from the Czech capital, and sensing correctly that Patton was keen to continue his attack Bradley telephoned him with a clear message: 'You hear me George... Halt!'[165] He did, but subsequently wrote that he should have been authorized to take the city 'and, if the Russians didn't like it, let them go to hell'.[166]

With his army split between those formations that had crossed the Danube river, deep in north Austria, and the corps in Czechoslovakia, Patton was delighted at the progress the Third Army had made by 7 May, and with some satisfaction he learned that a German surrender would come into effect the next day. The Third Army headquarters released the news, and with it an order for a general halt. When the fighting had stopped and initial celebrations had been enjoyed, Patton issued a general order to his troops. In it, he gave his thanks to the Third Army and said that it had inflicted 500,000 casualties, taken nearly one million prisoners and advanced 1,300 miles in 281 days, stating that this was the furthest in history that an army had advanced in such a short time. In making this claim, he studiously ignored the fact that Montgomery's Eighth Army had progressed 1,850 miles from El Alamein to Tunis in just 201 days.[167]

Patton ended the order: 'During the course of this war I have received promotion and decorations far above and beyond my individual merit. You won them; I as your representative wear them. The one honor which is mine and mine alone is that of having commanded such an incomparable group of Americans, the record of whose fortitude, audacity, and valor will endure as long as history lasts.'[168]

George S. Patton had survived the war and become a full general, but like Montgomery, he had a challenge adjusting to peace once again.

CHAPTER NINE

George S. Patton, Bernard Montgomery and the Post-War World

T HE FINAL SEVEN MONTHS of George Patton's life were marked by despair and controversy. Worn down by years of hard work and never more anxious than when the paths open to him did not lead to war, the general's mental health suffered grievously during the summer of 1945. Old age and peace did not suit an officer who had spent his life driven by an ambition that now, suddenly, was gone. Although he continued to lead the US Third Army from his headquarters – a former Waffen-SS officers' training school at Bad Tölz, thirty miles south of Munich – he deplored the fact that the US Army was rapidly decreasing its presence in western Europe while the threat posed by the Soviet Union was so great. Overseeing the slow dismemberment of an organization for which he had such an affinity and a huge affection gave him no satisfaction.

Having not seen his wife and family for three years, it would have been understandable had Patton been elated with his orders to return home for a month to promote war bonds, but his relationship with Beatrice had been strained for many years, and by 1945 the general's home was a headquarters and his joy was leading a combat formation. Thus, despite being lauded by the many hundreds of thousands he addressed on the tour of his homeland in June – 100,000 at the Los Angeles Coliseum alone[1] – the experience was painful. With his marriage in dire straits and confirmation that there was no appointment for him in the Pacific theatre, he struggled to see a future that he wished to embrace. He may have worn what *The Los Angeles Times* called 'the grim grin of the conqueror' during his speeches,[2] but inside he felt broken and as such spoke without concern for the implications – and he was disparaging about 'Allies, the Soviets, politicians, and even the next war'.[3] Just before returning to Europe in July, he told his daughters that he would not see them again, explaining in a macabre conversation: 'Well, my luck has run out… You are born with a certain amount of luck, like money in the bank, and you spend it and it's gone. It's too damned bad I wasn't killed before the fighting stopped, but I wasn't. So be it.'[4] The great fighting leader, it seemed, had lost his muse.

Back in Germany, Patton combined his command of the Third Army with the post of military governor of Bavaria. It was an important job, with responsibility for more than a million displaced persons – including former inmates of the concentration camps – along with the demilitarization and denazification of the region. What the general could not understand, however, was why experienced US troops were being sent back to the United States despite the strong presence of the Red Army in eastern Germany, nor why Germany's administrative and industrial infrastructure was being dismantled because it had been manned by Nazi Party members. 'If we let Germany and the German people be completely disintegrated and starved', Patton wrote in his diary on 22 September, 'they will certainly fall for Communism, and the fall of Germany for Communism will write the epitaph of democracy in the United States. The more I see of people, the more I regret I survived the war.'[5] He thought it more logical to face down the Soviets with the retention of strong forces in the West, and to assist Germany's recovery by keeping those who knew what they were doing in positions of responsibility despite their past 'affiliations'.

These were views that Eisenhower (the military governor of the US zone of occupation) told Patton to keep to himself – particularly as Patton's views about former Nazis were clouded by his own anti-Semitism – and to do nothing more than follow orders.

The errant general, however, seemed bent on creating another great controversy. Having shown his resentment towards his current appointments by being little more than a figurehead for both of his roles (preferring instead to read, write and play sport), he became increasingly vocal in saying that he had no intention of presiding over the emasculation of southern Germany. The surrender of the Japanese that September did not improve his belligerent mood, for despite being repeatedly told that he would not serve in the Pacific, he had retained a hope that Washington would change its mind. With no hope of seeing more combat, Patton wrote in his diary: 'Now all that is left is to sit around and await the arrival of the undertaker and posthumous immortality.'[6]

Eisenhower sought to shake Patton out of his malaise. Expecting him to act professionally in carrying out his peacetime duties, he wrote, 'I demand you get off your bloody ass and carry out the denazification program as you are told instead of mollycoddling the goddam Nazis.'[7] Patton ignored the prompt and, indeed, when visiting a camp containing 5,000 Nazis on 8 September, he was reported to Eisenhower for allegedly saying that it was 'sheer madness to intern these people'.[8] Soon after, the complex situation was further compounded when Eisenhower's headquarters was informed about the appalling conditions found by inspectors in one of Patton's displaced persons camps – and, moreover, that some of the guards were former SS men. At the explosive meeting between Eisenhower and Patton that followed, the latter blamed the sudden decline of the camps on the arrival of Jewish survivors, and said that he was looking to make a nearby village a concentration camp for them. Eisenhower could hardly believe what he was hearing, and had all the evidence he needed to suggest that Patton's judgement was impaired and to sack him, but he did not, preferring instead – out of both friendship and loyalty – to give him another chance. However, when on 22 September Patton held a press conference in which he publicly espoused support for former Nazis in the rebuilding of Germany, the time had come to remove the man who, according to *The New York Times*, 'was obviously in a post which he was unsuited by temperament, training or experience to fill. It was a mistake to suppose a free-swinging fighter could acquire overnight the capacities of a wise administrator.'[9]

Upset that he had to endure the shame of being relieved, Patton bade farewell to the Third Army on 8 October and, having been spared the humiliation of a recall to Washington, took up a new post at Bad Nauheim, twenty miles north of Frankfurt, as commander of the Fifteenth Army. It was a 'paper formation' consisting of little more than a headquarters staff, but Eisenhower thought it would suit Patton, as its task was to oversee the preparation of a history of the war in Europe – or, as Patton would write to Beatrice, 'a lot of stuff which no one will ever read'.[10] He approached his responsibilities with all the limited enthusiasm he could rally, but it did not take him long to realize that this was not a job for him, and so, once again, Patton became a mere figurehead for what was otherwise a hardworking organization largely run by his chief of staff, the ever-loyal Hap Gay.

While his staff trawled through mountains of documents and began to create a structure for their work, Patton travelled around Europe and prepared his war memoir, *War As I Knew It*, in which he was to write: 'It is sad to remember that, when anyone has fairly mastered the art of command, the necessity for that art usually expires – either through the termination of the war or through the advanced age of the commander.'[11] Many who had not known Patton previously were rather surprised that the larger-than-life general was so withdrawn, but Gay was increasingly concerned with how introspective his boss was becoming and later wrote that 'it was obvious he was undergoing deep and gnawing turmoil'.[12]

On 11 November 1945, twenty-seven years after the end of the First World War had upset his world, Patton celebrated his sixtieth birthday. He enjoyed the party thrown for him by his staff, and a subsequent visit to Sweden where he met up with former members of the 1912 Olympic pentathlon team, but, as Gay feared, the general was gradually being enclosed by a darkness he could not avoid. On 5 December, therefore, in what may have been a final attempt to reconcile him to his future, he wrote to Beatrice that he was coming home for Christmas and did not intend to return to Europe.

Patton had always believed that his destiny was to die on the battlefield. On 9 December, the day before he was to leave for home, Patton was travelling with Gay to a pheasant shoot when the car in which he was a passenger collided with an oncoming US Army truck in the Mannheim suburb of Käfertal. Only Patton suffered injuries, but his head and spine were badly damaged, prompting him to quip, 'This is a helluva way to die.'[13] Beatrice arrived in Germany a few days later, followed by the world's best spinal surgeons. Sometimes joking, but also prone to bouts of despondency, Patton nevertheless showed courage in the face of his trauma. His medical team were convinced, however, that if he survived, Patton would be paralysed from the neck down. Senior officers arrived to clog up the 130th Station Hospital's narrow corridors while the press gathered at its entrance, desperate for any insight into the general's condition, while Beatrice devoted herself to a vigil at her husband's bedside. A few close friends arrived to spend a short time with Patton, leaving shocked at the severity of his injuries, but then after ten days his condition suddenly worsened. Beatrice spent the afternoon of 21 December reading to him, and Patton passed away that evening.

George S. Patton was buried on Christmas Eve 1945 in the American Military Cemetery in Hamm near Luxembourg City – chosen by Beatrice because it contained the men with whom he had served during the Battle of the Bulge, his great achievement. *The New York Times* reflected: 'History has reached out and embraced General George Patton. His place is secure. He will be ranked in the forefront of America's great military leaders.'[14]

— ¤ —

By the end of the Second World War, Field Marshal Bernard Montgomery was an established national hero, the greatest British soldier since Wellington, an officer around whom the nation and the Army could rally in peace. Despite turning fifty-eight in November 1945, he was still fit, energetic and, critically, was ambitious and willing to draw on all his experience and abilities to contribute to Britain and the Army in a new context. In the post-war nuclear world, the old realities had been quickly replaced with a Cold War between the United States and the Soviet Union, making central Europe a potential battlefield once again. Other than being a staunch ally to those nations gathered around American might, which safeguarded Western democracy, Britain had to find a new place in the world order as its empire began to crumble and the financial implications of fighting two total wars in the space of thirty years became profound. The Army, meanwhile, needed to find its place within national defence, while endeavouring to fulfil the aims of government policy with a significantly reduced budget and undergoing widespread transformation. The Army was almost unrecognizable from that which Montgomery had joined while Queen Victoria was still on the throne, and the field marshal wanted to play his part in shaping its future.

Montgomery's first task in May 1945 after the German surrender was grappling with the immediate after-effects of that nation's defeat in the British zone of occupation in the north-west quadrant of the country: disarming a sullen enemy; overseeing the welfare of some 2.5 million displaced persons; undertaking the denazification of German institutions and culture; and re-establishing civilian control of the national infrastructure.[15] As military governor of the British zone, he had 80,000 British troops in three corps under his command in an Army that increasingly consisted of new recruits and was soon re-designated the 'British Army of the Rhine' (BAOR) with a headquarters located in the central north German town of Bad Oeynhausen. A dozen of Montgomery's senior staff officers who had been with him since the Western Desert were sent elsewhere in the early summer of

1945 – including Freddie de Guingand, to whom Monty wrote, 'No commander can ever have had, or will have, a better Chief of Staff than you were; you never spared yourself, in fact you wore yourself out completely for the good of the show. Together we achieved much; and together we saw the thing through to the end.'[16]

The changes necessitated in the headquarters, however, heralded a return to the centralized, highly controlled and suffocating environment that would only become less restrictive when new members of the team had been fully inducted and won his trust. It was a paternalistic style that few felt comfortable with, but the commander found necessary. 'Monty had got to the stage beyond wanting anyone's opinion except his own,' aide-de-camp Captain Johnny Henderson later recalled. 'At that stage he didn't... seem to ask people questions in the same way as if he wanted to know the answer. It was backing up his *own* convictions he wanted.'[17]

This was also true with the variety of non-military agencies and individuals with whom Montgomery needed to work. David MacDonald, an official working for the Allied Control Council (which governed the four Allied occupation zones in Germany and assisted with the political transition), called Montgomery 'a blinkered and bullying officer whose opinionated approach was extremely annoying. He thought he knew it all. He didn't.'[18] Disinclined to change what had worked so well for him before, Montgomery made some wonder how he had ever achieved what he had during the recent conflict. Spending increasing amounts of time by himself, he was soon perceived by colleagues as a rather sad middle-aged widower with few friends and an unhealthy obsession with his work.

Throughout Montgomery's life there had always been a rather cruel and despotic side to his character, which raised questions about his suitability for various appointments. During August 1945 when the professional head of the British Army, the Chief of the Imperial General Staff (CIGS) Alan Brooke, was beginning to think about his successor, he wrote of his protégé: 'Monty very efficient from Army point of view, but very unpopular with large proportion of the Army.'[19]

Too opinionated, too demanding and too difficult, the field marshal had a reputation for creating problems where none had previously existed, while expecting his will to be done in all situations. In the summer of 1946, however, with concerns about his suitability pushed to one side for the sake of giving Britain's most well-known soldier an opportunity in the top job, Montgomery replaced Brooke, and on taking up this strategic leadership role looked forward to his influence being felt across the British Army and Whitehall. Recently ennobled as Viscount Montgomery of Alamein and soon to become a Knight of the Garter, talented, stubborn and exceedingly self-confident, he felt that he possessed all the attributes required to lead the Army through change. Prime Minister Clement Atlee certainly hoped Montgomery was the right man for the job because he recognized the particularly difficult environment in which the CIGS would be working, but while he knew that the field marshal would provide a clear vision, he was less sure about his ability to compromise.

The role of CIGS – since 1964 titled 'Chief of the General Staff' – is a vital one at any time. The job has wide responsibilities – not limited to ensuring the health and effectiveness of the British Army, but also playing a part in wider defence and advising government on strategy – and the potential for immense influence. One of Montgomery's most pressing priorities was to consider what was required for the successful defence of western Europe in view of the Soviet threat, and its implications for the Army. But this had to be done while taking into account wider British defence policy, foreign policy, alliances, budgets, and the consequences of the Admiralty, War Office, Air Ministry and Ministry of Aviation being brought together under a single Ministry of Defence on 1 January 1947.[20] The service chiefs lost their direct access to the prime minister, and instead reported to a Minister of Defence who represented them at Cabinet. Montgomery needed to navigate all this for the Army, and he took his position in the Chiefs of Staff Committee – alongside Sir Arthur Tedder, Chief of the Air Staff, and Admiral of the Fleet Sir John Cunningham, the First Sea Lord – which met at least once a week.

While he argued the Army's case and his own views about strategy clearly, colleagues were frustrated by Montgomery's oversimplification of complex matters and his unwillingness to view issues from alternative perspectives. From the outset of his tenure, Monty's relationships were strained. Not only were the First Sea Lord and Chief of the Air Staff furious at his blatant self-publicity in early August, when he held a conference with the editors of the bestselling British newspapers (people still crowded to see him wherever he went), a week later he did them the discourtesy of sending his deputy, General Simpson, to a Chiefs of Staff meeting. Tedder and Cunningham were 'hopping mad and were extremely hostile to [Simpson]', wrote an observer,[21] and it set the tone for what was to come. During the two years Montgomery was CIGS, self-interested squabbles took hold, concessions could not be made and co-operation became impossible. 'The other Chiefs of Staff, they resented Monty,' testified Brigadier Nigel Poett, Director of Plans. 'That was part of the trouble, that they resented Monty very much indeed because Monty had been built up as a great national figure... [and] damned well saw that he remained a public figure!'[22]

Although each service chief played his part in this sorry situation, Montgomery's personality and the way he conducted business was usually at the root of the friction, and the field marshal would often find himself in a corner fending off verbal blows landed by the other two services. He disliked Cunningham for being too deep a thinker and not at all practically minded, while his antipathy towards Tedder went back to 1944 when the airman was Eisenhower's deputy and became such a vocal critic of Montgomery's performance in Normandy that he tried to have him sacked. 'Monty couldn't stand Tedder, had declared war on Tedder at an early stage,' Poett said. 'John Cunningham was very clever, and Monty didn't like his style of cleverness, didn't like him at all. John Cunningham didn't like Monty, Tedder didn't like Monty so it was not a very happy organisation – with Cunningham and Tedder ganging up on Monty.'[23] Personalities aside, the Chiefs of Staff Committee had worked during the war when its membership was united by one great task, but now the lack of an all-encompassing common purpose, and very little money, made division far easier.

Monty found it difficult to work with not only senior uniformed colleagues; he often found politicians too self-interested and thought they were forever looking at the implications of decisions rather than making them, while he regarded the civil service as obstructive and, while containing far too many 'experts', producing too few sensible plans – and that those they did develop were poorly executed. Montgomery was only truly happy in a headquarters of handpicked military staff where he was the boss, subordinates were loyal and everybody else fell into line behind his thinking. As such, he later described Whitehall as 'my least happy theatre of war' and added revealingly that 'it did not provide my sort of battle. I have never minded making myself an infernal nuisance if it produced the desired result... As a result of it all I was pretty unpopular when I left Whitehall.'[24]

Despite the friction, during Montgomery's time as CIGS he worked assiduously to improve the British Army conceptually so that it was 'fit for the future', keeping up to date with the latest military concepts and technological developments. He recognized that the character of war had recently changed and demanded a re-evaluation of the way in which the British Army fought, but had no truck with those who argued that due to nuclear weapons there was no role for the Army other than to 'mop up'. 'We must therefore be prepared, as in the past, for battle on land,' he intoned.[25] Montgomery shook the British Army out of its Second World War mindset through a variety of exercises, the first the aptly titled Exercise 'Evolution' (which emphasized air-land operations) in August 1946. This, the first major post-war British Army exercise, was followed by Exercise 'Spearhead' (an amphibious landing under nuclear conditions) run at the Staff College, Camberley the following summer. Both were designed, developed and overseen with Montgomery's usual attention to detail and desire to learn lessons.

In 1948 he established a committee under General Sir John Crocker (one of his former corps commanders from North-West

Europe) to prepare the ground for a refreshing of the British Army's fighting methods. Two years later the committee produced *The Conduct of War*, which advocated the breaking of the enemy's will to fight through manoeuvre and became the capstone publication that informed all other doctrine and influenced the British Army for more than a generation.

As professional head of the British Army, Montgomery travelled extensively as part of his strategic engagement role and developed a firm feeling about threats, security, politics and alliances. Of all his meetings while overseas, however, none was more important than one in late 1946 with Dwight Eisenhower, who had succeeded Marshall as Chief of Staff of the US Army. Montgomery characteristically exceeded his authority, and despite being told by Attlee not to discuss anything of policy importance, during his discussions in Washington the idea of a transatlantic alliance was born. He returned to London to face the wrath of the prime minister and the contempt of his fellow chiefs of staff but, as he later said, 'the ball had started to roll and Britain was still in the game'.[26]

The outcome of subsequent talks was a political and military agreement that eventually led to the establishment of the Western Union Defence Organisation (WUDO) in 1948. It consisted of United Kingdom, France, Belgium, the Netherlands and Luxembourg, with Montgomery taking up the chairmanship of the Commanders-in-Chief Committee when his term as CIGS ended. His primary concern was ensuring that the military resources of the five European nations were organized effectively to meet the strategic needs of the alliance. Although the Americans were not initially involved, they and the Canadians sent observers to WUDO's military headquarters in Fontainebleau to report back on developments with a view to the building of a larger and more powerful organization.

Montgomery's inevitable brashness with some senior WUDO colleagues did lead to unnecessary ill-feeling in senior ranks. In particular, General Jean de Lattre Tassigny, the French land forces commander, found the British field marshal and de facto Supreme Commander restrictive and domineering. As early as 1 October 1948, Montgomery's diarist was noting that de Lattre 'was not going to take orders from the Field-Marshal… A head-on collision', and then, at the end of the month: 'General de Lattre had challenged the Field-Marshal's authority: he must be brought to heel at once.'[27] Yet resentment continued to brew, leading *The New York Times* to explain, in an article titled 'MONTGOMERY RIFT WITH FRENCH SEEN; Split with Gen. de Lattre de Tassigny Involves Priority in Union Defense' on 30 April 1949, that 'for more than six months a controversy over their respective spheres has been in full swing between Field Marshal Viscount Montgomery, head of the Permanent Defense Organization of Western Europe, and Gen. Jean de Lattre de Tassigny, Commander in Chief of the Land Forces of the Western European Union. This dispute makes their cooperation difficult, if not impossible.'[28] Monty had caused Eisenhower a similar problem and, in a similar way, despite occasional flare-ups, the two men learned to work with each other. Indeed, successful WUDO exercises in 1949 and 1950 designed and led by Montgomery revealed what could be achieved in a short period of time, for despite personality clashes, the assertion of national interests and different working practices, the five nations were united in a common aim.

The advent of the North Atlantic Treaty Organization (NATO) in 1949 was testament to Montgomery's ambition to establish a meaningful enhancement to the Western alliance's military capabilities with the addition of several other nations, including the United States and Canada. With a new military headquarters established in 1951 at Rocquencourt, just west of Paris, titled 'Supreme Headquarters Allied Powers Europe' (SHAPE), Eisenhower became Supreme Allied Commander Europe and Montgomery, as the representative of a junior partner, his deputy (DSACEUR). It was an important appointment, critical to the prestige and influence of the United Kingdom, and would draw heavily on the field marshal's work from the previous couple of years.

Over the next seven years, until his retirement in 1958, Montgomery led the conceptual development of NATO's ground forces using his own annual SHAPE 'command post' exercises to improve what existed and act as a testbed for new ideas and concepts. They also became events at which NATO's senior commanders and defence ministers assembled at SHAPE to meet each other and learn about Monty's military vision in his closing address. 'In this context', Simon Moody has written of Montgomery's influence during this period, '[he] became NATO's blacksmith, dedicated to forging the alliance a new weapon.'[29] He also became the organization's key promoter, travelling widely to address parliaments, brief defence ministries and update headquarters – always looking to build understanding, develop co-operation and provide confidence about how NATO was confronting challenges and would do so in the future.

Montgomery insisted the Western alliance build a large and effective military force, but also the ability to out-think the Soviet Union in everything it did. 'One factor in which we can enjoy a great advantage, both at the outset and throughout', Monty always emphasized, 'is in brains.'[30] The field marshal was well received wherever he went, his former abrasiveness having been replaced with a warmness towards allies that was a recognition of the vital importance of close and trusting relationships between a community of nations. Indeed, after hearing him speak in Washington, US Army staff officer John D. Watson wrote: 'Despite what I had heard about Montgomery being cool towards the Americans, he could not have been more friendly or understanding. He seemed very well briefed and intelligent with a firm grasp on the situation. I left the meeting believing that the right man was in the right job and believe we all think the same.'[31]

During his years as Eisenhower's deputy at SHAPE, Montgomery never lost sight of the fact that the United States was the senior partner in NATO, and thus his relationship with Eisenhower was far less combative than it had been during the war because the two men understood each other. Montgomery also endeavoured to build good working relationships with Eisenhower's successors – first Matthew Ridgway and then Alfred Gruenther. At his insistence, for example, Gruenther established a special study unit known as the 'New Approach Group' (NAG) in 1953, which sought to further develop NATO's military strength in order to become a more credible deterrent and utilize the appropriate fighting methods and weaponry.[32] Throughout his time as deputy, Montgomery motivated and inspired NATO's nations to look to the future, harness new technology and never stagnate. He was equally keen to promote what he believed to be the enduring requirement for success: all the thinking, building and preparing was for naught, Montgomery argued, if armed forces failed to develop effective leaders. At a talk at the Royal United Services Institute (RUSI) in London in October 1954, for example, the field marshal said, 'Armies must develop a more lively and opportunistic type of battle leader than exists at present in both junior *and* senior ranks. Such a leader must have the imagination, the daring, and the resources to seize fleeting local opportunities; he must be trained to act independently and immediately within the framework of a general plan, rather than on precise and detailed orders or only after reference to a superior.'[33]

In saying this, Montgomery was advocating a type of leader with attributes and a mindset that would not have suited his own style of fighting during the Second World War, when he had trusted his commanders to use their own initiative only within the very clearly defined methods that he had dictated under his controlling centralized command. During his final four years as deputy, Montgomery was seeking to ensure that 'modern leaders' were produced, with the attributes that he outlined at RUSI. And his argument that leaders must be relevant to their times while also displaying the timeless qualities of effective leadership was not just one he made while in uniform – it was one that he returned to on countless occasions for the rest of his life.

Field Marshal The Viscount Montgomery of Alamein retired from active service on 18 September 1958 after fifty years' service.

He was determined not to slip into his dotage at his 'headquarters', as Monty often referred to his home – Isington Mill in East Hampshire. He continued to express himself through his writing, lobbying, lectures and sitting in the House of Lords, and attended to his legacy, keen to rebut the criticism his command during the North-West European campaign had attracted (including in the memoirs of Patton, Eisenhower and Bradley[34]) by encouraging the view that, despite mistakes, he was the most capable senior officer the Allies had. Montgomery's own memoirs were published in 1958, and with the rights licensed in many countries the book quickly became an international bestseller. Various individuals were consequently either hurt or made furious by what Montgomery wrote, with Claude Auchinleck threatening to sue over allegations he had plans to withdraw to Cairo when Monty took over the British Eighth Army. In the United States, many readers were angered by the book's belittling of Eisenhower's command, and particularly by the argument that his decision-making had extended the war in Europe for a year longer than had been necessary. Eisenhower had been elected US president in 1952, and the two men never exchanged another word.

Montgomery had never been overly concerned about falling out with former colleagues (or anybody else for that matter), and old age did not change him. He gained something of a reputation for failing to read the mood of audiences who attended his talks, wanting to relive wartime memories and rekindle old comradeship – the annual reunion of 3,000 Eighth Army veterans at the Royal Albert Hall, for example, at which the guest of honour instead gave a speech focused on current defence priorities and the art of war. He was gently advised on many occasions to talk about something more appropriate, but rejected the recommendations as firmly as he rejected sentimentality in any form. Having attended an event at which Montgomery was present, one former Highland infantryman reported to a friend: 'He remained every inch the field marshal, rather distant, combative and dominating affairs as though he had been invited into his own home. He was the host. Very odd, but then he was, wasn't he?'[35]

Unwilling to bend to the demands of others, he also resisted sharing the limelight with other senior officers. It was commonplace for Monty to 'send his regrets' if he learned (and he always asked) that another colleague or colleagues had been invited to an event, and he would never share the stage with a former subordinate. An exception was his return to El Alamein for the twenty-fifth anniversary of the battle in October 1967, shortly before the field marshal's eightieth birthday. His attendance, however, was dependent on Freddie de Guingand not being invited, as Montgomery increasingly liked to portray himself not so much as the captain of a team, but as a master of the battlefield reliant solely on his own skill and intuition. It was only after the intervention of the former commander of British Second Army, Miles Dempsey, that de Guingand was offered an invitation, and, other than formal occasions during which he was friendly to his former chief of staff, Montgomery largely ignored the man on which so many of his accomplishments were dependent.

Although his powers and stamina were waning during the 1970s, Montgomery continued to take on those academics, veterans, writers and commentators who disagreed with his view of history. In 1974, F. W. Winterbotham, a former RAF officer responsible for distributing Ultra intelligence, published a book detailing the importance of the code breaking in North Africa and Europe and revealing that the Allied victory 'was, in fact, a very narrow shave', raising the question 'whether or not we might have won had we not had Ultra'.[36] Montgomery's response was typically combative, arguing that it was just like any other information received about the enemy, and that the material itself was not vital but what was done with it. It was one last engagement in a very long and distinguished career.

Montgomery died at home on 24 March 1976 in his eighty-ninth year, and after a state funeral in St George's Chapel at Windsor Castle he was interred in his local churchyard at Binstead with a simple stone. Tributes were received from across the world, but one from Omar Bradley stands out. Putting old animosities aside, he wrote simply, 'Dear Monty. Goodbye and thanks. Brad.'[37]

Epilogue

BRITISH FIRST WORLD WAR veteran Guy Chapman described the experience of war as being like having a 'mistress', explaining: 'You may loathe, you may execrate, but you cannot deny her. No lover can offer you defter caresses, more exquisite tortures, such breaking delights. No wine gives fiercer intoxication, no drug more vivid exaltation.'[1] The influence of the 1914–18 war on Patton, Montgomery and Rommel was immense, for beyond the life-threatening wounds that each suffered at the front and the awards for gallantry that each received, it was an experience that confirmed to them that they wanted to be army leaders and to make a difference.

Patton, Montgomery and Rommel were demanding leaders. Their unswerving commitment to exert influence, demand high standards and realize challenging objectives put pressure on all those around them – sometimes unreasonably so – but they routinely achieved high performance and noteworthy outcomes. Yet despite the hierarchical character of the army and its demand for obedience, each officer understood that effective leadership in the military demands more than mere reliance on rank and orders. If leadership is the art of getting others to do things they would not otherwise do, and to do them willingly, all three officers became its effective exponents because they recognized that a bond of trust had to be established between themselves and their followers. As such, Patton,

Montgomery and Rommel worked diligently throughout their long careers to acquire the professional knowledge that would give them credibility, and the wisdom that would aid their judgement. It was a lifelong enterprise willingly undertaken by the three officers, and even if they occasionally mis-stepped on that path of self-improvement, it was a necessary journey.

It did not take Patton, Montgomery and Rommel long to recognize that as leaders they were servants to their followers and, as a consequence, that they needed to better understand what influenced the minds and behaviours of their people. In Patton's words, a leader needed to 'get under the hood to see what drives their people',[2] while Rommel argued that 'by skilful psychological handling... the performance of troops can be increased enormously',[3] and Montgomery asserted 'it is essential to understand human nature... If the approach to the human factor is cold and impersonal, then you can achieve nothing. But if you can gain the confidence and trust of your men and they feel their best interests are safe in your hands, then you have in your possession a priceless asset and the greatest achievements become possible.'[4]

Time and again, Patton, Montgomery and Rommel achieved remarkable success because they had won the trust of those they led – and so, whenever possible, they created a team of compliant subordinates who could be relied on not to undermine that trust. The three officers could therefore be criticized for failing to encourage and embrace diversity of thought and opinion, but while they led organizations primed for resolute action and achieved success, others dithered away opportunities and failed. As senior leaders, their dynamism was facilitated by chiefs of staff – whether Gay or Gaffey, Simpson or de Guingand, Gause or Speidel – who would check their commander's ideas, but habitually facilitated their will and operationalized their intent. After the war, Montgomery wrote of Freddie de Guingand: 'I trusted him completely; he seemed to know instinctively what I would do in any given situation, and he was always right. With such a Chief of Staff I could keep clear of detail; I left that all to him. The first requirement in high command is to have a good Chief of Staff. Without de Guingand, I doubt I could have done my part of the overall task.'[5]

As senior officers, having a trusted and empowered top team was vital to their ability to focus on their priorities, but while it may have been tempting to remain in their headquarters, the three generals never forgot that their infectious presence could have a huge motivational impact on the ground. Charles R. Codman, an aide to Patton during the last two years of the Second World War, later remarked on his general's 'uncanny gift for sweeping men into doing things they do not believe they are capable of doing, which they do not really want to do, and which, in fact, they would not do, unless directly exposed to the personality, the genius… of this unique soldier'.[6] Montgomery similarly impressed Warwick Charlton, his press officer in North Africa, who wrote: '[The general], who appears to be sometimes limited by intellect and not very emotional… did unleash all the things men really wanted to do, to believe in and so forth. They would have followed him to any damned place!... That's a rare thing, you know.'[7] Gerd von Rundstedt, meanwhile, argued that Rommel 'never failed to rouse men to great feats through his leadership and managed to extract the maximum of effort from them'.[8]

While their effect may have been similar, the leadership styles that Patton, Montgomery and Rommel assumed nonetheless differed because they reflected individual personalities. Patton's profanity-filled sentimental addresses to troops before battle, for example, were in contrast to Montgomery's dispassionate orations, while Rommel's speeches were sometimes clinically composed but could be mawkish. Each approach to the creation of that essential connection between leader and led had to be genuine if it was to be productive, and as such it provided an insight into the man. What unified their approaches, therefore, was an attempt to be true to themselves, for as Field Marshal Bill Slim told officer cadets graduating from the Royal Military Academy Sandhurst in 1952, '[Leadership] is, in effect, the extension of personality. Leadership is the most personal thing in the world, for the simple reason that leadership is just plain you.'[9]

However accomplished, Patton, Montgomery and Rommel were also flawed men, deeply so in some cases, with their leadership naturally mirroring their weaknesses – which included irascibility, a lack of consideration for the opinions and feelings of others, arrogance and selfishness. Each was also desperately seeking to write his own chapter in the annals of history, and so was not averse to allowing ambition to cloud his judgement. Indeed, both Patton and Montgomery relished the prospect of pitting their wits against Rommel in North Africa and so enhance their own reputations, and they also were competitive and spiteful towards each other. To Montgomery, Patton was a 'foul-mouthed lover of war', while Patton thought Montgomery a 'cocky little Limey fart',[10] and neither rated the other as a commander. The personalities of the two men were as different as their approaches to war-fighting, but they shared aggressive characteristics that provided Eisenhower and Brooke with myriad unpalatable issues to contend with over the final two years of the Second World War.

A combination of ambition, character flaws and pressurized circumstances ensured that Patton, Montgomery and Rommel all fell short of being model leaders, with even their patrons and closest colleagues unable to stop them from displays of various unbecoming behaviours. Patton's outrageous conduct in August 1943 towards battle-fatigued soldiers in Sicily was a reminder of just how easily hard-earned trust and respect could be overturned, and raised serious questions about his fitness to remain a senior leader. For Montgomery, meanwhile, his ill-judged press conference on 7 January 1945 during the Battle of the Bulge, during which he made erroneous claims that antagonized the Americans at a particularly sensitive time, revealed his peculiar and chronic lack of self-awareness. Rommel's inability to fully comprehend the strategic bigger picture and the implications of his persistent demands was bound to antagonize Berlin and ultimately raised questions about his trustworthiness. Indeed, while Patton, Rommel and Montgomery each demanded loyalty from their subordinates, they could be poor followers themselves, for each was capable of weaponizing the immense self-confidence which so inspired their followers, and using it against their superiors. Walter Bedell Smith, Eisenhower's chief of staff, doubtless reflected the feelings of many who served with the three officers when he said to Montgomery, 'You may be great to serve under, difficult to serve alongside, but you sure are hell to serve over.'[11]

Even as each man remains a controversial figure to this day, their achievements as leaders were undeniably remarkable. Often at their best when against the odds, under immense pressure and in the destabilizing presence of chaos and confusion, Patton, Montgomery and Rommel cut through the complexity, did not shirk from their responsibilities, applied sound judgement, made a decision and provided leadership. On balance, therefore, it is hard to disagree with Field Marshal The Lord Bramall's assessment of the three officers: 'Looking back on their accomplishments across decades of service it is difficult to come to any other conclusion than that their leadership was a triumph.'[12]

Notes

Introduction

1   Interview with Field Marshal The Lord Bramall, 17 April 2016.

2   This version of events is taken from Michael Tillotson, *The Fifth Pillar: The Life and Philosophy of The Lord Bramall KG* (Stroud: Sutton Publishing Limited, 2005), p. 47.

3   David V. Day and John Antonakis (eds), *The Nature of Leadership* (London: Sage, 2012), p. 5.

4   See Gabriel Morin, *Does Cultural Leadership Apply in the Context of Military Organization? A parallel study of the British and French Armies*, unpublished paper for the Centre for Army Leadership, 2016.

5   Harry S. Laver and Jeffrey J. Matthews (eds), *The Art of Command: Military Leadership from George Washington to Colin Powell* (Lexington, KY: University Press of Kentucky, 2008), p. 3.

6   ADP Army Leadership Doctrine (Ministry of Defence, edition 1, September 2016).

7   See Stephen Fitzsimons, *The Leadership Styles of Persian Kings in Herodotus*, unpublished PhD, University of Manchester, 2017; and Thomas E. Cronin and Michael A. Genovese, *Leadership Matters: Unleashing the Power of Paradox* (Abingdon: Routledge, 2012).

8   See Edgar H. Schein, *Organizational Culture and Leadership* (San Francisco: Jossey-Bass, 2004).

9   Jörg Muth, *Command Culture: Officer Education in the US Army and the German Armed Forces 1901–1940, and the Consequences for World War II* (Denton, TX: University of North Texas Press, 2011), p. 3.

10   See M. J. Gelfand, M. Erez and Z. Aycan, 'Cross-cultural Behavior', *Annual Review of Psychology*, Vol. 58 (2007), pp. 479–514; also R. J. House, P. J. Hanges, M. Javidan, P. W. Dorfman, and V. Gupta, *Culture, Leadership, and Organizations. The GLOBE Study of 62 Societies* (Thousand Oaks, CA: Sage, 2004).

11   See Albert S. King, 'Evolution of Leadership Theory', *Vikalpa: The Journal for Decision Makers*, Vol. 15, No. 2 (April–June1990).

Chapter One: Early Years and Junior Leaders, 1880s–1914

1 National Park Service, 'Hiram Cronk', https://www.nps.gov/people/hiram-cronk.htm [accessed 14 April 2019].

2 For more on this, see Hugh Brogan, *The Penguin History of the United States of America* (London: Penguin, 2001).

3 Susan J. Drucker and Robert S. Cathcart (eds), *American Heroes in a Media Age* (New York: Hampton Press, 1994), p. 139.

4 See King, 'Evolution of Leadership Theory', p. 45.

5 See numerous references to these works in various correspondence with his father, his aunt and others, George S. Patton Papers, Library of Congress, Family Papers, 1857–1979, Boxes 14–24.

6 See Carlo D'Este, *Patton: A Genius for War* (New York: Harper Perennial, 1996), pp. 45–49, who argues that Patton was dyslexic; and Stanley P. Hirshon, *General Patton: A Soldier's Life* (New York: HarperCollins, 2003), pp. 24–25, who argues that he was not.

7 See D'Este, *A Genius for War*, pp. 46–47.

8 68 per cent of all officers reaching general rank between 1898 and 1940 were West Point graduates. See Jörg Muth, *Command Culture*, p. 44.

9 Letter from George S. Patton to his father, dated 3 July 1904, George S. Patton Papers, Library of Congress, Family Papers, 1857–1979, Box 20.

10 See Muth, *Command Culture*, p. 67 et passim.

11 Ibid., p. 82.

12 See innumerable letters written by Patton over the period 1904–1909, George S. Patton Papers, Library of Congress, Box 20.

13 Letter from George S. Patton to his father, undated 1904, George S. Patton Papers, Library of Congress, Box 20.

14 George S. Patton's 'West Point Notebook', George S. Patton Papers, Library of Congress, Box 5.

15 'Elements of Strategy' textbook, Patton Papers, Special Collection, United States Military Academy West Point, New York.

16 D'Este, *A Genius for War*, p. 47.

17 See Muth, *Command Culture*, p. 77.

18 For more on this, see Russell F. Weigley, *History of the United States Army* (London: Batsford, 1967). By the summer of 1914, the US Army was approximately 98,000 officers and men strong.

19 See Arthur T. Coombe, *A History of the US Army Officer Corps, 1900–1990* (Carlisle, PA: Strategic Studies and US Army War College Press, 2014).

20 Undated entry from the first January–February 1909, George S. Patton's 'West Point Notebook', George S. Patton Papers, Library of Congress, Box 5.

21 Martin Blumenson, *The Patton Papers 1885–1940* (Boston: Houghton Mifflin, 1972), p. 222.

22 Ibid., p. 226.

23 George S. Patton's *Principles of Scouting*, dated February 1912, George S. Patton Papers, Library of Congress, Box 5.

24 Letter from Colonel Thomas Peterson to Mr Jake Lindt, dated 2 October 1912, author's collection.

25 Letter from George S. Patton to Beatrice Patton, dated 7 September 1912, George S. Patton Papers, Library of Congress, Box 15.

26 See George S. Patton Papers, Library of Congress, Box 66.

27 D'Este, *A Genius for War*, p. 145.

28 See Louis-Aimé Martin, *The Education of Mothers of Families, or, The Civilisation of the Human Race by Women*, trans. Edwin Lee (London: Whittaker, 1842), p. 19.

29 Bernard Law Montgomery, *The Memoirs of Field-Marshal The Viscount Montgomery of Alamein* (London: Collins, 1958), p. 17.

30 Montgomery, *Memoirs*, p. 11. For more on the Army during this period, see Timothy Bowman and Mark L. Connelly, *The Edwardian Army: Recruiting, Training, and Deploying the British Army, 1902–1914* (Oxford: Oxford University Press, 2012).

31 Alastair Horne, *The Lonely Leader: Monty 1944–45* (London: Macmillan), p. 7. See also Montgomery's school reports, The Montgomery Papers, Imperial War Museum, BLM 7/1.

32 Royal Military College Cadet Register, Volume 6 (1903–1907), War Office 151, The Sandhurst Collection, Royal Military Academy Sandhurst.

33 See Andrew George Duncan, *The Military Education of Junior Officers in the Edwardian Army*, unpublished DPhil, University of Birmingham, 2016.

34 The Akers-Douglas Committee on the Education and Training of Army Officers, which reported in 1902.

35 Duncan, *Military Education*, p. 23.

36 Ibid., p. 24.

37 Nigel Hamilton, *Monty: The Making of a General, 1887–1942* (London: Hamish Hamilton, 1981), p. 47.

38 The Royal Military College syllabus was now more suited to the military profession and consisted of: military administration; military law; military engineering; military topography; tactics; military history; geography; French or German language; drill; riding; and gymnastics. For references made to syllabus changes see Sandhurst: The Royal Military College: Full Inspection, HM Inspectorate, 1911, The National Archives, ED 109/5853.

39 Royal Military College Cadet Register, January 1907 – September 1908, The National Archives, WO151/8.

40 Duncan, *Military Education*, p. 157.

41 Talk by Montgomery to Officer Cadets and Directing Staff of the Royal Military Academy Sandhurst, Camberley, 17 July 1965. Notes taken by O/Cdt James Mills, Bolton Collection, Boston, Lincs.

42 Montgomery, *Memoirs*, p. 11.

43 Montgomery emphasized the development of his communication skills in a letter to Major Bill Gallagher dated 16 March 1953, papers of W. S. Gallagher, Bath, Somerset.

44 Montgomery, *Memoirs*, p. 29.

45 Hamilton, *The Making of a General*, p. 52.

46 There were consequently some lieutenants languishing in the rank in their late thirties while most commanding officers were in their mid-fifties.

47 Letter from Captain Tobias Smythe to his mother, April 1910, from the collection of Jane O'Neil (née Smythe), West Hampstead, London.

48 Montgomery letter to J. C. Worth discussing his leadership experience and referring to his time in India, dated 17 July 1934, author's collection.

49 Ibid.

50 Ibid.

51 Hamilton, *The Making of a General*, p. 54.

52 Interview with Gordon McDonald (transcript titled 'Montgomery and India'), dated 16 June 1969, a copy of which is in the papers of Field Marshal The Lord Bramall (uncatalogued in 2019), held at the University of Buckingham.

53 Montgomery, *Memoirs*, p. 31.

54 Hamilton, *The Making of a General*, p. 6.

55 David Irving, *The Trail of the Fox: The Life of Field-Marshal Erwin Rommel* (London: Weidenfeld and Nicolson, 1977), p. 9.

56 Rommel's sporting pursuits became increasingly adrenaline-fuelled, the young man happily embracing more risk in the mountains, skiing off-piste, cycling fast downhill or running to the point of physical collapse. See Dr David J. Williams, *The Development of Erwin Rommel's Risk-Reward Skill*, unpublished paper for the Centre for Army Leadership, 16 May 2019.

57 For more on the Germany Army during this period, see Martin Kitchen, *A Military History of Germany: From the Eighteenth Century to the Present Day* (Bloomington, IN: Indiana University Press, 1975).

58 This figure includes those undertaking compulsory active military service as well as those on the reserve lists.

59 Karl Demeter, *The German Officer Corps in Society and State 1650–1945* (London: Weidenfeld and Nicolson, 1965), p. 17.

60 Alexander Watson, 'Junior Officership in the German Army during the Great War, 1914–1918', *War in History*, Vol. 14, No. 4 (2007), p. 434.

61 See Muth, *Command Culture*, pp. 97–98.

62 Irving, *The Trail of the Fox*, p. 10.

63 Erwin and Lucie were to provided financial support for Gertrud, who became a welcomed member of the family. Walburga, however, never recovered from Erwin's rejection and committed suicide in 1928 having learned that her former lover was expecting a baby with Lucie.

Chapter Two: First Combat, 1914–16

1 Hirshon, *A Soldier's Life*, p. 67.

2 See George Patton's letter to Beatrice and his father during 1914–15, George S. Patton Papers, Library of Congress, Boxes 15 and 20.

3 Letter from George S. Patton to Beatrice Patton, dated 9 March 1915, George S. Patton Papers, Library of Congress, Box 15.

4 See letter to his father, dated 4 June 1916, George S. Patton Papers, Library of Congress, Box 20.

5 Blumenson, *The Patton Papers 1885–1940*, p. 291.

6 Letter from Billy Mendonca to Jacob E. Wall, dated 6 March 1916, Wall collection, Macon, Georgia.

7 Blumenson, *The Patton Papers 1885–1940*, p. 320.

8 George S. Patton, 'Personal Glimpses of Pershing', 1924, http://www.pattonhq.com/textfiles/pershing.html [accessed 2 July 2021].

9 Ibid.

10 See: Blumenson, *The Patton Papers 1885–1940*, p. 330; Hirshon, *A Soldier's Life*, p. 77; and D'Este, *A Genius for War*, pp. 173–74.

11 Letter from George S. Patton to Beatrice Patton, dated 13 April 1916, George S. Patton Papers, Library of Congress, Box 15.

12 *The Boston Globe*, 2 June 1916, p. 1.

13 Letter from George S. Patton to Beatrice Patton, dated 17 May 1916, George S. Patton Papers, Library of Congress, Box 15.

14 Letter from George S. Patton to his father, dated 12 July 1916, George S. Patton Papers, Library of Congress, Box 20.

15 Letter from John Pershing to George S. Patton, dated 1 October 1916, George S. Patton Papers, Library of Congress, Box 25.

16 See Hirshon, *A Soldier's Life*, p. 88.

17 Letter from Bernard Montgomery to his mother, dated 2 August 1914, The Montgomery Papers, Imperial War Museum, Part I, Section A, BLM 1/2.

18 Letter from Bernard Montgomery to his mother, dated 15 August 1914, The Montgomery Papers, Imperial War Museum, Part I, Section A, BLM 1/10.

19 Letter from Bernard Montgomery to his mother, dated 9 August 1914, The Montgomery Papers, Imperial War Museum, Part I, Section A, BLM 1/7.

20 For all movements and actions, see 10 Infantry Brigade War Diary: 1 Battalion Royal Warwickshire Regiment, The National Archives, WO95/1484/1.

21 Journal of Peter Symes PhD, January – September 1914, entry dated 24 August 1914, author's collection.

22 Letter from Bernard Montgomery to his father, dated 27 September 1914, The Montgomery Papers, Imperial War Museum, Part I, Section A, BLM 1/23.

23 Ibid.

24 Letter from Bernard Montgomery to his mother, dated 22 September

1914, The Montgomery Papers, Imperial War Museum, Part I, Section A, BLM 1/22.

25   10 Infantry Brigade War Diary.

26   *The London Gazette*, 1 December 1914, p. 10188, https://www.thegazette.co.uk/London/issue/28992/page/10188 [accessed 2 January 2019].

27   Hamilton, *The Making of a General*, p. 91.

28   Letter from Brigadier General Gerald Mackenzie to Bishop Montgomery, dated 29 January 1916, The Montgomery Papers, Imperial War Museum, Part I, Section A, BLM 1/31.

29   Letter from Bernard Montgomery to David Drake, dated 14 March 1916, private collection, TD papers, Winslow, Buckinghamshire.

30   Montgomery, *Memoirs*, p. 35.

31   Peter Caddick-Adams, *Monty and Rommel: Parallel Lives* (London: Arrow, 2012), p. 74.

32   See Lt-Col H. M. Davson, *The History of the 35th Division in the Great War* (London: Sifton Praed, 1926), p. 43.

33   Major Duncan Pearson, *Bernard Montgomery as First World War Staff Officer*, Humanities Research Institute Post Graduate Group, University of Buckingham, 16 August 2019.

34   Montgomery, *Memoirs*, p. 35.

35   Erwin Rommel, *Infanterie greift an* (Potsdam: Ludwig Voggenreiter, 1942), pp. 9–11.

36   Ibid., p. 10.

37   Ibid., p. 19.

38   Ibid., pp. 16–23.

39   Ibid., p. 81.

40   Ibid., p. 85.

41   Ibid., p. 91.

42   Ibid., p. 91.

43   Irving, *The Trail of the Fox*, p. 13.

44   Thomas Artmann diary entries, dated 1 and 2 November 1916, Artmann family archive, Paderborn.

45   Rommel, *Infanterie greift an*, p. 133.

46   Ibid., p. 137.

47   Ibid., p. 149.

Chapter Three: Hard-Won Experience, 1917–18

1   Letter from George S. Patton to Beatrice Patton, dated 29 January 1917, George S. Patton Papers, Library of Congress, Box 16.

2   For more see John J. Pershing, *My Experiences in the World War*, Volumes I and II (New York: Frederick A. Stokes Co., 1931).

3   Letters written by Patton during this period in Paris, George S. Patton Papers, Library of Congress, Boxes 16 and 25.

4   Letter from George S. Patton to Beatrice Ayer Patton, dated 27 September 1917, George S. Patton Papers, Library of Congress, Box 16.

5   D. P. Durand, *Patton's Tank School*, unpublished paper supporting a Royal Tank Regiment Staff Ride, November 2007, author's collection.

6   Letter from George S. Patton to Commander-in-Chief, American

Expeditionary Force, titled 'Command in the Tank Service', dated 3 October 1917, George S. Patton Papers, Library of Congress, Box 25.

7   Letter from George S. Patton to Beatrice Patton, dated 26 November 1917, George S. Patton Papers, Library of Congress, Box 16.

8   George S. Patton, *Patton on Armor: Light Tank Report 1917 and Tanks, Past, Present and Future 1928* (n.p., Province Publishing, 1980).

9   Letter from George S. Patton to Beatrice Patton, dated 14 January 1918, George S. Patton Papers, Library of Congress, Box 16.

10   George S. Patton Jr, *War As I Knew It* (London: W. H. Allen, 1948), p. 336.

11   Headquarters Army Tank School, Memorandum No. 1, dated 27 January 1918, George S. Patton Papers, Library of Congress, Box 47.

12   Letter from George S. Patton to Beatrice Patton, dated 14 January 1918, George S. Patton Papers, Library of Congress, Box 16.

13   The badge, Patton explained, represented 'the firepower of the artillery, the mobility of the cavalry, and the ability to hold ground of the infantry'. See D'Este, *A Genius for War*, p. 215.

14   Blumenson, *The Patton Papers 1885–1940*, pp. 500–501.

15   Hirshon, *A Soldier's Life*, p. 114.

16   Letter from George S. Patton to Beatrice Patton, dated 23 December 1917, George S. Patton

Papers, Library of Congress, Box 16.

17   Letter from George S. Patton to Beatrice Patton, dated 22 April 1918, George S. Patton Papers, Library of Congress, Box 16.

18   Blumenson, *The Patton Papers 1885–1940*, p. 562.

19   Ibid., pp. 581–82.

20   D'Este, *A Genius for War*, p. 242.

21   Blumenson, *The Patton Papers 1885–1940*, p. 59.

22   Patton, *War As I Knew It*, p. 340.

23   1st Lt Paul S. Edwards, 'Gallant and Exemplary Conduct of Col. Geo. S. Patton, Jr and the circumstances leading up to his being wounded in the Argonne attack – Sept. 26, 1918', dated 27 November 1918, George S. Patton Papers, Library of Congress, Box 49, Reel 1.

24   Michael Reynolds, *Monty and Patton: Two Paths to Victory* (Stroud: Spellmount, 2005), p. 63.

25   George S. Patton, 'My Father', written in 1927, George S. Patton Papers, Library of Congress, Box 68.

26   '"Bravest Man in the American Army" is Compliment Bestowed on New Jersey Boy by Tank Commander', *Indiana Evening Gazette*, 4 April 1919.

27   For details about this action, see D'Este, *A Genius for War*, pp. 258–60; and Blumenson, *The Patton Papers 1885–1940*, pp. 610–16.

28   Letter from George S. Patton to Beatrice Patton, dated 10 October 1918, George S. Patton Papers, Library of Congress, Box 16.

29 Letter from George S. Patton to General Francis Marshall, dated 12 April 1918, George S. Patton Papers, Library of Congress, Box 25.

30 Alan Maciver interview, conducted in 1975, Imperial War Museum, catalogue nos 3305.

31 Ibid.

32 Paul Harris, *The Men Who Planned the War – A Study of the Staff of the British Army on the Western Front, 1914–18*, unpublished PhD, King's College University of London, 2013, p. 9.

33 Ibid., p. 173.

34 Letter from Bernard Montgomery to his mother, dated 13 April 1917, The Montgomery Papers, Imperial War Museum, Part I, Section A, BLM 1/58.

35 Letter from Bernard Montgomery to his father, dated 13 April 1917, The Montgomery Papers, Imperial War Museum, Part I, Section A, BLM 1/61.

36 Captain J. C. Dunn, *The War the Infantry Knew 1914–1919: A Chronicle of Service in France and Belgium* (London: Abacus, 1994), p. xli.

37 Siegfried Sassoon, 'The General', in *The War Poems* (London: Faber and Faber, 1999).

38 See Captain Cyril Falls, *Official History of the Great War – Military Operations France and Belgium, 1917*, Vol. I (first published 1925; reprint Naval and Military Press, 2021).

39 Letter from Bernard Montgomery to James Moore, dated 1 May 1917, private collection, TD papers, Winslow, Buckinghamshire.

40 Letter from Bernard Montgomery to his father, dated 13 April 1917, The Montgomery Papers, Imperial War Museum, Part I, Section A, BLM 1/62.

41 Ibid.

42 Letter from Bernard Montgomery to his mother, dated 13 April 1917, The Montgomery Papers, Imperial War Museum, Part I, Section A, BLM 1/61

43 9 Corps War Diary, 1 May 1918 – 31 December 1918, The National Archive, WO95/837/1.

44 See Brigadier General Sir James E. Edmonds, *Official History of the Great War – Military Operations France and Belgium, 1918*, Vol. I (London: Macmillan, 1935).

45 Ibid.

46 9 Corps War Diary.

47 For more on this, see Gary Sheffield, *Forgotten Victory: The First World War – Myths and Realities* (Headline: London, 2002).

48 Montgomery, *Memoirs*, p. 38.

49 Letter from Bernard Montgomery to his mother, dated 3 September 1918, The Montgomery Papers, Imperial War Museum, Part I, Section A, BLM 1/65.

50 See Edmonds, *Military Operations France and Belgium, 1918*, Vol. 4.

51 Letter from Bernard Montgomery to his mother, dated 3 September 1918, The Montgomery Papers, Imperial War Museum, Part I, Section A, BLM 1/65.

52 See Alan H. Maude, *The History of the 47th (London) Division 1914–1919* (Ukfield: Naval and Military Press, 2009).

53 Photographs in packet titled 'Lille 28 October 1918 Eric Steele', author's collection.

54 Montgomery, *Memoirs*, pp. 36–37.

55 Rommel, *Infanterie greift an*, p. 173.

56 Interview (transcript) of Leo Krämer by James Brody, dated 17 August 1957, private collection of Mr Piers Brody.

57 Rommel, *Infanterie greift an*, p. 127.

58 Dandridge M. Malone, *Small Unit Command and Leadership: A Commonsense Approach* (New York: Presido Press, 1983), p. 17.

59 Rommel, *Infanterie greift an*, p. 196.

60 Daniel Allen Butler, *Field Marshal: The Life and Death of Erwin Rommel* (Havertown, PA: Casemate, 2015), p. 64.

61 Caddick-Adams, *Monty and Rommel*, p. 102.

62 Romania finally surrendered on 7 May 1918, and signed the Peace of Bucharest with the Central Powers.

63 See Rommel, *Infanterie greift an*, pp. 273.

64 Ibid., p. 274.

65 Major General Werner Widder, 'Auftragstaktik and Innere Führung: Trademarks of German Leadership', *Military Review* (September/October 2002), p. 4.

66 Rommel, *Infanterie greift an*, p. 335.

67 Ibid., p. 336.

68 Ibid., pp. 338–39.

69 Kurt Hesse, *Bildnis eines Soldaten* (Berlin: Deutscher Verlag, 1938), p. 15.

70 Rommel, *Infanterie greift an*, pp. 348–49.

71 Desmond Young, *Rommel: The Desert Fox* (New York: Berkley Medallion Books, 1971), p. 27.

72 Basil Liddell Hart (ed.), *The Rommel Papers* (London: Arrow Books), p. 201.

73 See Butler, *The Life and Death of Erwin Rommel*, p. 80.

Chapter Four: New Challenges – Leading in Peace, 1919–31

1 Charles F. Horne (ed.), *Records of the Great War*, Vol. VI (New York: National Alumni, 1923), p. 37.

2 *Illustrated London News*, 28 June 1919, p. 13.

3 Letter from George S. Patton to Beatrice Patton, dated 16 November 1918, George S. Patton Papers, Library of Congress, Box 16.

4 Blumenson, *The Patton Papers 1885–1940*, p. 642.

5 GHQ Tank Corps, AEF, General Orders 24, dated 17 December 1918, George S. Patton Papers, Library of Congress, Box 47.

6 Blumenson, *The Patton Papers 1885–1940*, pp. 648–49.

7 Letter from George S. Patton to Beatrice Patton, dated 9 February

1919, George S. Patton Papers, Library of Congress, Box 16.

8 Blumenson, *The Patton Papers 1885–1940*, p. 660.

9 Ibid., p. 713.

10 Stephen E. Ambrose, *Eisenhower: Soldier and President* (New York: Touchstone, 1990), p. 37.

11 Letter from George S. Patton to Nita Patton, dated 19 October 1919, George S. Patton Papers, Library of Congress, Box 14.

12 D'Este, *A Genius for War*, p. 288.

13 Steven Rabalais, *General Fox Corner: Pershing's Chief of Operations and Eisenhower's Mentor* (Havertown, PA and Oxford: Casemate, 2016), p. 162.

14 Blumenson, *The Patton Papers 1885–1940*, pp. 749–50.

15 See D'Este, *A Genius for War*, p. 314.

16 Ibid., p. 331.

17 Hirshon, *A Soldier's Life*, p. 171.

18 Blumenson, *The Patton Papers 1885–1940*, p. 778.

19 Ibid., p. 788.

20 Letter from George S. Patton to Dwight Eisenhower, dated 9 July 1926, George S. Patton Papers, Library of Congress, Box 25.

21 'On Leadership' lecture delivered at Schofield Barracks, November 1925, George S. Patton Papers, Library of Congress, Box 10.

22 Blumenson, *The Patton Papers 1885–1940*, p. 811.

23 Beatrice's father had left a $19 million fortune to his children, but with the death of his mother in 1928 George became wealthy in his own right due to a $200,000

inheritance. See Hirshon, *A Soldier's Life*, pp. 184 and 192.

24 G. S. Lambert wrote to his brother (Larry Lambert) in a letter dated 4 May 1930, the morning after a dinner at the Pattons: 'Beatrice Patton told me that George was a keen student of the economy and would raise the subject at any opportunity. Indeed, I was struck by our host's knowledge about matters fiscal, although I found the intense discussion rather dull.' Lambert family archive, Washington, DC, 1930–32 folder.

25 John Eisenhower interview, 5 June 1980, Dwight D. Eisenhower Papers, Library of Congress, MSS19604, Box 182.

26 Major G. S. Patton, and Major C.C. Benson, 'Mechanization and Cavalry', *Cavalry Journal* 39 (April 1930), http://www.pattonhq.com/pdffiles/vintagetext.pdf [accessed 28 January 2020].

27 Blumenson, *The Patton Papers 1885–1940*, p. 886.

28 Bradford Grethen Chynoweth, *Bellamy Park: Memoirs* (New York: Exposition Press, 1975), p. 133.

29 Major George S. Patton, 'The Probable Characteristics of the Next War and the Organization, Tactics, and Equipment Necessary to Meet Them', Army War College, 29 February 1932, http://www.pattonhq.com/pdffiles/vintagetext.pdf [accessed 28 January 2020].

30 Letter from George S. Patton to Beatrice, n.d but catalogued mid-1930, George S. Patton Papers, Library of Congress, Box 25.

31 First implemented in 1919 from a suggestion by Winston Churchill, the Secretary of State for War and Air, the 'Ten Year Rule' was a guideline, driven by a desire to cut costs, requiring the armed forces to assume that the British Empire would not be engaged in any great war during the next ten years. Despite concerns by detractors that the rule was naive and left the nation unprepared in the volatile world of international politics and diplomacy, by 1928 it had become self-perpetuating and remained extant unless *specifically* countermanded. It was abolished in 1931.

32 Bernard Montgomery, *The Path to Leadership* (London: Collins, 1961), p. 16.

33 See Edward Smalley, 'Qualified, but unprepared: Training for War at the Staff College in the 1930s', *British Journal for Military History*, Vol. 2, No. 1 (2015). For the importance of the Staff College during this period, see Brian Bond, *The Victorian Army and the Staff College, 1854–1914* (London: Routledge, 1972); and also David French and Brian Holden Reid (eds), *British General Staff: Reform and Innovation, 1890–1939* (London: Frank Cass, 2022).

34 Brian Montgomery, *A Field Marshal in the Family* (London: Constable and Company Limited, 1973), p. 181.

35 Ibid., p. 179.

36 Montgomery, *Memoirs*, p. 156.

37 Major General Douglas Wimberley, *Scottish Soldier: An Autobiography*, Volume VII: Final Miscellany Volume (n.p., 1974), p. 154.

38 '17th Infantry Brigade: Summary of Important Instructions', dated 30 June 1921, Imperial War Museum, EPS/2/2.

39 Brian Montgomery, *A Field Marshal in the Family*, pp. 182–83.

40 Ibid., p. 186.

41 Letter from Captain David Symes to his father, dated 23 October 1923, author's collection.

42 Ibid.

43 *Tactical Notes for the use in the West Riding Area and 49th (West Riding) Division*, October 1923, Archives of the York and Lancaster Regimental Museum, Ref 1758-1968 A-Q.

44 Letter from Bernard Montgomery to Basil Liddell Hart, dated 16 July 1924, Liddell Hart Centre for Military Archives, King's College London, 1/519/16.

45 Ibid.

46 Brian Montgomery, *A Field Marshal in the Family*, p. 188.

47 Ibid., p. 187.

48 Hamilton, *The Making of a General*, p. 188.

49 Brian Montgomery, *A Field Marshal in the Family*, p. 192.

50 Montgomery, *The Path to Leadership*, p. 10.

51 See Montgomery, *Memoirs*, pp. 193–94.

52 Hamilton, *The Making of a General*, p. 184.

53 Montgomery, *Memoirs*, p. 40.

54 See Lt. Col. F.W. Young, *The Story of Staff College 1858–1958* (Camberley: Gale & Polden Ltd, 1958).

55 Lt. Col. David Arbuthnot, interview (transcript) with Donald Childs, 16 August 1967, author's archive.

56 Ibid.

57 Smalley, 'Qualified, but unprepared', p. 63.

58 Major General Sir Francis de Guingand, *From Brass Hat to Bowler Hat* (London: Hamish Hamilton, 1979), p. 87.

59 Montgomery, *Memoirs*, p. 42.

60 Ibid., p. 41.

61 See Hamilton, *The Making of a General*, p. 213.

62 Montgomery, *Memoirs*, p. 41.

63 Donald Ure letter to Peter Mayhew, dated 6 December 1948, P. J. S. Mayhew archive, Sheffield.

64 For more on this, see Mark Jones, *Founding Weimar: Violence and the German Revolution of 1918–1919* (Cambridge: Cambridge University Press, 2016).

65 Butler, *The Life and Death of Erwin Rommel*, p. 100.

66 James S. Corum, *The Roots of Blitzkrieg: Hans von Seeckt and Military Reform* (Lawrence, KS: University of Kansas Press, 1992), p. 35.

67 Alaric Searle, 'Rommel and the Rise of the Nazis', in *Rommel: A Reappraisal*, ed. Ian Beckett (Barnsley: Pen and Sword Military, 2013), p. 12; and Ralf Georg Reuth, *Rommel: The End of a Legend* (London: Haus Books, 2005), pp. 22–23.

68 Transcript of Uwe Pfaffner interview with Major Peter Pfaffner (interviewee's son), 12/13 September 1966, author's collection.

69 *H. Dv. 487 Führung und Gefecht der verbunden Waffen (FuG)* (published in two parts: September 1931 and October 1933), Bundesarchiv, BArch RHD 4/1685.

70 Uwe Pfaffner interview with Major Peter Pfaffner.

71 Ibid.

72 Reuth, *The End of a Legend*, p. 110.

73 Young, *The Desert Fox*, p. 36.

74 Uwe Pfaffner interview with Major Peter Pfaffner.

75 Caddick-Adams, *Monty and Rommel*, p. 177.

76 Butler, *The Life and Death of Erwin Rommel*, p. 106.

77 Reuth, *The End of a Legend*, p. 110.

78 Irving, *The Trail of the Fox*, p. 22.

79 Butler, *The Life and Death of Erwin Rommel*, p. 106.

80 Ibid., p. 105.

81 Irving, *The Trail of the Fox*, p. 22.

Chapter Five: Taking Command, 1932–39

1 Letter from Col. David Robinson to Col. Frank Lee, dated 18 July 1932, George S. Patton Papers, Library of Congress, Box 25.

2 Dr Daniel Lees, *Patton's Hubris*, unpublished paper presented to the University of Buckingham postgraduate Modern War Studies

and Contemporary Military History course, 17 October 2014.

3   D'Este, *A Genius for War*, p. 351.

4   Hishon, *A Soldier's Life*, p. 207.

5   Letter from George S. Patton to Lt Col Peter Michaels, dated 10 July 1932, George S. Patton Papers, Library of Congress, Box 25.

6   Merle Miller, *Ike the Solider: As They Knew Him* (New York: Pedigree Books, 1988), pp. 264–65.

7   Dwight Eisenhower diary entry, dated 28 July 1932, Red Diary (September 1929 – April 1934), Dwight D. Eisenhower Library, Abilene, Kansas, Kevin McCann Papers, 1918–81, Box 1, Series I.

8   Merle, *Ike the Solider*, p. 265.

9   John F. Wukovits, *Eisenhower* (New York: Palgrave Macmillan, 2006), p. 43.

10   Interview with Henry Trisi by H. D. Poole, 12 October 1932, Oral History Archive, University of Southern Mississippi, Hattiesburg, Mississippi, File 1722-29/11.

11   Note (dated 1 October 1932) to an After Action Report (dated 18 July 1932) by George S. Patton, George S. Patton Papers, Library of Congress, Box 57.

12   Dwight Eisenhower diary entry, 28 July 1932.

13   Ibid.

14   D'Este, *A Genius for War*, p. 354. The successful removal of the Bonus Army led to 135 arrests and 55 protestor injuries, including a twelve-year-old boy who died having suffered respiratory difficulties due to the tear gas attack. Figures from *Senate Inquiry to Events in Washington D.C., 28 July 1932*, dated 21 August 1932, Senate Inquiry Papers, Library of Congress, MSS83736, Box 19/1.

15   D'Este, *A Genius for War*, p. 354.

16   *Time*, 16 April 1944, p. 23.

17   Carlo D'Este, *Eisenhower: A Soldier's Life, 1890–1945* (New York: Henry Holt, 2002), p. 117.

18   Efficiency Report, March 1934, George S. Patton Papers, Library of Congress, Box 49, Reel 1.

19   Letter from George S. Patton to Jon K. Smith, dated 10 June 1934, Smith and Bexton Family Archives, New York City.

20   The yacht is still sailing out of Viaduct Harbour, New Zealand.

21   Blumenson, *The Patton Papers 1885–1940*, p. 908.

22   Robert H. Patton, *The Pattons: The Personal History of an American Family* (New York: Crown, 1994), p. 233.

23   George Patton letter to John J. Pershing, dated 12 November 1936, John J. Pershing Papers, Library of Congress, Box 155.

24   Anti-semitism and racism were not widespread in the US Army officer corps, but neither were they uncommon. See various, including Joseph W. Bendersky, *The 'Jewish Threat': Anti-Semitic Politics of the US Army* (New York: Basic Books, 2001), and Jim Sudmeier, *Patton's Madness: The Dark Side of a Battlefield Genius* (Mechanicsburg: Stackpole Books, 2019).

25 Blumenson, *The Patton Papers 1885–1940*, p. 916.

26 Efficiency Report, 10 February 1937, George S. Patton Papers, Library of Congress, Box 49, Reel 1.

27 D'Este, *A Genius for War*, p. 363.

28 It focused on themes including: military education; leadership; tactics; and morale. See George S. Patton Papers, Library of Congress, Box 71.

29 Blumenson, *The Patton Papers 1885–1940*, p. 930.

30 Efficiency Report, November 1938, George S. Patton Papers, Library of Congress, Box 49, Reel 1.

31 Sgt Dick P. Mills, *Memories of the Army and the War*, unpublished memoir written in 1955, quoted in an email from Jessie Mills, 3 January 2017.

32 General Order 5, Fort Myer, Virginia, dated 18 March 1939, George S. Patton Papers, Library of Congress, Box 10.

33 See Blumenson, *The Patton Papers 1885–1940*, pp. 936–37.

34 D'Este, *A Genius for War*, p. 369.

35 Captain R. H. Phillips in a letter to his brother, Denis Phillips, dated 2 May 1948, Phillips family archive, Mobile Alabama. Captain Phillips served for eight months in Patton's headquarters before requesting a transfer despite the implications for his career. He was moved to an obscure staff job at Fort Leavenworth but 'was happy to be in a more healthy working environment'.

36 Letter from George Patton to Beatrice Patton, dated 27 July 1939, George S. Patton Papers, Library of Congress, Box 17.

37 Blumenson, *The Patton Papers 1885–1940*, p. 942.

38 Ibid., pp. 942–45.

39 Interview with Sergeant Jim Smith, conducted by Dr Robert Wells, 16 June 1955, Trigger archive, 1950 Box 1, New York City.

40 Sergeant Jim Smith, letter to his wife, Edna Smith, dated 18 October 1931, copy in author's collection.

41 See Karl Sabbagh, *Britain in Palestine: The Story of British Rule in Palestine 1917–1948* (London: Skyscraper Publications, 2012); also A. J. Sherman, *Mandate Days: British Lives in Palestine, 1918–48* (London: Thames and Hudson, 1997).

42 Bernard Montgomery letter to his mother, dated 10 April 1931, The Montgomery Papers, Imperial War Museum, BLM 1/74.

43 Lt Gen. Sir John Burnett-Stuart, Confidential Army Report on Bernard Montgomery, dated March 1932, The Montgomery Papers, Imperial War Museum, BLM 8/1.

44 Letter from Corporal Dennis Pease to his father, Frederick Pease, dated 6 December 1931, copy in author's collection.

45 Hamilton, *The Making of a General*, p. 219.

46 Lt Gen. Sir John Burnett-Stuart, Confidential Army Report, Bernard Montgomery, dated

March 1932, The Montgomery
Papers, Imperial War Museum,
BLM 8/1.

47 Hamilton, *The Making of a
General*, p. 234.

48 Toby Race, *My Time in the Army
and other Adventures* (London,
Race Publishing, 2000), p. 25.

49 Brian Montgomery, *A Field
Marshal in the Family*, pp. 214–15.

50 Trevor Royale, *Montgomery: Lessons
in Leadership for the Soldier's
General* (London: St. Martin's
Press, 2010), p. 32; and Hamilton,
The Making of a General, pp. 234–
35.

51 Letter from F. A. Pile to
G. D. A. Rees, dated 8 August
1932, Graham Rees family archive,
Chester.

52 Jonathan Fennell, *Fighting the
People's War: The British and
Commonwealth Armies and the
Second World War* (Cambridge:
Cambridge University Press, 2019),
p. 476.

53 Hamilton, *The Making of a
General*, p. 228.

54 Lieutenant David Serridge lasted
just three months with the
battalion before being transferred
back to England. He left the Army
a year later.

55 Quoted by Lt Col Dwin Bramall
in a lecture titled 'Fighting to
Win' delivered to 2nd Battalion
Green Jackets, 19 May 1965, The
Bramall Archive, The University of
Buckingham, Box 24.

56 Hamilton, *The Making of a
General*, p. 233.

57 Quoted by Lt Col Dwin Bramall,
'Fighting to Win'.

58 Hamilton, *The Making of a
General*, p. 230.

59 Brigadier Frederick Pile,
Confidential Army Report on
Bernard Montgomery, dated
March 1932, The Montgomery
Papers, Imperial War Museum,
BLM 8/1.

60 See Caddick-Adams, *Monty
and Rommel*, pp. 181–82, and
Hamilton, *The Making of a
General*, p. 240.

61 General Sir George Jeffrey,
Confidential Army Report on
Bernard Montgomery, dated July
1934, The Montgomery Papers,
Imperial War Museum, BLM 8/3.

62 Hamilton, *The Making of a
General*, p. 249.

63 Letter from Philip Fullard to
Derek Clayton, dated 18 May
1935, Clayton family archive,
Canterbury, Kent.

64 Brian Montgomery, *A Field
Marshal in the Family*, p. 227.

65 Montgomery, *Path to Leadership*,
p. 11.

66 Letter from Philip Fullard to Derek
Clayton, 18 May 1935.

67 *Instructions for individual training
issued by me as Brigadier, Comdg
9th Inf Bde*, The Montgomery
Papers, Imperial War Museum,
BLM 11.

68 Hamilton, *The Making of a
General*, p. 265.

69 Ibid., p. 269.

70 Ibid., p. 270.

71 Horne, *The Lonely Leader*, p. 27.

72 Montgomery, *Memoirs*, p. 44.

73 Hamilton, *The Making of a General*, p. 290.

74 Wavell was soon to give a prestigious Lees Knowles Lecture at Trinity College Cambridge, which was published by Penguin in 1941 under the title *Generals and Generalship*.

75 Lt Gen. Sir Archibald Wavell, Confidential Army Report on Bernard Montgomery, dated October 1938, The Montgomery Papers, Imperial War Museum, BLM 8/9.

76 Letter from Tom Turner to his brother, Terence Turner, dated 2 February 1939, Turner family collection, Birmingham.

77 Richard Mead, *The Men Behind Montgomery* (Barnsley: Pen and Sword Military, 2015), pp. 36–37.

78 See Ben H. Shepherd, *Hitler's Soldiers: The German Army in the Third Reich* (Yale: Yale University Press, 2016), variously in chapters 1 and 2.

79 Including Charles Messenger, *Rommel: Lessons from Yesterday from Today's Leaders* (London: St Martin's Press), p. 26.

80 Karl Kuhn diary entry, dated 18 November 1932, copy in author's collection.

81 Paul Uckelman diary entry, dated 2 July 1932, Vol. II, 1931–33, copy in collection of Mr Ross Dees, Hamburg.

82 Reuth, *The End of a Legend*, p. 26.

83 Searle, 'Rommel and the Rise of the Nazis', p. 16.

84 See Messenger, *Lessons from Yesterday*, p. 27.

85 J. L. McGarry, *Rommel: The Junior Commander* (n.p., 2017), p. 19.

86 Ibid., p. 45.

87 Ibid., p. 47.

88 See Butler, *The Life and Death of Erwin Rommel*, p. 114.

89 The SS filled the paramilitary role vacated by the SA.

90 McGarry, *The Junior Commander*, p. 63.

91 Butler, *The Life and Death of Erwin Rommel*, p. 131.

92 The book was published by a small Potsdam publishing house, Ludwig Voggenauer Verlag, as *Infanterie greift an*.

93 Searle, 'Rommel and the Rise of the Nazis', p. 19.

94 As Rommel's career began to take off, sales of *Infantry Attacks* continued to rise with the book becoming a bestseller in 1941 and with sales of 400,000 by 1945. See Searle, 'Rommel and the Rise of the Nazis', p. 18.

95 Reuth, *The End of a Legend*, p. 33.

96 See Lisa N. N. Pine, *The Family in the Third Reich, 1933–1945*, unpublished PhD thesis, London School of Economics, 1996, p. 86.

97 Young, *The Desert Fox*, pp. 44–45.

98 Reuth, *The End of a Legend*, p. 34.

99 David Fraser, *Knight's Cross: A Life of Field Marshal Erwin Rommel* (London: HarperCollins, 1994), p. 126.

100 Letter from Ralf Hass to Edda Naumann, dated 8 February 1939, Hass family archive, Berlin.

101 Ibid.

102 Reuth, *The End of a Legend*, p. 34.

103 See Searle, 'Rommel and the Rise of the Nazis', p. 25.

104 Ibid., p. 24.

105 See Reuth, *The End of a Legend*, p. 35.

106 See Searle, 'Rommel and the Rise of the Nazis', p. 24.

107 Reuth, *The End of a Legend*, p. 37.

108 Ibid.

109 See Lloyd Clark, *Blitzkrieg: Myth, Reality and Hitler's Lightning War, France 1940* (London: Atlantic Books), p. 8.

Chapter Six: A New War, 1940–41

1 Letter from George Patton to Malcolm McBride, dated 13 January 1940, McBride family archive, San Francisco.

2 D'Este, *A Genius for War*, p. 379.

3 Ibid., pp. 379–80.

4 Blumenson, *The Patton Papers 1885–1940*, p. 951.

5 Ibid., p. 956.

6 Ibid., p. 954.

7 Ibid., p. 956.

8 D'Este, *A Genius for War*, p. 381.

9 Gerald Mayes, *Henry L. Stimson and the Army, 1940–45*, unpublished paper for the British Commission for Military History, June 2002.

10 D'Este, *A Genius for War*, p. 382.

11 Letter from Major Larry Hind to his sister, Linda Ross, dated 20 September 1940, Ross family archive, Michigan.

12 See Hirshon, *A Soldier's Life*, p. 235.

13 'Armored Operation is Poland', seventeeen-page lecture to the officers and men of 2nd Armored Division, dated 3 September 1940, George S. Patton Papers, Library of Congress, Box 12.

14 Blumenson, *The Patton Papers 1940–1945*, p. 12.

15 Letter from Major Larry Hind to Linda Ross, 20 September 1940.

16 Captain 'Duke' Ellis letter to Major John Baulmer, dated 8 February 1941, Larry Baulmer collection, Denver, Colorado.

17 The top third was coloured cavalry yellow and overlaid with the number '2', below which was a tank track and a lightning bolt, while the lower left section was coloured infantry blue and the lower right artillery red.

18 Blumenson, *The Patton Papers 1940–1945*, p. 16.

19 Transcript of Gen. I. D. White oral history, dated 29 October 1977, and marked White Papers USAMHI, Carlisle, author's collection. The Isaac D. White Papers 1901–1990 are now held at the Norwich University Archives, Northfield, VT.

20 Speech 'Farewell to Members of the 2d Armored Division', dated 4 April 1941, George S. Patton Papers, Library of Congress, Box 73.

21 See D'Este, *A Genius for War*, p. 389.

22 Weigley, *History of the United States Army*, p. 87.

23   See Blumenson, *The Patton Papers 1940–1945*, p. 17.

24   *The West Georgian*, 14 January 1941, p. 4.

25   Blumenson, *The Patton Papers 1940–1945*, pp. 17–18.

26   '2d Armored Division Training Plan, March-April 1941', George S. Patton Papers, Library of Congress, Box 45.

27   Transcript of an interview conducted by Dr Paul Friend with Sergeant Ron. E. Heart, dated 17 August 1964, author's collection.

28   Blumenson, *The Patton Papers 1940–1945*, p. 24.

29   Ibid., p. 26.

30   Ibid.

31   Ibid., p. 32.

32   Ibid., p. 34.

33   See https://www.portablepress. com/blog/2015/11/the-beginning- of-life/ [accessed 18 May 2020].

34   For more, see Mary Kathryn Barbier, *George C. Marshall and the 1940 Louisiana Maneuvers* in the *Louisiana History: The Journal of the Louisiana Historical Association*, Vol. 44, No. 4 (Autumn 2003), pp. 389–410; and also Paul Dickson, *The Rise of the GI Army, 1940–4: The Forgotten Story of How America Forged a Powerful Army Before Pearl Harbor* (New York: Grove Press, 2021).

35   Untitled speech, dated 7 August 1941, George S. Patton Papers, Library of Congress, Box 45.

36   Quoted in a transcript of an interview conducted by Dr Paul Friend with Sergeant Ron. E. Heart, dated 17 August 1964, author's collection. Sgt Heart had trained to become a reporter and occasionally took shorthand notes either during or after speeches. Although the original notebook is now lost, Heart reads from the notebook in this interview.

37   Leonard Mosley, *Marshall: Hero for Our Times* (London: Hearst Books, 1982), p. 189.

38   Montgomery, *Memoirs*, p. 49.

39   Montgomery, *Path to Leadership*, p. 42.

40   Diary entry, 9 October 1939, Field Marshal Lord Alanbrooke, *War Diaries 1939–1945*, ed. A. Danchev and D. Todman (London: Weidenfeld and Nicolson, 2001), pp. 5–6.

41   Major David Boyd (SO2 Operations), *Reflections on War*, unpublished manuscript written in July 1945, Boyd family papers, Kendal, Cumbria, p. 17.

42   Quoted in a transcript of an interview conducted by Mr Tim Reynolds with Staff Sergeant Alf Tapp, dated 21 January 1992, Reynolds Archive, Chelmsford, Essex.

43   Ibid.

44   Quoted in Carl Leonard, *Montgomery's command philosophy in North West Europe, June 1944 – May 1945*, unpublished MA dissertation, University of Buckingham, December 2009.

45   Peter Carington, *Reflections on Things Past: The Memoirs of Lord Carrington* (London: Collins, 1988), p. 34.

46 Brian Montgomery, *A Field Marshal in the Family*, p. 253.

47 GHQ Deputy Chaplain General, British Expeditionary Force, dated 22 November 1939, The National Archive, WO167/31.

48 Diary entry, dated 23 November 1939, Alanbrooke, *War Diaries 1939–1945*, p. 19.

49 Montgomery, *Memoirs*, p. 59.

50 Montgomery, *Path to Leadership*, p. 126.

51 3rd Division Exercises Nos 1 and 2, 13/15 December and 19/21 December 1939, The Montgomery Papers, Imperial War Museum, BLM 16.

52 Diary entry, dated 13 December 1939, Alanbrooke, *War Diaries 1939–1945*, p. 24.

53 Hamilton, *The Making of a General*, p. 355.

54 Ibid.

55 Lt-Gen. Sir Brian Horrocks, *A Full Life* (London: Collins, 1960), p. 78.

56 Montgomery's involvement in France has been written with reference to his personal campaign diary (*Itinerary of Events*), 10 May – 3 June 1940, The Montgomery Papers, Imperial War Museum, BLM 19/2.

57 Major Guy Courage, *The History of 15/19 the King's Royal Hussars, 1939–45* (Aldershot: Gale and Polden Ltd, 1949), p. 20.

58 Diary entry, dated 15 May 1940, Alanbrooke, *War Diaries 1939–1945*, p. 24.

59 David Fraser, *Alanbrooke* (London: Harper Collins, 1997), p. 65.

60 Hamilton, *The Making of a General*, p. 365.

61 Interview with Edward J. Wood, dated 5 March 2004, author's collection.

62 Montgomery, *Memoirs*, p. 61.

63 Sir John George Smyth, *Leadership in War, 1939–1945: The Generals in Victory and Defeat* (London: St Martin's Press), p. 51.

64 Hamilton, *The Making of a General*, p. 379.

65 Kit Dawnay 'Inside Monty's Headquaters', in T.E.B. Howarth *Monty at Close Quarters: Recollections of the Man* (London: Leo Cooper, 1985), p. 8.

66 Horrocks, *A Full Life*, p. 86.

67 Clark, *Blitzkrieg*, p. 314.

68 3 Division War Diary, September 1939 – June 1940, British Expeditionary Force, France, WO167/218.

69 Montgomery, *Memoirs*, p. 71.

70 Hamilton, *The Making of a General*, p. 433.

71 For this period, see documents in The Montgomery Papers, Imperial War Museum, BLM 18.

72 Evan McGilvray, *Field Marshal Claude Auchinleck* (Barnsely: Pen and Sword Military, 2020), p. 58.

73 Ibid.

74 Montgomery, *Memoirs*, p. 72.

75 Roger Stillwell letter to Reginald Mason, dated 16 June 1948, Stillwell family collection, Hampstead, London.

76 *The Times*, 6 December 1940, p. 5.

77 Montgomery, *Memoirs*, p. 70.

78 'Minutes of a conference of officers of XII Corps held by

Montgomery', dated 5 May 1941, The Montgomery Papers, Imperial War Museum, LMD 18/2.

79 Horrocks, *A Full Life*, p. 98.

80 Hamilton, *The Making of a General*, p. 481.

81 Interview with Donny McDonald, dated 12 March 2004, author's collection.

82 Interview with Ethel Graves, dated 12 March 2015, author's collection.

83 Ian Milton, *Episodes from the War: The Memoirs of I. T .L. Milton*, unpublished manuscript dated 1962.

84 Fraser, *Knight's Cross*, pp. 160–61.

85 Interview with Otis Zoecke, dated 20 June 2006, author's collection.

86 Hart, *The Rommel Papers*, p. 6.

87 See Claus Telp, 'Rommel and 1940', in Searle, 'Rommel and the Rise of the Nazis', p. 48.

88 Fraser, *Knight's Cross*, pp. 172–73.

89 Hart, *The Rommel Papers*, p. 13.

90 Ibid., p. 16

91 Ibid., p. 20.

92 Karl-Heinz Frieser, *The Blitzkrieg Legend: The 1940 Campaign in the West* (Annapolis, MD: Naval Institute Press, 2005), p. 266.

93 See Clark, *Blitzkrieg*, p. 64.

94 Hart, *The Rommel Papers*, p. 17.

95 Clark, *Blitzkrieg*, p. 236.

96 Hart, *The Rommel Papers*, p. 22.

97 Ibid., p. 32.

98 Ibid., p. 34.

99 Ibid., p. 40.

100 Ibid., p. 43.

101 Clark, *Blitzkrieg*, p. 335.

102 Hart, *The Rommel Papers*, p. 66.

103 Diary entry, dated 16 July 1940, Luis Althaus diary (May – October 1940), Althaus family archive, Bonn.

104 Paul Henkelmann letter, 1 May 2013.

105 See Fraser, *Knight's Cross*, p. 206.

106 Ibid., p. 209.

107 Reuth, *The End of a Legend*, p. 67.

108 Letter from Paul Henkelmann to the author, dated 1 May 2010, author's collection.

109 Clark, *Blitzkrieg*, p. 245.

110 Diary entry, dated 16 October 1940, Luis Althaus diary (May – October 1940), Althaus family archive, Bonn.

111 Reuth, *The End of a Legend*, p. 46.

112 Hart, *The Rommel Papers*, p. 104.

113 See Niall Barrm, 'Rommel in the Desert – 1941', in *Rommel: A Reappraisal*, p. 67.

114 Interview with Carl Alpert, 18 November 2011, author's collection.

115 Fraser, *Knight's Cross*, p. 232.

116 Hart, *The Rommel Papers*, p. 111.

117 Diary entry, dated 15 April 1941, Joseph Goebbels, *The Goebbels Diaries, 1939–1941*, trans. and ed. Fred Taylor (London: Hamish Hamilton, 1982), p. 316.

118 Quoted by Carl Alpert during interview, dated 18 November 2011, author's collection.

119 Interview with Erich Stieglitz, conducted by Major Jim Trant, 16 August 1972 (as part of the Desert Army Research Association), Staff College Camberley Library Collection.

120 Heinz Werner Schmidt, *With Rommel in the Desert* (London: Panther Books, 1968), p. 56.

121 Reuth, *The End of a Legend*, p. 112.

122 Ibid.

123 Ibid., pp. 111–12.

124 Fraser, *Knight's Cross*, p. 254.

125 Robert Citino, *Death of the Wehrmacht: The German Campaigns of 1942* (Lawrence: University Press of Kansas, 2011), p. 123.

126 See Niall Barr, 'Rommel in the Desert – 1941', p. 74.

127 Hart, *The Rommel Papers*, p. 162.

Chapter Seven: Three in North Africa, 1942–43

1 Caddick-Adams, *Monty and Rommel*, p. 495.

2 Hart, *The Rommel Papers*, p. 18.

3 Diary entry, dated 7 February 1942, Joseph Goebbels, *The Goebbels Diaries*, ed. and trans. Louis P. Lockner (New York: Award Books, 1971), p. 85.

4 Reuth, *The End of a Legend*, p. 142.

5 Ibid., pp. 143–44.

6 Transcript of a telephone conversation between the author and Horst Wack on 9 January 2005, author's collection.

7 Hart, *The Rommel Papers*, p. 187.

8 Fraser, *Knight's Cross*, p. 319.

9 Hart, *The Rommel Papers*, p. 224.

10 Ibid., p. 232.

11 Ibid., p. 243.

12 Irving, *The Trail of the* Fox, p. 191.

13 See Ronald Lewin, *Ultra goes to War* (London: Hutchinson, 1978); and Frederick W. Winterbottom, *The Ultra Secret: The Inside Story of Operation Ultra, Bletchley and Enigma* (London: Orion, 2000).

14 Hart, *The Rommel Papers*, p. 283.

15 Reuth, *The End of a Legend*, p. 150.

16 Rommel's complaint was undoubtedly brought on by stress and made it difficult to digest his food. This meant that Rommel sometimes ate little, or not at all, leading to fatigue, problems sleeping and irritability.

17 Fraser, *Knight's Cross*, p. 362.

18 Ibid., p. 373.

19 Telephone conversation between the author and Horst Wack, 9 January 2005.

20 Hart, *The Rommel Papers*, p. 312.

21 Quoted by Dr David Weir-Brown in a talk titled 'Rommel's command style in North Africa: A Re-evaluation' to the Royal Military Academy War Discussion Group, December 1994.

22 Hart, *The Rommel Papers*, p. 321.

23 Fraser, *Knight's Cross*, p. 382.

24 Hart, *The Rommel Papers*, p. 351.

25 Ibid., p. 327.

26 Telephone conversation between the author and Horst Wack, 9 January 2005.

27 Quoted by Weir-Brown in 'Rommel's command style: A Re-evaluation'.

28 Heinz Linge, *With Hitler to the End: The Memoirs of Hitler's Valet* (Barnsley, Frontline Books, 2013), p. 127.

29 Hart, *The Rommel Papers*, p. 391.

30 Ibid., p. 411.

31 Ibid., p. 423.

32 See Peter Leib, 'Rommel in Normandy', in Searle, *Rommel: A Reappraisal*, p. 113.

33 Quoted by Weir-Brown in 'Rommel's command style in North Africa: A Re-evaluation'.

34 Fraser, *Knight's Cross*, p. 433.

35 Reuth, *The End of a Legend*, p. 64.

36 Bernard Montgomery, Diary Notes 3–20 September 1943, The Montgomery Papers, Imperial War Museum, BLM 44/1.

37 Martin Blumenson, *Salerno to Cassino* (Washington DC: Office of Chief of Military History, US Army, 1969), pp. 245–46.

38 Hamilton, *The Making of a General*, p. 503.

39 Montgomery, *Memoirs*, p. 75.

40 Horrocks, *A Full Life*, p. 99.

41 Major David J. Williams, diary entry, dated 16 February 1942, Williams family archive, Cromer, Norfolk.

42 Nigel Hamilton, *Master of the Battlefield: Monty's War Years 1942–1944* (London: McGraw-Hill, 1984), p. 338.

43 Winston S. Churchill, *The Second World War: The Hinge of Fate* (London: Penguin Books, 1985), p. 392.

44 The prime minister's preferred candidate, General William Gott, had been appointed before Montgomery, but was killed on 7 August before he could take command when an aircraft in which he was travelling was shot down.

45 Quoted in Hamilton, *Master of the Battlefield*, p. 137.

46 See Chapter 1, 'Leadership – What is It?' in Montgomery, *The Path to Leadership*, pp. 9–19.

47 Montgomery, *Memoirs*, p. 80.

48 Ibid., pp. 97–98.

49 Ibid., p. 98.

50 The new location was at Burg-el-Arab, where it nestled alongside the headquarters of the Desert Air Force to encourage understanding and mutual co-operation.

51 Quoted in 'Western Desert: Account of the Battle of Alam El Halfa Sept 1942 by Lt-Gen Sir Brian Horrocks, commanding 13th Corps', CAB 106/654, The National Archives.

52 Francis de Guingand, *Operation Victory* (London: Hodder & Stoughton, 1947), pp. 136–37.

53 See David French, *Raising Churchill's Army: The British Army and the War against Germany 1919–1945* (Oxford: Oxford University Press, 2000), p. 229.

54 Montgomery, *Memoirs*, p. 107.

55 Interview with Ronald Davies, 20 June 2015, author's collection.

56 De Guingand, *Operation Victory*, p. 268.

57 Interview with Terence Robertson, 25 June 2015, author's collection.

58 Letter from Bernard Montgomery to Col (rtd) Frederick Stead, dated 8 August 1962, Richmond family archive, Hereford.

59 De Guingand, *Operation Victory*, p. 279.

60 Hamilton, *The Making of a General*, p. 732.

61 Brian Montgomery, *A Field Marshal in the Family*, p. 278.

62 Hamilton, *The Making of a General*, pp. 749–50.

63 Mead, *The Men Behind Montgomery*, p. 63.

64 Niall Barr, *Pendulum of War: Three Battles of El Alamein* (London: Pimlico, 2005), p. 276.

65 Montgomery, *Memoirs*, pp. 127–28.

66 Alun Chalfont, *Montgomery of Alamein* (London: Weidenfeld and Nicolson, 1976), p. 180.

67 Montgomery most often appeared in a Grant tank when being photographed, but the vehicle was not appropriate for his day-to-day requirements.

68 Hamilton, *The Making of a General*, p. 780.

69 Ibid., pp. 796–97.

70 Ibid., p. 797.

71 Interview with John Robinson, 1 September 2015, author's collection.

72 Private papers of Colonel C. P. S. Denholm Young OBE, Imperial War Museum, Doc 24228.

73 Hamilton, *Master of the Battlefield*, pp. 50–51.

74 Peter Steadman, unpublished memoir, 'At War with Monty in the Desert' (written in 1949), Nicolson family archive, Canterbury, Kent.

75 French, *Raising Churchill's Army*, p. 252.

76 A later note to diary entry, dated 4 February 1943, Alanbrooke, *War Diaries 1939–1945*, p. 379.

77 Hamilton, *Master of the Battlefield*, p. 143.

78 D'Este, *A Genius for War*, p. 453.

79 *Desert War* promotional poster, author's collection.

80 Horrocks, *A Full Life*, p. 145.

81 Hamilton, *Master of the Battlefield*, pp. 180–81.

82 See Niall Barr, *Eisenhower's Armies: The American-British Alliance During World War II* (New York: Pegasus Books, 2015), p. 188.

83 Letter from Bernard Montgomery to Alan Brooke, dated 31 March 1943, personal correspondence of FM Alan Brooke, Liddell Hart Military Archives, King's College London, 8/1/1-4.

84 It was replaced by Eisenhower with a Dakota containing a jeep, which was far more suitable to shorter runways and allowed Montgomery to be on the move shortly after landing.

85 A later note to diary entry, dated 3 June 1943, Alanbrooke, *War Diaries 1939–1945*, p. 418.

86 Diary entry, dated 3 June 1943, Alanbrooke, *War Diaries 1939–1945*, p. 417.

87 See Dennis Porch, *The Path to Victory: The Mediterranean Theater in World War II* (New York, Farrer, Straus and Giroux, 2005), p. 43.

88 Montgomery, *Memoirs*, p. 166.

89 Quoted in a transcript of an interview conducted by Mr Tim Reynolds with Captain Leo Ross, dated 18 May 1992, Reynolds archive, Chelmsford, Essex.

90 See Lloyd Clark, *Anzio: The Friction of War – Italy and the Battle for Rome 1944* (London: Headline, 2006), pp. 8–12.

91 Quoted in interview conducted by Mr Tim Reynolds with Captain Leo Ross, 18 May 1992.

92 Montgomery, *Memoirs*, p. 185.

93 Blumenson, *The Patton Papers 1940–1945*, p. 302.

94 Some 70,000 Italian and 39,000 German troops had made good their escape to the Italian mainland through Messina. See Clark, *Anzio*, p. 12.

95 Brian Montgomery, *A Field Marshal in the Family*, p. 300.

96 See Clark, *Anzio*, pp. 31–61.

97 Royle, *Lessons in Leadership for the Soldier's General*, p. 104.

98 Diary entry, dated 4 October 1943, Col. Edwin James Dairy, Blue book, 1943, James family archive, Swanage, Dorset.

99 Letter from Bernard Montgomery to Alan Brooke, dated 29 September 1943, personal correspondence of FM Alan Brooke, Liddell Hart Military Archives, King's College London, 8/1/1-4.

100 French, *Raising Churchill's Army*, p. 250.

101 'The Campaign in Italy – 3rd Phase: 15 Oct–25 Nov 1943', diary notes, The Montgomery Papers, Imperial War Museum, BLM 43/1.

102 Ibid.

103 'Reflections on the Campaign for Italy, Sep–Dec 1943', The Montgomery Papers, Imperial War Museum, BLM 45.

104 'Personal Diary Notes; The Invasion of Italy – Phase 4, 26 Nov–31 Dec 43', The Montgomery Papers, Imperial War Museum, BLM 44.

105 Montgomery, *Memoirs*, p. 469.

106 De Guingand, *Operation Victory*, p. 302.

107 Porter B. Williamson, *General Patton's Principles: For Life and Leadership* (New York: Management & Systems, 1998) p. 44.

108 Email from Gerald P. Hooper quoting his father, Tech Sgt Jim Hooper, in his unpublished account of his Second World War experience, 'With Patton at War' (written 1961–62), Hooper family archive, Riverside, Los Angeles, California.

109 D'Este, *A Genius for War*, p. 409.

110 Email from Gerald P. Hooper quoting his father, Tech Sgt Jim Hooper.

111 Quoted in Blumenson, *The Patton Papers 1940–1945*, pp. 67–68.

112 Email from Gerald P. Hooper quoting his father, Tech Sgt Jim Hooper.

113 Gen. Brenton G. Wallace, *Patton and His Third Army* (Mechanicsburg, PA: Stackpole Books, 2000), p. 17.

114 Maj Gen. Ernest Harmon, *Combat Commander: Autobiography of a Solider* (NJ: Prentice Hall, 1970), p. 69.

115 'Beatrice Ayre Patton Reminiscences', George S. Patton Papers, Library of Congress, Box 23.

116 George S. Patton diary entry, dated 3 November 1942, Diary 24 September 1942 – 5 March 1943,

George S. Patton Papers, Library of
Congress, Box 1.

117 Ibid.

118 A later note to diary entry, dated
16 January 1943, Alanbrooke, *War
Diaries 1939–1945*, p. 360.

119 Omar N. Bradley, *A General's
Life: An Autobiography* (New York:
Simon & Schuster, 1984), pp. 99.

120 Blumenson, *The Patton Papers
1940–1945*, p. 187.

121 Quoted by Weir-Brown in 'Patton's
command style in North Africa: A
Re-evaluation'.

122 Ibid.

123 Ibid.

124 Blumenson, *The Patton Papers
1940–1945*, p. 222.

125 Letter from Dwight Eisenhower to
George S. Patton, dated 14 April
1943, George S. Patton Papers,
Library of Congress, Box 27.

126 George S. Patton diary entry, dated
15 April 1943, George S. Patton
Papers, Library of Congress, Box 1.

127 'Instructions to officers of Seventh
Army', dated 5 June 1943, George
S. Patton Papers, Library of
Congress, Box 45.

128 Kenneth Weisbrode, *Eisenhower
and the Art of Collaborative
Leadership* (London: Anthem Press,
2018), p. 260.

129 Letter from George S. Patton to
Beatrice Patton, dated 17 May
1943, George S. Patton Papers,
Library of Congress, Box 17.

130 'Speech to 45th Division, Seventh
Army – 27 June 1943', George S.
Patton Papers, Library of Congress,
Box 45.

131 Lieutenant Ralph Bialas,
'Recollections of General Patton',
privately published in 1950
(#3/50), author's collection.

132 Blumenson, *The Patton Papers
1940–1945*, p. 279.

133 Letter from George S. Patton to
Beatrice Patton, dated 19 July
1943, George S. Patton Papers,
Library of Congress, Box 17.

134 This account is taken from D'Este,
A Genius for War, pp. 533–34.

135 D'Este, *A Genius for War*, p. 536.

136 Quoted in Dwight D. Eisenhower,
Crusaade in Europe (New York:
Doubleday, 1948), p. 183.

137 Gerald Astor, *Terrible Terry Allen:
Combat General of World War II*
(New York: Presido Press, 2004),
p. 235.

138 See Bradley, *A General's Life*,
p. 198.

139 Lieutenant General L. K. Truscott,
*Command Missions: A Personal
Story* (New York, Lang 1954),
p. 135.

140 Letter from George S. Patton to
Beatrice Patton dated 18 August
1943, George S. Patton Papers,
Library of Congress, Box 17.

141 D'Este, *A Genius for War*, p. 530.

142 Blumenson, *The Patton Papers
1940–1945*, p. 138.

143 Bradley, *A General's Life*, p. 208.

144 George S. Patton diary entry, 29
September 1943, Diary 3 July – 12
November 1943, George S. Patton
Papers, Library of Congress, Box 1.

145 George S. Patton diary entry, dated
17 November 1943, Diary 13
November 1943 – 31 May 1944,

George S. Patton Papers, Library of Congress, Box 1.

146 George S. Patton diary entry, dated 28 December 1943, Diary 13

November 1943 – 31 May 1944, George S. Patton Papers, Library of Congress, Box 1.

Chapter Eight: Three in North-West Europe, 1944–45

1 Caddick-Adams, *Monty and Rommel*, p. 322.

2 Diary entry, dated 24 January 1944, Alanbrooke, *War Diaries 1939–1945*, p. 516.

3 Caddick-Adams, *Monty and Rommel*, p. 327.

4 Ben Metcalfe, letter to the author, dated 16 September 2000, author's collection.

5 Montgomery, *Memoirs*, p. 238.

6 Mead, *The Men Behind Montgomery*, p. 146.

7 John Buckley, *Monty's Men: The British Army and the Liberation of Europe* (Yale: Yale University Press, 2014), p. 32.

8 Hamilton, *Master of the Battlefield*, pp. 538–39.

9 Bradley, *A Soldier's Story*, p. 209.

10 Caddick-Adams, *Monty and Rommel*, p. 353.

11 Hamilton, *Master of the Battlefield*, p. 508.

12 Caddick-Adams, *Monty and Rommel*, p. 354.

13 Letter from Kenneth ('Red') O'Leary to the author, dated 17 April 2007, author's collection.

14 Ben Metcalfe letter to the author, 16 September 2000.

15 Buckley, *Monty's Men*, p. 264.

16 Journal of Captain Bill Fontaine (containing various thoughts and memories), from section titled 'Spring 1944', Fontaine family archive, Des Moines, Iowa.

17 Diary entry, dated 10 March 1944, Alanbrooke, *War Diaries 1939–1945*, p. 531.

18 Referred to by Lt Col Dwin (later Field Marshal the Lord) Bramall in notes from a conversation with Colonel D.W.S. Sanderson on 16 June 1959 while on the Directing Staff of the Staff College, Camberley. The Lord Bramall (uncatalogued in 2019), held at the University of Buckingham.

19 Facsimile of personal message from the C-in-C (B. L. Montgomery), dated 5 June 1944, author's collection.

20 Letter from Bernard Montgomery to his brother Harold, dated 6 October 1942, Tank Museum, Bovington.

21 Winston S. Churchill, *The Second World War: The Tide of Victory* (London: Cassell and Co, 1964), p. 19.

22 Diary entry, dated 18 July 1944, Major Peter Salmond diary, Salmond family archive, London, England.

23 Quoted in a letter from Ralph Canning to David Broad, dated 16 July 1952, Canning family papers, 1939–45 Box, Chester, Cheshire.

24 Quoted in Carl Leonard, *Montgomery's Command Philosophy in North West Europe, June 1944 – May 1945*, unpublished University of Buckingham MA dissertation, December 2009.

25 Diary entry, dated 27 July 1944, Alanbrooke, *War Diaries 1939–1945*, p. 575.

26 Ibid.

27 Referred to by Lt Col Dwin Bramall in notes from a conversation with Colonel D. W. S. Sanderson, 16 June 1959.

28 Lloyd Clark, *Arnhem: Jumping the Rhine 1944 and 1945* (London: Headline Publishing Group, 2009), p. 19.

29 Diary entry, dated 30 August 1944, Alanbrooke, *War Diaries 1939–1945*, p. 586.

30 Letter from Alan Brooke to Montgomery, dated 1 September 1944, The Montgomery Papers, Imperial War Museum, BLM 1/105.

31 Royle, *Lessons in Leadership*, p. 136.

32 Bradley, *A General's Life*, p. 256.

33 Buckley, *Monty's Men*, p. 243.

34 Terry Copp, *Cinderella Army: The Canadians in Northwest Europe, 1944–1945* (Toronto: University of Toronto Press, 2006), p. 245.

35 Royle, *Lessons in Leadership*, p. 133.

36 See Buckley, *Monty's Men*, pp. 251–52.

37 Quoted in Leonard, *Montgomery's Command Philosophy*.

38 Ibid.

39 Royle, *Lessons in Leadership*, p. 146.

40 Bradley, *A General's Life*, p. 270.

41 The Germans prepared under a veil of secrecy, which demanded that communications were limited to essentials and avoided radio transmissions.

42 Diary entry, dated 23–30 December 1944, Alanbrooke, *War Diaries 1939–1945*, p. 638.

43 Caddick-Adams, *Monty and Rommel*, p. 449.

44 'Field Marshal Montgomery's Press Conference, 7 Jan. 1945', The National Archives, CAB 106/1107.

45 Nigel Hamilton, *Monty: The Field Marshal, 1944–1976* (London: Hamish Hamilton, 1986), pp. 303–304.

46 'Field Marshal Montgomery's Press Conference, 7 Jan. 1945', The National Archives, CAB 106/1107.

47 Diary entry, dated 6 March 1945, Alanbrooke, *War Diaries 1939–1945*, p. 669.

48 Quoted in Leonard, *Montgomery's Command Philosophy*.

49 Royle, *Lessons in Leadership*, pp. 159–60.

50 Montgomery, *Memoirs*, pp. 328–29.

51 Letter from Raymond Wilkins to Dr Charles Barton, dated 17 April 1968, the Barton Archive, 1965–69, Box 12, Harrogate, Yorkshire.

52 John Toland, *The Last 100 Days: The Tumultuous and Controversial Story of the Final Days of World War II in Europe* (New York: Random House Publishing Group, 2014), p. 312.

53 Montgomery, *Memoirs*, p. 332.

54 Toland, *The Last 100 Days*, p. 314.

55 Ibid., p. 315.

56 Quoted in Leonard *Montgomery's Command Philosophy*.

57 Patrick Delaforce, *The Fourth Reich and Operation Eclipse* (Stroud: Fonthill Media: 2015), p. 97.

58 Royle, *Lessons in Leadership*, p. 165.

59 Bernard Montgomery, *Memoirs*, p. 335.

60 Quoted by Bill Downs in his article 'Montgomery Scorns Nazis, Exults, "This Is The Moment", *The New York Times*, 4 May 1945, University of Buckingham Library.

61 Montgomery, *Memoirs*, pp. 341–42.

62 21 Army Group log, dated 8 May 1945, Records of HQ 21st Army Group (SHAEF), US National Archives, microfilm 331.10.

63 https://ww2db.com/doc.php?q=331 [accessed 20 May 2021]. The invasion was expected by the following spring, and as such Hitler ordered the strengthening of the defences in the West over other fronts.

64 Wolf Hansen, interview with author, 16 April 2009, author's collection.

65 Terry Brighton, *Masters of Battle: Monty, Patton and Rommel at War*, (London: Penguin, 2009), p. 3.

66 Hans Speidel, *Invasion 1944: Rommel and the Normandy Campaign* (Westport, CT: Greenwood Press, 1971), p. 53.

67 Hart, *The Rommel Papers*, p. 453.

68 Messenger, *Lessons from Yesterday*, p. 162.

69 Hart, *The Rommel Papers*, p. 462.

70 Messenger, *Lessons from Yesterday*, p. 163.

71 Reuth, *Rommel: The End of a Legend*, p. 159.

72 Messenger, *Lessons from Yesterday*, p. 166.

73 Marianne Weiss, interview with author, 23 November 2000, author's collection.

74 Messenger, *Lessons from Yesterday*, p. 169.

75 Hart, *The Rommel Papers*, p. 476.

76 'Wonder weapons' (*Wunderwaffe*) referred to a variety of new weapons (including tanks, missiles and aircraft, most of which remained prototypes) in which Hitler put increasing faith in hanging his strategic fortunes. Few were successful, and those that did have promise were not produced in large enough quantities to have a significant impact.

77 Daniel Vasel, unpublished manuscript, 'Fighting in the invasion in France', dated 1961, copy in author's collection.

78 Speidel, *Invasion 1944*, p. 32.

79 Ibid., p. 72.

80 Ibid., p. 93.

81 Ibid., pp. 93–94.

82 See Peter Margaritis, *Crossroads at Margival: Hitler's Last Conference in France: June 17, 1944* (Createspace Independent Publishing, 2015).

83 Speidel, *Invasion 1944*, p. 99.

84 Caddick-Adams, *Monty and Rommel*, p. 418.

85 Fraser, *Knight's Cross*, p. 504.

86 Young, *The Desert Fox*, pp. 210–12.

87 Hart, *The Rommel Papers*, p. 493.

88 According to historian Roger Moorhouse in *Killing Hitler: The Plots, the Assassins, and the*

Dictator Who Cheated Death (New York: Bantam Books, 2006), p. 3, there were forty-two recorded assassination attempts on Hitler's life, with at least ten occurring during the Second World War.

89 Ian Kershaw, *Hitler, 1936–45: Nemesis* (London, W. W. Norton & Co, 2006), p. 693.

90 Fraser, *Knight's Cross*, p. 526.

91 Hans Speidel was eventually jailed having received the support of several influential senior officers, including Keitel, and became a leading figure in the post-war West German Bundeswehr.

92 Hart, *The Rommel Papers*, p. 500–501.

93 Hart, *The Rommel Papers*, p. 501–502.

94 Manfred Rommel, 'Deposition', written on 27 April 1945, copy in author's collection.

95 Hart, *The Rommel Papers*, p. 505.

96 Reuth, *The End of a Legend*, p. 211.

97 Ibid., p. 205.

98 Fraser, *Knight's Cross*, p. 554.

99 Ibid., p. 555.

100 For more on FUSAG and Operation Quicksilver, see Thaddeus Holt, *The Deceivers: Allied Military Deception in the Second World War* (New York: Scribner, 2004).

101 George S. Patton diary entry, dated 26 January 1944, Diary 13 November 1943 – 31 May 1944, George S. Patton Papers, Library of Congress, Box 1.

102 D'Este, *A Genius for War*, p. 573.

103 Ibid.

104 Letter from Michael Wilson to Mary Lewin, dated 16 January 1946, copy in author's archive.

105 George S. Patton Jr, *War As I Knew It* (London: W. H. Allen, 1948), p. 357.

106 Third Army Instruction No.1 from General George S. Patton, 6 March 1944, George S. Patton Papers, Library of Congress, Box 46.

107 Letter from George S. Patton to Beatrice Patton, dated 24 March 1944, George S. Patton Papers, Library of Congress, Box 18.

108 Kenneth Weisbrode, *Eisenhower and the Art of Collaborative Leadership*, p. 235.

109 Hirshon, *A Soldier's Life*, p. 461.

110 Thomas E. Ricks, *The Generals: American Military Command from World War II to Today* (New York: Penguin, 2013), p. 42.

111 Letter from George S. Patton to his son, George, dated 6 June 1944, George S. Patton Papers, Library of Congress, Box 21.

112 C. E. Dornbusch, *Speeches of George S. Patton Jnr, to his Third Army on the Eve of the Normandy Invasion* (New York: Hope Farm Press, 1963).

113 George S. Patton diary entry, dated 9 June 1944, Diary 31 May – 2 Oct 1944, George S. Patton Papers, Library of Congress, Box 1.

114 George S. Patton diary entry, dated 14 July 1944, Diary 31 May – 2 October 1944, George S. Patton Papers, Library of Congress, Box 1.

115 George S. Patton diary entry, dated 12 July 1944, Diary 31 May – 2

October 1944, George S. Patton Papers, Library of Congress, Box 1.

116 Ladislas Farago, *Patton: Ordeal and Triumph* (New York: Ivan Obolensky, 1963), p. 47.

117 Blumenson, *The Patton Papers 1940–1945*, p. 502.

118 D'Este, *A Genius for War*, p. 634.

119 Editorial, 'General Patton', *Washington Star*, 12 August 1944, p. 22.

120 Geoffrey Perret, *There's a War To Be Won: The United States in World War II* (New York: Ballantine Books, 1997), p. 367.

121 George S. Patton diary entry, dated 14 August 1944, Diary 31 May – 2 October 1944, George S. Patton Papers, Library of Congress, Box 1.

122 George S. Patton diary entry, dated 15 August 1944, Diary 31 May – 2 October 1944, George S. Patton Papers, Library of Congress, Box 1.

123 George S. Patton letter to Frederick Ayer, dated 1 September 1944, George S. Patton Papers, Library of Congress, Box 14.

124 Jeremy James, 'Eisenhower as Land Commander, 1 September 1944 – 8 May 1945', unpublished MA, 2012.

125 Cornelius Ryan, *A Bridge Too Far* (London: Hamish Hamilton, 1974), p. 78.

126 Alden Hatch, *George Patton: Old Blood and Guts* (New York: Sterling Publishing Company, 2006), p. 172.

127 D'Este, *A Genius for War*, p. 652.

128 Interview with Edward W. Mills, 21 August 2016, author's collection.

129 Letter from James Stark to Edward W. Mills, quoted in author interview with Edward W. Mills.

130 Patton, *War As I Knew It*, p. 355.

131 Letter from James Stark to Edward W. Mills, quoted in author interview with Edward W. Mills.

132 See D'Este, *A Genius for War*, p. 653.

133 See Geoffrey Perret, *There's a War To Be Won, The United States in World War II* (New York: Ballantine Books, 1997), p. 390.

134 George S. Patton letter to Ruth Ellen Totten, dated 1 December 1944, George S. Patton Papers, Library of Congress, Box 24.

135 George S. Patton diary entry, dated 17 December 1944, Diary 3 October 1944 – 5 February 1945, George S. Patton Papers, Library of Congress, Box 1.

136 Attended by Eisenhower, ACM Arthur Tedder (Eisenhower's deputy), Bradley, Devers, and Patton and several staff officers.

137 Stephen Ambrose, 'Eisenhower's Legacy', *Military Review*, LXX (October 1990), p. 5.

138 Michael Collins and Martin King, *Voices of the Bulge: Untold Stories from Veterans of the Battle of the Bulge* (Minneapolis, MN: Zenith Press, 2011), p. 134.

139 Bradley's headquarters was then located in Luxembourg City.

140 George S. Patton letter to Beatrice Patton, dated 21 December 1944, George S. Patton Papers, Library of Congress, Box 18.

141 Jerome Corsi and Dave Hoffman, *No Greater Valor: The Seige of*

Bastogne and the Miracle that Sealed Allied Victory (Edinburgh: Thomas Nelson, 2014), p. 168.

142 D'Este, *A Genius for War*, p. 690.

143 Letter from Billy Mayne to his brother, Jake Mayne, titled 'Fighting in Europe – the winter', dated 2 February 1962, copy in author's collection.

144 D'Este, *A Genius for War*, p. 690.

145 George S. Patton, letter to Beatrice Patton, dated 29 December 1944, George S. Patton Papers, Library of Congress, Box 18.

146 See Caddick-Adams, *Monty and Rommel*, p. 447.

147 Bradley, *A General's Life*, p. 367.

148 George S. Patton, letter to his son, George, dated 16 January 1945, George S. Patton Papers, Library of Congress, Box 21.

149 Patton, *War As I Knew It*, p. 355.

150 George S. Patton, letter to Frederick Ayer, dated 6 February 1945, George S. Patton Papers, Library of Congress, Box 14.

151 Corsi and Hoffman, *No Greater Valor*, p. 220.

152 Patton, *War As I Knew It*, p. 254.

153 Bradley, *A General's Life*, p. 412.

154 Interview with Edward W. Mills, 21 August 2016, author's collection.

155 Taped discussion about various aspects of their Second World War experiences between Arthur Colt and Donald Swann, dated 16 March 1953, Colt family archive, Kansas City, Missouri.

156 See Richard Baron, Abe Baum and Richard Goldhurst, *Raid! The Untold Story of Patton's Secret Mission* (New York: G.P. Putnam's Sons, 1981).

157 Ibid., p. 254.

158 'Behind the Lines, Between the Lines: Conversation with Abraham J. Baum', https://www.historynet.com/behind-lines-lines-conversation-abraham-j-baum.htm [accessed 3 March 2020].

159 Omar N. Bradley, *A Soldier's Story* (New York: Holt, 1951), p. 542–43.

160 Blumenson, *The Patton Papers 1940–1945*, p. 683.

161 *The Guardian*, 16 April 1945, p. 4.

162 *The Sunday Herald*, 29 April 1945, p. 2.

163 Letter from Patton to Mrs J. Kennedy, dated 25 April 1945, quoted in an email to the author from her grandson, Mr Gerry Kennedy.

164 Patton, *War As I Knew It*, p. 294.

165 Carlo D'Este, *Eisenhower: A Soldier's Life* (New York: Henry Holt & Co, 2002), p. 172.

166 Don M. Fox, *Final Battles of Patton's Vanguard: The United States Fourth Armored Division, 1945–1946* (Jefferson, North Carolina: McFarland, 2020), p. 273.

167 See George Forty, *Patton's Third Army at War* (Havertown, PA: Casemate P, 2015), p. 187.

168 Ibid., p. 189.

Chapter Nine: George S. Patton, Bernard Montgomery and the Post-War World

1 See Fox, *Final Battles of Patton's Vanguard*, p. 288.

2 *The Los Angeles Times*, 10 June 1945, p. 1.

3 Lieutenant General James Doolittle, quoted in D'Este, *A Genius for War*, p. 748.

4 D'Este, *A Genius for War*, p. 750.

5 George S. Patton diary entry, dated 10 August 1945, Diary 22 March – 26 September 1945, George S. Patton Papers, Library of Congress, Box 3.

6 Ibid.

7 Geoffrey Perret, *Eisenhower* (New York: Random House, 1999), p. 300.

8 D'Este, *A Genius for War*, p. 761.

9 J. Furman Daniels, *Patton: Battling with History* (Columbia, Missouri: University of Missouri Press, 2020), p. 195.

10 Letter from George S. Patton to Beatrice Patton, dated 10 October 1945, George S. Patton Papers, Library of Congress, Box 19.

11 Patton, *War As I Knew It*, p. 366.

12 Robert S. Allen's, 'Patton's Secret: "I'm Going to Resign from the Army"', no publication details.

13 Ibid.

14 *The New York Times*, 22 December 1945, p. 16.

15 See Barbara Marshall, 'German Attitudes to British Military Government 1945–47', *Journal of Contemporary History*, Vol. 15, No. 4 (October 1980).

16 Mead, *The Men Behind Monty*, p. 235.

17 Hamilton, *Monty: The Field Marshal*, pp. 591–92.

18 David MacDonald, conversation with Peter Chamberlain, dated 16 April 1969, The Bramall Archive, University of Buckingham, uncatalogued. For more on the British occupation, see Christopher Knowles, *The British in Occupied Germany, 1945–1948* (London: Bloomsbury Academic, 2017).

19 Diary entry, dated 23 August 1945, Alanbrooke, *War Diaries 1939–1945*, p. 720.

20 See C. F. Robinson, 'British Organization for Defense', *Public Administration Review*, Vol. 8, No. 3 (1948), p. 181.

21 Hamilton, *Monty: The Field Marshal*, p. 642.

22 Ibid., p. 643.

23 Ibid.

24 Caddick-Adams, *Monty and Rommel*, p. 461.

25 Simon J. Moody in 'Was There a "Monty Method" after the Second World War? Field Marshal Bernard L. Montgomery and the Changing Character of Land Warfare, 1945–1958', *War in History*, Vol. 23, No. 2 (2016), pp. 210–29.

26 Ibid., p. 215.

27 Hamilton, *Monty: The Field Marshal*, p. 731.

28 *The New York Times*, 30 April 1949, p. 3.

29 Moody, 'Was There a "Monty Method"', p. 218.

30 Ibid., p. 219.

31 John. D. Watson, quoted in lecture given by Dr Gilbert Miles at the Royal Military Academy Sandhurst on 19 October 1992 titled 'Field Marshal Montgomery and the Peace Makers'.

32 'The New Approach, 1953–1956', Supreme Headquarters Allied Powers Europe, NATO Doc 3340/11.3.

33 Bernard Montgomery, 'A Look Through a Window at World War II', *Journal of the Royal United Services Institute*, XCIX (November 1954), p. 50.

34 George Patton's *War As I Knew It* (1947), Dwight Eisenhower's *Crusade in Europe* (1948), and Omar Bradley's *A Soldier's Story* (1951) and *A General's Life: An Autobiography* (1983).

35 Letter from Major Alistair Thompson to Major Jerome Fairgood, dated 1 November 1958, Reginald Arbuthnot collection, Morningside, Edinburgh.

36 F. W. Winterbotham, *The Ultra Secret* (London: HarperCollins, 1974).

37 Royle, *Lessons in Leadership*, p. 178.

Epilogue

1 Guy Chapman, *A Passionate Prodigality: Fragments of Autobiography* (Barnsley: Pen and Sword Military, 2013), p. 98.

2 George S. Patton speech titled 'The Motivation of Troops', dated 16 May 1942, George S. Patton Papers, Library of Congress, Box 71.

3 Hart, *The Rommel Papers*, p. 168.

4 Quoted by Lt Col. Dwin Bramall in notes from a conversation with Colonel D.W.S. Sanderson, 16 June 1959.

5 Montgomery, *Memoirs*, pp. 166–67.

6 Blumenson, *The Patton Papers 1940–1945*, p. 850.

7 Hamilton, *Master of the Battlefield*, pp. 468–69.

8 Fraser, *Knight's Cross*, p. 369.

9 Address by FM The Viscount Slim to Officer Cadets of the Royal Military Academy Sandhurst, 14 October 1952.

10 Ben Macintyre, 'Montgomery v Eisenhower: two generals at war (with Hitler and each other), *The Times*, 20 January 2010.

11 Nigel Hamilton, *Master of the Battlefield*, p. xvii.

12 Interview with Field Marshal The Lord Bramall, 17 April 2016.

Select Bibliography

The literature about Patton, Montgomery and Rommel is vast, as is that about leaders and leadership. This bibliography includes a selection of those works the author found most useful in the preparation of this book, and includes all those referenced in the text.

Books

Alford, Richard (ed.), *To Revel in God's Sunshine: The Story of RSM J C Lord MVO MBE* (R. Alford, 1981).

Ambrose, Stephen E., *Eisenhower: Soldier and President* (New York: Touchstone, 1990).

Astor, Gerald, *Terrible Terry Allen: Combat General of World War II* (New York: Presido Press, 2004).

Axelrod, Alan, *Patton on Leadership: Strategic Lessons for Corporate Warfare* (New Jersey: Prentice Hall Press, 1999).

——, *Patton: A Biography* (London: Palgrave Macmillan, 2009).

Baron, Richard, Abe Baum and Richard Goldhurst, *Raid! The Untold Story of Patton's Secret Mission* (New York: G. P. Putnam's Sons, 1981).

Barr, Niall, *Pendulum of War: Three Battles of El Alamein* (London: Pimlico, 2005).

——, *Eisenhower's Armies: The American-British Alliance During World War II* (New York: Pegasus Books, 2015).

Beckett, I. F. W. (ed.), *Rommel: A Reappraisal* (Barnsley: Pen and Sword Military, 2013).

——, *A British Profession of Arms: The Politics of Command in the Late Victorian Army* (Norman, OK: University of Oklahoma Press, 2018).

Beevor, Antony, *Ardennes 1944: Hitler's Last Gamble* (New York: Viking, 2015).

Bendersky, Joseph W., *The 'Jewish Threat': Anti-Semitic Politics of the U.S. Army* (New York: Basic Books, 2000).

Blumenson, Martin, *Salerno to Cassino: United States Army in World War II, The Mediterranean Theater of Operations* (Washington, DC: Office of Chief of Military History, US Army, 1969).

——, *Breakout and Pursuit: United States Army in World War II, The European Theater of Operations* (Washington, DC: Office of Chief of Military History, US Army, 1970).

——, *The Patton Papers 1885–1940* (Boston, MA: Houghton Mifflin, 1972).

——, *The Patton Papers 1940–1945* (Boston, MA: Houghton Mifflin, 1974).

Bond, Brian, *The Victorian Army and the Staff College, 1854–1914* (London: Routledge, 1972).

Bowman, Timothy, and Mark Connelly, *The Edwardian Army: Recruiting, Training, and Deploying the British Army, 1902–1914* (Oxford: Oxford University Press, 2012).

Brighton, Terry, *Masters of Battle: Monty, Patton and Rommel at War* (London: Penguin, 2009).

Brogan, Hugh, *The Penguin History of the United States of America* (London: Penguin, 2001).

Buckley, John, *Monty's Men: The British Army and the Liberation of Europe* (New Haven, CT: Yale University Press, 2014).

Butler, Daniel Allen, *Field Marshal: The Life and Death of Erwin Rommel* (Havertown, PA: Casemate, 2015).

Caddick-Adams, Peter, *Monty and Rommel: Parallel Lives* (London: Arrow, 2012).

——, *Snow and Steel: The Battle of the Bulge 1944–45* (Oxford: Oxford University Press, 2015).

Camacho, Major Lawrence F., *The Leadership Development of Dwight D. Eisenhower and George S. Patton Jr.* (Royal Oak, NZ: Pickle Partners Publishing, 2015).

Chandler, David (ed.), *The Oxford History of the British Army* (Oxford: Oxford University Press, 2002).

Churchill, Winston S., *The Second World War* (London: Cassell and Company), 6 volumes: *The Gathering Storm* (1948); *Their Finest Hour* (1949); *The Grand Alliance* (1950); *The Hinge of Fate* (1950); *Closing the Ring* (1951); *Triumph and Tragedy* (1953).

Citino, Robert, *Death of the Wehrmacht: The German Campaigns of 1942* (Lawrence, KS: University Press of Kansas, 2011).

Clark, Lloyd, *Anzio: The Friction of War – Italy and the Battle for Rome 1944* (London: Headline, 2006).

——, *Arnhem: Jumping the Rhine 1944 and 1945* (London: Headline, 2008).

Collins, Michael, and Martin King, *Voices of the Bulge: Untold Stories from Veterans of the Battle of the Bulge* (Minneapolis, MN: Zenith Press, 2011).

Coombe, Arthur T., *A History of the US Army Officer Corps, 1900–1990* (Carlisle, PA: Strategic Studies Institute and US Army War College Press, 2014).

Copp, Terry, *Cinderella Army: The Canadians in Northwest Europe 1944–1945* (Toronto: University of Toronto Press, 2006).

——, and Bill McAndrew, *Battle Exhaustion: Soldiers and Psychiatrists in the Canadian Army, 1939–1945* (Montreal: McGill-Queen's University Press, 1990).

Corsi, Jerome, and Dave Hoffman, *No Greater Valor: The Siege of Bastogne and the Miracle that Sealed Allied Victory* (Edinburgh: Thomas Nelson, 2014).

Corum, James S., *The Roots of Blitzkrieg: Hans von Seeckt and Military Reform* (Lawrence, KS: University of Kansas Press, 1992).

Courage, Major Guy, *The History of 15/19 the King's Royal Hussars 1939–1945* (Aldershot: Gale & Polden Ltd, 1949).

Crang, Jeremy, *The British Army and the People's War 1939–1945* (Manchester: Manchester University Press, 2000).

Cronin, Thomas E., and Michael A. Genovese, *Leadership Matters: Unleashing the Power of Paradox* (Abingdon: Routledge, 2012).

Cushion, Nigel, *Undefeatable Spirit: The Story of 11 Days, of Albert, and the Lads from the Yards. The Norfolk Regiment, 1909–1919* (Norwich: Nelsonspirit Publishing, 2019).

D'Este, Carlo, *Patton: A Genius for War* (New York: Harper Perennial, 1996).

——, *Eisenhower: A Soldier's Life* (New York: Henry Holt & Co, 2002).

——, *Eisenhower: Allied Supreme Commander* (London: Cassell, 2004).

Daniels, J. Furman, *Patton: Battling with History* (Columbia, MO: University of Missouri Press, 2020).

Dannatt, Richard, *Boots on the Ground: Britain and Her Army since 1945* (London: Profile Books, 2017).

Davies, Frank, and Graham Maddocks, *Bloody Red Tabs: General Officer Casualties of the Great War 1914–1918* (Barnsley: Pen and Sword Military, 1995).

Davson, Lieutenant Colonel H. M., *The History of the 35th Division in the Great War* (London: Sifton Praed & Co Ltd, 1926).

Day, David V., and John Antonakis (eds), *The Nature of Leadership* (London: Sage, 2012).

Delaforce, Patrick, *The Fourth Reich and Operation Eclipse* (Stroud: Fonthill Media, 2015).

Demeter, Karl, *The German Officer Corps in Society and State 1650–1945* (London: Weidenfeld and Nicolson, 1965).

Dickson, Paul, *The Rise of the GI Army, 1940–1941: The Forgotten Story of How America Forged a Powerful Army before Pearl Harbor* (New York: Grove Press, 2021).

Dornbusch, C. E., *Speeches of George S. Patton Jnr, to His Third Army on the Eve of the Normandy Invasion* (New York: Hope Farm Press, 1963).

Downes, Cathy, *Special Trust and Confidence: The Making of an Officer* (London: Frank Cass, 1991).

Drucker, Susan J., and Robert S. Cathcart (eds), *American Heroes in a Media Age* (New York: Hampton Press, 1994).

Edmonds, Brigadier General Sir James E., *Official History of the Great War: Military Operations France and Belgium, 1918*, Volumes I–V (London: IWM Battery Press, Naval and Military Press, 1995).

Falls, Captain Cyril, *Official History of the Great War: Military Operations France and Belgium 1917*, Volumes I, II and III (London: IWM Battery Press, Naval and Military Press, 1992).

Farago, Ladislas, *Patton: Ordeal and Triumph* (New York: Ivan Obolensky, 1963).

Faulkner, Richard S., *The School of Hard Knocks: Combat Leadership in the American Expeditionary* Forces (College Station, TX: Texas A&M University Press, 2012).

Fennell, Jonathan, *Fighting the People's War: The British and Commonwealth Armies and the Second World War* (Cambridge: Cambridge University Press, 2019).

Fitton, Robert, *Leadership: Quotations from The Military Tradition* (New York: Avalon Publishing, 1990).

Forty, George, *Patton's Third Army at War* (Havertown, PA: Casemate Publishers, 2015).

Fox, Don M., *Final Battles of Patton's Vanguard: The United States Army Fourth Armored Division, 1945–1946* (Jefferson, NC: McFarland, 2020).

Fraser, David, *Knight's Cross: A Life of Field Marshal Erwin Rommel* (London: HarperCollins, 1994).

——, *Alanbrooke* (London: HarperCollins, 1997).

French, David, *Raising Churchill's Army: The British Army and the War against Germany 1919–1945* (Oxford: Oxford University Press, 2000).

——, *Military Identities: The Regimental System, the British Army and the British People c.1870–2000* (Oxford: Oxford University Press, 2005).

——, and Reid Brian Holden (eds), *British General Staff: Reform and Innovation, 1890–1939* (London: Frank Cass, 2002).

Frieser, Karl-Heinz, *The Blitzkrieg Legend: The 1940 Campaign in the West* (Annapolis, MD: Naval Institute Press, 2005).

Fuller, J. F. C., *The Foundations of the Science of War* (London: Hutchinson & Co, 1926).

Furnham, A., *The Psychology of Behaviour at Work* (Hove: Psychology Press, 2004).

Glover, Jonathan, *Humanity: A Moral History of the Twentieth Century* (London: Yale University Press, 2012).

Greenleaf, Robert, K., *The Servant as Leader* (Cambridge, MA: Center for Applied Studies, 1970).

Grint, Keith, *Leadership, Management and Command: Rethinking D-Day* (Basingstoke: Palgrave Macmillan, 2007).

Hamilton, Nigel, *Monty: The Making of a General, 1887–1942* (London: Hamish Hamilton, 1981).

——, *Monty: Master of the Battlefield, 1942–1944* (London: Hamish Hamilton, 1983).

——, *Monty: The Field Marshal, 1944–1976* (London: Hamish Hamilton, 1986).

Hatch, Alden, *General George Patton: Old Blood and Guts* (New York: Sterling Publishing Company, 2006).

Hirshon, Stanley P., *General Patton: A Soldier's Life* (New York: HarperCollins, 2002).

Holt, Thaddeus, *The Deceivers: Allied Military Deception in the Second World War* (New York: Scribner, 2004).

Horne, Alastair, *The Lonely Leader: Monty 1944–45* (London: Pan Military Classic, 2012).

Horne, Charles F. (ed.), *Records of the Great War*, Volume VI (New York: National Alumni, 1923).

House, R. J., P. J. Hanges, M. Javidan, P. W. Dorfman and V. Gupta (eds), *Culture, Leadership, and Organizations: The GLOBE Study of 62 Societies* (Thousand Oaks, CA: Sage, 2004).

Hughes, Richard L., *The Leader's Companion: Insights on Leadership through the Ages* (New York: Free Press, 1995).

Huntingdon, Samuel, *The Soldier and the State: The Theory and Politics of Civil-Military Relations* (Boston, MA: Harvard University Press, 1957).

Irving, David, *The Trail of the Fox: The Life of Field-Marshal Erwin Rommel* (London: Weidenfeld and Nicolson, 1977).

Jones, Mark, *Founding Weimar: Violence and the German Revolution of 1918–1919* (Cambridge: Cambridge University Press, 2016).

Keegan, John, *The Mask of Command: A Study of Generalship* (London: Pimlico, 2004).

Kershaw, Ian, *Hitler, 1889–1936: Hubris* (London: Penguin, 2001).

——, *Hitler, 1936–1945: Nemesis* (London: W. W. Norton & Co, 2006).

——, *The End: Germany, 1944–45* (London: Penguin, 2012).

Kirke, Charles, *Red Coat, Green Machine: Continuity in Change in the British Army 1700 to 2000* (London: Bloomsbury Academic, 2009).

Kitchen, Martin, *A Military History of Germany: From the Eighteenth Century to the Present Day* (Bloomington, IN: Indiana University Press, 1975).

Knowles, Christopher, *Winning the Peace: The British in Occupied Germany, 1945–1948* (London: Bloomsbury Academic, 2017).

Laughlin, Clara E., *Foch the Man: A Life of the Supreme Commander of the Allied Armies* (n.p.: BiblioLife, 2008).

Laver, Harry S., and Jeffrey J. Matthews (eds), *The Art of Command: Leadership from George Washington to Colin Powell* (Lexington, KY: University Press of Kentucky, 2008).

Lewin, Ronald, *Ultra Goes to War: The Secret Story* (London: Hutchinson, 1978).

McChrystal, Stanley, *Team of Teams: New Rules of Engagement for a Complex World* (London: Penguin, 2015).

McGarry, J. L., *Rommel: The Junior Commander* (n.p.: Military Matters, 2017).

McGilvray, Evan, *Field Marshal Claude Auchinleck* (Barnsley: Pen and Sword Military, 2020).

Mallinson, Allan, *The Making of the British Army* (London: Bantam Books, 2009).

Malone, Dandridge, M., *Small Unit Command and Leadership: A Commonsense Approach* (New York: Presido Press, 1983).

Manchester, William, *American Caesar: Douglas MacArthur, 1880–1964* (London: Hutchinson, 1979).

Margaritis, Peter, *Crossroads at Margival: Hitler's Last Conference in France: June 17, 1944* (n.p.: Createspace Independent Publishing, 2015).

Martin, Louis-Aimé, *The Education of Mothers of Families, or, The Civilisation of the Human Race by Women*, trans. Edwin Lee (London: Whittaker, 1842).

Maude, Alan H., *The History of the 47th (London) Division 1914–1919* (Uckfield: Naval and Military Press, 2009).

Mead, Richard, *The Men Behind Montgomery* (Barnsley: Pen and Sword Military, 2015).

Messenger, Charles, *Rommel: Lessons from Yesterday for Today's Leaders* (London: St Martin's Press, 2009).

Miller, Merle, *Ike The Soldier: As They Knew Him* (New York, Perigee Books, 1988).

Montgomery, Field Marshal The Viscount, *The Path to Leadership* (London: Collins, 1961).

Moorehead, Alan, *The Desert War: The Classic Trilogy on the North African Campaign 1940–43* (London: Sphere Books, 1968).

Moorhouse, Roger, *Killing Hitler: The Plots, the Assassins, and the Dictator Who Cheated Death* (New York: Bantam Books, 2006).

Moran, Lord, *The Anatomy of Courage: The Classic WW1 Study of the Psychological Effects of War* (London: Constable, 2007).

Morselli, M., *Caporetto 1917: Victory or Defeat?* (London: Frank Cass, 2001).

Mosley, Leonard, *Marshall: Hero for Our Times* (London: Hearst Books, 1982).

Muth, Jörg, *Command Culture: Officer Education in the US Army and the German Armed Forces 1901–1940,* and the Consequences for World War II (Denton, Texas: University of North Texas Press, 2011).

Neillands, Robin, *The Battle for the Rhine 1944: Arnhem and the Ardennes: The Campaign in Europe* (London: Cassell, 2005).

Parker, Peter, *The Old Lie: The Great War and the Public-School Ethos* (London: Continuum, 2007).

Patton, George S., *Patton on Armor: Light Tank Report 1917 and Tanks, Past, Present and Future 1928* (n.p., Province Publishing, 1980).

Patton, Robert H., *The Pattons: The Personal History of an American Family* (New York: Crown, 1994).

Perret, Geoffrey, *There's a War to Be Won, The United States Army in World War II* (New York: Ballantine Books, 1997).

Perret, Geoffrey, *Old Soldiers Never Die: The Life of Douglas MacArthur* (London: Andre Deutsch, 1996).

Perret, Geoffrey, *Eisenhower* (New York: Random House, 1999).

Pimlott, John (ed.), *Rommel: In His Own Words* (London: Greenhill, 1994).

Porch, Dennis, *The Path to Victory: The Mediterranean Theater in World War II* (New York, Farrar, Straus and Giroux, 2005).

Puryear, Edgar, *American Generalship: Character Is Everything: The Art of Command* (New York: Presidio, 2001).

Rabalais, Steven, *General Fox Corner: Pershing's Chief of Operations and Eisenhower's Mentor* (Havertown, PA: Casemate Publishers, 2016).

Reuth, Ralf Georg, *Rommel: The End of a Legend* (London: Haus Books, 2005).

Reynolds, David, *In Command of History: Churchill Fighting and Writing the Second World War* (London: Allen Lane, 2004).

Reynolds, Michael, *Monty and Patton: Two Paths to Victory* (Stroud: Spellmount, 2005).

Ricks, Thomas E., *The Generals: American Military Command from World War II to Today* (New York: Penguin, 2013).

Royle, Trevor, *Montgomery: Lessons in Leadership for the Soldier's General* (London: St Martin's Press, 2010).

Sabbagh, Karl, *Britain in Palestine: The Story of British Rule in Palestine 1917–1948* (London: Skyscraper Publications, 2012).

Sassoon, Siegfried, *The War Poems* (London: Faber and Faber, 1999).

Schein, E., *Organizational Culture and Leadership* (San Francisco: Jossey-Bass, 2004).

Shamir, Eitan, *Transforming Command: The Pursuit of Mission Command in the U.S., British, and Israeli Armies.* (Redwood City, CA: Stanford University Press, 2011).

Sharp, Lieutenant Colonel Langley, *The Habit of Excellence: Why British Army Leadership Works* (London: Penguin, 2021).

Shepherd, Ben H., *Hitler's Soldiers: The German Army in the Third Reich* (Yale, CT: Yale University Press, 2016).

Sheffield, Gary, *Forgotten Victory: The First World War – Myths and Realities* (London: Headline, 2002).

——, *Command and Morale: The British Army on the Western Front, 1914–18* (Barnsley: Pen and Sword Military, 2014).

Sherman, A. J., *Mandate Days: British Lives in Palestine, 1918–48* (London: Thames and Hudson Ltd, 1997).

Showalter, Dennis, *Patton and Rommel: Men at War in the Twentieth Century* (New York: Penguin, 2006).

Smyth, Sir John George, *Leadership in War: 1939–1945. The Generals in Victory and Defeat* (Newton Abbot: David and Charles, 1974).

Speiser, Peter, *The British Army of the Rhine: Turning Nazi Enemies into Cold War Partners* (Champaign, IL: University of Illinois Press, 2016).

Spiers, Edward, *The Late Victorian Army: 1868–1902* (Manchester: Manchester University Press, 1992).

Stewart, Adrian, *Six of Monty's Men* (Barnsley: Pen and Sword Military, 2011).

Stiehm, J., *The US Army War College: Military Education in a Democracy* (Philadelphia, PA: Temple University Press, 2002).

Stolfi, Russel H. S. A., *Bias for Action: The German 7th Panzer Division in France & Russia 1940-1941* (Dudley Knox Library: Marine Corps University Perspectives on Warfighting, 1991).

Sudmeier, Jim, *Patton's Madness: The Dark Side of a Battlefield Genius* (Mechanicsburg, PA: Stackpole Books, 2019).

Taylor, Robert L. and William E. Rosenbach (eds), *Military Leadership: In Pursuit of Excellence* (Oxford: Routledge, 2009).

Terrain, John, *1914–1918 Essays on Leadership and War* (London: Trustees of the Western Front Association, 1998).

Thompson, Julian, *Forgotten Voices: Desert Victory* (London: Ebury Press, 2011).

Tillotson, Michael, *The Fifth Pillar: The Life and Philosophy of The Lord Bramall KG* (Stroud: Sutton Publishing Limited, 2005).

Toland, John, *The Last 100 Days: The Tumultuous and Controversial Story of the Final Days of World War II in Europe* (New York: Random House, 2014).

Von Hassell, Agostino, and Ed Breslin, *Patton; The Pursuit of Destiny* (Edinburgh: Nelson Current, 2010).

Wallace, General G. Brenton, *Patton and His Third Army* (Harrisburg, PA: Military Service Publishing Co., 1946).

Wavell, General Sir Archibald, *Generals and Generalship* (London: Penguin Special, 1941).

Weigley, Russell F., *History of the United States Army* (London: Batsford, 1967).

Weisbrode, Kenneth, *Eisenhower and the Art of Collaborative Leadership* (London: Anthem Press, 2018).

Welch, David, *The Third Reich: Politics and Propaganda* (Oxford: Routledge, 2002).

White, Arthur S., *Bibliography of Regimental Histories of the British Army* (Ukfield: Naval and Military Press, 2001).

Wilkes, John, and Eileen Wilkes, *Rommel and Caporetto* (Barnsley: Leo Cooper, 2001).

Williamson, Porter B., *General Patton's Principles: For Life and Leadership* (New York: Management & Systems, 1998).

Winterbotham, Frederick W., *The Ultra Secret* (London: HarperCollins, 1974).

Wukovits, John F., *Eisenhower* (New York: Palgrave Macmillan, 2006).

Young, Desmond, *Rommel: The Desert Fox* (London: Harper, 1950).

Young, Lieutenant Colonel F. W., *The Story of Staff College 1858–1958* (Camberley: Gale and Polden Ltd, 1958).

Articles and Chapters

Ambrose, Stephen, 'Eisenhower's Legacy', *Military Review* (Headquarters Department of the Army), Volume LXX, No. 10 (October 1990).

Barbier, Mary Kathryn, 'George C. Marshall and the 1940 Louisiana Maneuvers', *Louisiana History: The Journal of the Louisiana Historical Association*, Vol. 44, No. 4 (Autumn 2003).

Bender, Jason M., 'Non-Technical Innovation: The Prussian General Staff and Professional Military Education', *Small Wars Journal* (14 September 2016).

Blitzwalkers, 'Captain Evans, Monty and the Flying Fortress' (10 June 2015), http://blitzwalkers.blogspot.com/2015/06/captain-evans-monty-and-flying-fortress.html.

Bungay, Stephen, 'The Executive's Trinity: Management, Leadership – and Command', *The Ashridge Journal* (Summer 2011).

Copp, Terry, '"No Lack of Rational Speed": First Canadian Army Operations, September 1944' *Journal of Canadian Studies,* Vol. 16 (Fall 1981).

Dunford Jr, General J., 'From the Chairman: The Pace of Change', *Joint Force Quarterly*, No. 84 (January 2017).

French, David, 'Officer Education and Training in the British Regular Army 1919–39', in G. Kennedy and K. Neilson (eds.), *Military Education: Past, Present and Future* (Westport, CT: Praeger, 2002).

French, David, 'The Regimental System: One Historian's Perspective', *Journal of the Society for Army Historical Research*, Vol. 84, No. 340 (2006).

Gelfand, M. J., M. Erez and Z. Aycan, 'Cross-Cultural Behavior', *Annual Review of Psychology*, Vol. 58 (2007).

Hackett, Lieutenant General Sir John, 'Origins of a Profession', in *The Profession of Arms* (Washington, DC: Center of Military History, 1986), pp. 3–8.

King, Albert S., 'Evolution of Leadership Theory', *Vikalpa: The Journal for Decision Makers*, Vol. 15, No. 2 (April–June 1990).

Marshall, Barbara, 'German Attitudes to British Military Government 1945–47', *Journal of Contemporary History*, Vol. 15, No. 4 (October 1980).

Meehan, Helen Montgomery, 'The Ancestors of Field Marshal Montgomery of Alamein', *North Irish Roots*, Vol. 11, No. 1 (2000).

Montgomery, Bernard, 'A Look Through a Window at World War II', *Journal of the Royal United Services Institute*, Vol. XCIX (November 1954).

Moody, Simon J., 'Was There a "Monty Method" after the Second World War? Field Marshal Bernard L. Montgomery and the Changing Character of Land Warfare, 1945–1958', *War in History*, Vol. 23, No. 2 (2016).

Morin, G., and V. Chanut, 'Who Drives an Officer's Career, the Individual or His Institution? The Case of French Officers', *International Review of Administrative Sciences* (July 2018).

Murray, Patrick. G., 'The Louisiana Maneuvers: Practice for War', *Louisiana History: The Journal of the Louisiana Historical Association*, Vol. 13, No. 2 (Spring 1972).

National Park Service, 'Hiram Cronk', https://www.nps.gov/people/hiram-cronk.htm.

Norris, Jacob, 'Repression and Rebellion: Britain's Response to the Arab Revolt in Palestine of 1936-39', *Journal of Imperial and Commonwealth History*, Vol. 36, No. 1 (2008).

Patton, George S., 'Personal Glimpses of Pershing' (1924), http://www.pattonhq.com/textfiles/pershing.html.

————, 'The Probable Characteristics of the Next War and the Organization, Tactics, and Equipment Necessary to Meet Them' (29 February 1932), http://www.pattonhq.com/pdffiles/vintagetext.pdf.

————, and Major C. C. Benson, 'Mechanization and Cavalry', *Cavalry Journal*, Vol. 39 (April 1930), http://www.pattonhq.com/pdffiles/vintagetext.pdf.

Portable Press [blog], 'The Beginning of Life' (24 November 2015), https://www.portablepress.com/blog/2015/11/the-beginning-of-life/.

Reynolds, Major General Michael, 'George Patton's End Run: The Story of his Final Days', *WWII History*, https://warfarehistorynetwork.com/2016/07/21/george-s-pattons-end-run-the-story-of-his-final-days/.

Robinson, C. F., 'British Organization for Defense', *Public Administration Review*, Vol. 8, No. 3 (1948).

Santoro, Gene, 'Behind the Lines, Between the Lines: Conversation with Abraham J. Baum', Historynet (21 April 2017), https://www.historynet.com/behind-lines-lines-conversation-abraham-j-baum.htm.

Smalley, Edward, 'Qualified, but Unprepared: Training for War at the Staff College in the 1930s', *British Journal for Military History*, Vol. 2, No. 1 (2015).

Watson, Alexander, 'Junior Officership in the German Army during the Great War, 1914–1918', *War in History*, Vol. 14, No. 4 (2007).

Weir, David, 'Leadership in a Desert War: Bernard Montgomery as an Unusual Leader', *Review of Enterprise and Management Studies*, Vol. 1, No. 1 (November 2013).

Widder, Major General Werner, 'Auftragstaktik and Innere Führung: Trademarks of German Leadership', *Military Review*, Vol. 82, No. 5 (September/October 2002).

Autobiographies, Memoirs, Journals and Diaries

Alanbrooke, Field Marshal Lord, *War Diaries 1939–1945*, ed. Alex Danchev and Daniel Todman (London: Weidenfeld and Nicolson, 2001).

Bradley, Omar N., *A Soldier's Story* (New York: Holt, 1951).

————, *A General's Life: An Autobiography* (New York: Simon & Schuster, 1983).

Bramall, Field Marshal Lord, *The Bramall Papers: Reflections in War and Peace*, ed. Robin Brodhurst (Barnsley: Pen and Sword Military, 2017).

Carington, Peter, *Reflections on Things Past: The Memoirs of Lord Carrington* (London: Collins, 1988).

Chapman, Guy, *A Passionate Prodigality: Fragments of Autobiography* (Barnsley: Pen and Sword Military, 2013).

Chynoweth, Bradford Grethen, *Bellamy Park: Memoirs* (New York: Exposition Press, 1975).

DAK War Diary No. 1, Entries 1941, https://rommelsriposte.com/d-a-k-war-diary-entries-1941/.

de Guingand, Francis, *Operation Victory* (London: Hodder and Stoughton, 1947).

——, *From Brass Hat to Bowler Hat* (London: Hamish Hamilton, 1979).

Dunn, Captain J. C., *The War the Infantry Knew 1914–1919: A Chronicle of Service in France and Belgium* (London: Abacus, 1994).

Eisenhower, Dwight D., *Crusade in Europe* (New York: Doubleday, 1948).

——, *The Eisenhower Diaries*, ed. Robert H. Ferrell (New York: Norton, 1981).

Goebbels, Joseph, *The Goebbels Diaries*, ed. and trans. Louis P. Lochner (New York: Award Books, 1971).

——, *The Goebbels Diaries, 1939–1941*, ed. and trans. Fred Taylor (London: Hamish Hamilton, 1982).

Harmon, Major General Ernest, *Combat Commander: Autobiography of a Soldier* (Englewood Cliffs, NJ: Prentice Hall, 1970).

Hesse, Kurt, *Mein Hauptmann: Bildnis eines Soldaten* (Berlin: Deutscher Verlag, 1938).

Horrocks, Sir Brian, *A Full Life* (Barnsley: Leo Cooper, 1960).

Howarth, T. E. B., *Monty at Close Quarters: Recollections of the Man* (London: Leo Cooper, 1985).

Liddell Hart, B. H. (ed.), *The Rommel Papers* (London: Arrow Books, 1987).

Linge, Heinz, *With Hitler to the End: The Memoirs of Hitler's Valet* (Barnsley, Frontline Books, 2013).

Montgomery, Bernard, *The Memoirs of Field-Marshal The Viscount Montgomery of Alamein* (London: Collins, 1958).

——, *Montgomery and The Eighth Army: A Selection of Correspondence from the Diaries, Correspondence and other Papers of Field Marshal The Viscount Montgomery of Alamein, August 1942 to December 1943*, ed. Stephen Brooks (London: The Bodley Head for the Army Records Society, 1991).

Montgomery, Brian, *A Field Marshal in the Family* (London: Constable and Company Limited, 1973).

Patton Jr, George S., *War As I Knew It* (London: W. H. Allen, 1948).

Pershing, John J., *My Experiences in the World War*, Volumes I and II (New York: Frederick A. Stokes Co., 1931).

Race, Toby, *My Time in the Army and Other Adventures* (London: Race Publishing, 2000).

Rommel, Erwin, *Infanterie greift an* (Potsdam: Ludwig Voggenreiter, 1937).

Schmidt, H. W., *With Rommel in the Desert* (London: Panther Books, 1968).

Speidel, Hans, *Invasion 1944: Rommel and the Normandy Campaign* (Westport, CT: Greenwood Press, 1971).

Truscott, Lieutenant General L. K., *Command Missions: A Personal Story* (New York: Lang, 1954).

Wimberley, Major General Douglas, *Scottish Soldier: An Autobiography*, Volume VII: Final Miscellany Volume (n.p., 1974).

Unpublished PhDs and MAs

Duncan, Andrew George, *The Military Education of Junior Officers in the Edwardian Army*, DPhil, University of Birmingham, 2016.

Fitzsimons, Stephen, *The Leadership Styles of Persian Kings in Herodotus*, PhD, University of Manchester, 2017.

Harris, Paul, *The Men Who Planned the War: A Study of the Staff of the British Army on the Western Front, 1914–1918*, PhD, King's College London, 2013.

Leonard, Carl, *Montgomery's Command Philosophy in North West Europe, June 1944–May 1945*, MA dissertation, University of Buckingham, December 2009.

Morin, G., *La fabrication du leader et du leadership: analyse des processus de transformation dans trois grandes organisations*, Phd, Université Panthéon-Assas Paris II, 2016.

Pine, Lisa N. N., *The Family in the Third Reich 1933–1945*, PhD, London School of Economics, 1996.

Speiser, P., *The British Army of the Rhine and the Germans (1948–1957): From Enemies to Partners*, PhD, University of Westminster, 2012.

Unpublished Papers and Talks

Allen, Robert S., *Patton's Secret: 'I'm Going to Resign from the Army'* (n.p.d.).

Bialas, Lieutenant Ralph, *Recollections of General Patton*, privately published in 1950, #3/50.

Durand, D. P., *Patton's Tank School*, unpublished paper supporting a Royal Tank Regiment Staff Ride, November 2007.

Hooper, Tech Sergeant Jim, *With Patton at War*, Hooper Family Archive, Riverside, Los Angeles, 1961–62.

Lees, Dr Daniel, *Patton's Hubris*, paper presented to the University of Buckingham postgraduate Modern War Studies and Contemporary Military History course, 17 October 2014.

Mayes, Gerald, *Henry L. Stimson and the Army, 1940–45*, paper for the British Commission for Military History, June 2002.

Miles, Dr Gilbert, 'Field Marshal Montgomery and the Peace Makers', a talk delivered at the Royal Military Academy Sandhurst, 19 October 1992.

Mills, Sergeant Dick P., *Memories of the Army and the War*, 1955.

Morin, Gabriel, *Does Cultural Leadership Apply in the Context of Military Organization?' A Parallel Study of the British and French Armies*, Centre for Army Leadership, 2016.

Pearson, Major Duncan, *Bernard Montgomery as First World War Staff Officer*, a talk delivered at Humanities

Research Institute Post Graduate Group, University of Buckingham, 16 August 2019.

Steadman, Peter, *At War with Monty in the Desert*, Nicolson Family Archive, Canterbury, Kent, 1949.

Vasel, Daniel, *Fighting in the invasion in France*, unpublished manuscript, 1961.

Weir-Brown, David, 'Montgomery's Command Style: A Re-evaluation', a talk delivered at the Royal Military Academy Sandhurst, May 1992.

——, 'Rommel's command style: A Re-evaluation', a talk delivered at the Royal Military Academy Sandhurst, December 1994.

——, 'Patton's Command Style in North Africa: A Re-evaluation', a talk delivered at the Royal Military Academy Sandhurst, War Discussion Group, June 1998.

Williams, Dr David J., *The Development of Erwin Rommel's Risk-Reward Skill*, Centre for Army Leadership, May 2019.

Author's Collection

Letters

Paul Henkelmann to author, 1 May 2013.

Billy Mayne to his brother, Jake Mayne, 2 February 1962.

Ben Metcalfe to author, 16 September 2000.

Corporal Dennis Pease to his father, Frederick Pease, 6 December 1931.

Colonel Thomas Peterson to Mr Jake Lindt, 2 October 1912.

Sergeant Jim Smith to his wife, Edna Smith, 18 October 1931.

Captain David Symes to his father, 23 October 1923.

Michael Wilson to Mary Lewin, 16 January 1946.

Interviews

Lieutenant Colonel David Arbuthnot, with Donald Childs, 16 August 1967 (transcript).

Field Marshal The Lord Bramall, with author, 17 April 2016.

Ronald Davies, with author, 20 June 2015.

Wolf Hansen, with author, 16 April 2009.

Sergeant Ron. E. Heart, with Paul Friend, 17 August 1964 (transcript).

Ethel Graves, with author, 12 March 2015.

Donny McDonald, with author, 12 March 2004.

Edward W. Mills, with author, 21 August 2016.

Uwe Pfaffner, interview with Major Peter Pfaffner, 12–13 September 1966 (transcript).

Terence Robertson, with author, 25 June 2015.

John Robinson, with author, 1 September 2015.

Horst Wack, with author, 9 January 2005 (transcript of telephone conversation).

Marianne Weiss, with author,
    23 November 2000.

Edward J. Wood, with author, 5 March
    2004.
Otis Zoecke, with author, 20 June 2006.

Miscellaneous

Karl Kuhn, 1932 diary.
'Journal of Peter Symes PhD', January–
    September 1914.
Photographs in packet titled 'Lille
    28 October 1918 Eric Steele'.

Desert War 1943 promotional poster.
Manfred Rommel, 'Deposition',
    27 April 1945.

Archival Collections

(References to individual collections can be found in the chapter notes)

The Papers of Field Marshal The Lord
    Bramall, the Bramall Collection,
    University of Buckingham.
Personal Correspondence of Field
    Marshal Alan Brooke, Liddell Hart
    Military Archives, King's College
    London.
Papers of Field Marshal Sir Claude
    Auchinleck (1919–71), University of
    Manchester Library, GB 133 AUC.

The Montgomery Papers, Imperial War
    Museum.
George S. Patton Papers, 1807–1979,
    Library of Congress.
Dwight D. Eisenhower Papers, Library
    of Congress.
Dwight D. Eisenhower Library, Abilene,
    Kansas, Kevin McCann Papers,
    1918–81.
Liddell Hart Centre for Military
    Archives, King's College London.

Archival Sources

Official Collections

Royal Military College Cadet Register,
    January 1907–September 1908, The
    National Archives, WO151/8.
Royal Military College Cadet Register,
    Volume 6, 1903–1907, War Office
    151, The Sandhurst Collection, Royal
    Military Academy Sandhurst.
Sandhurst: The Royal Military College:
    Full Inspection, H. M. Inspectorate
    1911, The National Archives, ED
    109/5853.

10 Infantry Brigade War Diary: 1
    Battalion Royal Warwickshire
    Regiment, 1 August 1914 – 31
    December 1914, The National
    Archives, WO95/1484/1.
104 Infantry Brigade: Headquarters War
    Diary, 1 January – 30 June 1916, The
    National Archives, WO95/2482/1.

104 Infantry Brigade: Headquarters War Diary, 1 July – 31 December 1916, The National Archives, WO95/2482/2.

104 Infantry Brigade: Headquarters War Diary, 1 January – 30 April 1917, The National Archives, WO95/2482/3.

104 Infantry Brigade: Headquarters War Diary, May – June 1917, The National Archives, WO95/2482/4.

104 Infantry Brigade: Headquarters War Diary, 1 July – 31 August 1917, The National Archives, WO95/2482/5.

104 Infantry Brigade: Headquarters War Diary, 1 September – 30 September 1917, The National Archives, WO95/2482/6.

104 Infantry Brigade: Headquarters War Diary, 1 October – 30 November 1917, The National Archives, WO95/2482/7.

104 Infantry Brigade: Headquarters War Diary, 1 December – 31 December 1917, The National Archives, WO95/2482/8.

104 Infantry Brigade: Headquarters War Diary, 1 January – 28 February 1918, The National Archives, WO95/2483/1.

104 Infantry Brigade: Headquarters War Diary, 1 March – 31 March 1918, The National Archives, WO95/2483/2.

104 Infantry Brigade: Headquarters War Diary, 1 April – 31 May 1918, The National Archives, WO95/2483/3.

104 Infantry Brigade: Headquarters War Diary, June 1918, The National Archives, WO95/2483/4.

104 Infantry Brigade: Headquarters War Diary, July 1918, The National Archives, WO95/2483/5.

104 Infantry Brigade: Headquarters War Diary, 1 August – 30 September 1918, The National Archives, WO95/2483/6.

104 Infantry Brigade: Headquarters War Diary, 1 October 1918 – 31 March 1919, The National Archives, WO95/2483/7.

9 Corps War Diary, 1 May 1918 – 31 December 1918, The National Archives, WO95/837.

47 Division War Diary, 1 September to 31 October 1918, The National Archive, WO95/2705/3.

RAMC/1212/11 ADMS, 47th (London) Division, France 1917–19, RAMC Archives, Army Medical Services Museum, Keogh Barracks.

GHQ Deputy Chaplain General, British Expeditionary Force War Diary, dated 22 November 1939, The National Archive, WO167/31.

17th Infantry Brigade: Summary of Important Instructions dated 30 June 1921, Imperial War Museum, EPS/2/2.

Tactical Notes for the use in the West Riding Area and 49th (West Riding) Division, October 1923, Archives of the York and Lancaster Regimental Museum, Ref 1758-1968 A-Q.

H. Dv. 487 Führung und Gefecht der verbunden Waffen (FuG) (published in two parts: September 1931 and October 1933), Bundesarchiv, BArch RHD 4/1685.

Senate Inquiry into Events in Washington D.C., 28 July 1932 dated 21 August 1932, Senate Inquiry Papers, Library of Congress, MSS83736, Box 19/1.

General I.D. White oral history, 29 October 1977, Isaac D. White Papers 1901–1990, Norwich University Archives, Northfield, VT.

Western Desert: Account of the Battle of Alam El Halfa Sept 1942 by Lt-Gen Sir Brian Horrocks, commanding 13th Corps, The National Archives, CAB106/654.

'Field Marshal Montgomery's Press Conference, 7 Jan. 1945', The National Archives, CAB106/1107.

Field Marshal The Viscount Slim, address to Officer Cadets of the Royal Military Academy Sandhurst, 14 October 1952, Sandhurst Collection.

The New Approach, 1953–1956, Supreme Headquarters Allied Powers Europe, NATO, Doc 3340/11.3.

3 Division War Diary, September 1939– June 1940, British Expeditionary Force, France, The National Archives, WO167/218.

Alan Maciver interview 1975, Imperial War Museum, 33051.

Interview with Henry Trisi by H. D. Poole, 12 October 1932, Oral History Archive, University of Southern Mississippi, Hattiesburg, Mississippi, File 1722-29/11.

Family Collections

Luis Althaus diary, May–October 1940, Althaus family archive, Bonn.

Thomas Artmann diary, Artmann family archive, Paderborn.

Major David Boyd, 'Reflections on War', unpublished manuscript July 1945, Boyd family papers, Kendal, Cumbria.

Letter from Ralph Canning to David Broad, 16 July 1952, Canning family papers, 1939–45 Box, Chester, Cheshire.

Taped discussion between Arthur Colt and Donald Swann, 16 March 1953, Colt family archive, Kansas City, Missouri.

Captain 'Duke' Ellis, letter to Major John Baulmer, 8 February 1941, Larry Baulmer collection, Denver, Colorado.

Journal of Captain Bill Fontaine, Fontaine family archive, Des Moines, Iowa.

Letter from Philip Fullard to Derek Clayton, 18 May 1935, Clayton family archive, Canterbury, Kent.

Letters from Ralf Haas to Edda Naumann, 3 April 1939, Haas family archive, Berlin.

Letter from Major Larry Hind to his sister, Linda Ross, 20 September 1940, Ross family archive, Michigan.

Diary of Colonel Edwin James, Blue book, 1943, James family archive, Swanage, Dorset.

Leo Krämer, interviewed by James Brody (transcript), 17 August 1957, private collection of Mr Piers Brody.

Letter from G. S. Lambert to his brother, Larry Lambert, 4 May 1930, Lambert family archive, Washington, DC, 1930–32 folder.

Letter from Billy Mendonca to Jacob E. Wall, 6 March 1916, Wall collection, Macon, Georgia.

Ian Milton, 'Episodes from the War: The Memoirs of I. T. L. Milton', unpublished manuscript, 1962, private collection, TD papers, Winslow, Buckinghamshire.

Field Marshal The Viscount Montgomery of Alamein, talk to Officer Cadets and Directing Staff of the Royal Military Academy Sandhurst, Camberley, 17 July 1965, notes taken by Officer Cadet James Mills, Bolton collection, Boston, Lincolnshire.

Letter from Bernard Montgomery to David Drake, 14 March 1916, private collection, TD papers, Winslow, Buckinghamshire.

Letter from Bernard Montgomery to Major Bill Gallagher, 16 March 1953, papers of W. S. Gallagher, Bath, Somerset.

Letter from George S. Patton to Jon K. Smith, 10 June 1934, Smith and Bexton family archives, New York City.

Letter from George Patton to Malcolm McBride, 13 January 1940, McBride family archive, San Francisco.

Captain R. H. Phillips, letter to his brother, Denis Phillips, 2 May 1948, Phillips family archive, Mobile, Alabama.

Captain Leo Ross, interviewed by Tim Reynolds, 18 May 1992, Reynolds archive, Chelmsford, Essex.

Diary of Major Peter Salmond, Salmond family archive, London, England.

Letter from Roger Stillwell to Reginald Mason, 16 June 1948, Stillwell family collection, Hampstead, London.

Letter from Major Alistair Thompson to Major Jerome Fairgood, 1 November 1958, Reginald Arbuthnot collection, Morningside, Edinburgh.

Letter from Captain Tobias Smythe to his mother, April 1910, Jane O'Neil (née Smythe) collection, West Hampstead, London.

Staff Sergeant Alf Tapp, interviewed by Tim Reynolds, 21 January 1992, Reynolds archive, Chelmsford, Essex.

Letter from Tom Turner to his brother, Terence Turner, 2 February 1939, Turner family collection, Birmingham.

Paul Uckelman, Journal Vol. II 1931–33, copy in Mr Ross Dees' collection, Hamburg.

Letter from Donald Ure to Peter Mayhew, 6 December 1948, P. J. S. Mayhew archive, Sheffield.

Letter from Raymond Wilkins to Dr Charles Barton, 17 April 1968, Barton archive, 1965–69, Box 12, Harrogate, Yorkshire.

Major David J. Williams, War Diary, Williams family archive, Cromer, Norfolk.

Miscellaneous

Führer Directive No. 51, issued 3
   November 1943, https://ww2db.
   com/doc.php?q=331

Newspapers and Magazines

The London Gazette, 1 December 1914.
The Boston Globe, 2 June 1916.
Illustrated London News, 28 June 1919.
Indiana Evening Gazette, 4 April 1919.
Das Reich, 23 May 1940.
The West Georgian, 14 January 1941.
Time, 16 April 1944.
Washington Star, 12 August 1944.

The New York Times, 4 May 1945.
The Guardian, 16 April 1945.
The Sunday Herald, 29 April 1945.
The Los Angeles Times, 10 June 1945.
The New York Times, 22 December
   1945.
The New York Times, 30 April 1949.

Acknowledgements

This book has been a very long time in research and writing. So long, that at times I wondered whether I would ever finish it due to the demands of other responsibilities. Prime among them was establishing the Centre for Army Leadership (CAL) at the Royal Military Academy Sandhurst, an endeavour through which I forged a firm friendship with Field Marshal the Lord Bramall. Over the last three years of the great man's life, we spent many happy hours discussing leadership and, eventually, the three subjects of this book. Our meetings took place at his home and his local pub, The Feathers, with each conversation making its own special contribution to the most rewarding period of my career.

I am delighted to have this opportunity to thank all those who spared some of their valuable time to provide me with advice and support across the six years it took to produce *The Commanders*: the late Field Marshal the Lord Bramall; Gen Sir Nick Carter; Gen Sir Mark Carleton-Smith; Lt Gen Stuart Skeates; Maj Gen (rtd) Paul Nanson (the first Director Army Leadership); Maj Gen Bill Wright; Maj Gen (rtd) Duncan Capps; Brig Robin Lindsay; Brig Lisa Keetly; Brig Mike Cornwell; Col Rob Alston; Lt Col Will Meddings; the late Lt Col Dr Jane Hunter; Lt Col Jamie Nowell; Lt Col Justin Baker; Lt Col Langley Sharp; Lt Col Henry Llewelyn-Usher; Lt Col Erica Bridge; Lt Col Charlie Colbeck; Lt Col Joanna Munce; Maj Paul McFarland; Maj Ben Acton; Capt Sam Wilson; WO1 Sarah Cox; Capt Andy Stephen; WO1 Chris Nicol; WO1 Sheridan Lucas; Dr Linda Risso; Mrs Danielle Jackman; Mrs Emma Boyd, Ms Gail Bolger; Mrs Vivita Taganekurukura; Col Matt Ketterer; Col Dave Crome; Col Dr Miles Hayman; Mark Watton; Lt Cdr Jim Denney; Wg Cdr Phil Poole; Dr Zoe Szuster-Stone; Dr Joanna Harvey; the many talented CAL secondees and officer cadets, and CAL Fellows: Dr Victoria Carr; Mr Gavin Paton; Mr Scott Sherriff; Dr Matthew Anderson; Dr Gabriel Morin; and Mary Hunter.

Academic friends and colleagues were particularly generous to me during this busy time and I would like to express my appreciation for: Professors John Adamson; Saul David; John Drew; Julian Richards; Gary Sheffield and Matthias Strohn; colleagues in the Centre for Historical Analysis and Conflict Research (CHACR), and my University of Buckingham research students: Dr Paddy Walker; Yvonne Walsham; Dr Colin Carnall; David Wells; David Fisher; Jonny Briggs; Maj Claudia Harvey; Richard Jones; and Colin Howe. I am also grateful to Col (rtd) Chris Croft, former director of the US Center for the Army Profession and Leadership (CAPL) at Fort Leavenworth, the CAPL's current director Col Samuel Saine, and his team including Col (retd) John Hixon; Clark M. Delavan; and Dr Mellisa Wolfe. James Mellor and Kate Parry proved to be inestimable research assistants in the US, as did Derek Sands and Kate Moore in the UK and Daniel Meyer in Germany. Without the remarkable cache of information that these experts unearthed, this book would be very much the poorer. My thanks also to the many families and individuals who have allowed me to quote from their letters, papers, collections and archives. Their names can be found in the bibliography.

A book with the scope of *The Commanders* would have been impossible to write without the invaluable assistance provided by a host of libraries and archives and I would like to thank the following for their good humour and professionalism: John Pearce and Sue Lloyd at the Central Library RMAS and the new Richard Holmes Library at Robertson House, Camberley; and Peta Yates at the University of Buckingham Library. I would also like to acknowledge the assistance provided by the following libraries and archives: the Prince Consort's Library, Aldershot; the London Library; the Royal United Services Institute Library; the Senate House Library, University of London; the University of Manchester Library; the British Library; the Dwight

Eisenhower Library; the Library of Congress; the US Army Center of Military History; the Maughan Library, King's College, London; the Liddell Hart Centre for Military Archives, King's College, London; the National Archive; the Imperial War Museum Archive; and the National Army Museum.

This book would never have been published without the dedication of my inspirational agent, Charlie Viney, and my outstanding (and hugely patient) editors on both sides of the Atlantic: George Gibson in New York and James Nightingale in London. I also grateful for the indispensable contributions made to this book by Emily Burns, copy editors Gemma Wain and Sarah Chatwin, index complier Chris Bell and map designer Keith Chaffer.

I am fortunate to have a remarkable family supporting me in everything I do, and they receive my love and gratitude: Pauline and John Clark – my parents; my brother Brent and his family in England – Caroline, Tilda, Orla and Jasper; and Alastair Muir-Taylor and his family in the US – Lisa Ann, Tom, Georgia, Genie and Sophie. I end, however, by thanking the magnificent bunch who keep me grounded, give me encouragement and make me so proud every day: Freddie, Charlotte, Henry and, of course, Catriona. This book is for you.

Wigginton Bottom
June 2022

Illustrations

George S. Patton Jr in Virginia Military Institution uniform, 1903. (*VMI Archives 0001968*)

Erwin Rommel as a cadet, Danzig, 1910. (*World War II Database*)

Bernard Montgomery at St Paul's School, 1906. (*Express/Getty Images*)

Patton and Beatrice Ayer, 1910. (*VMI Archives 0003228*)

Captain Bernard Montgomery while serving as brigade major, 1917. (© *Hulton-Deutsch Collection/Corbis via Getty Images*)

Lieutenant George Patton at US field headquarters in Mexico, 1916. (*Library of Congress, Prints and Photographs Division*)

Oberleutnant Erwin Rommel on the Italian Front, 1917. (*Wikimedia Commons*)

Lieutenant Colonel George Patton, 1918. (*National Archives at College Park*)

Lieutenant Colonel Bernard Montgomery, c.1931. (© *IWM MH22844*)

Patton and General Billy Mitchell, c.1935. (*VMI Archives 0001052*)

Major General George Patton during the 'Louisiana Maneuvers', 1941. (*Bettmann/Getty Images*)

Adolf Hitler leads a review party of Major Erwin Rommel's Jäger Battalion, September 1934. (*Bundesarchiv 183-1987-0313-503*)

Major General Erwin Rommel in St Valery, June 1940. (© *IWM RML 342*)

Lieutenant General Bernard Montgomery in North Africa, 1942. (© *IWM E19699*)

Rommel inspecting his Afrika Korps troops with Italo Garibaldi, March 1941. (© *IWM HU 39482*)

Rommel with the 15th Panzer Division, Libya, November 1941. (*National Archives at College Park, NWDNS-242-EAPC-6-M713a*)

Montgomery during the Battle of El Alamein, 5 November 1942. (*National Army Museum*)

President Roosevelt, Major General George Patton, Brigadier General William Wilbur and General George C. Marshall during the Casablanca Conference, January 1943. (*Library of Congress, Prints and Photographs Division*)

Lieutenant General George Patton in North Africa, March 1943. (*Library of Congress, Prints and Photographs Division*)

Hitler congratulates Rommel on his promotion to field marshal, Berlin, September 1943. (*Sueddeutsche Zeitung Photo/Alamy Stock Photo*)

Montgomery with Patton, Palermo, Sicily, 28 July 1943. (*US Army/Interim Archives/Getty Images*)

Major General Troy Middleton, Lieutenant General Omar Bradley and Patton. (*Strategy Bridge*)

Montgomery and Patton, Palermo airfield, 28 July 1943. (*Center of Military History of the United States Army, via Wikimedia Commons*)

Montgomery with General Sir Harold Alexander at an advance airfield in Sicily, July 1943. (*Australian War Memorial, MEA0229*)

Rommel with Fritz Bayerlein, North Africa. (*Rommel North Africa: Bundesarchiv 146-1977-158-07*)

Patton, Brigadier General Hobart R. Gay and Brigadier General Paul D. Harkins, Germany, March 1945. (*From the collection of Gary Schulze*)

Brigadier General Sir Francis de Guingand, Tripoli, Libya, January 1943. (© *IWM E 22000*)

Allied commanders in London for a planning conference, 2 January 1944. (© *IWM CH 12110*)

Rommel and officers inspecting beach defences in Normandy, April 1944. (*Bundesarchiv 1011-719-0243-33*)

Rommel inspecting German 21st Panzer Division, Normandy, 30 May 1944. (*Bundesarchiv 1011-300-1865-08*)

Montgomery speaking to Allied correspondents, Normandy, 11 June 1944. (*Bundesarchiv 1011-300-1865-08*)

Montgomery playing with his two puppies, Normandy, 6 July 1944. (© *IWM B 6542*)

George VI inspects US Fifth Army troops with Lieutenant General Mark Clark, Italy, July 1944. (© *Usis-Dite/ Bridgeman Images*)

Montgomery, Patton and Omar Bradley, Normandy, 7 July 1944. (*Library of Congress, Prints and Photographs Division*)

Patton, Bradley and Eisenhower, Bastogne, December 1944. (© *IWM EA 52043*)

Field Marshal Sir Alan Brooke, Montgomery, Winston Churchill, General William H. Simpson, Aachen, Germany, 30 March 1945. (© *IWM HU 90425*)

Portrait of Rommel, 6 June 1942. (*Bundesarchiv 246-1977- 018-13A*)

Rommel with his family at home in Herrlingen, 5 June 1944. (*Popperfoto via Getty Images*)

State funeral of Rommel in Ulm, 18 October 1944. (© *IWM RML 40*)

Churchill, Montgomery and Brooke on the banks of the Rhine, 26 March 1945. (© *IWM BU 2636*)

Montgomery and Prince Bernhardt of the Netherlands inspect the Arab stallion previously owned by Rommel, 2 August 1945. (© *IWM BU 9531*)

Montgomery with President Truman on a visit to the White House, 11 September 1946. (*The Print Collector/ Alamy Stock Photo*)

Index